An Introduction to

EARLY CHILDHOOD STUDIES

Sara Miller McCune founded SAGE Publishing in 1965 to support the dissemination of usable knowledge and educate a global community. SAGE publishes more than 1000 journals and over 800 new books each year, spanning a wide range of subject areas. Our growing selection of library products includes archives, data, case studies and video. SAGE remains majority owned by our founder and after her lifetime will become owned by a charitable trust that secures the company's continued independence.

Los Angeles | London | New Delhi | Singapore | Washington DC | Melbourne

An Introduction to

EARLY CHILDHOOD STUDIES

Edited by

SACHA POWELL & KATE SMITH

4TH
EDITION

SAGE

Los Angeles | London | New Delhi
Singapore | Washington DC | Melbourne

Los Angeles | London | New Delhi
Singapore | Washington DC | Melbourne

SAGE Publications Ltd
1 Oliver's Yard
55 City Road
London EC1Y 1SP

SAGE Publications Inc.
2455 Teller Road
Thousand Oaks, California 91320

SAGE Publications India Pvt Ltd
B 1/I 1 Mohan Cooperative Industrial Area
Mathura Road
New Delhi 110 044

SAGE Publications Asia-Pacific Pte Ltd
3 Church Street
#10-04 Samsung Hub
Singapore 049483

Editor: Jude Bowen
Associate editor: George Knowles
Editorial assistant: Catriona McMullen
Production editor: Nicola Carrier
Copyeditor: Jill Birch
Proofreader: Thea Watson
Indexer: Gary Kirby
Marketing manager: Lorna Patkai
Cover design: Wendy Scott
Typeset by: C&M Digitals (P) Ltd, Chennai, India
Printed in the UK

The first edition was published in 2004 and reprinted in 2005, 2007 and 2008.
The second edition was published in 2009 and reprinted in 2010 and twice in 2012.
The third edition was published in 2014 and reprinted in 2014, 2015 and 2016.
This fourth edition published 2018.

Library of Congress Control Number: 2017938915

British Library Cataloguing in Publication data

A catalogue record for this book is available from the British Library

ISBN 978-1-4739-7482-1
ISBN 978-1-4739-7483-8 (pbk)

At SAGE we take sustainability seriously. Most of our products are printed in the UK using FSC papers and boards. When we print overseas we ensure sustainable papers are used as measured by the PREPS grading system. We undertake an annual audit to monitor our sustainability.

CONTENTS

ABOUT THE EDITORS

Sacha Powell is Professor of Early Childhood Care and Education, and Director of the Research Centre for Children, Families and Communities at Canterbury Christ Church University. Her research focuses on policies and practices in the care and education of babies and children up to three. Her recent publications include the *Routledge International Handbook of Philosophies and Theories of Early Childhood Education and Care* (2016). Sacha is Chair of the UK's Association for Professional Development in Early Years (www.tactyc.org.uk) and a member of the Research Committee of The Froebel Trust (www.froebel.org.uk). Her first degree was in Modern Chinese with Japanese and she continues to collaborate with colleagues in early childhood settings, universities and local education bureaus in China.

Kate Smith is a Senior Lecturer within the School of Childhood and Education Sciences at Canterbury Christ Church University. Prior to working in Higher Education she was a primary school teacher in London and Kent, coordinating Art and Literacy provision. Kate's research interests lie in young children's activities as 'makers' and how we can enable children's creativity, language and literacy within early education settings. Her PhD explored young children's activity as writers in their first year of school, and she is currently researching 'playful' writing opportunities in reception and year one classrooms with a group of teachers using Froebelian principles.

ABOUT THE CONTRIBUTORS

Angela Anning is Emeritus Professor of Early Childhood Education, University of Leeds. She worked as a teacher in all phases of primary, secondary and tertiary education. She was involved in primary teacher education, childhood studies and professional development at Leeds University. Her research interests are the professional knowledge of those working in early childhood services, multi-agency teamwork, early childhood curricula and in particular art education/children's drawing. She was one of the core team involved in the National Evaluation of Sure Start. She has published extensively in the field of early childhood services and education.

Carol Aubrey is Professor Emeritus at the University of Warwick and has been Visiting Professor at Birmingham City University and Professorial Fellow at Liverpool Hope University. She trained as a primary school teacher and educational psychologist and spent a number of years in primary teacher education, with a particular focus on the early years, first at University College Cardiff and then at the University of Durham. Her research interests lie in the policy-to-practice context of early childhood education and care, including multi-agency working, leadership, early learning and development, with an interest in mathematics development and inclusion/special educational needs.

Polly Bolshaw is a Senior Lecturer in Early Years at Canterbury Christ Church University (CCCU), who teaches predominantly on the BA (Hons) Early Childhood Studies programme. Prior to this, she completed the *New Leaders in Early Years* programme at CCCU and worked as an Early Years Professional in a Sure Start Children's Centre. Her research interests include the experiences of people who work with young children and study early childhood, early childhood education for sustainability, and services within the UK that aim to support children and their families.

Thea Cameron-Faulkner is a Senior Lecturer in the School of Arts, Languages and Cultures at the University of Manchester. Her research is situated within a constructivist approach to language development and focuses on the role of the social and physical environment in the early stages of the developmental process.

Alison Clark is a Visiting Research Associate at UCL Institute of Education, London. Her research interests include listening to children, children's experiences of place and the development of participatory research methods. Working with Professor Peter Moss at Thomas Coram Research Unit she developed methods for listening to young children in research called the Mosaic approach. She is interested in how qualitative research methods can facilitate communication between young children and adults in a range of professional roles and international contexts with recent research collaborations in Denmark and Norway.

Tricia David has worked in the field of Early Childhood Education and Care for over forty years. Having officially retired, she is honoured to have been awarded the titles of Emeritus Professor at Canterbury Christ Church University and was previously Honorary Emeritus Professor of Early Years Education at the University of Sheffield. Tricia's publications have included studies of international comparisons and, more recently, the review for *Birth to Three Matters* and *Routledge International Handbook of Philosophies and Theories of Early Childhood Education and Care*. Her 1990s works on multi-professionalism, apparently still read during current developments in provision, are spurring others to create contemporary studies in this complex and exciting field.

Marilyn Fleer holds the Foundation Chair of Early Childhood Education at Monash University, Australia, and is the President of the International Society for Cultural Activity Research (ISCAR). Her research interests focus on early years learning and development, with special attention on play, pedagogy, culture, science and technology. She can be contacted at marilyn.fleer@monash.edu.

Ruth Ford is a Reader in Developmental Psychology at Anglia Ruskin University, Cambridge, UK. She studies the cognitive development of young children, including children at risk of learning impairments, focusing on the development of memory and executive functions. Her research also encompasses early intervention projects that aim to help parents interact with their children in ways that promote better thinking and learning. She has a BSc (Hons) and PhD from the University of New South Wales in Sydney, Australia.

Justine Howard is a Senior Lecturer at the Centre for Child Research at Swansea University and the Programme Director of their Masters in Developmental and Therapeutic Play. She is a Chartered Psychologist and Associate Fellow of the British Psychological Society, holding a first degree in psychology, a postgraduate diploma in research methods and a PhD in the psychology of education. She is also trained in Developmental and Therapeutic Play. Her research is principally concerned with children's perceptions of play and how these perceptions are influenced by social and environmental interaction. Her recent experimental work focuses on the benefits of playful practice. She is also the editor of *The Psychology of Education Review*.

Sonia Jackson is Emeritus Professor at the Thomas Coram Research Unit, UCL Institute of Education, London, UK. She has led numerous research studies on the health and education of children and youth in out-of-home care, including the EU-funded YiPPEE project, and has published extensively on these as well as early childhood development and care. Recent publications include: *People Under Three: Play, Work and Learning in a Childcare Setting*; *Improving Access to Further and Higher Education for Young People in Care* and *Educating Children and Young People in Care: Learning Placements and Caring Schools*. She is also active as an advocate for disadvantaged children and a patron of organisations that promote their wellbeing. Her current research on young children in foster care explores an overlooked subject crossing conventional subject boundaries, and is published in the *The SAGE Handbook of Early Childhood Policy*.

Nicola Kemp is a Senior Lecturer in Early Childhood at Canterbury Christ Church University and Director of the MA in Early Childhood Education. She works across the University, leading Education for Sustainable Development (ESD), as well as co-leading the 'Ecopedagogy' research theme group. A geographer by background, Nicola is interested in children's experiences of the natural environment and has developed the *Connecting Children and Nature Network for Kent*, bringing together staff, students and a range of local organisations for knowledge exchange and curriculum development. Her other research interests include forest school, home education, alternative curricula and Education for Sustainable Futures.

Jackie Marsh is Professor of Education at the University of Sheffield. Over the past two decades she has led numerous research projects that have examined young children's literacy practices in the digital age in homes, communities and early years settings. Many of her projects involve collaborations with schools and children's media industry partners, including her latest ESRC-funded project on young children's use of tablets (www.techandplay.org). Jackie is Chair of the COST Action IS1410, *The Digital Literacy and Multimodal Practices of Young Children* (www.digil-itey.eu), a network of researchers in 33 countries who are collaborating to further knowledge in this area.

Helen Moylett is an independent early years consultant and writer. She has been an early years teacher, a local authority senior advisory teacher and a Senior Lecturer in primary and early years education at Manchester Metropolitan University. In 2000 she left academia to become head of an early years centre. In 2004 she joined the National Strategies. She was centrally involved in developing the Early Years Foundation Stage as well as many of the National Strategies materials associated with it. Helen is a former President of the British Association of Early Childhood Education and a tutor at the Centre for Research in Early Childhood (CREC) in Birmingham. She has written and edited various early years books including *Characteristics Of Effective Early Learning: Helping Young Children Become Learners For Life* (2013).

Martin Needham is Associate Head of School for Childhood, Youth and Education Studies at Manchester Metropolitan University. He trained and worked as an Early Years and Primary teacher in Nottinghamshire, London and Pakistan. This was followed by development roles in education management and leadership in Pakistan and then with early education, extended schools services and children's centre provision in England. A Principal Lecturer since 2014, he has frequently taught on multi-agency working in the early years at undergraduate and post-graduate levels. Martin has published work on multi-agency working, young children's learning, professionals engaging with parents and leadership in the early years, conducting research projects in these areas funded by the DfE and NHS Scotland. He has recently been involved in early education policy contexts exploring early learning and workforce development in the UK and internationally.

Siobhan O'Connor is a Senior Lecturer in Early Childhood Studies at Canterbury Christ Church University. Her research interests include the development of an inclusive curriculum for early childhood studies degree programmes, notions of professionalism in the early years and the concept of quality in early childhood care and education.

Jayne Osgood is Professor of Education in the Centre for Education Research & Scholarship at Middlesex University. Previously she has worked at the National Foundation for Educational Research and London Metropolitan University's Institute for Policy Studies in Education. She is also currently Professor II at Oslo & Arkerhus University College, Norway; Visiting Professor at The Education University of Hong Kong and Visiting Professor at Western Sydney University, Australia. Jayne's recent publications include the 'Reimagining Quality in Early Childhood Education' Editorial for *Contemporary Issues in Early Childhood (2016)* 17:1, 1–8 and 'Putting post humanist theory to work to reconfigure gender in early childhood: when theory becomes art becomes method' in *Global Studies of Childhood (2015)* 5:3, 346–60 with M. Giugni.

Helen Penn is Professor Emerita of Early Childhood at the University of East London, and is about to take up an appointment as Visiting Professor at the Institute of Education, UCL. She was previously a teacher and a senior administrator of ECEC services, before becoming an academic. She has worked for a number of international organisations on large-scale international aid projects on early childhood, most recently with UNICEF. She is currently working on a work memoir, to be published by Routledge in 2018, and is co-editing a book with a Norwegian colleague: *Early Childhood: A Review of Theories, Policy and Practice in Development Work*, to be published by Palgrave Macmillan also in 2018.

Dendy Platt is Honorary Senior Research Fellow in Social Work at the University of Bristol. He has taught on the MSc in Social Work and MSc in Advanced Social Work with Children & Families. He has worked as a social worker and team leader in local authority social services departments, and in project director roles with Save the Children, and with Barnardo's. He has undertaken research and writing on social work assessments and decision-making in relation to children and families, on family support, and on social workers' engagement with families. He is currently working on a project supporting social workers to assess parental capacity to change in situations where there are child welfare concerns, and has developed a practice approach called C-Change.

Sally Robinson is a Principal Lecturer who leads the Public Health team at Canterbury Christ Church University, and an experienced external examiner to other universities. Sally's research has included investigating children's perceptions of eating and body image, healthy early years settings, healthy eating and language learning in European schools, children's views of older people, childhood obesity and the needs of teachers who are working with children with life limiting or life threatening conditions. Her publications include *Healthy Eating in Primary Schools* (2006) and *Educating Children with Life-Limiting Conditions* (2017). She also works with young children as a play therapist.

Iram Siraj OBE is Professor of ECE at UCL Institute of Education. Iram's recent research projects have included leading on the Evaluation of the Foundation Phase across Wales and she was principal investigator of the major DCSF 17-year study on Effective Pre-school, Primary and Secondary Education (EPPSE 3–16, 1997–2014), the E4Kids study (ARC Linkage, Melbourne University 2009–2014) and of the influential Researching Effective Pedagogy in the Early Years project (REPEY, 2002). She is a visiting professor at the University of Wollongong and divides her time between the UK and Australia, where she leads several research studies, mainly in New South Wales and Victoria. Her DfE publications on effective pedagogy in primary schools (EPPSEM study, Siraj-Blatchford et al., 2011) and 'unpacking' the influences on the trajectories of children performing 'against the odds' (Siraj and Mayo et al., 2014) have received international recognition. She is a specialist, early years adviser to governments and ministers in the UK and overseas.

Nigel Thomas is Professor Emeritus of Childhood and Youth at the University of Central Lancashire and founder of The Centre for Children and Young People's Participation. Nigel's research interests are principally in child welfare, children's rights, children and young people's participation, and theories of childhood and intergenerational relations. His publications include *Children, Family and the State: Decision-Making and Child Participation* (Macmillan 2000, Policy Press 2002); *Social Work with Young People in Care* (Palgrave 2005); *Children, Politics and Communication: Participation at the Margins* (Policy Press 2009); and *A Handbook of Children and Young People's Participation: perspectives from theory and practice* (with Barry Percy-Smith, Routledge 2010). Nigel is Chair of the Editorial Board of the journal *Children & Society*, a visiting Professor in the Centre for Children and Young People at Southern Cross University and an Honorary Professor in the School of Education and Lifelong Learning at Aberystwyth University.

Yordanka Valkanova is a Senior Lecturer in Childhood Studies at Canterbury Christ Church University. Previously she lectured at Roehampton University and was an Assistant Professor at Plovdiv University, Bulgaria. Her publications include *Accession and Migration: Changing Policy, Society and Culture in an Enlarged Europe* (2009) as well as numerous articles. Her research has focused on the history of childhood in Russia and Eastern Europe and digital literacy.

Joanne Westwood is Assistant Director for Social Work Education at the University of Salford. Previously she worked at the University of Stirling and the University of Central Lancashire. Joanne is a qualified social worker and worked with children, young people and their families in both statutory and voluntary agencies. Her research and teaching interests include advocacy, law and child welfare policies and practices. She has undertaken research on migrant children, global childcare systems and children's experiences of domestic violence in the UK.

GLOSSARY

Abjection	Depositing something, which makes us feel degraded, on the other side of an imaginary border. The French psychoanalyst and feminist Julia Kristeva proposes that we first experience abjection at the point of separation from the mother.
Accommodation	In Piaget's theory, the process of changing existing schemas or creating new schemas in response to new information.
Assimilation	In Piaget's theory, dealing with new environmental situations by using existing cognitive organisation.
Biocentric/ Ecocentric (rights)	A biocentric perspective considers living things (e.g. people, plants) to be most important whereas an ecocentric perspective gives equal weight to all aspects of the ecosystem, including non-living components (e.g. geological features).
Causal determinant	Pre-existing factor that brings about change (causes the change).
Centration	In Piaget's theory, focusing attention on just one aspect of an object or event.
CHES	Child Health and Education Studies (The 1970 British Cohort longitudinal study).
Cognates	Words that have a common etymological origin.
Concrete operations stage	The third stage in Piaget's theory of cognitive development, from 7 to 11 years. The child can now use adult internally consistent logic but only when the problem is presented in a concrete way.
Conservation	In Piaget's theory, awareness that altering an object's or substance's appearance does not change its basic properties.
Continuity– discontinuity issue	The issue of whether development involves gradual, cumulative change (continuity) or distinct stages (discontinuity).
Cultural capital	The accumulated and embodied knowledge, skills and behaviour, which facilitate social mobility in a given cultural context.
Deferred imitation	Imitation that occurs after a lengthy time delay.
Dialectical theory	A theory that assumes that all social relationships (in which development occurs) have inherent contradictions.

Diffractive/ Diffraction	A concept offered by Barad (2007) that has been taken up by feminist researchers in recent research falling within the new materialist/post humanist paradigm. In physics diffraction is the way that waves (sound, water, light) combine as they interweave and the way in which waves appear to bend and spread when an obstruction is encountered. As waves meet they interfere with one another. This interference is never only destructive; it is also generative. For social scientists diffraction offers a useful metaphor for thinking-with and opens up research to include a wider range of agents and actors than humans and textual representations alone. In research with children, such as that undertaken by Davies (2014), diffractive thinking is deployed to consider how different ways of knowing, being and doing interact, overlap, and constructively and destructively interfere with one another.
Discourse	Written and spoken communications which may have a powerful influence over others.
Discursively constructed childhood	Transformation of concepts of childhood, expressed in everyday situations and interactions, and promoted by mass media, institutions and politicians.
Distributed leadership	A collective enterprise that operates at different organisational structures and levels, through situations, relationships and processes.
Early Help Assessment (EHA)	A tool for identifying the needs of children and families intended to lead to particular forms of support.
ECEC	Early childhood education and care (integrated childcare and early education).
Egocentrism	In Piaget's theory, the tendency to focus on one's own perspective.
Emergency Protection Order (EPO)	If a child is deemed by the court to be at serious risk of harm, an EPO is a means of ensuring immediate protection by removing the child to a safe place or keeping them in situ.
Empirical progression	Claiming progression of an individual or group (e.g. in learning or development in particular maths skills) on the basis of statistical data.
Epigenesis	A theory based on the belief that developmental changes are the result of interactions between a person's genes and environmental influences.
Epistemology	A branch of philosophy that concerns sources of knowledge. Specifically, epistemology is concerned with what certain knowledge makes possible, how knowledge is generated, what sources of knowledge are drawn upon, and the limitations of knowledge in any given field of study. An episteme is a school of thought/body of ideas that determine which knowledge is intellectually certain at any particular time.

EPPE — Effective Provision of Preschool Education: an influential, longitudinal research project.

Equilibration — Using the processes of accommodation and of assimilation to produce a state of equilibrium or balance.

Ethico-onto-epistemological — A concept offered by Barad (2007) which argues for the interconnection of ethics, ontology and epistemology. In its hyphenated form the term conveys a central new materialist idea, that is: what is in the world (ontology) and what we understand about what is in the world (epistemology) cannot be separated as things that do not affect one another. Barad argues that things emerge in the world and are both shaped by what we know and what they are. She argues that everything, every encounter is shaped by politics and therefore we have a responsibility to recognise our role in how the world, and how we understand the world is shaped.

Ethnocentrism — To evaluate cultural groups based on a belief they are inferior to your own. This occurs because humans place their own beliefs, values and customs at the centre of things causing an inherent bias towards their own cultural practices.

Eugenics — A movement that is aimed at improving the genetic composition of the human race.

Executive control — The ability to exercise coordination so as to perform various tasks successively, multi-task or switch to and fro between tasks successfully.

EYFS — Early Years Foundation Stage framework – national curricular framework for children from birth to five in England.

Feminist post-structuralism — A perspective that emerged in the late 20th century in response to the predominance of structuralism. Structuralism is founded upon ideas of certainty and truth, whereas post-structuralism argues that there is no one universal set of ideas about humanity that can apply to every place, culture and time. Furthermore, post-structuralists argue that universal explanations (or dominant views) lead to the oppression or invisibility of differences. For feminists, these differences relate to gender. Feminist post-structuralism therefore questions objective 'truths' upon which individuals construct ideas about the world and which act to privilege men and boys.

Formal operations stage — The final stage in Piaget's theory of cognitive development, from age 11 years. Thinking now involves formal internally consistent adult logic and abstract thinking.

Formative assessment	Decisions based on observation which identify children's learning and development so far. The basis of planning in the here and now and to support children's future progress.
Froebel	Friedrich Froebel (1782–1852) was a German pioneering pedagogue who introduced 'kindergartens' and a comprehensive philosophy for educating young children.
Gestalt	A whole that is equal to more than the sum of its parts (in psychology).
Global society	This term can represent a view that globalisation has led to all societies being seen as parts of a single entity.
Globalisation	How ideas from one or more (usually more economically powerful) context are transferred to (usually less powerful) others and come to dominate or take precedence over local beliefs and practices.
Hegelian dialectic	A method of argument employed by the German philosopher Georg Wilhelm Friedrich Hegel (1770–1831) that brings together thesis, antithesis and synthesis. It suggests that the thesis must always attract an antithesis, and this tension must always result in a synthesis, which in turn becomes a new thesis.
Hegemony (hegemonisation)	Stems from ideas posed by Italian Marxist, Gramsci; the concept refers to the means by which one powerful social group imposes its particular perspectives, beliefs, or political and economic conditions upon another.
Heteronormativity	Concerns the way that everyday interactions, practices and policies construct individuals as heterosexual; this process is integral to the way that heterosexuality is normalised and naturalised, and non-heterosexual relationships are rendered deviant, abnormal and unnatural.
Hidden curriculum	The indirect or unspoken spread of particular beliefs and values within the contexts of teaching and learning.
Historiography	The writing of history.
Human purchase	Refers to the connection we feel to a particular issue or subject. The aspirational (rather than tangible) nature of sustainability means people often find it hard to find a human connection and to see it as significant in the context of their everyday lives.
Humanist	A scholar of the humanities; an advocate or follower of the principles of humanism, who concentrates on human activities and possibilities, usually downplaying or rejecting the importance of God.
Indigenous cosmologies	Are generated from within native cultural communities and typically take the form of artistic and literary expression in which traditional culture and knowledge are embodied. Indigenous knowledge is transmitted from one generation to the next via handmade textiles, paintings, stories, legends, ceremonies, music, songs, rhythms and dance.

Intelligence	Problem-solving skills and the ability to learn from and adapt to the experiences of daily life.
Lexicon (adj. lexical)	An individual's mental inventory of word forms and their associated meaning.
Ludic/epistemic (play)	(Based on the work of Corinne Hutt in the 1970s) ludic play refers to imaginative play that does not involve learning; epistemic play involves exploration of the world and yields learning.
Mental operations	In Piaget's theory, mental processes that simulate actions in the real world.
Metacognition	Higher order thinking skills involving, for example, thinking about thinking.
Mirror neurons	Brain cells which are activated by observing the actions/behaviour of others.
Mudiad Ysgolion Meithrin	Welsh Medium (Language) Playgroups.
Multi-level modelling	A term for statistical modelling that involves more than one level of variables.
Multimodal (literacy)	The rich variety of skills and knowledge that people have and acquire when engaging with/using literacy (e.g. spoken, digital).
Naturalistic observation	Observation that takes place in a child's everyday contexts as opposed to a laboratory or clinical context.
Nature–nurture issue	The issue of how a child's cognitive development is affected by their biological inheritance (nature) and their environment (nurture).
Neo-Vygotskian	Followers of Vygotsky have elaborated his theories into a more comprehensive body of work in which advances in holistic development are mediated, through social interaction, by supportive adults or more experienced peers.
Neural interconnectivity	The connections and communications between neuronal cells in the brain.
Neuronal pathways	Networks of brain cell connections that facilitate the processing of information and patterns of behavior.
Non-participant observation	The observer is not actively involved in the activity that is being observed.
Normative	Relates to an idea that a standard rule or norm exists/is created (and the ways that people's beliefs and behaviours conform to this or differ from it).
NSPCC	National Society for the Prevention of Cruelty to Children – a UK charity.
NVQ	National Vocational Qualification(s).

Object permanence	In Piaget's theory, an awareness that objects continue to exist even when they can no longer be seen.
OECD	Organisation for Economic Cooperation and Development.
One-Child Policy	A succession of policies designed to slow the birth rate in the People's Republic of China, which mostly limited couples to one child, especially those living in densely populated urban areas.
Ontology/ ontological	Can be defined as the science or study of being; it deals with the nature of reality. Ontology is a system of beliefs that reflect an individual's interpretation about what constitutes a reality. Ontology is associated with the central question of whether social entities need to be perceived as objective or subjective; as truths or social constructions.
PACEY	(formerly National Childminding Association) Professional Association for Childcare and Early Years.
Paradigm	A way of thinking and viewing the world (or a belief system) that includes particular orientations, theories and so forth, which (in research terms) shape the way that studies are conceptualised, designed, conducted and reported. Examples include positivism (seeking to categorise, predict or test), interpretivism (seeking understanding of phenomena) and critical theory (aiming to expose inequality/to emancipate).
Para-professionals	People who are not qualified to take responsibility for the entirety of a professional role but to whom certain aspects of the role might be delegated (by qualified professionals), e.g. teaching assistants.
Participant observation	The observer is part of the action taking place.
Peer tutoring	Teaching of one child by another.
Perception	The brain's interpretation of sensory information.
Perezhivanie	(From Vygotsky) A lived experience in the social situation of development.
Plowden Report	Influential 1967 report on all aspects of primary education in England by the Central Advisory Council for Education, which was chaired by Lady Plowden.
Post-colonial	Refers to the time after, and the effects of, European colonisation. More generally, it is concerned with exposing the continued influence and power of the former colonisers over the economies and cultures of decolonised states.

Pre-operational stage	The second stage in Piaget's theory of cognitive development, from 2 to 7 years. The child can cope with symbols (such as using language) but cannot cope with adult internally consistent logic (operations).
Qualitative	Explores and tries to describe the qualities of something, including underlying meanings, sometimes according to different perspectives, often using various research methods to better understand or explain a phenomenon.
Quantitative	Attempts to capture, organise or categorise and investigate according to quantities and using specific measures.
Queer theory	Reinforces the idea that identities are not fixed or stable but rather are shifting, contradictory, dynamic and socially constructed. Informed by theorist s such as Judith Butler, queer theory holds that all identities are perfomances and disrupts the idea that gender and sexuality are inherently fixed. This perspective provides a critical lens through which to begin to see everyday processes in everyday contexts as producing particular (heteronormative) ideas about gender.
Recapitulation (in play)	Where actions reflect evolutionary behaviours that for most children are now extinct, such as playing at being a hunter-gatherer.
Reversal/ reversibility	The ability to undo, or reverse mentally, an action or operation.
Romantic Movement	A retrospective term describing change in ideas that emerged from writers, poets and artists in the late 18th and early 19th century, characterised by the focus on individual thought and feelings. The 18th century French philosopher, Jean-Jacques Rousseau had a profound influence on 'the Romantics' and representations of childhood.
Scaffold(ing)	The context provided by an adult or other knowledgeable person that helps the child to develop his or her cognitive skills.
Schema (cognition)	In Piaget's theory, organised knowledge used by children and adults to guide their actions.
Schema (language)	A partially abstract grammatical representation based on a range of word-based constructions.
Secularism	A principle that advocates strict separation of the state from religious institutions.
Semantic battle	Dispute about the meanings of words and phrases in language.
Sensorimotor stage	First stage in Piaget's theory, at which children learn to co-ordinate their sensory and motor abilities.

Seriation	In Piaget's theory, the ability to order stimuli along a quantitive dimension (such as length).
Serious case review	Serious case reviews are a statutory procedure for the review of serious cases such as a child death or very serious neglect, with a view to local services identifying improvements in practice that may prevent recurrence.
Social constructionism	A school of thought, a theory of knowledge, which suggests that meaning is socially defined and organised, and therefore is subject to social change.
Social constructivism	A theoretical view about knowledge creation, which holds that knowledge is constructed through people's interactions with one another and their contexts shape these constructions.
Socio-genealogical	Concerned with people's connections to their personal, socio-cultural and biological heritage and histories.
SSLP	Sure Start Local Programmes. Sure Start was a flagship social policy of the New Labour Government. It was intended to deliver multiple services for young children and their families and began in 1999 with area-based programmes in the poorest localities in England.
Structured observation	Observation which uses a particular format, e.g. an involvement scale, or technique, e.g. time-sampling.
Summative assessment	Based on everyday formative assessment when practitioners take stock of children's overall progress at a particular point in time.
Symbiotic relationship	A relationship between two organisms that may be mutually beneficial or vital for the survival of one or more of the organisms involved.
Symbolic function	In Piaget's theory, the ability to mentally represent an object that is not present.
Theory of Mind (ToM)	Having an understanding that others' thoughts, intentions, and beliefs are different from one's own.
Theseus, Hercules, Achilles and Perseus	Theseus, Hercules, Achilles and Perseus were Greek founder-heroes, all of whom battled and overcame foes that were identified with an archaic religious and social order.
Working memory	A mental workspace in which information is temporarily stored and manipulated.
Zone of proximal development (ZPD)	In Vygotsky's theory, capacities that are not yet functioning fully in the child but can be developed with adults' assistance.

INTRODUCTION

SACHA POWELL AND KATE SMITH

The purpose of this introductory text is to provide students of early childhood as well as practitioners working daily with young children with a broad understanding of the perspectives and practices in early childhood today. The book, now in its fourth edition, testifies to the on-going interest and growth in undergraduate and postgraduate programmes in early childhood, reflecting what was noted in previous editions, that there is a continuing high placing of early childhood on the political agenda. This revised edition is made up of twenty-two chapters each written by key thinkers in the field of early childhood. These chapters not only illustrate different aspects of early childhood, and demonstrate the diverse landscape in the field, but also tackle some clearly identified interwoven themes. We hope that the book will give the reader a rich insight into this complex and fascinating area of study that continues to evolve, strengthen and challenge.

Early childhood studies is shaped by multiple discourses within health, education, social care, psychology, sociology, geography, law, and philosophy. It is unique in its multidisciplinary approach but also in what it seeks to explore. Early childhood studies has always had at its foundation a search for making meaning of young children's lives. Exploring the early years of human life asks us to contemplate important questions about how we value this stage of existence, and how we perceive young children as distinct from adults throughout their earliest experiences and activities. Consequently, there are some challenging questions that need to be asked about how we frame early childhood in our enquiries – for instance – do we view young children as developing, knowing, or rightful? The perspectives that are taken lead to specific choices of how to support our youngest citizens' welfare, their learning, and their voice and so our fundamental ideas of early childhood underpin the systems and structures that surround them. These questions also provoke us to reflect on our own personal beliefs and principles in the work we do on a day-to-day basis with young children, helping us to identify what is needed to build essential relationships with children and babies, a necessity for them to flourish as individuals, and for us to be fulfilled in working alongside them as they flourish.

Knowing that there are different lenses through which young children are 'imagined' makes for a field of study that is often difficult and problematic rather than comfortable and straightforward.

In this book we make no apologies for creating demands on the reader to think hard about the differing ways in which young children are viewed, as to properly interrogate government policies and localised practices we must critically engage in the alternative ways of seeing on offer. The following chapters recognise the dilemmas within the field, whilst trying to get to the heart of what really matters in the work that goes on with children. The overall aim of the book is to make us stop and think about early childhood in diverse ways, and to develop conversations with others around theory, policy and practice, and in so doing recognise the further questions that need to be asked.

There are four key themes that we recognise as being addressed in the book as a whole, with each chapter adding to these areas of discussion. The themes identified are: political, social and economic changes; the social construction of childhood and children's rights; the impact of **globalisation**; and dominant and competing theories.

POLITICAL, SOCIAL AND ECONOMIC CHANGES

Many of our authors note that political, economic and environmental factors matter in shaping young children's lives and opinions about early childhood. The political context of this new edition, in 2018, is one which was probably unimaginable a few years ago. The move to 'Brexit' in the UK alongside the election of Donald Trump as President of the USA have been viewed widely as a rejection by many in the electorate of the policies that surround globalisation, and have shaken many assumptions about democratic processes and consensus. We are in a world that appears increasingly separated and fragmented, where populist politics is on the rise and the liberal values that have been the bedrocks of certain strategies and practices in the developed north are being upended. At the time of writing we are left wondering how this will impact on early childhood education and care. We have yet to see the ramifications of these electoral choices; however, living with these uncertainties is sharpening our focus in regard to the essential beliefs and values that shape our shared social responsibilities, and is perhaps re-invigorating our discussions about how (and whether) the state, communities, families and the individual might (or should) support young children and their families, not only in our own country but across the globe.

It is apparent from Sonia Jackson's summary in Chapter 11, that currently there is a continuing political commitment to early childhood in many countries worldwide and among international organisations like UNESCO and the World Health Organization (WHO). The reasons for this interest are diverse and contested but arguments include a moral responsibility for young children's welfare, legal duties to make certain provisions for them and long-term aspirations about the contribution of citizens to a country's economic growth and stability in a globally competitive 'marketplace'. Although there is wide variation in the proportions of GDP (Gross Domestic Product) that are reportedly invested in early childhood services in different countries (see, for example, UNICEF, 2008; European Commission, 2014; **OECD**, 2016), there can be no doubt that there has been significant financial investment in provision over the last decade for the first years of life, including the months before birth. What is also apparent is an increasing strategic use of funding to support young children born into economic disadvantage and increase the places on offer in early years provision, particularly for children under the age of three. However, Helen Penn (Chapter 4) argues that we look again at the drivers behind widespread and substantial 'investment' in early childhood programmes, some of which have ignored or overridden local traditions and customs at their peril.

Although countries recognise funding needs there is disparity across the world in terms of equality of access to good standards of care, welfare and education for young children and their families at home and in their communities. As Sally Robinson notes in Chapter 15, a 'life course' perspective not only exposes social, economic and environmental determinants of (health) inequality but also attempts to redress these by advocating policies that support a progressive universal approach to the re-configuration and re-distribution of services for families with young children. There are challenges however. The emphasis on integrated working across agencies, between professionals and bridging the private, statutory and voluntary sectors have been impacted by the policies of austerity and shrinking local authority budgets as a result of the financial crash in 2008. Alongside this, moving out of professional silos is also notoriously troublesome, whether at departmental level in government or within a community-based 'team around a child/family' as Angela Anning and Martin Needham discuss in Chapter 19.

The rising political narrative in support of 'school readiness', with policies to boot, for example having two year olds in school, was noted in the last edition and continues to raise pedagogical concerns around the narrowing of the provision for young children to what can be accountable and measurable. In Chapter 9 Justine Howard looks at the complex qualities of play and its importance in providing young children with autonomy as learners, and Iram Siraj offers us a reminder in Chapter 13 of the importance of our role as advocates of theoretically reasoned and thoroughly researched practices based on learning relationships with young children. Professionals are increasingly aware of the demands of meeting assessment requirements conflicting with their own pedagogical orientations and Part 4 of the book attempts to offer some support in untangling these kinds of challenges and dilemmas with exemplars and suggestions that are deeply rooted in theory.

THE SOCIAL CONSTRUCTION OF CHILDHOOD AND CHILDREN'S RIGHTS

A second prominent theme throughout this edition, as in previous editions of the text, concerns childhood as a social construct. From a social constructionist perspective, what we think we know and believe to be true is not fixed and simply internalised; our beliefs are the product of our experiences and social interactions and are (re-)constructed by and through these. This is illustrated in Chapter 16 by Siobhan O'Connor and Polly Bolshaw, who look at the differing arguments for inclusion. Many authors in this edition reflect on how 'childhood' is a concept that exists and is characterised in particular ways by historical (Chapter 2) and contemporary beliefs (Chapters 4 and 5), and is not simply a 'natural' aspect of human existence. So what constitutes childhood in different cultures – if indeed the first years after birth are constructed as such – varies in time and place. Differences can be found around the world in relation to what babies and young children are believed to be, to be capable of doing, are permitted or enabled to do, are prohibited or protected from and this is not purely a response to biological immaturity (Chapter 1). It is also dependent on the existence of a construct of 'adulthood' and how childhood is conceived in comparison. This is starkly evident in discussions around children's rights highlighted by Nigel Thomas in Chapter 12. But it can also be seen throughout the book in relation to social processes and discourses that distinguish children from others, for example, by having specific welfare needs as articulated by Dendy Platt in Chapter 14.

THE IMPACT OF GLOBALISATION

The social construction of childhood can be linked to a further issue noted by several writers: the increasing emphasis on and effects of globalisation (see, in particular, Chapters 1 and 4). Young children and their families across the world are on the move either as a result of forced displacement due to environmental threat or conflict, or to seek better opportunities in life. Jackie Marsh recognises the rapid expansion of digital technologies in Chapter 5 that have provided children with opportunities to extend their communication and strengthen their relationships with others remotely. Considering global childhoods and recognising alternative childhood experiences challenges our perceptions about what we consider to be 'normal', often based on our own experience, and thus what are 'good' practices and approaches. This is illustrated in Chapter 4 through Helen Penn's discussion of good models of parenting. Global perspectives may also facilitate the 'borrowing' of early childhood policies, provision or practices from different cultures and countries. However, while a critical engagement with alternative ideas may be viewed positively, concerns have been raised by Joanne Westwood and Helen Penn (Chapters 1 and 4) about the export of theories and practices, and with them particular embedded values, especially when this is from the relatively wealthy North to the relatively poor South. For example, the imposition of what are seen as dominant theories of child development that may infer that there is a 'universal' child (Chapter 1). These theories, along with concepts such as 'culture' and 'quality', are now being explored and problematised both from a sociological perspective as outlined by Nigel Thomas in Chapter 3 and from a post-modern perspective as described by Jayne Osgood in Chapter 22.

DOMINANT AND COMPETING THEORIES

There are certain 'dominant' theories, particularly theories of child development as discussed extensively in Chapters 6 to 10, which are extremely powerful in the discourses that surround young children. The ideas – contained within these developmental theories, which promote the importance of nurturing social and emotional relationships and the role of cultural environments in structuring these through communication and language – are highly pertinent to our understanding of early years practice both in families and in organised settings. Increasingly, however, the authority given to these ideas is being challenged by writers who draw from alternative **paradigms** to offer differing views of young children that are more encompassing of them as beings as well as becomings (see Jayne Osgood – Chapter 22 – and Nicola Kemp – Chapter 21).

This edition, with these new chapters, creates further understandings of how differing theories contrast and come together; it is this challenging debate that gets to the core of what early childhood is, and can be, as a field of study.

It is imperative that these theoretical problems are recognised by the early childhood workforce to aid their ability to be critically reflective as demonstrated by Carol Aubrey in Chapter 20, to be able to listen to the voices of children, as discussed in Chapter 18 by Alison Clark, and to develop skills in child observation (Helen Moylett provides useful examples in Chapter 17). Within this text some writers consider a range of perspectives and propositions when discussing a particular issue – for example, when exploring children's cognitive development or how they acquire language (Chapters 6 and 8). However, it is also possible to identify competing theories when pursuing an area of interest across different chapters. This is well illustrated in relation to the issue of play. For example, it is maintained that play is fundamental to young children's learning, health and development – cognitive, social and emotional (Chapters 6, 7 and 9) – as well as to the development of adaptable and flexible thought (Chapter 9). It is also indicated that play is central to an inclusive curriculum (Chapter 16). We are warned, however, that not all play promotes learning and development and that when considering children's education, the prioritising (and even the existence) of 'free play' is challenged (Chapter 13). Indeed, when considering play in a global context, the idea that children should be allowed simply to play, rather than making a contribution to the family and community, is raised for consideration (Chapter 4).

Of course, these tensions between competing theories and discourses remind us of the demands and significance of inter-agency and multidisciplinary working (Chapter 19). They also emphasise the complexity, challenges and excitement of the interdisciplinary study of early childhood! The variation in the chapters within the book – and indeed the dissonance that can emerge from thinking about childhood from diverse perspectives – provides, we hope, a juncture from which to consider our own positions; for we are all deeply implicated in the reconstruction of narratives about who (or what) a young child is and early childhoods are for. And so we would encourage readers to step back, to think hard and critically about the ideologies underlying the frames and frameworks that may mould (or reflect) our beliefs. In so doing, choosing not simply to reject those ideologies but to work hard to understand their origins, evolutions and implications so as to be better prepared to recognise, contest and move forwards from those with which we might feel uncomfortable and the reasons for feeling this way. Or, as Erica Burman (2001) has entreated: 'far from jettisoning our cultural legacies (which is an impossible, and probably undesirable, demand), we can perhaps instead use these to better effect to look within, and beyond, ourselves and our categorisation systems, and emerge better equipped to work with those who have historically been devalued and excluded in order to build others'.

ORGANISATION OF THE BOOK

This fourth edition of the text is edited by Sacha Powell with a new co-editor, Kate Smith, whose field of interest is in children's language, literacy and play. Thanks go to Nigel Thomas and Trisha Maynard for their significant contribution to the first three editions; their ideas and words still resonate through this book.

As emphasised already, the twenty-two chapters presented here cover a very extensive territory, ranging from the history of childhood to the place of play in the early years curriculum. The book begins with perspectives on childhood (Chapters 1–5) and then considers developmental theories (Chapters 6–10). Policies, structures and provision are considered next (Chapters 11–16), followed by chapters that provide practice examples or metaphors to illustrate theory (Chapters 17–22).

Readers will find that the inter-relationships between child development, historical and cultural perspectives on childhood, local and national policy and the nature and quality of provision, and the implications of all this for professional practice, are emphasised throughout the text.

Each individual chapter aims to introduce its subject to an interested reader who may have limited previous knowledge of the area, to indicate to them some of the important areas of debate within that specific arena. Some chapters include case studies, models of policy or services, or examples of practice, which will hopefully be useful in bringing theoretical approaches into the real world of working with young children. All conclude with a summary of key points raised in the chapter to aid understanding, and suggestions for further reading. The full list of sources from each chapter is at the end of the book.

For this fourth edition all the chapters have been updated by the authors from the third edition. We are extremely pleased to have their continued expertise on board; we are grateful to Nigel Thomas, Helen Penn, Ruth Ford, Tricia David, Thea Cameron-Faulkner, Justine Howard, Sonia Jackson, Iram Siraj, Alison Clark, Carol Aubrey, Joanne Westwood, Yordanka Valkanova, Dendy Platt, Sally Robinson, Siobhan O'Connor (joined also by Polly Bolshaw), Helen Moylett, Angela Anning (joined by Martin Needham for this edition), Jackie Marsh and Marilyn Fleer for this. We are also very pleased to have two new contributions, mentioned previously, written by Nicola Kemp and Jayne Osgood. We believe that their chapters enhance the book by offering us insights into fresh and alternative views of early childhood, ones that are increasingly being explored in research and study.

Each author is an expert in their own field. Their professional backgrounds are diverse, reflecting the multidisciplinary nature of the subject and the strong interchange between theory and practice. Although there are differences of emphasis in the chapters that follow, one overriding perspective still runs through the whole book. This is our theoretical and practical commitment to respecting children and seeing children as competent participants in all matters relating to their health, care, welfare and education. We continue to promote the importance of investment in young children's lives, both through study and resources, convinced that this is necessary for the health and wellbeing of all in society, with a clear message that hearing children's voices – their gestures and expressions – provides us with the knowledge necessary to identify the best ways to think about and make this investment.

PART 1

PERSPECTIVES ON CHILDHOOD

CHILDHOOD IN DIFFERENT CULTURES

JOANNE WESTWOOD

CONTENTS

INTRODUCTION

The perception of childhood as a period of dependence and innocence has a long history. Being strongly associated with the **Romantic Movement** of eighteenth-century Europe it resonates with more recent Western theories of child development, ideas about child rearing and policies relating to the care and education of children. The advent of a **global society**, however, demands that we examine and reflect on our own belief systems and those which inform our individual and institutional practices with children. This chapter begins with a discussion of globalisation and culture (see also Chapter 4) and then sets out reasons why a cross-cultural understanding of childhood, children and child rearing is a prerequisite for any form of intervention in children's lives. Understanding the importance of culture can challenge our own preconceived ideas about childhood in a global context and help us to determine what we expect from children and their place and rights in society.

GLOBALISATION

Globalisation is the extension of relationships and patterns of social practice and meaning across the world space; what happens in one part of the world has an impact somewhere else (Ritzer, 2008). Globalisation is a layered and uneven process which connects the local to the global (James, 2006) and in doing so brings a range of concerns and issues to the local context. The process of globalisation shifts societies and individuals closer together through the mediums of technology, transport and communication, moves both resources and people and is tied to consumption. Global products and brands and the (re)location of Western business interests to the developing world are all the outcome of globalisation, and the mechanics of globalisation mean that Western business and financial interests drive forward trade and exchange, arguably at the expense of the interests and benefits of local economies. The impact of globalisation is felt by non-developed and non-industrialised countries and it is maintained that power is retained by Western countries (Ritzer, 2008), although critics suggest that this perspective unhelpfully renders consumers as passive and powerless (Buckingham, 2007).

While there are clear benefits of globalisation, particularly in relation to communication and speed, there are disadvantages: specifically the 'hegemonisation' which occurs when one world view or one product/brand dominates. The US burger chain McDonald's provides a good example of **hegemony** at work in a global market. For example, McDonald's opened stores in China which had a big impact on the ways that families spend their disposable income. Marketing was child-oriented in the early days and China's 'Little Emperors' (a result of the so-called **One-Child Policy**) began to make demands of their parents in hitherto unseen ways. This changed traditional family dynamics and hierarchies and McDonald's not only brought a form of hegemony and change in dietary intakes but also cultural change that was more akin to family life in the USA than traditional Chinese families (Guo, 2000). Buckingham (2007: 44) suggests that: 'rather than relying simply on physical occupation, the US is now seen to sustain its hegemony through a process of ideological and cultural domination'.

As we can see, hegemony in a global context is not restricted to commodities but also extends to beliefs and ideas about social and cultural practices. There is thus potential for conflict in relation to childhood and ideologies and theories of child development and practice, where dominant views emanating from Western traditions and beliefs stifle local, traditional and culturally specific practices.

CULTURE, ETHNOCENTRISM AND CULTURAL RELATIVISM

Cultural theory suggests that a universal human culture is shared by all societies and that social practices support societies' structures (i.e. families, faiths) and fulfil individual needs. How then is culture defined?

Culture (see also Chapters 4 and 10) is how individuals understand who they are and how people give their lives meaning. Culture defines social groups – that is, the cultural group people belong to (macro culture). Culture is also understood as a set of practices, beliefs, plans and rules which a social group agree upon and which mark them out as unique. Culture gives groups a sense of identity and belonging and pride; it is learned, can be taught and acquired by members of the group (Rai and Pannar, 2010). Children acquire culture through exposure to, and observation and adoption of, behaviours and activities, as well as participation with their community and individuals, and by verbal and non-verbal communication.

Culture provides security and familiarity, is transmitted from one generation to another and is therefore dynamic: one generation may add or develop aspects and ideas about the world depending upon the context. Culture is patterned, uses symbols to convey meaning and continues over time, it is innovative and creative and can change in response to wider influences and societal demands (Rai and Pannar, 2010). For example, the provision of day care for pre-school children became the norm in the UK when the labour market required women to enter the workforce. The culture of child rearing practice being carried out largely by women in the home during the post-war period changed as the economic and political pressures were focused on female employment. This was not a straightforward process, as the development of day care for pre-school children was ideologically and politically opposed (Lewis, 2012) but by the start of the twenty-first century a childcare industry was fully established to provide a range of day care options for families, reflecting a significant cultural shift (see Chapter 11).

Cultures and cultural practices are studied by anthropologists; for example, Mary Douglas (1966, reissued 2006) studied the rituals and cultural practices and behaviours we know as taboos of the Lele tribe in Africa. Douglas argued that rather than being bizarre and primitive, beliefs about taboos, particularly those related to personal hygiene and the protection of females, developed to protect vulnerable members of the social group and to assure its future. Hendry (2008) explores cultures, traditions and their meaning and symbolism more widely drawing on anthropological research in Mexico, Japan and Morocco. Initiation rites, for example, vary widely but exist across many societies to signify a stage of development in childhood or in the transition towards adulthood. In some traditions these rites are gruelling physical tests or mutilations but they provide continuity and familiarity to the social group, tribe or clan.

It is not always easy for a 'newcomer' to learn the rules of the group; consider the example of a child in the UK who has been looked after at home before entering a reception class. In education settings children may, for example, have to learn that in whole class activities they need to signal their desire to speak and then wait to be asked or that they need permission to visit the toilet.

'Ethnocentrism' and 'cultural relativism' are concepts which also require definition if we are to understand how culture and cultural practices are both defended and criticised.

WHAT IS ETHNOCENTRISM?

Ethnocentrism is the belief that one's own culture and way of behaving is the correct way; all others are judged by this standard. Ethnocentrism generally legitimates a Western 'gaze' or interpretation of a problem or issue – concealing and, in doing so, preventing the articulation of indigenous responses. An example might be where there are concerns about HIV orphans in sub-Saharan Africa; whereas the local community may assert that the care of orphans lies with the extended family and kinship network, Western responses may include the development of institutionalised care. In cultures where extended family members (aunties, uncles, grandparents) traditionally provide care for children this ethnocentric response is deeply flawed as it disrupts customs and practices which have long ensured cultural and community continuity.

Issues related to working children also challenge our cultural perspectives about childhood and what is deemed acceptable and appropriate. Children who work transgress the boundaries and notions of childhood; indeed, the issue of child work/labour has been a longstanding point of conflict and tension in the West with international agencies and institutions at the forefront of the activity to remove children from the workplace. However, while there are good reasons to prevent exploitative child labour there are some benefits for children and their families and communities particularly in the case of poverty where children feel pride at being able to make a contribution to their family or when their work pays for their education.

WHAT IS CULTURAL RELATIVISM?

James and James (2012: 35) define cultural relativism as:

> The recognition that societies differ in their cultural attitudes towards social phenomena and therefore no universal criteria can be applied to compare one cultural view with another. Culture can therefore only be judged through reference to their own standards.

They provide an example of the age of marriage which varies across Europe, with a fairly standard age of 16. In the Indian sub-continent it is not unusual for girls to be married at 12. In the Western context this may be seen as abusive and exploitative and campaigners suggest that early marriage leads to earlier child birth which impacts on the health of females. However, the cultural practices of early and arranged marriage have been practised as a means to bring families and kinship groups closer together and ensure the continuance of the tribe, clan or group.

It is important to ensure that when we accept and defend cultural practices, we are not legitimating harmful behaviours. An example of this is found in the Laming enquiry (2003) where the concerns about Victoria Climbié were not expressed or communicated, as the deferential behaviour she presented when with her aunt was accepted by the professionals she had contact with as the norm in her culture (see Chapter 14). The child was clearly frightened by the presence of her aunt, but the extent and reasons for these fears were only articulated after Victoria's death.

The complexity of cultural relativism can be seen in relation to the practice of female circumcision which is common in some parts of Africa. The practice in some cultures is related to transition from childhood to adulthood and beliefs about healthy childbirth. Campaigning organisations in the 1970s and 1980s renamed the practice 'female genital mutilation' and drew political attention to the physical harms caused by the practice (Keck and Sikkink, 1998). The practice is now condemned by activists from within the culture and so its legitimacy as a rite of passage for girls is challenged (James and James, 2012).

CHILDHOOD AND CHILD REARING IN CROSS-CULTURAL CONTEXTS

As indicated above, our own views of childhood will have been formed within a particular cultural context and will therefore often be seen as how things 'are' and 'should be'. However, there are many reasons why as practitioners we should broaden our understanding of child development and child rearing practices and also extend what we know and believe about childhood in other cultures.

First, if we accept that developmental theories are contextually and culturally specific (see Chapters 6–10), then we can see that there are limits to how these theories are applied. The concept of the self as connected to others, which is common in many African cultures, develops as part of a rich socialisation process which begins after birth. The mother of the infant communicates the heritage and kinship lineage, emphasising the uniqueness and nobility of his or her birth. Members of the kinship network live in close proximity to facilitate continued social support including childcare between members, as well as retaining links to ancestral heritage (Gbadesgin, 1998 cited in Owusu-Bempah, 2007). This is in contrast to the early experiences of infants in Western cultures who live in a nuclear family with (usually) two parents and develop attachments exclusively with them.

Attachment theory, based on the work of John Bowlby (1965[1953]) (see Chapter 7), has been challenged as being overly reliant on Western notions of the family, disregarding the varying ways in which global communities, tribal groups and societies rear children. Notions of reciprocity, and the significant role kinship networks undertake, are marginalised in the dominant child rearing theories with which Western education and science are aligned. Owusu-Bempah (2007) argues that **socio-genealogical** connectedness is crucial for children's adjustment to separation from their family or kinship networks. This theory can assist us in our interventions with children who have experienced their parents' divorce and separation as well as more permanent 'endings' they have experienced through international migration, long-term fostering and adoption.

Understanding that children need to have information and culturally rich experiences which respect their heritage and history is a relevant issue for children who may be brought up by carers who do not share their culture, and as such care givers and practitioners would need to ensure that children's environments and activities draw on multiple cultural experiences.

Second, ecological models of child development have supplemented more traditional theories of attachment and incorporate the notion of the child interacting with, and adapting to, the environment. Erikson's (1995) life stage development theory, for example, suggests that all children go through similar stages or sequences, and each culture has developed its own way of both monitoring and protecting children as they transit each stage. The ecological perspective (Bronfenbrenner, 1979) also suggests that culture and the environment are important factors to consider and development tasks are adapted to suit the environment in which children are reared. More recently, Owusu-Bempah (2007) suggests that child development relies as much on the environment and the nurturing that children receive as it does on the knowledge and understanding they have about their heritage, cultural origins and the sense of being connected to their genealogical roots (see Chapter 10).

Timimi (2009) illustrates the way in which Islamic cultural practices and traditions assist children through various stages of development. These stages have been linked to children developing an understanding of the importance of truthfulness and co-operation and the sophisticated cognitive abilities to discern, show respect and demonstrate social skills. Once these understandings are attained, the child is deemed ready to move to the next phase of development. Within this culture, Timimi points out, indulgent parenting in a social environment that is characterised by high acceptance, low pressure and low competitiveness encourages children to want to show respect to adults and to demonstrate obedience. This is in contrast to Western traditions of child rearing which often over emphasise the importance of individuality, independence and self-esteem in children.

Timimi (2009) maintains that non-Western societies welcome a range of childhood behaviours and more consensual and hierarchical interpersonal relationships. Children in these social systems are accepted just for being who they are, rather than what they may become, or in achieving certain developmental milestones. Although it is also important to consider that in many faiths, cultures and practices of child rearing the normality of heterosexuality predominates and so the gendered socialisation of children emphasises the reproduction of **normative** gendered behaviours (Kehily, 2009).

The third reason for examining child rearing and childhood in other cultures is that if we value one cultural perspective or approach to child rearing over another this inevitably leads to 'ethnocentrism' – the belief that one's own way of life is the only or superior way – and this precludes respect for and integration and/or adoption of traditional practices which have worked well in a range of circumstances and environments. In 1930 the anthropologist Margaret Mead published the findings of her study of the Manus people of New Guinea and suggested that modern societies could learn from the child rearing practices of this tribe:

> the successful fashion in which each baby is efficiently adapted to its dangerous way of life is relevant to the problems which parents here must face as our mode of life becomes increasingly charged with possibilities of accident. (Mead, 1954: 13)

This leads to the fourth reason for challenging what we think of as 'taken for granted' knowledge. In many Western societies the family is generally defined through blood relations and it is this family which is morally and economically obliged to care for children. In many non-Western societies the notion of family is broader than blood relations, and includes reciprocity between kinship and extended family networks that have roles and responsibilities towards children and their siblings (see Chapter 4). Some social work interventions for children without parental care have been criticised for transposing Western models of childcare which marginalise and undermine traditional approaches to caring for children (EveryChild, 2012). Abebe and Aase (2007) discuss this in relation to the role of the extended family in caring for children whose parents have died from HIV/AIDS in Ethiopia. Child rearing practices in Ethiopia have long included the traditions of sending children to live with relatives distinguished as 'front line' who are blood relations and 'fictive kinships' defined as:

> people who have no blood relationship with each other but have deliberately created social ties that would enable them to co-operate with each other during normal times as well as during periods of stress. (Abebe and Aase, 2007: 2060)

In the UK in recent years family placement work with children who cannot be looked after by their families has started to recognise the important role that wider familial networks play in supporting children and their parents in caring for children, drawing on these and other indigenous approaches found in Africa and New Zealand.

In order to embrace difference and diversity and benefit from the rich sources of knowledge and tradition it brings, we must at all costs resist drawing on our own experience of childhood and our child rearing as the solitary measure of comparison. Mead's work and the work of other anthropologists who study children and their social and cultural life in their own environments bring a wealth of insights to the differences and variations in childhood, family and community life in a global context. We know from the work of Mead that the Manus people looked after their children very well, preparing them for later life when they would be responsible for continuing traditions and practices.

However, what are we to make of children being trained for a harsh rural life and their exposure to the natural environment which Western traditions of child rearing would baulk at as dangerous and irresponsible? Mead (1954) reported that Manus children could eat when they liked, play when they liked and sleep when they saw fit. In a Western context this may be seen as neglectful behaviour on the part of the parents and children exposed to this regime would likely be subject to a battery of psychological tests to assess the immediate and long-term damage to them. It thus falls to practitioners to consider how these different approaches may be used to inform and shape our approach to working with and on behalf of children.

THE LOSS OF CHILDHOOD: WORK AND MIGRATION

In Western societies, the 'loss of childhood' is often used to describe the way in which children are denied a childhood as they have to assume adult responsibilities. The notion of the 'loss of childhood' is a term often applied to children who work and, as noted above, a Western ethnocentric perspective on child work has led to international calls for the abolition of child labour. However, the reasons for children working are often associated with structural factors and individual aspiration as well as culture and tradition and so global and national attempts to ban children from the workplace may do more harm than good.

Ethnographic research provides a broad cultural context for understanding childhood and children's agency (Nieuwenhuys, 1996; Manzo, 2005) and has informed research on child labour in developing countries and on child work and migration (Liebel, 2004; Hashim, 2006). These studies highlight the role of extended family networks in supporting children's migrations and desire to work. The longer term benefits of migration to children, their families and communities have also been evidenced. Children in Burkina Faso who left their village to work away from home for a year returned with new skills and were more respected by their elders. The migration was often seen by parents and the returning children as *rites de passage* (De Lange, 2005). Busza et al. (2004) found that children's own aspirations and hopes for a better future for themselves and their families were the primary reasons for them to migrate abroad for work. Children's migrations for work were facilitated by intermediaries and extended family members, who often advocated around payment issues and offered support during their migrations in general.

The intervention of states and their agents and attempts to prevent children from working have had negative impacts, for example: children's economic contribution to their family being reduced or removed; children being unable to pay for their education. Western ideals about childhood which inform these interventions neglect to consider the cultural differences which encourage children to make a contribution to their household and education. Western approaches which simply seek to remove children from the workplace and 'give them back their childhood' undermine the social action which children can and do engage in to address structural economic conditions including their bargaining with employers around several issues including working conditions and wages (Liebel, 2004).

UNCRC AND CHILDREN'S RIGHTS

The UN Convention on the Rights of the Child (UNCRC) (UN, 1989) provides the framework for a minimum set of universal standards and entitlements for children and signatory countries agree to base their national legislation on these standards. The UNCRC recognises children as holders of rights, rather than being objects of international law (see Chapter 12). In relation to the focus adopted in this chapter, however, the UNCRC may be criticised on several counts.

First, many countries have used the UNCRC to measure progress in improving the life chances and opportunities for children (Twum-Danso, 2009). However, the UNCRC might actually undermine the expectations, aspirations and ambitions of children who can never hope to realise the idealised rights enshrined in the Convention. The monitoring committee (Committee on the Rights of the Child – CRC) is unable to report on the progress countries are making; developing countries simply do not have the resources to monitor progress and there is a lack of clarity in terms of which national government department is responsible for addressing any issues or challenges which are presented in countries' monitoring reports. The capacity of developing countries to invest in infrastructure services such as health and education is also compromised by the availability of national resources.

A view of children both as having rights but, because of their immaturity and innocence, of being incapable of exercising their rights, ensures that the UNCRC affords children protection as well as equal status with adults (Twum-Danso, 2009). For many children, the realisation of their rights and the Western idealised notions of childhood as a space of freedom, innocence and dependence remain outside their grasp. The situations of children in certain countries have worsened considerably in the last few decades and globally many children lack real economic and political power. Financial and structural interventions and programmes are generated though adult-centred concerns and force children into exploitative labour, while international conflicts, such as in Syria, Afghanistan and Iraq, expose them to poverty and dislocation.

The UNCRC and children's rights perspectives have also been criticised for ignoring the realities of children's lives where they are socio-economic actors. The dominance of developmental **discourses** which reproduce images of children and childhood as (being in) a state of dependence and immaturity simultaneously mutes the expressions of social action and participation which children demonstrate in the vast range of social institutions which cater to and for them. The UNCRC is individualised and based around entitlement and social justice and is not aligned with the sense of community reciprocity and responsibility which characterises child rearing and concepts of childhood in non-Western contexts (Kjørholt, 2007).

CONCLUSION

This chapter has outlined key reasons why we should understand the differences children experience growing up in their cultures. Studying childhood in different cultures is pertinent given the various impacts of globalisation and the international migratory movements of people who bring with them cultures and traditional patterns of child rearing which are often in contrast to notions of what is accepted as normal in our own cultures. As this chapter has discussed, our understanding of childhood necessarily includes recognition that this is not a fixed, one dimensional phase of life which starts and ends with achieving a particular stage of development; these stages, while arguably universal, are also culturally and socially defined. Instead, we may talk of childhoods and childhood experiences, while also acknowledging that these are socially constructed.

Childhood can be a period of innocence and dependency but this is not the experience of all children and importantly nor should it be. Cultural and traditional beliefs systems which engender responsibility, reciprocity and self-discipline shape different childhoods and ensure the reproduction of culture and community cohesion strategies. Child rearing can take many forms and is defined and fostered through traditional practices and by drawing on a range of development theories, some of which are peculiar to a given culture or social group. The challenge for practitioners is to recognise and embrace these differences and the diversity they bring to childhood experiences.

Key points

- Globalisation leads to benefits, opportunities and disadvantages for children and their families, especially where power is retained by developed countries.
- Beliefs are influenced by culture; ethnocentrism and cultural relativism can affect the ways we think about and understand childhood and children's lives, and have an impact in/on childcare and welfare policies and practice.
- Different cultures bring a diversity to our understanding of parenting and child rearing practices which support and sustain cultures and important traditions.
- Attachment and child development theories are Western concepts and diverse cultures in different global contexts are not always applicable where children assume caring, familial or work responsibilities generating family income.
- Children and their rights are conceptualised from Western ideological perspectives which align with norms and expectations of childhood and which are not easily transferable or applicable to other cultures.

Recommended reading

Kwame Owusue-Bempah's (2007) book *Children and Separation: Socio-Genealogical Connectedness Perspective* (see reference list) raises important issues about the cultural limitations of traditional Western, psychological child development theories and introduces socio-genealogical connectedness.

CHILDHOOD THROUGH THE AGES

YORDANKA VALKANOVA

CONTENTS

INTRODUCTION

This chapter examines different historical interpretations of childhood and identifies and evaluates some of the salient themes and forms of discourse that have surrounded the major traditions of research into childhood. I will argue that the general tension between the existing social and material world, and the possibility for changing this world, have had an effect on the conceptualisation of childhood throughout the ages. In much previous analysis the emphasis is located on what is commonly perceived as the Western world. Space precludes discussion of childhood outside North America and most of Europe and in an attempt to reach a clear sense of detail, the focus is selective and stresses locations where, due to the documentary sources, the patterns of childhood were more apparent. It is also significantly about education and schooling.

TOWARDS A CONCEPTUALISATION OF CHILDHOOD

I will begin by offering a necessarily historical account of the scholarly discussion of the notion of childhood. Two centuries ago, it would have been unheard of to begin a discussion with a conceptualisation of childhood. Human infants have a long period of dependency relative to other animals and childhood was defined mainly in terms of biology (James et al., 1998; Bjorklund, 2011). In the main, children were expected to work as soon as possible which meant that what we call childhood, a comparatively long period free from labour, was unknown. Although ideas about children's education and development are one of the oldest areas of consideration in philosophy (for example, by Plato, Aristotle or Confucius), as many societal expectations of what future adults should look like were involved, the notion of childhood, as we shall see later in this chapter, was an area of intense debate.

Recent interest in the discussion of the **ontology** of childhood – or what it is – and its **epistemology** – or how we know about it – can be traced back to the post-modern context of the 1960s, and more precisely to the interest in childhood ignited by the influential book written by Philippe Ariès (1962), a French family historian, entitled *Centuries of Childhood: A Social History of Family Life*. Ariès used representation of childhood in medieval art to support his argument that childhood was socially constructed in the seventeenth and eighteenth centuries, and therefore that it was considered to be varied across time and space; it was not biologically given. Social constructionists, like Philippe Ariès, believe that constructs are social products, but through their application in scholarly or everyday discussions they become real. Yet, since the publication of Ariès's book, this assertion has been questioned by many (see Newton, 2014; and also Immel and Whitmore, 2013). Interest in Ariès's work stimulated research into historical interpretations of the concept of childhood and looked at its cultural and social dimensions. However, as **social constructionism** itself teaches us, the proposition that childhood is constructed implies that it does not exist *per se*.

Nevertheless, it is clear that some historians of childhood have found social constructionism to be a valuable tool that allows them to conceptualise the material properties associated with childhood, their representations and the various discourses of childhood (see, for example,

Cunningham, 2005). Moreover, social constructionism has been institutionalised in universities in the sociology of childhood for some time now (see Chapter 3). Still, it has not proved possible to produce the meaning of an immaculate conception of childhood.

Grounded in the post-modern discourse framed by the work of Michel Foucault, and later of Bruno Latour, historians such as Neil Postman (1985) employed 'adulthood' as a 'counter concept' to examine the extent to which society sets up markers of childhood, and in addition to this, to acknowledge the proposition that both concepts participate in a **semantic battle**. Indeed, Postman found it analytically useful to distinguish between them and offered the idea of 'adultisation'. Many early years educators found this especially insightful in the establishment of the concept of childhood (see Cannella, 1997). Postman, following Ariès, further argued that children as young as six and seven were regarded as being no different to adults in the time prior to the Renaissance. The argument was based on the anecdotal assertions that no child rearing institutions were known before then, and that children had no special status in society. Thus, the potential of historical research in enriching the discussion of an ontology and epistemology of childhood requires further exploration.

To understand the impact of the social environment on children's identity construction it is necessary to investigate what mechanisms catalyse the transformational function of the social. The cultural-historical dialectical method grounded in the studies of the Russian psychologist Lev Vygotsky (1997[1926]), offers a promising tool for social constructionist investigation. More precisely, Vygotsky's theory assumes future-oriented intentions to explain identity development. It would appear that in terms of **Hegelian** dialectic, from which Vygotsky borrowed his conception, change in identity could be explained through social change and through identifying social contradictions that constitute development. In agreement with Vygotsky's theory, some ideas such as Zelitzer's (1985) proposition that children's 'merit' is determined by the fulfilment and satisfaction their existence brings to parents' lives, and Steedman's (1995) suggestion that childhood is used by the parents as an external locus of their selfhood, are valuable additions to Vygotsky's conception of the self. Seen in this light, childhood would appear as an antagonist to Neil Postman's view, a dialectical contradiction between the view of 'the future' on one side and 'the reality' on the other, as Freud (1924) also observed. Further, in recognition of the child's agency, I would suggest that childhood should be regarded as a process of co-construction of selfhood, a consideration potentially important if we would like to practise the discipline of early childhood studies (see Chapter 3 on the 'new' paradigm).

THE HISTORIOGRAPHY OF EARLY CHILDHOOD

ANCIENT TIMES AND THE MEDIEVAL ERA

Ancient and medieval **historiography**, as well as the anthropological sciences, suggest that the concept of childhood did not originate with industrialisation or during the Enlightenment, as the social constructionists argued in the 1960s and 1970s. Authors, like Ariès, were apparently unaware of the historical writings on medieval and ancient childhood but interestingly enough, even the general philosophical writing in antiquity made little impact on their thesis.

The Greek philosopher Plato's perception of childhood is a convenient example of a reflection of the discourse that underpinned the contemporary understandings of children and childhood. In his vision of an ideal state, presented in *The Republic*, his most popular book, Plato (2007) paid particular attention to the role that education could have in the functioning of the governance of the state. He postulated three stages of biological and psychological development from early childhood to adult life. At the first stage, from birth to the age of three, the child is vulnerable and needs protection and attention. The adult's general role is to amuse, empower and encourage fearless behaviour. Plato described the nursery stage, from three to six years, as a time for play and storytelling. Education starts at the primary school stage, from six to thirteen years. Then, children should be engaged in the study of a variety of subjects, including numbers, geometry, and cubes, morals, music and gymnastics. Physical exercise, he thought, was good for the mind, body and soul. The next stage, from thirteen to sixteen years, was for more complex studies of mathematics, dialectics and arts. From sixteen to twenty years, young men were to be provided with military training. Plato regarded play as a guided pedagogic principle, applicable in all subjects and ages, and developed the idea that children should not be trained through force, but rather through play. This further indicates Plato's understanding of children's specific educational needs and the role of education in the construction of childhood in the ancient world.

As a result of the influence of the growth of the archaeology of childhood, statements about children as significant social agents in ancient history have become commonplace. Such a display of facts becomes integral to the current historiographical account of multiple contexts, and articulates the complexity of the notion of childhood in antiquity. The representations of childhood apparent in the stories about **Theseus, Hercules, Achilles and Perseus** (Graves, 1960), and in visual art, **discursively construct** a sense of heroic identity, built on desirable qualities such as bravery, noble morality, handsomeness and a certain degree of clever ingenuity. However, the archaeological scholarship suggests that there are certain contradictions between the images of desirable identity offered by adults, and practices such as play and domestic activities documented in the 'everyday discourse' situated in material culture. Moreover, the female and male staged transition to adulthood is documented in textual sources (see Gaius Petronius' *Satyricon* or Apuleius' *The Golden Ass*), and in ancient Greek and Roman myths.

MEDIEVAL CHILDHOODS

Relatively precise documented representations of childhood in the Middle Ages do exist today, however, medieval historians suggest that initiation practices, which prepared adolescent girls and boys for their gender roles in their societies, have not been examined closely by the social constructionists. For example, the Jewish Ashkenazi Bar Mitzvah ritual of eating cookies formed as the letters of the Hebrew alphabet and covered with honey could be viewed as a sacred symbol of becoming literate, and therefore demonstrates the power of education in the child's life (for Aleph-Bet rituals see especially Marcus, 1996 and Westerman, 2001). In addition, there were circumcision practices for both boys and girls (see Karras, 2003) that alert us to gender specific expectations in relation to future religious roles in society, but they also could be viewed as consideration of the continuity of childhood, or even as a staged childhood. Furthermore, completely at odds with Neil Postman's thesis that no child rearing institutions existed in antiquity and the Middle Ages, medieval historiography maintains that there were patterns of professional childcare in the Middle Ages. For instance, the rural 'baby rooms' in France (Fildes, 1995) where urban mothers would leave their children with wet nurses could be considered as child rearing 'institutions'. Therefore, to believe that no concept of childhood existed in antiquity and the Middle Ages is a remarkably tenacious misconception.

THE RENAISSANCE CHILD

We may gain some insights into the continuity of the traditions of the conceptualisation of childhood by examining the notion of the Renaissance child. The Renaissance was a time of change in Europe, considered largely as taking place between the fourteenth and sixteenth centuries, and initiated in Florence, Italy, with a revival of interest in classical Greek and Roman antiquity. Examinations of documentary evidence reveal what was special about child rearing in the Renaissance. Ultimately, rigid class structure and social stratification in terms of poverty and gender inequality had a profound effect on how Renaissance childhood was experienced.

The admiration of ancient values provided a rationale for the Renaissance conceptualisation of childhood. The main goal of education was a polymath, a *homo universalis*, or a person who was skilled in numerous fields or disciplines (Briggs and Burke, 2000). Indeed, the mirror of antiquity reflected the concept of the ideal aristocratic child, seen as an essential element in the evolution of society aiming for a new future. In his book *Civil Life*, composed in 1429, Matteo Palmieri (2012), a famous Renaissance **humanist**, outlined the qualities of the ideal citizen, and among other characteristics of respectable citizenship, Palmieri advocated good parenting. He emphasised the importance of education for active participation in the life of the city. Associating childhood with education, he maintained that education must start from an early age, because early years education was crucial for building human qualities that contribute to the betterment of society. In addition, Renaissance men and women distinguished themselves from the previous generations by developing an ardent interest in the individuality of the child (Klapisch-Zuber, 1987). According to Palmieri (2012), parents must observe children's behaviour in order to understand their development. As he put it: 'The child begins to make known his wishes and partly to express them in words. The whole family listens and the whole neighbourhood repeats his sayings' (1825[1429]: 233). Furthermore, he maintained, fathers should teach their children the alphabet and reward them with kisses and laugher. This display of a rather 'feminine' notion of fatherhood is apparent in Palmieri's book, but it is also an observable feature in many other sources. One possible explanation of this phenomenon is offered by Klapisch-Zuber (1987) who suggested that the adoration and interest in young children was prompted by the cult of the Virgin Mary, developed in the late Middle Ages. Indeed, a clear psychological distinction between adults and children was embedded in the Renaissance discourses. This public expression of the knowledge of childhood is seen even in the deviation from the humanist paradigm in the work of Giovanni Dominici (1927[1401]), who designed methods of religious education, where play, including games and toys for children, were included.

Specific social and gender differences were notable in Renaissance education patterns. While the rich noble families provided their sons with training in rhetoric and instruction in philosophy and ancient languages, the urban merchant classes chose for their boys a more pragmatic mode of education, with an emphasis on learning mathematics to satisfy the practical needs of the family businesses. Girls, generally, were educated at home or in convents. The boys from poorer or artisanal families, as well as the girls, would receive an education that suited their status. The Renaissance childhood, the polymath pattern, therefore, was reserved for the nobles. Also, due to poverty, parental mortality or other unfortunate events, many children experienced childhoods which diverged from the standard biography. However, some children from lower classes were able to become scholars, as is the case with Desiderius Erasmus Roterodamus (1469–1536). Still, the advanced, but ultimately aristocratic ideas of the wholeness of the child, in which personal and civic hopes for a better future were embedded, had an impact on the few, rather than on the many. The concept of Renaissance childhood was pregnant with a dialectical contradiction between the expectations for 'the future' on one side, and the reality on the other.

THE CHILD OF THE ENLIGHTENMENT

Born in post-Renaissance times, in the seventeenth century, the Enlightenment was a breakthrough in thinking: a cultural movement, characterised by a diffusion of information, **secularism** and the view that all authority must be subject to the test of reason. The Scientific Revolution played a major role in providing tools for examining the epistemological status of ideas of child rearing and education. 'Nature' was a category that dominated the discourse; however, little attention was paid to the precise use of nature and its **cognates**. In particular, nature was viewed as a corrective to the general law, an instrument of liberation, a concept around which to create a fairer society (Munck, 2011). Works of philosophers, such as John Locke (1632–1704), Voltaire (1694–1778) and Jean-Jacques Rousseau (1712–1778) challenged ideas grounded in tradition, fostered intellectual interchange and placed an emphasis on the rights of humanity. Jean-Jacques Rousseau's ideas conveyed in his book *Emile* (1964[1762]) placed an emphasis on children's experience, and aimed at educating the natural man (Valkanova, 2015). Freedom and love should help children unfold their good nature. According to Rousseau, formal tutoring should be avoided; however, the tutor arranges and manipulates the environment to stimulate self-development. Furthermore, books should play little or no part in the child's education, which he thought should be dominated by doing and activity.

A personal diary written by a boy in the Netherlands, starting in 1791, at the age of ten, and kept for several years, exemplifies the way Rousseau's discourse on natural education served to construct childhood at the time (Baggerman and Dekker, 2009). The child was raised by parents who gave him a Rousseauian upbringing, inspired with admiration for nature and scientific progress. Receiving an education preparing him for the clerical profession, the boy documented in his diary his hopes and desires for the future. However, all he wished was to spend as much time outdoors as possible, and to become a farmer when he grew up. The diary captured insightful reflections of the boy's explorations of the world situated in his paternal home and beyond. His reading, designed for both education and pleasure, was broad and combined classical and religious literature. His growth occurred in a loving, supporting environment, surrounded by siblings, extended family members and friends. This diary shows us an example of childhood established as a category in its own right, reflecting the dominant view of child rearing as an agent in changing society.

One of the first systematic contributions to the science of childhood produced during the Enlightenment was the work of Dietrich Tideman (1748–1803), a German philosopher and physician, professor in the University of Marburg. Tideman kept a journal of his son's sensory, motor, language and cognitive behaviour during the first thirty months of the toddler's life. Such attempts to generate knowledge about childhood gave cause for historians to think harder about processes and interactions that were previously hidden.

THE VICTORIAN CHILD

The notion of the Victorian child has a variety of aspects. First, Victorian childhood has been interpreted in a Marxist mode (Mabbott, 2010). The arguments centre on the influence the middle classes had during the Victorian age. Queen Victoria's reign (1837–1901) was a time of unprecedented political and economic transformations in England. As a result, the growing capitalist industries needed a cheap labour force to satisfy market demand and achieve international competitiveness. Children were often preferred and employed at low rates and long hours. The Victorian middle classes saw their role as enabling the working classes to realise their potential. Factory reform movements prompted legislative changes to improve children's working conditions and introduce free, compulsory education for all (see the Factory Acts from 1878). Compulsory schooling was highly important in terms of creating a childhood of increasing dependency, and one separated from the world of work (Heywood, 2001). However, the efforts put forward were then applied to satisfy middle-class interests. Such arguments viewed the middle classes as a powerful force, aimed at creating a society based on worth rather than on one's birth (Rose, 1991).

Second, quite often historians of childhood made the effect of romanticism and mysticism on child rearing practices their cornerstone (see Malkovich, 2013; also Austin, 2003). Indeed, the middle classes distinguished themselves from the 'wealthy and corrupt' upper aristocratic classes through constructing individual uniqueness. Authenticity, discovered through a rebirth of medieval ideas and ideals, was used as an image that represented the middle classes' uniqueness as something that was reliable and genuine, and thus acceptable. Discourses embedded in popular magazines such as *Lady's Magazine* revealed assumptions about the future of society evident in the constructions of the concept of childhood. The romantic themes were also apparent in the discourse associated with the arrival of the German educator Friedrich **Froebel**'s (1782–1852) kindergarten, and his idea of early childhood education in Britain. Froebelian pedagogy, as developed by Froebel and his followers across Europe, America and Asia, involved a number of constituents that help us understand why Victorians found this method attractive. For example, a Froebelian syllabus encouraged reasoning, and stressed 'nature', in relation to the conceptualisation of a rather dialectical unity of subjective and objective. It also emphasised holism over autonomism. Play was the natural activity on which teaching and learning should be based. Especially designed objects – gifts – were used to encourage creativity and technological development while emphasis was placed on self-activity as an essential educational process. These qualities were extremely important in the Victorian era of social reforms. Although Froebel's method was popular, the kindergartens opened in Britain during that time were largely for middle-class children. Nevertheless, Froebel societies, established across the country, made a very successful attempt to bring Froebelian ideas on early childhood education to the general public through providing a highly professional training to kindergarten teachers, and also through a vast publishing agenda. Romantic discourse, therefore, paved the way for professionalisation of early childhood education and care.

THE PROGRESSIVE CHILD

The cultural and industrial transformation at the end of the nineteenth and the beginning of the twentieth century brought about a new conceptualisation of childhood, in which progressive education had its full share. Progressive education, which is rooted in the works of Jean-Jacques Rousseau, Johann Heinrich Pestalozzi (1746–1827) and Friedrich Froebel, was initiated by John Dewey (1859–1952), an American philosopher, who opened a 'Laboratory School', as he named it, in Chicago in 1896. Previously associated with the romantic ideal, the conceptualisation of childhood now shifted its agenda, under the impact of the rise of psychology and the research on children associated with it, and it proclaimed a shared faith in human agency and a growing understanding of the value of rationality as an important part of successful social and government reforms. Children were encouraged to construct identities in ways that were associated with socially engaged **intelligence** and self-activity.

Progressivism and the new education gained immense popularity in America and throughout Europe and Asia. Many of Froebel's followers, who embraced the philosophy of the new education, such as Patty Smith Hill in the USA, Emmy Walser in Switzerland and Luisa Schleger in Russia, adapted Froebel's ideas to the new notion of Dewey's school (Valkanova and Brehony, 2006). The progressive ideas of childhood were also accommodated within the Marxist labour school philosophy, elements of which were embedded in the pre-schools established by the Soviet regime in Russia after the Revolution of 1917 (Valkanova, 2009). Dewey's ideas were strongly presented in the discursive construct of childhood in Bolshevik Russia. The Soviet reforms in the early childhood sphere sought to establish an education system, in an attempt to engineer the ideal human being, the 'new man' and the 'new woman'. The consideration of labour as an important activity for the development of the child was proposed by a number of academics, including Lev Vygotsky, who advocated the labour school in his book *Educational Psychology* (1997[1926]). Like Froebel, he maintained that work emerged from play, especially from manipulative and pretend play. Thus, by emphasising certain traits, the legacy of progressive discourse brought forth a new construction of the child's role in society and revealed a positive recognition of the child's agency.

THE NORMALISED CHILD

The growth of psychology as a science at the end of the nineteenth century, and the subsequent development of an interest in 'intelligence testing', provided those professionals working with young children with a new explanatory model of how diverse phenomena in child development fitted into unifying normative patterns (Beaty et al., 2006; Smuts and Smuts, 2006). Overall, the 'scientific method' came as an alternative to the descriptive 'observation method' that was used until then to make assumptions about developmental characteristics of children. Testing was viewed as a promising device in preparing the child for future adjustment in society. The first attempts to develop reliable scales for measuring capability were made in the middle of the nineteenth century. However, one of the most influential sets of measures was introduced in 1884 by the British scientist Francis Galton (1822–1911), a cousin of Charles Darwin and was used to identify deviancies in the development of children. Such tests, as well as the testing method founded by the French psychologist Alfred Binet and his assistant Theodor Simon in 1904, marked the increasing demand for 'meaningful' diversity labels in the search for optimal educational arrangements for challenging children who deviated from the norm.

Indeed, as a result of the influence of intelligence testing on education practices, statements about normal and abnormal became commonplace. The idea of deviance, viewed as a new trajectory of early years pedagogy, played a central role in the work of the Italian physician and educator Maria Montessori. Montessori applied the above dichotomy to establish the notion of a normalised child, which she regarded as a new level of humanity (Brehony, 2000). As she put it: 'Normalisation is the single most important result of our work' (Montessori, 1967[1949]: 204). Montessori made her idea of the normalised child hugely popular by suggesting some ways in which education acted as a mediator between the child and society (Zener, 1999). According to Montessori, only the normalised child becomes a responsible and productive member of society (Montessori, 1967[1949]).

Unfortunately, the normative childhood was a major impulse behind a controversial episode of human history, that of the **eugenics** movement. Eugenics, defined by its contributors as the science of 'improving' the human race, emerged at the beginning of the twentieth century. The supporters of the eugenics movement believed that every 'defective' child is a burden. These ideas became popular in the United States and Europe (Mintz, 2004), and many public figures agreed that the state had to remove the 'defects' from the human race in order to build a stronger society. Sadly, the eugenics movement spread to Germany and found a home in Nazi ideology in the 1930s (Searle, 1976; Lowe, 1980).

Most recently, normality has been interpreted in relation to 'school readiness'. This concept, also referred to as 'readiness to learn' and 'readiness for school', has entered the official discourse of pre-school education; with standardised 'readiness assessments' used to identify whether children are fit to enter school in a number of countries. In the United States, in 1994, federal legislation which codified delayed entry to school was passed by Congress. The validity of the arguments that children should be taught earlier has been intensively questioned in the UK as well (Duncan et al., 2007). The discourse of normality, therefore, is still influential in constructing contemporary experiences and meanings of childhood. However, it would appear that 'normality' in relation to child development is an unstable concept that relies on contexts for its meaning and interpretations.

NEO-LIBERAL CHILDHOOD

The neo-liberal child is a concept which conveys assumptions about his or her future role as an agent that has a mission to rescue society from obscurity. Neo-liberals attempt to delegate power from the state to the individual and encourage the marketisation of children's services (Hendrick, 2003). In its most general sense, the neoliberal child is positioned as an active and creative individual. Vincent and Ball (2007) offer the metaphor of the Renaissance child in an attempt to explain some neo-liberal middle-class parenting patterns. They highlight parents' enthusiasm for enabling intense extra-curricular support for their under-fives. The authors link this passion of parents to a desire to establish clear boundaries between the working and middle classes. Admittedly, Vincent and Ball do widen the scope of the concept of the Renaissance child by referring to 'otherness' in the process of identification, in this case a process of co-identification, if we acknowledge the parents' efforts to help their children establish a middle-class self-definition. Indeed, the construction of the Renaissance child is used as **abjection** of the working-class self-definition.

Skelton and Francis (2012) further show that it is possible to account for the division of education accomplishments on the grounds of masculinity. They apply the concept of the Renaissance child to mount a compelling argument, which shows the important role gender plays in the neo-liberal production of subjectivity. Both examples show that **social constructivism** can help us reach beyond particular historical contexts, and ultimately transform our understanding of the whole tradition of childhood studies.

CONCLUSION

This chapter has provided examples of the way in which children have been positioned by diverse discourses concerning the construction of concepts of childhood, schooling and education. As the analysis in this chapter has shown, it would be difficult to find a concept that would not be relevant to any of the contemporary traditions. Significant for understandings of how childhood was conceptualised over the ages is the outline of the subject–object relation offered by Vygotsky's concept of 'the self', which allows us to look at how different identities arose and developed, and how they fitted into the larger system of what is considered as 'manhood'. Consequently, the traditions of studying childhood need to be examined in their continuity. This is why it is so important to pay attention not only to the ideas of childhood produced by the 'great minds', by its nature an ontological exploration, but also to see the development of the traditions in studying childhood as a cumulative process of epistemological understanding.

————— Key points —————

- Ancient and medieval historiography as well as the anthropological sciences alert us that the concept of childhood did not originate with industrialisation or during the Enlightenment.
- The scientific revolution played a major role in providing tools for examining the epistemological status of ideas of child rearing and education.
- The cases and examples identified, such as the neo-liberal concept of the 'Renaissance child', show that social constructivism can help us reach beyond particular historical contexts, and ultimately transform our understanding of the whole tradition of childhood studies.

————— Recommended reading —————

Michael Wyness's (2011) text *Childhood and Society: An Introduction to the Sociology of Childhood* gives a comprehensive account of social constructionism, illustrated with examples drawn from research with children.

SOCIOLOGY OF CHILDHOOD

NIGEL THOMAS

CONTENTS

INTRODUCTION

The aim of this chapter is to introduce some key elements of the sociological study of childhood and to see how it can help us to achieve a better understanding of childhood and children's lives. I look first at how sociologists have traditionally studied childhood (or more often, have failed to). I consider some of the problems with socialisation theory and with views of childhood as a preparation for adult life, and the critique of socialisation theory from an interactionist perspective. I also look at some recent work in psychology and anthropology which has dealt with some of the same issues. I then review what has been called the 'new paradigm' of the sociology of childhood, and take stock of some of the research that has been, and is being done, using this framework.

WHAT IS SOCIOLOGY?

In general terms, sociology is concerned with the study and understanding of *social processes* and *social structures*. These may be studied at a number of different levels:

1. The 'macro' level is concerned with demographic patterns (population and so on) and with global changes in social patterns and relations.

2. The 'meso' level looks at social institutions – the family, work, leisure, schooling and so on.
3. The 'micro' level studies social interaction – sometimes in a very detailed way.

The key organising concepts used by sociologists include:

1. Ideas about social relations – authority, social cohesion, conflict.
2. Social categories such as class, ethnicity and gender.

3. Broader social processes – for instance, 'modernisation'.

Early European sociologists such as Emile Durkheim and Max Weber, at the beginning of the twentieth century, were interested in social organisation and in the relationship between the individual and society. They asked questions such as: 'What binds people together in social groups?', 'How do people come to share belief systems, and why are belief systems different?', 'Why do people obey authority?' In the middle of the century the dominant voices were American – sociologists such as Talcott Parsons who aimed to build a comprehensive theory that would explain everything from global social structures to the detail of social relations in terms of *function*, and critics such as C. Wright Mills who were more interested in the conflicts of interest between different groups in society. In the 1960s a branch of sociology developed that was concerned much more with social interaction – for instance, Erving Goffman studied how individuals present themselves in society, and Harold Garfinkel focused on the minute detail of interaction, in particular the rules governing conversations.

More recently the dominant voices have included Michel Foucault, with his complex exploration of power and knowledge and, in Britain, Anthony Giddens. Giddens' central preoccupation is with one of the key tensions in social theory, which he characterises as the relationship between *structure* and *agency*. On the one hand, our lives are governed by social structures and social processes, so that it might be said that we have no existence outside society. On the other hand, these social structures and processes are nothing but the result of human activity. So which is prior – do individuals create society, or does society create individuals? Are we free agents, or are our lives determined? A moment's reflection may suggest to us that in some way both statements are true – but the task then is to explore the relationship between them. Another sociologist of major significance is Pierre Bourdieu, who has responded to this question by developing the concept of *habitus*, by which he means the layers of acquired dispositions from which we draw our routines for thinking, speaking and acting. As he puts it, *habitus* is 'embodied history, internalized as a second nature and so forgotten as history … the active presence of the whole past of which it is the product' (Bourdieu, 1992: 56). So we do make choices, but from a repertoire which is more or less limited by our social positioning and experience.

What has all this to do with childhood? From a cursory reading of much of the sociological literature, one might say 'very little'. Many of the standard texts have in the past had no index entry for childhood, or if they have it has been simply a cross-reference to 'the family' or 'education'. This has begun to change, but only slowly, and it is rare to find any book of general sociology with a chapter on childhood. The questions about social structures and social processes have not been asked specifically in relation to childhood; the questions about social relations, authority and power have not been applied to adult–child relations; and the social categories used – class, ethnicity, gender – have not been extended to include childhood. Where we do find books in the past about 'the sociology of childhood' they tend to be specifically about the process of *socialisation* (for instance, Bossard and Boll, 1966). Children are studied, not as actual and participating members of society, but as *prospective* members. What is interesting about children, from this perspective, is the process by which they are made into adults.

SOCIALISATION THEORY

A child is born into a world that already exists. From the point of view of society, the function of socialisation is to transmit the culture and motivation to participate in established social relationships to new members. (Elkin, 1960: 7)

The central idea of classical socialisation theory (note it is often spelt 'socialization', especially in American texts) is that we are in effect *produced* in childhood by social conditioning. It is only through this process that we become *social*, and, because human beings are essentially social animals, this means that it is only through this process that we become fully human. More specifically, we are socialised into understanding and accepting the conventional norms and values of our particular society, and into becoming part of a culture; we are socialised into our particular role(s), social status and social class; and, according to some, our own individual personality is also the result of a socialisation process. The idea that individual personality is the result of socialisation was put forward most strongly by the behaviourist J.B. Watson, who wrote:

Give me a dozen healthy infants, well-formed, and my own specified world to bring them up in, and I'll guarantee to take any one at random and train him to become any type of specialist I might select – doctor, lawyer, artist, merchant-chief and, yes, even beggarman and thief, regardless of his talents, penchants, tendencies, abilities, vocations, and race of his ancestors. (*Behaviorism* [1930], quoted in Elkin, 1960: 46)

Socialisation theory identifies a number of socialising institutions or 'agencies of socialisation': principally the family, the school, the peer group and the mass media. Some theorists distinguish between *primary* socialisation, which includes the laying down of fundamental characteristics of personality, basic values and so on; and *secondary* socialisation, representing the continuing effect of group interaction and culture on our habits, thoughts and values throughout life. Most of the attention tends to be on primary socialisation; some conceive of this as taking place throughout childhood and into adolescence, while others confine it to early childhood. For instance, Bossard and Boll argue that 'the social conditioning of the personality during the first years of life is of primary importance … the basic patterns of personality are laid during the period of childhood', and that 'the sociological processes of personality formation can best be studied during the earlier stages' (Bossard and Boll, 1966: 7–8). From this perspective the family is clearly the most important socialising institution.

Socialisation theory came under increasing criticism in the 1970s from sociologists who took an *interactionist* approach, such as Norman Denzin. Studies of adult–child interaction and child–child interaction, and reflections on them, led to dissatisfaction with 'socialisation' as a model for what was observed to take place. Mackay (in Waksler, 1991) uses the example of an observed interaction between a child and a teacher about the child's understanding of a story, to show how the teacher treats the child as incompetent throughout in respect of the task, but how in fact an analysis of the interaction shows that it presumes a high degree of competence on the child's part to make it work.

Matthew Speier puts the criticism forcefully. He argues that traditional interests in development and socialisation have neglected 'the interactional foundation to human group life':

The traditional perspectives have overemphasised the task of describing the child's developmental process of growing into an adult at the expense of a direct consideration of what the events of everyday life look like in childhood … the intellectual and analytic position of sociologists is essentially ideological in the sense that they have used an adult notion of what children are and what they ought to be that is like that of the laymen in the culture. (Speier, 1976: 170)

In other words, it is the job of sociologists to bring distinctive analytic tools, and an open and enquiring mind, to the study of childhood, rather than simply recycle conventional ways of seeing and understanding.

PSYCHOLOGISTS, SOCIOLOGY AND CHILDHOOD

The key organising concepts of developmental psychology (see also Chapter 6) are very different from those used by sociology – concepts such as *learning*, *conditioning* or sometimes *unfolding*. Most discussions of child psychology start with Piaget, whose key insight was that the child learns to understand the world better as she or he progresses through a series of developmental stages characterised by increasingly sophisticated conceptual schemes. Margaret Donaldson and others revised Piaget, using research that showed that children were able to understand concepts that had been thought to be beyond their reach, if the tasks were presented in a way that 'made sense' to the child. This linked with the ideas of Vygotsky, an early contemporary of Piaget, about the '**zone of proximal development**' – the area into which the child is able to move on with support.

There are other differences between Piaget and Vygotsky. Piaget is sometimes thought to view the child as a solitary learner, and Vygotsky is seen as adding a social perspective on the process of development. In fact Piaget did emphasise a social element in learning, but he also seemed to see what was learned as in some sense *natural* – there is a natural progression from one conceptual framework to another, which it is the child's task to discover. For Vygotsky what the child learns is above all a culture, and therefore the role of other people in learning is indispensable. Building on these ideas, a number of psychologists including Jerome Bruner, Martin Richards and Paul Light began to explore the social dimension of psychological development in more depth.

It might on the face of it appear that psychology has converged with socialisation theory, in that it has gone from seeing development as a natural process of 'unfolding', or of the child discovering what is already there in the world, to a focus on the process of transmission of cultural norms and ways of seeing and doing things. In fact the new psychology is very different from traditional socialisation theory precisely because of what Piaget taught us about the child's active participation in learning, and Vygotsky's revelation of the processes of dialogue and negotiation inherent in cultural learning. These strands in the theory are much more convergent with, for instance, the interactionist perspective of Denzin than they are with classical socialisation theory. Barbara Rogoff (1989) writes of 'the joint socialization of development by young children and adults'; she argues that the child from the earliest age is an active participant in the socialising processes of development (see also Chapter 7).

ANTHROPOLOGISTS, SOCIOLOGY AND CHILDHOOD

Anthropology is literally 'the study of people'. It developed as an academic discipline in the late nineteenth and early twentieth century. First in the field was physical anthropology (the study of variations in physical types around the world), followed closely by cultural anthropology (the study of habits and mode of life), from which developed modern social anthropology with its focus on kinship relationships and belief systems. From the beginning anthropology developed a distinctive method based on close observation and detailed recording in 'field notes', known as *ethnography*. The focus was very much on 'primitive' or 'tribal' societies – people who are 'different' from 'us' in what were thought to be significant ways, although in recent years the same methods and concepts have been applied to Western societies.

Like sociologists, anthropologists for many years were backward in applying their concepts and methods to children and childhood. Anthropologists tended to rely on adult informants, to study adult behaviours and beliefs, to be interested in the social networks of adults, and to share adult concerns with their subjects. In 1973 Charlotte Hardman argued that children were a 'muted group' who had been ignored by anthropologists and given no voice in the anthropological record. She suggested that children deserved to be studied in their own right as a group with their own *culture*, their own network of relationships, their own beliefs and their own values (see Hardman, 1978). Gradually, anthropologists have turned their attention to childhood and the lives of children. This has been important for the study of childhood because it implies:

1. Looking at children not just as developing adults or adults-to-be, but as people in their own right.
2. Looking at children not just in their families or at school, but in their peer group, in work, in interaction with other children and with adults both within and outside their family group.
3. Taking children's own explanations and their beliefs seriously, in the same way that anthropology respects adults' accounts of their own culture.

THE 'NEW PARADIGM'

The contemporary sociology of childhood is distinguished by two central ideas. The first is that childhood is a social construction. Historical and cross-cultural studies have shown us that the 'nature' of childhood is enormously variable according to the social context, and that childhood is in a sense socially defined and created. The biological processes involved in growing up and getting older are real; but the pattern and the meaning of these changes are structured and mediated by society and culture. The second idea is the increasing recognition we have seen in sociology, psychology and anthropology that children must be seen as social actors in their own right. Children's lack of active presence in society has been mirrored by their lack of active presence in theory.

These two insights are the key elements in a *new paradigm* for the sociology of childhood, which was clearly articulated by Alan Prout and Allison James (1990). They described it as an 'emergent' paradigm, because it was still in the process of formation. Prout and James identified distinctive features of the 'new paradigm' as follows:

1. Childhood is understood as a social construction. It provides an interpretative frame for contextualising the early years of human life. Childhood, as distinct from biological immaturity, is neither a natural nor universal feature of human groups but appears as a specific structural and cultural component of many societies.
2. Childhood is a variable of social analysis. It can never be entirely divorced from other variables such as class, gender or ethnicity. Comparative and cross-cultural analysis reveals a variety of childhoods rather than a single and universal phenomenon.
3. Children's social relationships and cultures are worthy of study in their own right, independent of the perspective and concerns of adults.
4. Children are and must be seen as active in the construction and determination of their own social lives, the lives of those around them and of the societies in which they live. Children are not the passive subjects of social structures and processes.

5. Ethnography as a methodology allows children a more direct voice and participation in the production of sociological data than is usually possible through experimental or survey styles of research.

6. Childhood is a phenomenon in relation to which the double hermeneutic of the social sciences is acutely present (see Giddens, 1976). That is to say, to proclaim a new paradigm of childhood sociology is also to engage in and respond to the process of reconstructing childhood in society (Prout and James, 1990: 8-9).

This perspective has produced a great deal of stimulating research, much of it in Northern Europe and Scandinavia. Simultaneously, sociologists in North America have continued to develop research and theoretical work in understanding childhood. Corsaro (2017) made a substantial contribution to thinking about the relationship between *structure* and *agency* in childhood, with his concept of *interpretive reproduction*. The idea behind this concept is that children work to reproduce themselves, their culture and their social relationships, but that in doing so they interpret them for themselves. As he puts it:

1. Children actively contribute to cultural production and change.
2. They are constrained by the existing social structure and by societal reproduction.
3. Within these constraints, children's participation is *creative* and *innovative*.

STUDYING CHILDREN IN SOCIETY

The methods used by sociologists to study children in society vary in relation to a number of different factors, in particular the level of analysis:

1. At the *micro* level research is concerned with the study of children as individuals or in social interaction. Research may be **qualitative** or **quantitative**, but is more likely to be qualitative. Such research often favours methods of communication that are accessible to children and elicit their competence - for instance drawing, writing and using stories.

2. At the *meso* level research concerns the study of children's lives on a larger scale, in relation to institutions such as school, family or the media, in activities such as leisure, sport or travel, or in terms of 'problems' such as poverty, illness, disability, homelessness, divorce and separation, crime, abuse, pornography, war and famine. Such research tends to use survey methods, statistical data or the compilation of findings from a number of 'micro' studies.

3. At the *macro* level research concerns the study of children's lives on a larger scale. This might include historical changes in the nature of childhood and in patterns of child-adult relations, or global and generational relationships between children and adults. This research uses statistical data, or analytical and theoretical work based on existing theory or research.

Most of the research we will consider in this chapter is at the *micro* level, because that reflects most of the work in the new paradigm. However, there is also important work at the other levels.

CHILDREN AND THEIR PEERS

Corsaro (2017) uses his concept of 'interpretive reproduction' in studying children's *peer cultures*. For Corsaro, peer culture is defined in interaction, taking different forms at different ages. Children's early participation in peer culture is mediated by adults – taking place, for instance, in pre-school settings to which parents arrange access for their children. In these settings children may first encounter ideas of sharing and collective ownership, and of friendship. The central themes in children's 'initial peer cultures', according to Corsaro, are: attempts to *gain control* of their lives, attempts to *share* that control with each other, and the importance of *size* and of the idea of 'growing up'. He explores these themes through studies of play routines, of children's protection of their interactive space, and of sharing routines and rituals. Corsaro shows how children learn about autonomy and control through challenging and mocking adult authority and by confronting fears and conflicts in fantasy play. In contrast to the traditional psychologist's view of children's innate capacities unfolding as they mature, or the traditional sociologist's view of roles and values being inculcated by external social institutions and processes, he emphasises the importance of viewing such phenomena such as conflict and friendship as *collective* and *cultural* processes.

In later age stages Corsaro focuses on social differentiation: gender differentiation, status hierarchies, core groups and 'rejected, neglected or controversial' children. He advises caution about assuming that these processes are the same everywhere, arguing that cultural differentiation is always important. However, some themes tend to be consistently present: for instance, in pre-adolescent peer cultures he notices the different patterns and issues that typically emerge in the seven to thirteen age group, the greater stability of friendship patterns and the phenomenon of 'best friends', of friendship groups and alliances and of gossip.

CHILDREN IN FAMILIES

Sociologists might ask different kinds of questions about children in families, depending on what paradigm they are using. For instance, someone using a *socialisation* paradigm might ask questions like: How are children socialised? How do families 'raise' children? What difficulties do parents encounter in 'raising' children? What are the different patterns of family socialisation? How does family socialisation interact with school and peer culture?

Someone working within a *family sociology* paradigm might ask questions such as: Why do parents have children? What is the significance of changes in family composition? What are the different patterns of family life and how are they experienced?

On the other hand, for those following the new paradigm of the sociology of childhood the salient questions might be: What is the meaning of 'family' to children? How are the lives of children in families negotiated? What is the relationship between children's lives in their families and children's other social worlds? What is the relationship between how childhoods are negotiated in families and the social construction of childhood?

Exploring the implications of the new paradigm for the relationship between childhood and family sociology, James and Prout (1996) draw attention to the ways in which children construct and manage their identities differently in different settings – school, family, peer group and so on – and also in response to the particularities of individual families. O'Brien et al. (1996), in the same volume, report on research into children's views on what counts as a family. Presented with vignettes of different household types and relationships (married couples with and without children, unmarried couples with children, single parent and step families, separated parents), children were asked whether these counted as families or not. Younger children tended to emphasise conventional criteria such as marriage, while older ones placed more stress on quality of relationships. Children's views tended to reflect their own personal experiences, and in discussion children were prepared to adapt their views in response to each other's arguments. Smart et al. (2001) studied children's perspectives on divorce and separation, and used children's accounts of family life to show how childhood is changing and the status of children in families is being transformed.

Regardless of the approach taken, some features will be important from any perspective, illustrating common concerns of all sociologists:

1. Changes in family life.
2. Changes in family composition.
3. Children's place in families.
4. Children who are outside families.

CHILDREN IN SCHOOL

Now let us look at the kind of questions that sociologists might ask about children in school. The socialisation paradigm produces questions like: How are children socialised in schools? How do schools inculcate social values and norms in children? How does school socialisation interact with family socialisation? Traditional sociology or social policy approaches, on the other hand, might lead one to ask: What is the nature of the school as an institution – how does it operate, where does the power lie? What are the objectives of schooling, and how are they effectively achieved? What is the effect of schooling on social inequalities (in terms of class, gender, ethnicity)?

The new paradigm asks questions like: What is the meaning of 'school' to children? How are the daily lives of children in schools patterned? How is the experience of children in schools structured in terms of, for example, age, gender, ethnicity? How is meaning negotiated in the classroom between children and teachers? What is the relationship between children's lives in the classroom and in the playground? How does school have an impact on transitions in children's lives? What is the relationship between how childhoods are negotiated in schools and the social construction of childhood?

To take just one example, Seung Lam and Pollard (2006) analyse the transition from home to kindergarten, in terms of children crossing a cultural boundary and, in effect, commuting between two cultural settings. The authors present a conceptual framework for understanding children as agents in the transition, employing elements from socio-cultural theory such as the concept of *rite of passage*. They conclude that:

> children bring to kindergarten what they learned (including patterns of strategic action, competencies, child identity) at home. They are active in making sense of, responding and adapting to the new kindergarten classroom in terms of separation from caregiver, transition programme, physical environment, play and learning, rules and routines and relationships. This is a dynamic and continuous negotiation process of adaptation. (Seung Lam and Pollard, 2006: 137)

CHILDREN AND NEW MEDIA

There is a growing body of sociological work on children's relationship with communications and digital media – television and video, the internet, mobile phones and so on (see Chapter 5). Reflecting the preoccupations of the 'new paradigm', much of the focus is on how children use these new media to extend their social networks and their interaction with a wider world, and sometimes on how they adapt technology to new purposes and in unexpected ways.

CHILDREN, PLACE AND ENVIRONMENT

There is a healthy interchange between sociology and geography in the field of childhood studies. The growing sub-discipline of 'children's geographies' has its own (eponymous) journal and many other publications (for example, Holloway and Valentine, 2000). Research here is concerned with children's use of place and space, which, as sociologists and anthropologists have noticed, are key factors in shaping children's lives. Related to this is a substantial body of research and practice around children's relationships with their environments and the part which children may play in environmental change at all levels. The journal *Children, Youth and Environments* is of key significance here.

RECENT DEVELOPMENTS AND FUTURE DIRECTIONS

The flourishing of new sociological approaches to childhood has tended to be dominated methodologically by small-scale research with children in different settings, and theoretically by an emphasis on children's agency. At the same time there have always been sociologists whose focus was on the bigger picture, and who continued to ask questions about the structure of society and children's place in it (for example, Qvortrup et al., 1994; Qvortrup, 2005). Recently there has been increased questioning of the emphasis on 'agency' (Oswell, 2013) and a renewed interest in how children's lives are more or less determined by social structure, a growing interest in the concept of *generation* and relationships between generations (Alanen and Mayall, 2001; Mayall, 2002) in ideas of children's citizenship (Cockburn, 2013), and even an attempt to rehabilitate the concept of 'socialisation' (James, 2013).

There is a growing body of work that applies sociological theory to the understanding of young children's lives, especially in daycare and early education settings, e.g. Clark et al. (2005). There is also continuing interest in the cross-cutting of the category 'childhood' with other kinds of social stratification – gender, ethnicity, (dis)ability and class. Lareau (2000; 2003) has shown how in the USA social class is significant in shaping the patterns of children's lives in the present, as well as their opportunities in the future. The same may apply in the UK and other countries.

Other writers are concerned with the ways in which childhood is changing, and the impact of social change on childhood. Lee (2001) argues that as adult lives become more fluid and uncertain the old dichotomy, with childhood seen as a preparation for adult life, becomes increasingly irrelevant, and arguments for seeing children as 'being' rather than 'becoming' need to be reframed. Prout (2005) questions the adequacy of a purely social understanding of childhood for understanding lives that are so shaped by technology, and argues for conceptualising contemporary childhood in ways that take account of the inseparable part played by artefacts and machines. Nonetheless, a sociological framework is still of key importance in understanding contemporary childhood.

CONCLUSION

Sociology can help us to understand children's lives and children's place in society in a fuller and more rounded way – especially a sociology that takes as its starting point that children are people and participants in social life, not just 'adults in the making'. Sociological insights have much in common with recent work in psychology and anthropology and there has been some convergence between the disciplines. However, the distinctive sociological emphasis on social structures and social processes remains important.

This chapter introduces some of the ideas behind contemporary sociological research in childhood, and offers examples of the work that is being done. Further reading is suggested below.

Key points

- In general terms, sociology concerns the study and understanding of social processes and structures. These may be studied at different levels: 'macro', 'meso' and 'micro'.
- Most sociologists have failed to study children or childhood, except occasionally through the lens of 'socialisation', which sees children as passive recipients of adult influence.
- In the 1970s American sociologists made powerful critiques of this approach and work in the UK and Scandinavia in the 1980s added impetus for change. New thinking in psychology and anthropology emphasised the importance of seeing children as active participants in their own development and upbringing.
- A 'new paradigm' for the social study of childhood was announced by James and Prout in 1990. This perspective has produced much stimulating research at the 'macro', 'meso' and especially the 'micro' level, seeing children as 'being' rather than simply as 'becoming'.
- Examples of the new understanding include work on children's peer relationships, children's lives in families, at school and in work. More recently there has been a focus on children's place in the social structure, and intergenerational relations, and to combining the ideas of 'being' and 'becoming'.
- A growing body of work applies sociological theory to the understanding of young children's lives, to the cross-cutting of age with other social divisions such as race, class, gender and disability.

Recommended reading

Corsaro's theorising of children's agency in social structure and culture is powerful and illuminating, and the fact that much of his research is with pre-school children makes it particularly relevant to students of the early years: see Corsaro, W. (2017) *The Sociology of Childhood* (Fifth Edition). USA: SAGE.

THE GLOBALISATION OF EARLY CHILDHOOD EDUCATION AND CARE

HELEN PENN

CONTENTS

INTRODUCTION

'Globalisation' has many economic definitions and there are many interpretations about its impact, but here I use it in a limited sense to mean that ideas of and descriptions about early childhood, which are mainly European or North American in origin, are misused to describe childhood everywhere (see Chapter 1). The shorthand terminology for the differences and divisions between different parts of the world changes constantly. Previous terms have been: first/third world; developed/developing countries; majority/minority world; north/south; and currently high income/middle income and low income countries. (A new definition of 'high wealth/low wealth' is now being mooted!) In this chapter the shorthand I now use is low/middle/high income countries. But any shorthand attempt to describe the world's diversity – and its obligations – is problematic. Shorthand is necessary, but it has drawbacks too; some low income countries have some extremely rich citizens, and some rich countries have some very poor ones.

HOW CHILDHOODS VARY

One of the most puzzling aspects about how children grow and learn is the importance of context. Take a very simple example, that of food. All children need to eat, but how their food is obtained and prepared, when they eat, what they eat, where they eat, how they eat and what they are taught to think about what they eat is almost entirely determined by where they live and whom they live with. A child living in the UK is likely to have a diet high in processed foods, will graze throughout the day and be petulant about many foods; a child in Italy will be encouraged to savour food, and consider its consumption as a social occasion; a child living in France will eat to the clock; and a child living in Spain will also eat to the clock, but the clock will be set to a much later time. The staple food – the bulk – that children eat may be based on wheat, rice, sorghum, barley, maize, millet, potato, yam, or many other kinds of crop. Children living in nomadic groups in very cold regions of the world will thrive on a diet extremely high in animal fat. Those accustomed to one type of food may view another staple food as inedible (I shall never forget being given raw whale blubber in Northern Canada by an Inuit woman, and being told that it was 'soul food' and she always felt better for having eaten it. I could barely swallow it!). In some parts of the world there is a surplus of food, but in many parts of Africa or Asia, a child will typically experience hunger as an everyday aspect of life, and will never have a choice about the food she or he eats.

Food preparation and consumption, as Goody (1982) pointed out in his classic anthropological text, are deeply embedded in cultural and geographical contexts. This extraordinary variation in food and eating habits means that it is difficult to set nutritional or any other kind of norms that it is possible for all children to follow, except at the very broadest level of generality. Children need certain levels of essential nutrients for growth – although even that minimum level is debatable – but the form in which they obtain them is anything but standard.

The example of food consumption is a metaphor for other aspects of young children's lives. The argument being put forward in this chapter is that whilst there are some very general features of early childhood, all of them are shaped and modified by cultural context. So much so, that rather than understanding the generalities, it may be more useful to understand the particularities. Bruner argues that 'perhaps even more than with most cultural matters, child-drearing practices and beliefs reflect local conceptions of how the world is and how the child should be readied for living it' (Bruner, 2000: xi).

Having argued for cultural differences, I also want to give a word of caution about using the word culture. 'Culture' is itself a difficult concept (see Chapters 1 and 10), on the verge of being unusable. 'Culture' describes a set of related beliefs and practices of a particular community, although not everyone in the community will understand or practise them in the same way. These beliefs and patterns are manifested in surface differences – diet, games, clothes, eating habits and folklore – but they also draw on implicit and embedded assumptions and values, what the historian Catriona Kelly (2007) calls the 'elusive invisible network'. 'Culture' is usually thought of as belonging to a particular geographical space or country, but from a historical perspective, people are always on the move, and calamity is always round the corner. As Nederveen Pieterse (2004) has claimed in his book *Globalization and Culture: Global Melange*, 'cultures' are always porous, hybrid, shifting, and contradictory and reflect the frequently forced interchanges of ideas and practices that take place over time. For instance, almost all European countries now have large immigrant populations, and even small countries like Ireland or Finland are changing rapidly, so much so that one commentator has coined the phrase 'super-diversity' in order to describe the changes that have occurred in Europe (Vertovec, 2012). The Syrian refugee crisis is another instance of this continuous upheaval.

It is not only populations, but the nation state itself that is a relatively recent historical imposition, a reflection of past battles and especially of colonialism and empire. Countries like India, Nigeria, Sudan or Iraq or the (now ex) Soviet Union, brought together – sometimes very unhappily – many very different communities, traditions, languages, and religions, and talking about a particular country and its traditions is almost meaningless, such is the arbitrariness of national boundaries. So culture is rarely static or unchanging, it shifts from one generation to the next, from one place to another, and always varies over time. It is displayed differently by one individual to another, but is (just about) coherent enough to be recognised and at least partly described. Rather than use the word 'culture' in this chapter, I prefer to use words like 'local community' or 'cultural context' even although these words, too, should be used with care.

INTERNATIONAL PERSPECTIVES – A GLOBAL VIEW

Much of the work in child development focuses at a micro-level, about the understandings and interpretations of what children can do and the kinds of explanations that can account for their behaviour. LeVine and New point out that the study of child development has been largely confined to 'America, Europe and other Western countries who comprise less than ten per cent of all children in the world' (2008: 1). In their book they try to redress the balance by collecting together accounts of anthropologists working in unusual (to us) corners of the world. They sum up these accounts as follows:

- Every human society recognises a distinction between children and adults and the age-linked emergence of children's abilities to learn, work, and participate in community activities. At the same time societies vary considerably in the way they interpret children's readiness and ability to do these things.
- Schooling is a relatively recent idea. Until the late twentieth century most children participated in economic and domestic tasks; most were involved in multi-age children's groups; and the distinction between work and play was often blurred.
- Childhood environments differ considerably. In material terms, where children live, whether they have water, sanitation and shelter, what they eat and whether they have enough, what kind of health care is available to them; and in cultural terms, who they consider to be part of their family, how they speak and who to and in what language etc. will vary tremendously between societies.
- The ideas of parents are strongly influenced by culture; norms of parenting reflect and help to sustain the moral standards of a community. Parents have strong views about following these norms, yet they also reinterpret them and adjust them to changing circumstances.
- Children are not passive recipients of cultural practices – they are active interpreters. They acquire the conventions of communication and norms of behaviour that give them entrée to their local social world, but they use and modify them for their own purposes.

LeVine and his colleagues are trying to broaden the traditional discussions about child development, and to point out the narrowness of the knowledge base (Arnett-Jansen, 2015). LeVine comments elsewhere (LeVine, 2003) that what characterises child rearing in rich countries is an extraordinary focus on the individual, on an individual child's needs and wishes and preferences. Over and over again in advice to practitioners in early childhood guidance manuals it says that 'Every child should be treated as an individual'. It is continually stressed that each child is unique, that each child is an individual, each child is different etc. But there are other communities and contexts where the reverse holds true, where individuality is not prized, and collective obligations are prioritised over personal concerns. The community is paramount. Children are, in the words of the anthropologist Paul Riesman, 'learning to be a relative' (1992: 146). This view of how children should be and act is built into the very languages which children speak, and which contain in their very grammar terms of relationship and deference (e.g., different ways of saying 'you' according to whom you are speaking – older, younger, boy, girl, etc.).

More recently Serpell and Adamson-Holley (2015) and Correa-Chavez et al., (2015) have produced empirically derived definitions of children's learning in low and middle income countries where very different expectations and traditions of learning from those in rich countries hold true. These authors suggest that another shibboleth of early childhood in rich countries is that of 'learning through play'. Children's interests and activities are not regarded as necessarily distinct from those of adults, as in the notion of free play. Instead, children learn – and enjoy learning – by contributing to adult activities and through being helpful. Serpell, working in Zambia, and Rogoff working in Latin America, stress that learning happens by contributing to normal adult/household/communal activities. Serpell explores socially responsible activities as a paradigm for learning for children starting school. Rogoff develops her ideas of guided participation, and describes a process which she calls 'observing and pitching in'. In a **reversal** of conventional understanding, if children do not have a recognisable place in adult/collective activities, they are likely to feel – and behave – as excluded and redundant. Their self-esteem comes from being helpful and being seen to earn their keep in their community.

As mentioned above, language encapsulates culture and community. Many languages have more tenses than English, and this in turn requires more subtlety in the interpretation and **recapitulation** of events. Other languages are also more heavily gendered, and have many modes of addressing other people when English just relies on 'you' as a main form of address. Other languages are more rhythmic and musical, more given to recitation and performance than to private and solitary reading.

Language structures thinking and communication. In one way, children in low income countries might be regarded as fortunate; often they grow up in bilingual or multi-lingual environments (Bloch, 2007). Depending on the language you speak, you see and hear the world differently. English is a global language, 'the new Latin' as it is sometimes called. Because English is now so ubiquitous, most native English speakers see no reason to learn another language. But if ways of thinking and relating to other people is built into language, those who are multi-lingual are automatically at an intellectual advantage. Those who come from oral traditions tend to be acute listeners, and to remember accurately. Pre-school and schooling experiences sometimes damage rather than enhance language learning by a narrowing of methods, including a failure to appreciate the importance of oral learning, rhyme, chanting and recitation.

In richer countries, artistic self-expression is seen as a form of individuality, rather than as a community undertaking. So nurseries might value the daubs of young children as a first attempt at self-expression, and expect children to be proud if these daubs are displayed to others. But if the artistic expressiveness is a communal one – for example weaving, or choral singing or intricate group dancing requiring complex rhythmic performance, or indeed writing down an ideographic language which requires careful calligraphy on paper – if it is a skill which requires considerable mastery of form before it is recognisable, then it makes little sense to praise ineffectual efforts. Instead what counts is what Barbara Rogoff (1990) has called 'guided participation', a very careful instruction in the correct way to do things and gentle discouragement of what is wrong.

Another profound example of different understandings and perceptions of childhood is in the understanding and practice of religion. Like many writers from rich countries, I consider that education should be entirely secular; people are at liberty to hold whatever religious views they wish, but they should do so privately. As Scourfield et al. (2013) put it:

> To many people a typical British child in the primary school year may spend her time, when not in school, playing with toys ... but she does not read religious texts, or learn a classical language she is unlikely to ever converse in and does not have a strong sense of the presence of God ... There is a risk that any idea of typical childhood falls into stereotyping of course, but the idea of a child being socialised into a monotheistic worldview from birth and then when old enough, attending classes several times a week to learn to read the Qur'an in classical Arabic is certainly outside the mainstream of secular western childhood. (2013: 1)

For many Muslim communities, for example, the idea of young children being cared for and learning without being schooled into an understanding of God's beneficence is unwelcome (Ebrahim, 2017).

APPLYING INTERNATIONAL STANDARDS AND MEASUREMENTS

The above examples are just a few of the ways in which child rearing is perceived as profoundly different across the world. In a recent article (Penn, 2011) I track the use of ideas about early childhood by international non-governmental organisations such as the highly influential World Bank, UNICEF, UNESCO, Save the Children and other agencies which promote early childhood care and education programmes in low income countries. The rationales for promoting early childhood can be grouped as developmental-cognitive; socio-economic; and human rights. Both the developmental-cognitive argument, based on standard notions of developmental progress and cognitive abilities; and the socio-economic argument, based on standard notions of economic progress, have their origins in research and assumptions of rich countries, and have difficulties in coming to terms with diversity, or, in the case of the socio-economic arguments, do not consider it at all. Even the child rights arguments have their origins in Western liberal thought, and have been subject to criticism, and as a result there is now a separate African Charter on the Rights and Welfare of the Child (ACHPR, 1990), which emphasises responsibilities as well as rights.

There is a remarkable communality amongst the rationales adopted by international agencies, a promotion of standard precepts about children's understanding and children's needs which frequently fails to acknowledge local realities. For instance, I have discussed the World Bank Early Child Development programme in one country, the African state of Mali, and attempt to show in detail how particular local understandings of childhood are simply unregistered or obliterated (Penn, 2012).

A recent example which relates to early years is the UNICEF Early Learning Developmental Standards (ELDS) and school readiness programme. The ELDS programme originated out of concerns in the USA about developing tools and learning outcomes to measure the progress of pre-school children, so that they were 'ready' for school. The assumption was that if more is known about the intake of children starting school, and a baseline can be created, then it should be easier to measure how well the school itself is doing in educating its children. The ELDS standards were intended as a measuring instrument to understand the outcomes of various pre-school experiences and to inform steps to develop better programmes. This essentially American problem of school readiness was taken up by many USA based international aid agencies. UNICEF seized on the idea and in 2003–2004 launched its *Going Global* programme to measure school readiness, although school starting ages and school systems differ widely across countries.

The UNICEF ELDS standards were initially developed by academics at Harvard and Columbia Universities. The standards covered physical, cognitive, emotional and social domains. UNICEF piloted the tests in six countries, and then launched them globally. Each country was supposed to adapt the ELDS standards for its own use, and then roll them out nationally. Given the intended reach of the programme, a great deal of money appears to have been spent by UNICEF in promoting it (although the detailed accounts are unavailable). I was involved in assessing the programme in Bosnia and Herzogovina, and spoke at a conference in Sarajevo in 2015 and on Bosnian television about the findings. Predictably, although a lot of work had gone into developing the standards, and trying to adapt them for local use, they did not reflect sufficiently the current circumstances – in this case a crumbling Soviet kindergarten system, and a rapidly growing private system. Because of the dedication of local UNICEF staff in the region, a considerable effort had gone into trying to make ELDS work, but in many other – very different – countries ELDS never got off the ground or was quietly abandoned. The *Going Global* programme was completely abandoned in 2015, after an undeclared amount of money had been spent on it, and references to it on the UNICEF website are now almost impossible to find. At the time of writing, the final evaluation report on the project has not been published.

The UNICEF example is an unfortunate one, but there is a small sub-industry, especially amongst development economists, in trying to develop and refine standardised, international measurements for use in assessing the efficacy of early childhood intervention projects. A recent conference convened by the Institute of Fiscal Studies (June 2016) referred to research studies in Ghana, China, and a tranche of Latin American studies, trying to identify and cost which aspects of early childhood interventions gave best value for money. Most of the discussion centred on the research methods themselves, and their mathematical efficacy, rather than on the underlying principles and values of **ECEC** that were being measured. Titles of these large-scale, very expensive research projects included 'Quality pre-school for Ghana: Advancing research methods to support policy change', 'Improving the quality of centre-based care in Colombia', 'Evaluation of dosage, implementation and continuous quality improvement in public preschool', 'Teacher quality and learning outcomes in kindergarten'. Predictably, the findings from all these papers were that there were few statistically reliable results, and the statistically reliable results which did exist were not consistently found across the papers.

The common response to poor performance of children on standardised tests of school readiness is to ascribe the failure to parental ignorance. Parents are assumed to be ignorant of what is necessary to support their young children, and be unaware of, or unable to discriminate between the quality of interventions open to them. But as the work of Serpell (above) and others suggests, parents' beliefs and circumstances are very different from those of the school – and even more so from the researchers' – linguistically, cognitively, and socially.

As a conference attendee, I was tempted to make a comparison with the search at the CERN Atomic Reactor for the Higgs Boson particle. There are many thousands of physicists and other scientists working in Switzerland on the search for this mysterious particle, which, if found, would revolutionise the study of physics and fundamentally alter our view of the universe. It is not too fanciful to suggest that the developmental economists and cognitive psychologists are searching, with great methodological sophistication, for their own Higgs Boson particle, the type of ECEC intervention which will change lives and alter our understanding and ability to manipulate the way in which children learn and grow. But while the former is a legitimate enquiry, bearing results, the latter can only ever be a fool's errand, because values and assumptions about what is worthwhile in ECEC are local as well as global. Rigorous research is essential to test out assumptions, and especially important in the case of early childhood interventions in low income countries; but unless it is broad-based and interdisciplinary research, it is not likely to yield very much in the way of usable findings.

WOMEN, WORK AND CHILDCARE

Paradoxically, at the same time as there have been attempts to apply ideas like ELDS about early childhood to low and middle income countries without due consideration of circumstances, there is also a crisis occurring in many low income countries which does mirror conditions in richer countries. In most low and middle income countries there has been enormous internal and external migration, from rural areas to the cities, and from poor countries to rich ones. In China for example in the last two decades over 30 million people have migrated from villages to the cities, losing most of their rights and entitlements to health care and education in doing so. China is the most dramatic example of internal migration, but a similar pattern has happened elsewhere. The result is what one commentator has called '*the feminization of poverty*' (Razavi, 2011). The result of migration, (but other factors too), has been that women in low income countries have often lost their family and community support networks, and struggle to earn some kind of income whilst supporting their children as single parents. The extent of this phenomenon is considerable; possibly as many as 35 million young children worldwide left unattended, or cared for in dangerous conditions by slightly older children (Samman et al., 2016). Ironically this unprecedented demand for day care is largely ignored by international aid agencies, which instead predicate their responses on an old-fashioned middle-class view of family life, with father-earner and stay at home mother. There is hardly any mention of working mothers in the ELDS literature. The rhetoric, much of it from external donors such as the World Bank, is about the need for early childhood interventions (Garcia et al., 2008) and these rationales rarely relate to direct support for women and childcare. By default most provision in low income countries is provided by private entrepreneurs. People pay for what they can afford, and poor people who cannot afford to pay fees either receive a very poor service or none at all. In this way inequality is exacerbated (Woodhead and Streuli, 2013).

The hegemony – the power and influence – of the international agencies based in rich countries is almost total and unchallenged. In neglecting local circumstances and understandings, the result of course is that programmes fail and like ELDS, they are jettisoned (Penn, 2011). The issue of knowledge transfer in education, and in particular the export and import of educational ideas from rich to poorer countries has attracted considerable attention from scholars (Phillips and Ochs, 2004; Steiner-Khamsi, 2004; Steiner-Khamsi and Silova, 2008) although to date very little work has been done in the field of early childhood. Steiner-Khamsi argues that educational ideas are never straightforwardly transferred from one country to another, but there is always a mixture of adaptation, incorporation and resistance, according to local contexts. These local contexts are not 'untouched' relics of a traditional past, but are themselves the product of many past influences and current socio-demographic pressures. She uses the example of education in Mongolia to describe how educational reforms prescribed by the World Bank and other international agencies were nominally accepted because of the much needed money being offered, but the reforms were in fact subverted or not implemented. For example, she describes attempts by donors to introduce 'community participation' into schools, but there is no word in Mongolian for 'community'. The nearest translation was 'home-place' which rendered the planned interventions by donors meaningless. The reforms just petered out. Although donors are willing to export ideas, the process is rarely reciprocal, and local ideas are regarded as quaint rather than warranting serious attention.

Because globally imported initiatives and reforms mostly do not work, or do not work in the way that donors anticipate, the usual response is to blame the recipients. Ferguson (1994; 2015) makes the point that the very high failure rate of aid projects, not just in early childhood, but across the board, is because of aggressive reliance on scientific and technical progress to satisfy human needs, upgrade livelihoods and resolve social dilemmas. He argues that in low income countries cash transfers i.e. giving unconditional benefits to the poor such as old age pensions and child benefits – for example in South Africa – makes more difference in combating chronic poverty than any actions by aid agencies.

The DfID *Young Lives* project, which has followed up 12,000 children over a fifteen-year period in Peru, Ethiopia, Andhra Pradesh and Vietnam, using a wide range of methods, qualitative and quantitative, has shown that early childhood, whilst important, does not necessarily contribute to future wellbeing if other risk factors are present; or conversely if circumstances improve children can make up for lost opportunities. Chronic poverty is complex, multi-faceted, and likely to be recurring, and no one solution is likely to be effective. Jones and Vilar argue in relation to their work in Peru for the *Young Lives* project:

> It is critical to unpack culturally specific understandings of core cultural concepts with which a research project is engaging (such as 'children', 'family' and 'work') and how these are subject to competing interpretations and reinterpretations in societies undergoing rapid social, political, economic and demographic transitions. (2008: 45)

CONCLUSION

This chapter has discussed the expectations and understandings about young children's lives and what they need and how different cultural contexts shape these assumptions. Yet most of the academic and policy discussion that takes place in early childhood does so in a Euro-American context which emphasises technical solutions that do not sufficiently recognise the situation of many children.

This lack of recognition of local context is important because when donors from rich countries try to export ideas about early childhood (or education more generally) to low and middle income countries, they frequently fail in their attempts, in wasteful and costly ways.

The issue of early childhood in low and middle income countries is also important because of the very rapid urbanisation that is taking place in most countries of the world. Just as there has been a minor revolution about women's roles in rich countries, which has prompted the development of early childhood education and care, so there is a rather different kind of revolution going on in low income countries. Life in the slums and poor quarters of big cities in low income countries is very problematic, particularly for mothers, and the kind of care and education offered to young children who live in potentially hostile environments is a matter of real concern for anyone concerned about childhood.

These are the complex issues that anyone discussing the globalisation of childhood faces: what contexts are relevant, what assumptions are being made, and how can chronic poverty and instability be addressed?

Key points

- Childhood is often generalised but it is characterised by particularities: childhood varies enormously from place to place.
- Culture is a debated concept and cultures – or local communities and cultural contexts – are often in a state of flux.
- Ideas about childhood can travel and colonise different contexts. Rich countries tend to emphasise children's separateness. For example, their individuality or the importance of learning through play (not work). This view can override the beliefs of people in contexts where community and children's relatedness to others is paramount.
- The assumptions about childhood of rich countries are translated into influential, international interventions and conventions, which neglect local realities in many parts of the world.

Recommended reading

Samman, E., Presler-Marshall, E., Jones, N. with Bhatkal, T., Melamed, C., Stavropoulou, M. and Wallace, J. (2016) *Women's Work: Mothers, Children and the Global Childcare Crisis*. London: ODI. Available online: https://www.odi.org/global-childcare-crisis

CHILDHOOD IN THE DIGITAL AGE

JACKIE MARSH

CONTENTS

INTRODUCTION

This chapter reflects on the nature of childhood in the digital age. It offers an overview of research that has explored children's use of digital technologies in homes and communities and considers the main issues that have emerged regarding this use. The chapter also reflects on potential future developments in this field. The aim of the chapter is to provide an introduction to the key issues and debates in a topic that frequently gives rise to misconceptions, and to signal the research questions that might be important in the years ahead. First, however, the nature of the digital age is considered.

THE DIGITAL AGE

The social, cultural and economic changes wrought over the past forty years as digital technologies have developed at a fast pace are wide-ranging. The technological transformations, which have created a paradigm shift as significant as the move from oral to written cultures, or the invention of the printing press, have impacted upon a range of areas. In terms of the economy, the employment landscape has changed exponentially since the industrial age. Given that numerous tasks are now automated through technologies and many aspects of business can be conducted over the internet, a globalised approach has been adopted by many industries, leading to the outsourcing of tasks to countries in which workers have a lower standard of living than Western countries. New forms of employment have arisen in the West, such as the development and management of social networking sites. The 'dot-com bubble', which occurred during the last years of the twentieth century, led to the commercial growth of the internet and e-commerce. The internet is becoming increasingly important in the financial landscapes of ordinary households, with a major shift to online banking and purchasing. Tech City (2016) report that in 2016, the digital technical economy supported 1.56 million jobs, with the sector creating employment at a rate that was almost three times that of other sectors.

In a similar fashion, digital technologies have had a major impact on our social and cultural lives. Individuals are now networked with a range of other people, both known and unknown, through the use of text and video messaging, and social network sites, such as Instagram, Facebook, Snapchat, Twitter and WhatsApp. Developments in digital photography mean that it is simple to store and send photographs using the internet and the ease of using digital video recording apps on mobile phones has encouraged many to record and upload videos to video sharing sites such as YouTube, including children (Marsh, 2015). The music industry has been transformed through the ability of consumers to access music digitally, leading to the widespread practice of downloading music illegally. These phenomena have been characterised as signalling a move from consumerism to production, with the growth of the 'produser' (Bruns, 2006) – the individual who is both a consumer of mass media and a contributor to media culture through the production of digital texts and artefacts (see Chapter 18 for the use of such technology in research with children). It is inevitable that these changes have had an impact on young children's lives and in this chapter, an overview of young children's access to, and use of, digital technologies will be provided. First, however, we need to consider the broader social and cultural context which shapes this use. The following section considers some of the key messages given about young children's use of technology by the mass media.

MEDIA DUPE OR MEDIA SAVVY? MEDIA DISCOURSES OF CHILDHOOD IN A DIGITAL AGE

Moral panics (Cohen, 1987) regarding children's use of technologies are a recurrent feature of media coverage in the UK. These have included concerns about the perceived negative impact of media on children's emotional, physical, social, linguistic and cognitive development, in addition to worries about the way in which children are becoming positioned as economic targets by multinational companies (Kenway and Bullen, 2001). Moral panics have always occurred in relation to the cultures of children and young people, as Springhall (1999) outlines, but the intensity with which media reports have dealt with this matter in the twenty-first century indicates that there has been a material shift in the moral panic discourse. For example, in January 2008, media reports of a spate of teenage suicides in a town in Wales led to headlines such as 'Police fear internet cult inspires teen suicides' (Britten and Savill, 2008), as many of the teenagers involved had used the social networking site Bebo. Police subsequently denied that they had identified the internet as a key common component across the suicides, but this did not prevent extensive media coverage which suggested that this was the case. Similarly, in more recent years, the increase in young children's use of tablets has led to concerns about 'iPad addiction' (Joshi, 2016; Palmer, 2016).

Luke and Luke (2001) suggest that the reactions against children and young people's engagement with new technologies can be traced to the growing gap between the communicative practices of adults and youth, with the former based on traditional print-based practices and the latter moving increasingly to on-screen reading and writing. This argument has some resonance with the discussions regarding 'digital natives' and 'digital immigrants' (Prensky, 2001), in which children are characterised as being digitally competent, in contrast to many adults who struggle with the use of new technologies. However, this notion has been subject to widespread critique, given that age does not always correlate to confidence with and use of technologies (Thomas, 2010). Lankshear and Knobel (2011) have used the concept of 'mindsets' to describe this disjuncture, with the term 'insider mindsets' characterising learners who recognise the changes to communication that technologies have brought and thus transform practices accordingly and the phrase 'outsider mindsets' indicating individuals who have a propensity to continue to treat the world in much the same way as before, with digital technologies failing to promote fundamental changes to practices. The discussion in relation to mindsets enables a nuanced account of generational differences in the digital age, recognising that age cannot always be tied to confidence with and use of technologies.

It can be seen, therefore, that media representations concerning childhood and technology present conflicting messages. On the one hand, children are viewed as digital experts, navigating a range of technologies with intuitive expertise, and on the other they are positioned as the innocent victims of a globalised and highly commercialised technology industry, driven to zombified or aggressive cognitive states through an addictive use of various media. Inevitably, the reality is very much more complex, with patterns of use and competence shaped by individual and social circumstances. The next section of the chapter considers the research on children's use of digital technologies and identifies the ways in which the context of this use is all-important.

CHILDREN'S ENGAGEMENT WITH DIGITAL TECHNOLOGIES IN HOMES AND COMMUNITIES: AN ECOLOGICAL PERSPECTIVE

Despite the widespread prevalence of digital technologies as they have developed over the last decades, there is still a limited amount of research on young children's engagement with them (Holloway et al., 2013). There are some large-scale national reviews of young children's use of technologies in the US and England (Marsh et al., 2005; Rideout, 2014; Marsh et al., 2015a; Ofcom, 2015). A larger number of smaller-scale studies have been conducted across a wide range of countries including those with a focus on the UK (Livingstone et al., 2014; Marsh et al., 2015b), Europe (Chaudron, 2015), Australia (Davidson et al., 2014) and Qatar (Savage, 2012). In the following discussion, an ecological analysis of children's use of digital technologies is outlined, drawing from the work of Bronfenbrenner (1979), in order to understand the way in which different domains of practice shape children's experiences with digital literacy. Ecological theories indicate that attention needs to be paid to the inter-relation of a range of factors which shape individuals' engagement with technology. Nardi and O'Day (1999: 49), for example, suggest that an ecology is 'a system of people, practices, values, and technologies in a particular local environment'. Interaction with technology is never context-free and the relationships between social agents, tools, technological practices and local contexts are complex and determine the nature of its use.

Bronfenbrenner (1979) suggested that the environment in which a child grew up impacts upon his or her development in a number of ways. He argued that individuals exist within overlapping ecological systems that are 'a set of nested structures, each inside the next, like a set of Russian dolls' (Bronfenbrenner, 1979: 3). The first of these structures is the microsystem; this is the immediate environment surrounding the child or children under study. It refers to the immediate interpersonal interactions with significant others in the environment and this environment can vary according to the unit of analysis, e.g. it can be the home, a classroom and so on. The mesosystem links two different microsystems together. An example of this might be the relationship between homes and early years settings. The third level, the exosystem, consists of settings in which children are not active participants but which impact significantly on children's lives. For example, parents' workplaces might have a significant impact on child rearing practices. Finally, the macrosystem is the larger cultural and social context that impacts on the way in which children live. These systems are not intended to operate in a hierarchical manner but instead overlap to create complex and inter-related planes of experiences which inform children's development.

MICROSYSTEM

Microsystems are the smallest unit of analysis and are environments that are closest to the child. The microsystem of the home is one in which, in general, the majority of children in the UK are offered access to digital technologies and are supported in the use of these technologies by parents. For example, in the 'Technology and Play' study, which involved a survey of 2,000 parents and carers of nought- to five-year-olds in the UK (Marsh et al., 2015a) and in-depth case studies of six families, children had access to a wide range of technologies in the home including laptops and tablets. Children were keen to engage with technologies in ways that fostered social interaction with parents and siblings. Technology was mentioned by parents as a means of developing shared cultural understandings and for families who spoke languages other than English, the media offered a significant means of engaging with both language and culture. Therefore the home as a microsystem was, for the majority of children, a rich site for technological experiences. In the microsystem, socio-economic status (SES) is a significant factor in the types of technological activities in which children engage. Patterns of access and use differ across technologies, with children in social groups C2DE, working-class children, being less likely to own the more expensive iPads, for example, and more likely to own cheaper types of tablets (Marsh et al., 2015a). Across all social groups, however, the microsystem of the home offers a range of opportunities for children to become competent in the use of a variety of digital technologies. Ofcom (2015), in a survey of children's media use across the UK, report that:

- 96 per cent of children live in homes with access to the internet through a PC, laptop, tablet or smartphone.
- At least 3 in 4 children aged 3–15 live in a household with a tablet computer.
- The use of tablet computers to play games is increasing (35 per cent of 5–15-year-olds), whilst the use of portable game players is decreasing (down 11 per cent in a year for the same age group).
- 42 per cent of 5–15-year-olds have a mobile phone and of these, 35 per cent own a smartphone.
- 44 per cent of 5–15s watch on-demand television content.

Children acquire a range of skills and knowledge as a result of this engagement, including skills in the use of hardware and software and the ability to read/view and produce **multimodal**, multimedia texts. In Table 5.1, a summary is provided of the range of texts that young children view/read and write using digital technologies in the home.

A further noteworthy aspect of children's experiences of digital technologies in the microsystem is the fact that texts are connected across various media. For example, if a child is interested in the television programme *Peppa Pig*, he or she can also encounter the narrative on a DVD, computer game, internet site or iPad app. Kinder (1993) developed the concept of 'transmedia intertextuality' to describe this process. This phenomenon means that there are various entry points to any text and children's understanding of narrative may be developed in complex ways, as various media offer specific experiences of narrative. For example, a child might listen to a story retold from a third-person viewpoint, such as a narrator, and then encounter the same story through a computer game in which he or she can adopt a first-person perspective.

Children's play across digital media is also multi-layered and the toys and artefacts linked to favourite media texts enable children to replay characters and stories in a creative manner.

Children are spending increasing amounts of time online and some of them are gravitating to social networking sites that are aimed at older age groups. In a recent study of the online activities of 180 primary school children aged five to eleven (Burke and Marsh, 2013), it was found that a third of the five- to eight-year-olds stated that they had their own Facebook page, yet the entry age for this site is thirteen years. However, on further examination, it was clear that the children's Facebook pages had been set up by their parents and that the parents were managing and overseeing the children's use of the site, including their friendships. Seven-year-old Katy, for example, reported how her mum was aware of her Facebook page as she had set it up and managed her friendship network. Katy used the site to chat to family members, such as her aunties. In this instance, it would appear that Facebook was a family literacy practice and that this was a relatively safe use of the site by Katy and her family. Nevertheless, it cannot be assumed that all parents would have effective oversight of their children's use of the site and there are certainly concerns about introducing children to practices such as online gambling, which are prevalent in such social networking sites. This, therefore, is an example of the way in which children's use of digital technologies can be both productive and potentially counter-productive, dependent upon other aspects of their ecological system.

Table 5.1   Young children's digital viewing/reading and writing in the home

Technology	Texts read	Texts written
Television/DVD/Blu Ray	• Words and symbols on remote control • Electronic programming guide • Text included in games on satellite/cable channels (red button) and smart TVs • Words, signs and symbols in programmes and advertisements	• Writing in search feature of smart TVs
Computer/laptop/tablet	• Alphabet on keyboard • Text on websites • Text instructions for programs • Text in programs	• Random typing of letters • Writing of name • Writing lists, letters and stories • Typing letters/words/phrases in online sites such as games and virtual worlds • Mulitmodal texts created, such as drawings, photographs and films
Handheld computers	• Text instructions for programs • Text in programs	

Technology	Texts read	Texts written
Mobile phones/smartphones	• Text on screen, e.g. text messages • Signs and symbols on the keypad	• Pressing random letters, pretending to text • Choosing emoticons • Mulitmodal texts created, such as drawings, photographs and films
Electronic games, e.g. LeapPad	• Alphabet on keyboards and text on screen, e.g. alphabet and word games	• Typing in letters and words
Console games/virtual reality headsets and games	• Text instructions for programs • Text in programs	
Musical hardware, e.g. MP3 players/radios/karaoke machines	• Words and symbols on operating systems • Words on screen with karaoke machines	
GPS technologies, e.g. TomTom	• Text on screen, e.g. navigation page	
Other domestic electronic devices, e.g. microwave, washer	• Words, signs and symbols on the devices	

MESOSYSTEM

In Bronfenbrenner's model, the mesosystem connects the interactions between two microsystems. Children, therefore, can interact with individuals, text and artefacts which relate their home experiences to another microsystem, such as neighbourhood and community groups, or schools. Bronfenbrenner (1979) uses the example of a child learning to read to illustrate this. Children's reading ability is influenced by a number of factors, including the nature of the relationship between home and school attitudes to, and practices of, reading. Children who are supported in learning to read at home are more likely to succeed in the task at school. In relation to young children's use of digital technologies, the mesosystem may provide opportunities for children to extend their digital competences or it may limit them, according to the context. For example, some studies have indicated the way in which early years settings and schools do not always support young children's engagement with digital technologies and this may have a detrimental effect on children's confidence and progression in digital literacy (Levy, 2011). A stark example of the disjuncture between contexts in the mesosystem can be found in Wohlwend's (2009) account of children from print-centric early years classrooms in the US, who longed to play with the new technologies and media that were part of their everyday experiences outside of school. She offers an account of one child who, thwarted by the limitations of digital technologies on offer in the classroom, drew his own mobile phone:

> He gave an oblong piece of paper rounded corners and penciled a 3 by 3 array of squares below a much larger square to represent a numeric pad and an LCD screen. Additional phone features

(receiver, compact size) were emphasized by adding play actions: he held the opened paper flat in the palm of his hand, raised his hand to his ear, talked into the paper for a few seconds, then snapped it shut with one hand, and tucked it into his pocket. (Wohlwend, 2009: 125)

The five- to seven-year-old 'early adopters' in Wohlwend's study used paper and pencil to create mobile phones, iPods and video games in order to bring their own digital microsystems into this early years setting. However, Johnson (2010) suggests that even when children have access to new technologies in the classroom, it might not always lead to enthusiastic engagement. She conducted a survey in which thirty-eight, six- and seven-year-old children in Australia completed a ten-item rating scale on internet use at home and school. Her findings indicate that 'children who frequently use and enjoy the Internet at home avoid using the Internet at school, particularly with respect to email but with the exception of playing games' (Johnson, 2010: 290). The reasons for this pattern could be varied and include sensitivity to the differences in contexts across home and school; for example, children may prefer the privacy of home for the purpose of sending an email, or it may be the case that the technological hardware and software in homes and schools are very different and thus children do not easily transfer their practices across the domains. For the small number of children who have no, or little, access to online services at home, or have limited use of technologies, it is even more important that early years settings and schools offer opportunities to engage meaningfully with a range of digital media.

EXOSYSTEM

The exosystem, according to Bronfenbrenner, consists of settings and contexts in which children are not active participants but which impact significantly on children's lives. Parental education and/or employment outside of the home may have an impact on young children's use of digital technologies in the home. For example, in a study of under-eight's digital literacy practices in seven countries, it was found that level of education was an influencing, although not determining, factor in parents' digital engagement with children, with more educated parents having a greater set of skills and thus a higher level of digital engagement with children (Chaudron, 2015). Parents in this study who had particular expertise in digital technology through employment were also more confident about managing their children's use of technology (Livingstone et al., 2015).

MACROSYSTEM

The final nested structure in Bronfenbrenner's model, the macrosystem, refers to the wider social and cultural context in which the child operates. As the previous discussion in the chapter suggests, influences on this level may be negative, given the emphasis in the mass media and popular writings of many cultures on the perceived harmful effects of the use of technology on children's social, physical, linguistic and cognitive development (e.g. Palmer, 2006). In Plowman et al.'s (2010) case studies of young children's use of technology in the home, some parents expressed anxieties about children's use of technologies, including concerns about the possibility of over-use, perhaps as a result of this mass media bias. In an Australian study (Fox et al., 2011) three teachers and ten parents of pre-school children were interviewed about their views of technology. Teachers were positive about the use of technology, but the mothers were opposed to its use at home. It is of interest that eight of the ten mothers had experienced university, three at postgraduate level. It may be that issues of social class were pertinent here, as in other studies, middle-class parents have been more likely to comment on the potentially adverse effects of technology, while many working-class parents were resistant to negative messages in the media and emphasised the importance of their children developing digital skills relevant for employment in the twenty-first century (Marsh et al., 2005).

Drawing from an ecological conceptual framework (Bronfenbrenner, 1979), it can be seen that children's experiences of technology are shaped by the contexts in which they live, both the contexts in which they are present and those external contexts that shape their immediate environment. Each child's engagement with technology is unique to his or her ecological system and this will inform how children's engagement with technology is shaped. Thus, the task of basing decisions about policy and practice on this information is a challenging one, and one which demands careful assessment of these interlocking structures and systems if early years settings and schools are to respond appropriately to children's technological experiences. Early years educators need to ensure that they attend to the specific circumstances of individual children's interactions with technologies outside of early years settings in order to offer them appropriate provision. For example, practitioners could develop a knowledge base that enables them to determine the confidence levels of parents in the use of technologies and where they identify families in which levels of confidence are lower, offer support such as family learning activities that extend parents' abilities to use technologies alongside their children. In this way, the digital divide that exists due to the interaction of access to technologies with other significant factors, such as the historical technological experiences of family members, can begin to be bridged in some way in order to promote technological competence and expertise in digital literacy for all.

FUTURE DEVELOPMENTS

Research in the field over the past few years has identified the way in which many young children are increasingly drawn to online play (Burke and Marsh, 2013; Marsh et al., 2015b). Studies indicate that young children engage in a similar range of play activities online as they do offline and that these spaces can be productive sites for social engagement (Marsh, 2013; Marsh et al., 2016). Further, the online sites are connected to a range of offline texts and artefacts. In addition, there is growing interest in physical toys which have some kind of online presence or digital connection, such as the Furby robotic toy, which links to an app and enables children to feed and water the Furby using virtual food and drink. The rise of this 'Internet of Toys' means that it is not possible to make a clear distinction between children's online and offline play and digital literacy practices, as the boundaries between these domains are becoming blurred in the digital age. This trend will develop further in the years ahead, although there have been concerns raised with regard to data privacy and security implications, given that some of these toys collect data on the child. This has already led, in one instance, to a potential security breach in relation to children's chat logs and photographs (Khoury, 2015).

In the years ahead, it is also conceivable that children will be able to play with a wider range of interfaces that facilitate imaginative play. For example, virtual reality headsets, such as Google Cardboard or Oculus Rift, are becoming increasingly popular. Whilst the technology is still fairly new, these headsets enable children to play interactive games in a range of spaces and they are able to project themselves into imaginative virtual scenarios, such as Disney films (Robinson, 2016). Studies will be required that enable early years educators to understand the impact of these developments on children's play across space and time.

A further development will relate to the increasing role that robots will play in children's lives. Robots are becoming more sophisticated and are already being used in a range of offline contexts, such as servicing the needs of older people. In years ahead, children will be able to program and play with robots in ways that are not possible currently. Some scholars have expressed concern about these developments. For example, Turkle (2011) suggests that an increasing use of robots may impact on children's ability to develop intimacy and trust in offline relationships. Researchers in the early childhood field will need to attend to this and related issues in future studies.

Finally, 3D printing is becoming ever more accessible as the costs are reduced. This technology has great potential for young children, as they can use the machines to create their own 3D models. Such developments relate well to the rise of the 'maker' movement, in which anyone with access to the right tools and resources can create artefacts, often in 'makerspaces' or 'Fab Labs'. These spaces offer great potential for learning (see Peppler et al., 2006). Research in this area has largely focused on teenagers and young people and there is a need to consider the impact of engagement in such spaces by young children in future studies (see a study which explores this topic: 'Makerspaces in the Early Years: Enhancing Digital Literacy and Creativity' (MakEY: http://makeyproject.eu)).

These developments demonstrate that technology is becoming ever more pervasive, mobile and transparent in everyday life and that in years ahead, children's engagement in digital play will increasingly take place across a range of environments, both indoor and outdoor, online and offline and across time. Technology will enable these environments to become increasingly integrated, so that it will become necessary to understand childhood as it is played out across these spaces.

CONCLUSION

This chapter has considered the nature of childhood in the digital age. Given the extent to which many young children are competent and confident users of a range of technologies because of their experiences in the home and communities from their earliest years, it is important for early years educators to understand the implications for research, policy and practice. In many ways, digital technologies have not changed the essential elements of childhood, such as the need for deep attachments to family members, the importance of enjoying a strong face-to-face friendship network and having opportunities to engage in creative and imaginative play using a range of natural and manufactured resources. Rather, developments in digital technologies have provided opportunities to extend these elements and strengthen them across a range of contexts. This is not to suggest that technology has only a positive impact on childhood; of course it brings with it risks such as overuse, online bullying and a potential reduction in outdoor play in natural environments. Nonetheless, what the chapter emphasises is that technological developments also bring opportunities and it is important that early childhood educators take an informed and measured approach to this topic.

Key points

- Young children are engaged in digital culture from birth and develop a wide range of skills, knowledge and understanding through use of digital technologies.
- There is a need to understand the influences on children's use of technology from different perspectives that focus on the home, the immediate environment outside of the home and the wider society. For example, children's levels of access to digital technologies and use of these in homes impacts on their skills and confidence. If early years settings and schools do not offer sufficient opportunities to engage with digital technologies, then those children who lack access to them at home will be further disadvantaged. Parental work and employment outside of the home impacts on their ability to support young children's use of technologies. Finally, the attitudes towards technology in the wider culture can shape children's access to and use of digital technologies if parents become fearful of the negative messages they read about media use.
- Technological developments are leading to the blurring of boundaries between online and offline spaces. This creates both opportunities and risks for children. Children are able to play with a range of hardware and software that promotes imaginative and creative play, but online play means that toy companies are sometimes able to collect data about children's activities for commercial purposes.
- Future research in this field should focus on children's engagement with the 'Internet of Toys', robots, 3D printers and virtual reality in order to determine the impact of these technologies on children's play, development and learning.

Recommended reading

Marsh, J. and Bishop, J.C. (2014) *Changing Play: Play, Media and Commercial Culture from the 1950s to the Present Day*. Maidenhead: Open University Press. This book traces the continuities and discontinuities in children's play over time and considers the impact of technology on play in recent years.

PART 2

THE DEVELOPING CHILD

YOUNG CHILDREN'S COGNITIVE DEVELOPMENT

RUTH FORD

CONTENTS

INTRODUCTION

The term *cognitive development* refers broadly to the growth of children's cognition between birth and adolescence, including **perception**, attention, language, reasoning and memory (Bjorklund, 2011). Because cognitive development has such diverse aspects, it has not yet been explained fully by any single theory. This chapter gives an overview of some of the foremost accounts in the field before focusing on two important domains of cognitive development which have been researched intensively in recent years; social cognition and self-regulation. It concludes by drawing attention to practical applications of cognitive developmental research and directions for future study.

THEORIES OF COGNITIVE DEVELOPMENT

Theories of cognitive development can be contrasted by their stances on several issues, particularly: (1) the relative contribution of heredity versus the environment (i.e., **nature** *versus* **nurture**), (2) whether development is steady or stage-like, (3) the role of domain-general versus domain-specific processes, (4) the extent to which children initiate opportunities for their own learning, and (5) the impact of the socio-cultural context. As will become evident, different opinions regarding these matters have led to remarkably diverse views on the nature and development of children's thinking.

PIAGET'S THEORY: THE CHILD AS SCIENTIST

Swiss psychologist Jean Piaget initiated the study of cognitive development in the 1920s. He carried out large-scale studies of children's thinking and detailed examinations of his own children's development. Piaget's pioneering theory has been hugely influential, because it provided many thought-provoking ideas that have stimulated research programmes to the present day. Piaget's theory acknowledges contributions of both nature and nurture to intellectual ability, describes **continuity** and **discontinuity** in development, and stresses the active contribution of the child to its intellectual growth (for example, Piaget, 1952). Piaget's training in biology and philosophy informed his approach to the study of psychology. His background in biology led to an interest in the relations between evolution and human cognitive development, leading him to speculate that children are motivated to acquire knowledge because such behaviour is adaptive. His background in philosophy, particularly in logic, inspired him to search for internal consistency underlying children's errors in problem solving. Piaget's theory is described as *constructivist* in depicting the child as actively constructing knowledge in response to experiences, and *domain-general* in assuming the existence of cognitive processes that apply to a wide variety of problems. Piaget's work began gaining attention during the 1960s partly because it rejected ideas that had dominated psychology for the previous thirty years (for example, behaviourist models of learning). The essence of Piaget's theory is the notion of the 'child as scientist', carrying out simple tests to discover how the world works.

According to Piaget, continuity in development arises from three processes: assimilation, **accommodation** and equilibration. ***Assimilation*** occurs when new experiences are integrated into existing knowledge, *accommodation* occurs when children modify their knowledge in response to new experiences that cannot be assimilated, and ***equilibration*** reflects the child's attempts to balance assimilation and accommodation to create stable understanding. For example, a young child might believe that only animals are living things because only animals move in ways that preserve their life. Her ideas develop as she encounters new kinds of animals and assimilates these examples into her '**schema**' for living things. However, when she discovers that plants move in ways that promote their survival too she experiences a state of disequilibrium (uncertainty) and then accommodates her knowledge structures to the new information about plants and decides that since this movement signifies life, plants must be living things.

For Piaget, cognitive development is discontinuous with four discrete stages (***epigenesis***). His theory assumes that later stages of development build on earlier achievements and these stages are universal (true for all human cultures) and age-invariant (passed through in the same order by all children).

The first stage is the ***sensorimotor stage***, which lasts from birth to approximately the age of two years. During this stage, infants think only about objects and events in their immediate environment. Through assimilation, accommodation and equilibration, infants construct progressively more sophisticated links between sensation and motor activity (sensorimotor schemas), enabling them to develop ideas about time, space and causality. As they grow older, infants integrate simple reflexes such as gazing and grasping to achieve more advanced behaviours such as visually guided reaching, they attain an understanding that objects continue to exist even when they cannot be seen (the concept of **object permanence**), and they test ideas about cause and effect, for example, by shaking and biting a rattle to discover how to produce a noise.

By their second birthday, most infants have entered the ***pre-operational*** stage, which lasts until approximately the age of seven years. Children become capable of representing their experiences mentally using imagery and language. Piaget referred to this as ***symbolic function*** and argued that it could be observed in **deferred imitation** and frequent engagement in make-believe play. For example, if a three-year-old girl holds a banana to her ear and speaks into it as if it was a phone then she indicates that she is capable of mentally representing the banana as something else. Once the symbolic function is in place, Piaget's theory suggests that subsequent cognitive development involves the acquisition of new modes of thinking, known as ***mental operations***. Pre-operational children are misled by superficial appearances during problem solving because they lack the important mental operations necessary for logical reasoning. For example, until they acquire the ability to mentally undo an action, children are unable to understand that the amount of liquid in a container does not change when it is poured into a container of a different shape (that is, a failure of ***conservation***). Three other important features of the pre-operational stage are ***egocentrism***, the inability to take another person's point of view, ***centration***, the tendency to focus attention on a single aspect of a problem at a time, and *animism*, the tendency to attribute life-like qualities to non-living things.

During the ***concrete operational*** stage, typically lasting from the ages of seven to twelve years, children demonstrate the use of logic when dealing with problems involving concrete objects and events, and they succeed in conserving number, volume, mass and area. Children also begin to pass tests requiring ***seriation*** (i.e. sorting objects along a particular dimension such as length), *transitive inferences* (identifying logical relations between objects) and *class inclusion* (understanding superordinate versus subordinate class membership, such as animal versus dog). However, they do not yet show evidence of thinking in abstract or hypothetical terms and cannot easily combine information systematically to solve a problem.

Finally, on entering the **formal operational** stage of development at approximately the age of twelve years, children are able to consider abstract constructs and to formulate and test hypotheses in a scientific manner. For example, if given a pendulum with varying weights and lengths of string they can then deduce what determines the rate of oscillation. Their ability to think hypothetically also leads them to query the way society is structured and to ponder philosophical questions about truth, justice and morality.

Many of the studies that have been stimulated by Piaget's theory have concluded that he underestimated young children's capabilities because he failed to take into account their memory and language limitations. Whereas Piaget's basic findings in relation to the sequence of development have been extensively replicated, other research has challenged his notion of stages of development, his emphasis on domain-general reasoning abilities, and his neglect of the contribution of social interactions to children's thinking. These points have been addressed in turn by information-processing approaches, core-knowledge approaches and socio-cultural approaches to cognitive development.

INFORMATION-PROCESSING APPROACHES: THE CHILD AS A COMPUTATIONAL SYSTEM

Information-processing approaches reject Piaget's ideas about abrupt transformations in cognitive development and instead posit a gradual improvement of basic cognitive processes, memory and knowledge (Halford and Andrews, 2010). In terms of core issues, development is assumed to reflect both nature and nurture, to be continuous rather than discontinuous, and to involve active problem solving by the child.

Notions about information processing hold that as children grow older they become more efficient at encoding information from the environment, faster in their speed of mental processing, better able to apply learning and memory strategies, and more knowledgeable. For example, knowledge acquisition is associated with significant gains in memory capabilities during childhood – young children become better at remembering novel events as they develop *scripts* or mental representations of the usual sequence of activities for commonly experienced routines like attending a birthday party or visiting the doctor.

The majority of information-processing theories of cognitive development assume sequential processing of information but connectionist or neural-network models aim to mimic the physiological workings of the human brain by invoking parallel processing (Elman, 2005). Neo-Piagetian information-processing views, which account for stage-like development in terms of continuous improvements in processing capacity, have also been influential. Finally, dynamic systems theories reject ideas about linear causality (where x causes y) and, instead, suggest that mutually interdependent parts of the cognitive system co-operate in a non-linear fashion to produce new, emergent properties (Lewis, 2000).

CORE-KNOWLEDGE THEORIES: THE CHILD AS A PRODUCT OF HUMAN EVOLUTION

Similar to both Piaget's and information-processing theories, core-knowledge theories assume that the child is an active agent in their own development who strives to learn. Uniquely, however, such approaches argue that children are born with learning abilities already in place that are specialised for particular domains of thought. Innate forms of domain-specific knowledge are believed to have arisen in response to human evolutionary history, without which it is presumed infants would have difficulty in beginning to make sense of the world. Innate knowledge is suggested to be crucial to the development of such skills as face recognition, taxonomic classification and language.

Core knowledge has been argued to provide the foundation for children's intuitive or naïve theories about how the world works (i.e. the *theory* approach to development – Wellman and Gelman, 1998). Naïve theories operate in *core domains* like physics, psychology and biology; for example, from a very early age children appear to understand that the world contains physical objects that occupy space and move in response to external forces, that people's behaviour is driven by their goals and desires, and that objects can be broadly classified as either animate or inanimate. Evidence that young children have surprising competence in particular aspects of their cognitive development is hard to explain in terms of Piaget's general stage-based theory.

According to theory approaches, cognitive development proceeds as the acquisition of new knowledge enables children to refine and extend their rudimentary theories to create better ones. Such approaches form part of a larger class of theories in the rapidly growing field of evolutionary developmental psychology. As a whole, this approach seeks to explain how specific cognitive skills have developed in response to environmental pressures (Geary and Bjorklund, 2000). Evolutionary developmental psychology distinguishes between biologically primary abilities (that is, cognitive skills determined by evolution, such as language) and biologically secondary abilities (that is, cognitive skills determined by culture, such as reading). It is assumed that the development of primary abilities requires little nurture from the environment whereas the development of secondary abilities requires a higher level of external support. Additionally, research in developmental cognitive neuroscience has shed light on maturation of brain structures and functions (Johnson and de Haan, 2011) while neuroconstructivism seeks to understand interactions between genes, behaviour and the environment (Westermann et al., 2007).

SOCIO-CULTURAL THEORIES: THE CHILD AS A SOCIAL BEING

The theories reviewed so far have uniformly stressed children's active role in their own development as they identify problems and attempt to solve them independently. In contrast, socio-cultural theories highlight the importance of communicative interactions with other people (Bornstein and Bruner, 1989). Socio-cultural perspectives share the notions of *guided participation* (how adults assist children to achieve higher levels of skills than they would attain on their own) and *cultural tools* (including language and other symbol systems, artefacts, skills and values with cultural significance – Rogoff, 1990).

The socio-cultural approach to understanding cognitive development was initiated by the Russian psychologist, Lev Vygotsky. Although Vygotsky was a contemporary of Piaget, his work received little attention in the Western world until it was translated into English as *Mind in Society* (Vygotsky, 1978). Vygotsky was intrigued by the idea that young children are born into a social world in which adults are motivated to help them learn. Whereas Piaget claimed that a child constructs knowledge by actively engaging with the environment, Vygotsky suggested that development is a joint endeavour between the child and his or her caretakers during social interchanges. Vygotsky acknowledged the contribution of nature to development, believing infants enter the world equipped with basic cognitive functions such as the ability to remember. These basic abilities are nurtured into higher mental functions during social interactions and dialogues between a child and his or her parents, teachers and other representatives of culture. Thus, through these interactions, children internalise increasingly mature and effective ways of thinking.

Vygotsky (1986) reasoned that social interactions benefit children's thinking due to the input of language and he postulated the existence of three stages of language-thought development. In the first stage, called *external speech*, thinking comes from a source outside the child. In the second stage, called *private speech*, children talk to themselves as a way of directing their own thinking. In the final stage, called *internal speech*, children have internalised their thought processes.

Vygotsky also introduced the idea of the *zone of proximal development*. This refers to an area of functioning just beyond the child's current level to which they are capable of progressing given appropriate assistance from other people with greater knowledge. Vygotsky defined it as 'the distance between actual developmental level as determined by independent problem solving and the level of potential development through problem solving under adult guidance or in collaboration with more capable peers' (Vygotsky, 1978: 86). Vygotsky thus assumed that in most instances children's potential level of functioning exceeds their actual level of functioning.

Subsequent work in the Vygotskian tradition drew attention to the role of *intersubjectivity* in social interactions, that is, mutual understanding arising from joint attention to the same topic. It additionally described *social scaffolding*, that is, the process by which adults provide a temporary framework to support a child's thinking at a higher level than they can yet reach on their own (Wood et al., 1976). **Scaffolding** takes the form of explaining the goal of the task, demonstrating how the task should be done and carrying out the more difficult aspects of the task. At first, children require extensive support to attain a higher level of thinking about a particular problem but, over time, they come to require less assistance until eventually they can complete the task on their own. Children who receive appropriate scaffolding show faster acquisition of new skills than do children who learn independently (see Chapter 13 for a discussion of adult roles in children's learning).

Vygotsky's theory is an example of a ***dialectical theory***; it emphasises the development of cognition under social influence. Other socio-cultural approaches can be described as *contextualist*; they stress the wider influence of environmental contexts on development. Interest in contextualism was prompted by the publication of *The Ecology of Human Development*, by Urie Bronfenbrenner in 1979. As described in Chapter 5 (this edition), Bronfenbrenner viewed cognitive development as proceeding within a nested series of contexts, reflecting three main levels of the environment. First, the *microsystem* comprises the various settings in which the child directly participates, such as home, school and neighbourhood. Second, the *exosystem* comprises systems that affect the child indirectly by virtue of their influence on microsystems. Such settings include the extended social network of the family. Finally, the *macrosystem* comprises the cultural environment of the child, for example, characteristics of a particular socio-economic or ethnic background. Bronfenbrenner also identified *mesosystems*, which represent interactions between two or more microsystems, and subsequently he incorporated the *chronosystem*, referring to influences on development that are specific to a particular historical period (Bronfenbrenner, 1986). For example, children growing up today differ from previous generations in their extensive exposure to television and computers. Notably, Bronfenbrenner advocated a transactional view of development in that he believed children, caregivers and the environment have a mutual influence on one another (Bronfenbrenner and Morris, 1998) and the child is not a passive recipient of environmental forces but to some extent selects their experiences. For example, a child who is raised by parents who encourage reading might develop an enjoyment of literature that later leads them to seek out friends with similar interests.

DEVELOPMENT OF SOCIAL COGNITION

The term *social cognition* refers to the cognitive processes that deal with social information. Such processes underpin all social interactions and, over the last two decades, have been one of the most widely investigated topics in developmental psychology. Tomasello et al. (2005) argued that the extraordinary dominance of the human species over other animals has resulted not from our greater intelligence *per se* but from our ability to create and participate in social groups and institutions. On this account, humans are uniquely disposed to understand and share the intentions of others, making it possible for them to engage in sophisticated forms of social behaviour. *Shared intentionality*, which emerges in infancy, means that children are primed to learn through observation and to co-operate with others in activities that instruct them in new skills. In evolutionary terms, shared intentionality may have been crucial to humans' development of language and other symbol systems, as well as complex tools and technologies.

Further to shared intentionality, effective social interactions appear to involve a **theory of mind** or the understanding that human behaviour is governed by a complex system of mental states, such as desires, knowledge, beliefs and emotions (Wellman, 2002). Such understanding enables us to make sense of what people say and do and is vital for successful interpersonal relations (see Chapter 7 on 'mind reading'). As adults, we are aware that other people may have a view of the world that differs from our own, or from reality. The importance of theory of mind is reflected in our frequent use of mental-state terms in everyday language (e.g. John looked for his keys in his coat pocket because that is where he *thought* they were; John is opening the biscuit tin because he *wants* a biscuit).

It has been argued that young children lack a fully-fledged theory of mind, as shown by their poor performance on tests of the understanding of false belief. False-belief tests gauge children's appreciation of the fact that people can possess and act on beliefs that do not reflect reality. One of the most commonly employed false-belief tasks is the unexpected transfer task, devised by Wimmer and Perner (1983). In the original version, children watched a story conveyed by puppets. The story featured a little boy called Maxi who put his bar of chocolate in a blue cupboard in his kitchen and then left the scene. Maxi's mother entered the kitchen and moved his chocolate bar to a green cupboard. Upon Maxi re-entering the kitchen, children were asked to predict where Maxi would look for his chocolate. Wimmer and Perner found that 58 per cent of the children aged four to five years incorrectly responded that Maxi would look for the object in its actual location (the green cupboard), whereas 92 per cent of the children aged six to nine years correctly responded that Maxi would look for the object in its original location (the blue cupboard). Such findings have been widely replicated over the years leading to the conclusion that children younger than five to six years find it hard to acknowledge the existence of mental states that are discordant with what they know to be true.

Investigations of children's theory of mind have raised the usual issues central to cognitive development. First, there is controversy regarding whether acquisition of theory of mind is continuous or stage-like. Based on the finding that the majority of typically developing children start to understand false belief around the age of four-and-a-half years, some researchers have argued that there is a radical shift in the child's thought processes at this time and that younger children fail to possess a representational understanding of mind (the *representational deficit view* – Perner, 1991). The opposing argument is that the rudiments of theory of mind are evident in infancy and develop gradually over the course of childhood. Supporting the latter view, children as young as thirty-six months of age can pass false-belief tests if critical aspects of such tests are made more meaningful. Given that children younger than four years can engage in pretence and identify a variety of basic mental states and emotions, many researchers prefer to postulate continuity in the development of theory-of-mind capabilities during early childhood.

Second, there is debate surrounding whether theory of mind relies on domain-specific or domain-general cognitive processes. Whereas domain-specific accounts assume the existence of a specialised brain or cognitive system devoted solely to theory-of-mind reasoning, domain-general accounts argue that theory-of-mind problems are solved by all-purpose cognitive mechanisms. Domain-specific accounts include the proposals that theory of mind depends on a dedicated cognitive module (*modular theory* – Scholl and Leslie, 1999) or, alternatively, a set of causal, explanatory rules pertaining uniquely to human behaviour (*theory theory* – Gopnik and Wellman, 1992). Regardless of whether there is an element of domain specificity to theory of mind, a role of domain-general processes is suggested by evidence that young children's performance on false-belief tests is positively related to their **working memory** capacity and powers of inhibitory control. Such evidence implies that success on false-belief tests depends to some extent on children's ability to remember the sequence of events and to suppress their (salient) knowledge of current reality in order to respond to their (less salient) knowledge of past events (Carlson and Moses, 2001).

Finally, research into theory of mind highlights issues of nature versus nurture. A contribution of heredity to theory of mind is suggested by behaviour genetics studies (Hughes et al., 2005) and by brain imaging studies that implicate a specific network of brain areas (namely, the medial pre-frontal cortex and temporal poles) as underpinning theory-of-mind abilities (Frith and Frith, 2001). Nevertheless, environmental influences appear substantial, as indicated by speedier theory-of-mind development in children whose mothers refer more frequently to mental states in everyday conversation (see, for example, Ruffman et al., 2002). Conversely, theory-of-mind development is severely delayed in deaf children from hearing families who have restricted opportunities for communication at home (Peterson and Siegal, 1995). The finding that theory of mind is impaired in deaf children who are deprived of information about other people's mental activities provides strong evidence for an important contribution of nurture to theory of mind.

DEVELOPMENT OF SELF-REGULATION

The term *self-regulation* refers to the ability to curb impulses and to behave in a careful and considered manner (Garon et al., 2008). Cognitive aspects of self-regulation include the ability to sustain attention to independent goal-directed activity and resist distraction, whereas affective self-regulation represents the capacity to manage emotions and to respond effectively in situations that have important personal consequences (Zelazo et al., 2005). Self-regulation is an important function of the pre-frontal cortex, a region of the brain that deals specifically with the effortful control of thought and behaviour and that shows significant maturation during the pre-school years (Zelazo et al., 2008).

The development of self-regulation has been of prime interest to researchers given evidence of its important role in children's adjustment to and subsequent success at school (Duncan et al., 2007; Duckworth and Carlson, 2013). In a classic study, Mischel et al. (1989) presented four-year-olds with two marshallows on a plate and told them that they could either eat one marshmallow straight away or wait 15 minutes to eat both marshmallows. When followed up as adolescents, participants who had been able to wait (i.e., exhibiting *delay of gratification*) showed superior scholastic performance. More recently, Blair and Razza (2007) examined the relations between cognitive and affective self-regulation on one hand, and attainments on tests of mathematics, phonemic awareness and letter knowledge on the other, in five- to six-year-old children. After controlling for verbal ability and fluid intelligence, they found that cognitive self-regulation was positively correlated with all three domains of academic ability. Indeed, the capacity for self-regulation during childhood predicts a broad range of measures of health and wealth well into adulthood, even after taking account of IQ and social class (Moffitt et al., 2011).

In light of such findings, it has been suggested that early intervention programmes for children deemed at risk of educational failure should strive to develop the self-regulatory skills that are needed for successful adjustment to the classroom (Blair, 2002; Noble et al., 2005). This seems feasible given evidence of strong environmental influences on the development of self-regulation (Farah et al., 2006; Bernier et al., 2010). Studies have sought to nurture self-regulation using computer-based training (Rueda et al., 2005) and appropriate forms of play and social interaction. As an example of the latter approach, Diamond et al. (2007) evaluated the effects of a specially designed pre-school programme (Tools of the Mind) inspired by the work of Vygotsky. Children whose pre-school teachers encouraged them in interactive dramatic play, and in the use of private speech and external aids to control behaviour, subsequently had better self-regulation than children who followed a standard pre-school curriculum.

APPLIED ISSUES AND FUTURE RESEARCH DIRECTIONS

All theories of cognitive development are agreed that the physical and social environments are important forces in children's learning, highlighting the importance of enriching their pre-school experiences. As already discussed, evidence that social interactions figure largely in the development of theory of mind and self-regulation has led to calls for appropriate interventions for children who show impairments in these domains. Research in the socio-cultural tradition has further revealed that children's cognitive development can be enhanced by programmes that promote responsive parenting and exposure to guided learning interactions (Boland et al., 2003; Landry et al., 2008; Ford et al., 2009).

Theories of cognitive development have profound implications for the education of young children even after formal schooling commences. Education has been heavily influenced by Piaget's theory, with its suggestion that allowing children to interact with the environment will facilitate their learning, its notion of cognitive *readiness* for determining when and what children should be taught, and its detailed analysis of children's emerging concepts about number and physical causality. Information-processing theories have introduced detailed, trial-by-trial methods of exploring learning (*microgenetic* methods – Siegler, 2000), core-knowledge theories have provided important information regarding young children's ability to reason about unobservable causes of events, while discoveries within developmental cognitive neuroscience have identified learning experiences that can stimulate specific brain regions to improve aspects of academic performance. Finally, socio-cultural theories of cognitive development can be credited with drawing educators' attention to the importance of make-believe and socio-dramatic play as well as prompting moves to encourage co-operative learning and **peer tutoring** in schools. Moreover, a growing awareness of the ecological context of development has led to efforts to involve members of the wider community in the educational system with the aim of developing a culture of learning both within and beyond the classroom.

CONCLUSION

Theories of cognitive development grapple with issues of nature versus nurture, continuity versus discontinuity, active versus passive development, domain-general versus domain-specific learning, and the role of the socio-cultural context. Pioneering studies by Piaget led him to propose that there are four distinct stages of cognitive development, with young children behaving as amateur scientists who carry out simple experiments on their world to discover how it works. Subsequent investigation in the information-processing tradition suggested that development is continuous rather than stage-like and that it can be understood in terms of age-related improvements in processing mechanisms, memory capacity and knowledge. Additionally, research into innate competences has indicated that infants are born possessing certain kinds of knowledge that facilitate their learning in particular core domains. Finally, the work of Vygotsky and Bronfenbrenner has implicated a contribution of social and cultural factors to children's learning. Vygotsky argued that cognitive development occurs within social interactions with more capable others that guide children into increasingly mature ways of thinking.

In conclusion, the study of children's thinking and cognitive development is a dynamic and evolving field that covers a diversity of topics. All accounts have important insights to offer and recent writings have emphasised the need for theoretical integration. One aim is to explicate the reciprocal relations between a child's biological make-up and social environment, for example, the effects of a child's temperament on the instructional strategies favoured by their caregivers (Gauvain, 2005; Bjorklund, 2011). Other emerging themes include the nature of environmental influences on brain development, particularly stress, and the interplay between sources of vulnerability and sources of resilience (Shonkoff and Phillips, 2000; Blair, 2010). Increasing our understanding of these important issues should pave the way for improved policy and practice in relation to the education and nurture of young children.

Key points

- The term cognitive development refers broadly to the development of children's thinking and reasoning.
- There are many competing theories of cognitive development with different assumptions about how change occurs.
- One of the most important questions concerning cognitive development relates to the roles of nature and nurture. Most theorists are agreed that nature and nurture work together and are well documented in the study of how children acquire a theory of mind and their development of self-regulation.
- Finally, theories of cognitive development have important applications to education.

Recommended reading

Bjorklund (2011) provides a comprehensive review of children's cognitive development with attention to interactions between biological and social/environmental influences.

BABIES' AND YOUNG CHILDREN'S EMOTIONAL AND SOCIAL DEVELOPMENT

TRICIA DAVID WITH SACHA POWELL

CONTENTS

INTRODUCTION

This chapter explores current evidence from research concerning what is probably the most important aspect of a child's development during the first years of life – emotional development and the ways in which this impacts upon other areas of development and learning, such as social and cognitive development. Above all, it highlights the crucial nature of close and loving relationships because these are the models which will cast either sunlight or long shadows over a child's future experiences: how and what they learn about themselves and the social worlds they inhabit.

While a review of historical texts shows that those in the early childhood education and care (ECEC) field have long claimed to prioritise social and emotional development (see, for example, Taylor et al., 1972), the new emphasis from government and its bodies (e.g. DfES, 2004; Ofsted, 2005; DCSF, 2008a; Field, 2010; DfE and DH, 2011; DH, 2011b) indicates that such a focus is more than the wish to enable all children to be comfortable in their own skins. Preparation for school is said to be dependent on an appropriate level of social and emotional development, as is school achievement. Additionally, later psychiatric care, involvement in crime and anti-social behaviour – all drains on the public purse (Hummel et al., 2011) – may be long-term results from socially and emotionally impoverished early years. In her paper focusing on emotional wellbeing and mental health, Soni (2012: 180) argues that the introduction of the EYFS provides a 'golden opportunity for practitioners to link together information, provided via the media, research and government, concerning the increased incidence of mental health problems and the value practitioners can offer in supporting children under five in promoting children's mental health.' Sad and troubled babyhoods should concern us all, but not simply because of their consequences, more importantly because we would want all our children to experience joy in themselves, in their relationships and in living. However, while happy childhoods are an admirable goal for a society, what is important is understanding how we learn to cope with experiences which make us 'sad or mad'. Unfortunately, sadness and anger are likely to be among every human being's life experiences. So being able to cope and understand why and how our emotions affect us, how we can improve our own wellbeing, becoming resilient and knowing what we can do to make ourselves feel happy, are key elements in protecting ourselves emotionally. Further, since overwhelming negative emotions can over-ride our abilities in other areas, such as the social and cognitive aspects of our lives, being able to analyse our feelings and deal with them ultimately impacts on our achievements.

One could argue that this kind of emotional development matters for everyone in society, for themselves and for the 'common good'. Martha Nussbaum (2013), the American philosopher, argues that love matters for justice, while similarly claiming (2010) that the Arts and Humanities are components of liberal education that matter for democracy.

NEW THINKING, OLD THINKING: WELLBEING AND RESILIENCE – LEARNING TO COPE, LEARNING TO BE HAPPY

With the opportunities afforded by multidisciplinary approaches to health and development, including contributions from neuroscience, some leading researchers in the field of emotional wellbeing suggest we can pre-empt later emotional difficulties. In his book *Flourish: A Visionary New Understanding of Happiness and Well-being*, which is a culmination of years of work to date, Seligman (2011) argues that misery is politically insidious and that we should be helping children – and adults – learn how to apply his PERMA model: Positive emotions; Engagement and flow in activities which match our abilities and which we enjoy; Relationships with others – central to being human; Meaning – having a purpose that amounts to more than ourselves; and Achievement – recognising what we can do, using and celebrating such achievements. Seligman claims that self-discipline is twice as important as IQ in its influence on accomplishments – and this too links back to having the ability to analyse and overcome negative feelings. He calls his field 'Positive Psychology'.

In a similar vein, Allan Shore (2016) has brought together research evidence from a range of disciplines – including psychology and neurobiology – which he argues can be applied to prevent the kind of pathologies that can arise when life is barren and meaningless. He also draws on the new science of *epigenetics*, highlighting the effects of negative emotions on both physical and mental disorders later in life which can have their origins in maladaptive emotional processes learnt early in life, when certain genes may have been epigenetically activated or deactivated, impacting on inherited DNA.

Lucy Bailey and Emma Judge founded the charity 'How to Thrive' in 2009, based on Seligman's Positive Psychology in order to train teachers to build resilience in children through realistic thinking, adaptive coping skills, and social problem solving. With young children this might involve activities such as sharing a story, followed by discussion, about falling out with a friend. So far research evaluating their project is yielding very positive results and not simply about whether the children feel happier and more able to cope but also in academic achievements.

Having experienced psychological illness and stress as an undergraduate, Evans (2013) turned to philosophy. He claims that exploring ideas about how to live 'the good life' and the messages of the ancient Greek thinkers would benefit all children and students, helping them analyse the ways in which their own emotional reactions were ruling their lives. Clearly we are not suggesting 'philosophy for babies' but since young children from the age of around 18 months old are capable of 'mind-reading' (Reddy, 2010; Tyler, 2016) – they can use what they know about the people closest to them to 'wind up' or manipulate them – additionally, they can be helped to discuss their own feelings and reactions to emotionally charged experiences.

BORN TO BE SOCIAL AND TO FORM EMOTIONAL ATTACHMENTS

From the moment of birth, babies are intensely interested in other people. In the first months of life they are trying to form close relationships and they are beginning to develop an individual sense of self. At the same time they are coming to know if those individual selves have any agency, or power, over their own lives. During these early months of life, a baby will learn from interactions with parents and carers, developing an understanding of self and of how relationships work – or do not. Such interactions involve cognitive as well as social and emotional processes. Almost twenty years ago Judy Dunn (1999) pointed out that compartmentalising children's areas of development for research purposes was not taking account of their interwoven influences. Books by Goleman (2004; 2007) have provided the field with comprehensive reviews of research about emotional and social development, including studies from neuroscience, which reinforce the importance of these foundational aspects of young children's lives. Discussing 'webs of attachment' Goleman (2007: 114) writes:

> laughing and crying come spontaneously in primal moments of social connection ... Distress at separation and joy at bonding both bespeak the primal power of connection.

Human emotions are the basic building blocks of a person's entire, holistic development. Human beings seem to be born to be social. In the first months of life, babies make distinctions between people/objects, self/other (Stern, 1985). They appear to need to form *attachments* to the people who are familiar and significant to them (usually a parent or other relative at first) and these *attachments* at four months old are said to be good predictors of their emotional bonds and their ability to regulate their emotions at a year old (Braungart-Rieker et al., 2001). In the everyday interactions of being sensitively cared for, they begin to be aware of themselves; and despite the fact that researchers a quarter of a century ago argued that children do not develop a sense of self (recognise themselves as separate people with an individual identity) until their second year, more recent research indicates that this amazing feat begins soon after birth (Sigelman and Rider, 2008). These first attachments provide a 'model' which will be drawn upon later in life.

Around two years of age, children begin to realise that others may judge them. Shame and guilt begin to constrain negative or immoral behaviour and empathy to inhibit cruelty. When adults – and older children – adjust their behaviour sensitively to what they perceive as the baby's needs and wishes, we say they are behaving *contingently*, not only showing warmth and affection but also modelling for the younger child.

ATTACHMENT

One of the most important figures in Western psychology, John Bowlby, formulated and wrote extensively for decades about his theory of attachment (see, for example, Bowlby, 1951; 1965[1953]). Bowlby proposed that attachment is an innate device intended to protect the immature offspring of a species by attracting adults who will ensure their survival. Later, however, Bowlby (1988) himself agreed that attachment research had shown up flaws in his theory and that instead of the idea of specific, crucial phases of development he had come to prefer a theory of developmental pathways. Bowlby's admission alerts us to the need to be wary of expecting any theory to be capable of explaining 'everything'. Furthermore, attachment theory was used politically, especially during the 1950s and in a way that was never intended, to discourage women from employment outside the home.

Nevertheless, attachment theory continues to exert an effect to this day, as evidenced by the 'key person approach' in early years policy and practice and as Baron-Cohen (2011: 48) states, Bowlby's work was remarkable and his predictions have been 'amply proven' and are extremely important socially. He depicts Bowlby's theory thus:

what the care-giver gives his or her child in those first few critical years is like *an internal pot of gold* ... This ... is what gives the individual the strength to deal with challenges ... It overlaps with what London psychiatrist Michael Rutter refers to as 'resilience'.

So despite some reservations, attachment remains a useful concept in trying to understand babies' need to relate positively to people closest to them and in recognising how early interactions provide building blocks for a sense of self and models for later social competence (Page, 2016). The work of psychodynamic therapists and the contributions of psychoanalysis are also important in thinking about attachment (Elfer, 2016). For example, Shore (2011) suggests that, as a result of new technology, we now know there is a neural site in the orbitofrontal cortex of the brain and its growth is dependent upon a child's experience. A carer's 'attunedness' and responsiveness will result in positive emotional development; lack of such experiences, however, result in limited ability to cope with distress, anger, terror and shame, although sensitive relationships later in life can help to ameliorate this. The recent discovery of **mirror neurons** in the brain, which both perceive the world and act upon it, mean babies, like all humans, empathise and begin to have compassion for those with whom they identify; but also they can 'feel' for those who are different from themselves (Keysers, 2011). Reddy (2010) cites Trevarthen as proposing that, as babies only a few weeks old can detect emotional states from others' faces, there is possibly an evolutionary element at work – such shared emotions indicate the meaningful perception of the other person's feelings – thus promoting social connectedness.

Babies can have a network of attachments made up of different members of 'the family' – all the familiar people who share the baby's life (see, for example, the film *Babies* – Chabat and Balmes, 2009). These social experiences are influential in the process of achieving healthy social development (NICHD, 2006). When they are only a few months old babies start making preferential attachments. They behave in ways that are designed to attract the preferred person's attention – smiling, cooing, trying to make eye contact – and will be pacified by that person's voice, a look from them or the presentation of a toy, for example. Some of these preferred attachment figures will be older children in a household. Different attachment figures will elicit different responses from a baby. Passionate crying by a baby when a parent arrives to collect them from an ECEC setting may indicate the strength of an attachment rather than anything amiss (Davies, 1999).

Research by Trevarthen (2009) and his colleagues over the last thirty years has been especially valuable to the field of early childhood. For example, from two months of age, around the time they also engage in social smiling, infants are sensitive to *social contingency* (responsiveness to the infant's signals), especially to the timing of emotional *attunement* in two-way exchanges. These attuned exchanges indicate the development of *primary intersubjectivity* – the rudiments of turn taking, sensitive timing and responsiveness to the other's behaviour, especially facial expressions. Intersubjectivity is thought to be the foundation of early social interaction. Such early, playful interactions are called 'proto-conversations' and they gradually offer the young child opportunities for anticipating and predicting and they form the basis for social and cognitive advances that occur during the first year. Caution is needed however, since while some researchers suggest attachment is universal, others argue that it is expressed differently in different cultures (Wang and Mallinckrodt, 2006) (see Chapters 1, 4 and 22).

CHILDREN AND FAMILIES 'AT RISK'

Some children may be at risk in terms of their social and emotional development for a number of reasons. For example, children born into families who have been informed soon after their baby's birth that their child has an identifiable impairment or life-threatening illness are often left to deal with powerful emotions which may impact upon the attachment process. Despite two Children Acts (HM Government, 1989; 2004), both of which have stressed the requirement for professionals from different services to work together more effectively in the 'best interests' of children, it appears that England still lags behind other countries in its ability to ensure this in practice (see Chapters 11 and 19). Research, training and resources in this area are said to have been neglected (Atkinson et al., 2002), although Messenger (2012), while agreeing over the need for training, suggests the personal qualities, confidence and experience of those involved are important in this respect.

Children affected by autism, who may appear aloof and indifferent and who do not seek out meaningful interactions with other children or with adults may also need extra support, because they do not perceive their world in the same way that other children do (Tyler, 2016). They are unaware of, or do not understand, others' social interactions, gentle teasing, jokes and feints because they have no sense of what is happening in the mind of another person. Meanwhile, shy children may have overactive amygdalas (Kagan, 2010) and high levels of activity in this brain area can inhibit their ability to cope. They need to be with other children who can cope so that their brain mechanisms develop and overcome these inhibitions. Baron-Cohen (2011) explains that prolonged early stress affects the way the hippocampus functions so that the stress hormone cortisol is released into the blood stream by the adrenal gland. Additionally, in one part of the amygdala the nerve cells start branching more than is normal. However, as Kagan (2010) argues, while biology, or temperament, may impact on early reactions and abilities, it need not determine them in the longer term, and Karmiloff-Smith (2010) suggests caution in using brain studies, as there is a need to look at neural trajectories over time through developmental neuroimaging, rather than 'snap-shots' at isolated points in a life.

Children who are described as being in 'hard to reach' or 'vulnerable' families may attract special effort on the part of outreach workers and practitioners (Boag-Munroe, 2012), particularly in families where parents did not themselves experience warm and sensitive parenting, or where they are experiencing high levels of stress. Some parents may describe their babies as irritable or difficult and, because of anxiety, respond aggressively rather than being able to calm them. Such experiences can lead to low resilience later in life (Hagekull et al., 1993). Alertness and responsiveness to individual risk factors are vital but it is also imperative to exert caution in any interpretation of their (potential) effects. A comprehensive report on the development of a screening tool for health visitors noted that while some outcome predictions may be possible, the influence of different sets of factors varies according to the outcome being considered. From a study of maternal indicators and young children's developmental outcomes, using the Millennium Cohort Data, Kiernan and Mensah (2011: 60) suggest that: 'it may be more appropriate to take a more holistic approach to understanding how families influence their children's development and wellbeing' and Maddox (2016) argues that a process called 'relational well-being' would be better than the idea of the existence of a fixed, personal quality called 'resilience'.

INDEPENDENCE AND INTERDEPENDENCE

One of the most striking changes during the transition from babyhood to early childhood is a child's growing sense of self (Dunn, 1993). Individual children become aware of how others view them and, as emphasised earlier, it is usually the parent–child relationship that provides the basis for fostering a sense of self-competence and worth. Along with this growing sense of self, the child will be trying to gain a sense of independence, wishing to be seen as capable by others – and told so in words and actions when attempting to be independent. These experiences enable children to learn that they are competent members of society and this promotes their ability to interact successfully with peers throughout middle childhood (Mikulincer and Shaver, 2007). Children develop self-awareness and social awareness in conjunction with a sense of their own agency. When parents and practitioners allow them to assert some power and control over their own lives, they learn to be self-regulating and autonomous. This process will incorporate elements of conflict and its resolution for, as Kernan et al. (2011: 3) explain, young children's relationships encompass:

> understandings and experiences of nurturance, care and learning in interactions and interpersonal relations; conflicts and negotiation; pleasure and rejection; friendships and play; group phenomena; independence and interdependence; and identity and belonging.

By eighteen to twenty-four months old, young children usually recognise themselves in mirrors, begin to use 'I', 'me' and 'mine' and use their own name. They also start to assert their own wishes. A few more months on and they begin to develop their gender identity and to show awareness of racism in their society. They can 'learn to be strong and independent through positive relationships' (DfE, 2017: 6) (see Chapter 17); being independent, able to think, act and speak 'bravely' for oneself is important. So too is being able to co-operate and collaborate, listen to, respect and learn from the ideas or contributions of others and to support others in expressing these. Both independence and interdependence are important for the 'common good'.

BELONGING

Wrapped up in the process of emotional, social and personal development is the child's sense of 'belonging'. Families today are very different from the families of even a generation ago, and as Jagger and Wright (1999: 3) point out, 'The family is neither a pan-human universal nor a stable or essential entity … Families and family relations are, like the term itself, flexible, fluid and contingent'. However, since research shows how important familiar, loving, significant people are to babies and young children, it is vital that, as a society, we explore ways of ensuring that they feel they are part of a 'family' or 'community', however it is constituted. Families, like communities, develop their own cultures – ways of being and behaving. Young children are made to feel they belong when they are able to participate in that culture, they know 'what we do and how we behave' (see, for example, Black and Lobo, 2008).

What matters to a young child is the act of parenting, not the gender identity of who does it or if parents are in a heterosexual or same-sex partnership/marriage. Despite this, some research has focused on differences between fathers (as males) and mothers (as females), reporting that most fathers behave differently towards their children compared with mothers. However, as Anderson (1996) points out, it can be the mother who acts as a gatekeeper, either including or excluding the father and thus encouraging or discouraging a meaningful relationship between a father and his child. According to Belsky (1996), fathers whose infants are securely attached to them are usually more extrovert and positive about their home lives than fathers whose children are insecurely attached to them. The strength of attachment to one parent is usually a good indicator of attachment to the other and the relationship between a mother or father and their first-born appears to set the tone for the attachments of later offspring (Brumbaugh and Fraley, 2006). When a new baby joins a family, the older sibling/s may show ambivalence – natural, given that such a newcomer may be usurping the older child's position. However, with family support and encouragement even children younger than three show they can adapt their talk and behave endearingly towards the new baby, picking up the cues and modelling behaviours of other family members.

Over twenty years ago, the leading contributors to New Zealand's ECEC curriculum, Te Whariki, argued that all children need to have a feeling of belonging, because it 'contributes to inner well-being, security and identity' (New Zealand Ministry of Education, 1996: 54). More recently, however, these authors reiterated that Te Whariki constructs children as 'powerful and participating', criticising their government's emphasis on vulnerability and risk (May and Carr, 2016: 322). They argue that cuts in funding for professional development have led to concerns about implementation. In a similar way, research by Denham et al. (2015) suggests that practitioners need to be aware that emotional knowledge tends to vary with age, gender, socio-economic risk status and **executive control** and, importantly, is related to later educational success. Teaching young children about emotions yields success in social and later school life and Martucci (2016) provides evidence from shared story-book reading leading to understandings of cognitive, affective and desire states of mind.

MIND-READING AND MIND-MINDEDNESS

Mind-reading in this context means having the ability to infer the desires or wishes of another person, usually a person one knows very well. Young children become experts at reading the minds of their parents, siblings and friends, using this knowledge to ingratiate themselves or to tease and annoy. So mind-reading forms part of the social fabric of life. Of course, all siblings have their quarrels – and sometimes fights. The incidence of fighting between sisters and brothers is higher than that between friends outside the home, although the incidence for boys is roughly the same as that with peers. As Dunn (1984: 144) adds, 'It is because they understand their siblings so well, and because they feel so strongly about them, that their relationship is so significant and so revealing'.

Attendance at an ECEC setting affords babies and young children opportunities to make friends and to play with other children. Again, Dunn (1993) tells us that young children's friendships are important to them and often children as young as four have friends they made when only two. Friends are also important when children move to a new ECEC setting or to school. Those who, on transition, had a friend who moved setting with them fared much better in comparison with those who did not move with a friend, and Dunn found that they remembered that it was the presence of the friend that made them happy in the new setting. She also explored the ways in which family members related to one another and recognised these were reflected in interactions in nurseries. Children who enjoyed high levels of involvement with their mothers were more likely to be conciliatory and to compromise with friends. They also engaged in longer and more elaborate bouts of shared fantasy play and conversations.

A similar effect was found when Howes et al. (1994) explored children's relationships with their ECEC practitioners. Where the practitioners modelled socialisation the children seemed to be more accepting towards each other and when they felt secure in their setting they displayed complex play with other children, with whom they were also more gregarious than children who did not experience positive relationships with staff.

Harris (1989) explains how different cultures build on what may be a universal, innate ability to recognise positive and negative emotional states. He also discusses the ways in which the emotions of guilt and shame are used to socialise children and different cultures use these to varying degrees. By the time they are two years old children are learning the 'scripts' assigned to different emotions by their family or community, that are learned to make one acceptable. Sometimes they will use 'transitional objects' to help them in this regulation of the emotions. These might be dummies, favourite soft toys or comforters that have been self-chosen.

Children who have warm, affectionate relationships with their parents have been found to be more likely to have high self-esteem, to be better socially adjusted and to achieve academically (Mortimer, 2001). In the review of the literature for *Birth to Three Matters* (DfES, 2003), we used Siegel's (1999) important studies to point out that if parents – and one might surmise this could also apply to practitioners – did not enjoy warm, close relationships with their own parents, then encouraging them to reflect on their narratives of their own childhoods and to understand how they feel can help them become more positive, so that they are able to engage in the loving, sensitive interactions which will benefit their children's emotional wellbeing and personal and social development (David et al., 2003).

For ECEC settings, the issues related to staff relationships with children and the difficulties of shifts, holidays and other complications require debate. Elfer et al. (2011) advocate the Key Person approach to enable close relationships, which the babies and young children need to develop. They suggest that the benefits of the Key Person approach allow for supplementing rather than replacing loving care and learning that children experience at home. It is through the actions and talk of familiar adults, whether family members or staff in an ECEC setting, that young children develop their emotional and social abilities and their physical and cognitive powers. Adults who are capable of being 'mind-minded' – that is, they show they think of young children as 'feeling, intentional and sentient, as opposed to purely physical beings' (Degotardi and Sweller, 2012: 253) – support and encourage such all-round development. They follow each child's interest and try to help individuals achieve their goals, often talking them through their struggles – for example, 'Oh, you're trying to reach the red teddy … (moves red teddy closer) – that's it, now you've got teddy!'

Training for staff should involve 'reflective supervision' in which trainees need to be helped to recognise high quality infant experiences and to reflect on their own work-based practices, to link theory to practice, so increasing their ability to appreciate the children's perspectives. Further, Degotardi and Sweller (2012) found that staff will often demonstrate greater 'mind-mindedness' when working with older children, thus apparently perceiving babies and toddlers as less capable. Such assumptions could also be challenged in reflective supervision.

In England, Ofsted inspectors are now required to check on children's bonds with their Key Persons (Tassoni, 2013), looking for evidence, such as frequent eye contact, delight in being together, showing they have a strong connection. These are highly desirable features of provision but not always practicable (Goouch and Powell, 2013) and indeed impoverished adult–child ratios may further jeopardise such contingent interactions.

CONCLUSION

This chapter has examined different perspectives and understandings of social and emotional development in young children. It has emphasized the connectedness of babies and young children to other people, especially the significant carers in their lives, who may constitute a wide range of emotional partners who fulfil different roles. The ways these people think about and behave towards babies and young children can reinforce (or refute) cultural traditions; and can support the development of mutuality, a sense of self, of trust and self-worth as well as providing the foundations for other relationships in the present and in the future.

Key points

- Human beings are born to be social and to form emotional bonds. They are equipped with *mirror neurons*, brain cells which are activated by observing the actions/behaviour of others, so that we share each other's minds and have a 'deeply connected social mind ... the feat of our brain, the emotional connection with others is, to a large extent, what makes us human' (Keysers, 2011: 5-6).
- Early relationships with sensitive, loving others form the model for later relationships; pleasurable interactions during the first two years provide the scripts which children adopt in their later friendships (the adults and older children involved act as models).
- Children who, early in life, have been encouraged by emotionally sensitive parents and carers to explore and enjoy their world will take greater pleasure in goal-directed behaviour later in life and they will persist at difficult tasks; they will also be more competent socially and cognitively.
- Being unable to cope with overwhelming emotional experiences can affect health later in life and produce *epigenetic* effects.
- Staff in ECEC settings sometimes need to help children integrate into the group and they need to be aware of how friendships can help children cope with transitions. They can also foster emotional and social understanding through stories and discussion, so helping children appreciate their own and others' feelings.

───────── **Recommended reading** ─────────

Vasudevi Reddy's *How Infants Know Minds* (2010) explains how emotional engagements can show babies' early and increasing awareness of other people's intentions.

LANGUAGE DEVELOPMENT IN THE YOUNG CHILD

THEA CAMERON-FAULKNER

CONTENTS

INTRODUCTION

For decades, researchers from a range of disciplines have been intrigued by the process of language development and the insight it can provide for our understanding of human cognition. The field of child language research is rich with competing theories, all of which aim to address the key question in the field: what are the processes and knowledge base that underlie the development of language in humans? In this chapter I will outline three approaches to the study of language development: the behaviourist approach, the formalist approach and the constructivist approach. While each of these labels subsumes a network of related theories, the categorisation provides a useful starting point. Following the theoretical overview, the discussion will be widened to encompass cross-cultural aspects of language development and their impact on our understanding of the process in general.

THEORETICAL APPROACHES TO LANGUAGE DEVELOPMENT

In some ways the most logical place to start this discussion is by considering what kind of linguistic knowledge is ascribed to adults. By considering the type of knowledge a child must acquire we can then focus on the manner in which they traverse the path of development from preverbal infants to fully-fledged members of their linguistic community.

THE BEHAVIOURIST APPROACH

In the behaviourist tradition, most typically associated with Skinner (1957), language is situated within the behaviourist rubric of classical and operant conditioning, that is learning evoked through 'stimulus and response' and 'reward/punishment' processes. Classical conditioning is claimed to underlie the child's ability to associate a stimulus (like a noise or object) with an arbitrary verbal sign (a word or phrase). For example, consider a caregiver and child playing with a rattle. The child holds and shakes the rattle and looks towards the caregiver. The caregiver then comments on the object, 'Yes, it's a *rattle*. Do you like the *rattle*?' Over time the child begins to associate the form *rattle* with the object and acquires a new word form. Thus, the early stages of language development involve the child imitating a linguistic form presented in response to a particular stimulus.

The response of the caregiver to the child's utterances further shapes the child's linguistic system through the process of operant conditioning as forms eliciting 'rewards' are retained while forms resulting in 'punishment' are avoided. Thus, if the child produces a linguistic form that approximates a word and is appropriate in a given context, she or he will be rewarded in some way by the adult (such as a positive verbal response 'yes', the presentation of a requested item or the continuation of a conversation). Conversely, if a child produces a form that does not represent the child's target language or is not produced in response to the appropriate stimulus then it is more likely that she or he will not be rewarded (for example, the adult may ignore the utterance, ask for clarification or fail to produce the item that the child attempted to request).

So, from the traditional behaviourist perspective, language development was viewed as a process involving imitation of input forms and subsequent shaping of the linguistic system through feedback from more experienced conversational partners.

THE FORMALIST APPROACH

Skinner's most famous critic, Noam Chomsky, launched a devastating attack on the behaviourist account of language development in his 1959 review of Skinner's book *Verbal Behavior* (1957). Chomsky claimed that the behaviourist characterisation of language was too simplistic and did not capture the underlying complexities of linguistic knowledge. In his review Chomsky proposed that our knowledge of language was highly abstract, consisting of algebraic rules and abstract categories that no child could learn without considerable innate knowledge. Consequently, Chomsky claimed that humans must be endowed with a genetic blueprint of language, known as Universal Grammar (UG). It was claimed that the linguistic information contained within UG went beyond the concrete linguistic expressions produced in everyday speech and captured the underlying rules and regularities which shape all natural languages.

As with all dynamic approaches to theoretical issues, the formalist approach is continually evolving. One of the more recent approaches is the Principles and Parameters theory (Chomsky, 1995) in which UG is claimed to consist of two types of information: first, structural information which equips the child with a set of general linguistic principles, and second a set of parameters ('switches') which allow the child to 'set' certain aspects of their linguistic knowledge to particular values in response to their language of exposure. To take a concrete example, consider the variation in word order across languages.

In English, verbs follow subjects as in (1):
1   It fell.

Whereas in Irish subjects follow verbs (2):
2   Thit sí.

Fell-it.

'It fell.'

Through exposure to their target language the child would subconsciously switch the appropriate parameter in line with the word order patterns attested in their language and thus be said to have acquired the word order (and associated values known as 'headedness') of their native language. In this way the input a child receives acts as a trigger as opposed to the sole source of linguistic evidence available to the child.

Chomsky bolstered his linguistic theory by positing a number of claims pertaining to the linguistic input received by young children. First, Chomsky claimed that the input children receive is degenerate, that, is the language children hear contains incomplete utterances, grammatical errors, false starts and many other features of everyday informal speech (Chomsky, 1965). Therefore, if the child's only available source of linguistic knowledge is the ambient language then how could they be sure which utterances were grammatical and which were not? In addition to this, Chomsky and other UG researchers claim that the input does not contain the wide range of structures necessary for a child to work out the underlying categories and rules of their target language:

> People attain knowledge of the structure of their language for which no evidence is available in the data to which they are exposed as children. (Hornstein and Lightfoot, 1981: 9)

Together these two claims are known as the 'Poverty of the Stimulus' argument and are presented as a challenge to any approach to language development in which the input plays a central role.

Chomsky also claimed that children do not receive explicit feedback on the grammaticality of their utterances. For example, a child who produced errors related to negation (*I not do it*) is not informed consistently of the correct form (*I didn't do it*). This claim is referred to as the 'no-negative evidence' problem and is widely upheld within the formalist tradition:

> I think that the assumption that negative evidence is not available to the child's learning mechanisms is warranted. There are, no doubt, cases in which parents correct their children (e.g., over-regularized affixing). However, there is anecdotal evidence that even in such cases, children are oblivious to such corrections. (Pinker, 1984: 29)

As Pinker points out, even when feedback is on offer there is evidence to suggest that this input is not always positively received as the well-quoted example from McNeill indicates:

Child: Nobody don't like me.
Mother: No, say 'Nobody likes me.'
Child: Nobody don't like me.
(dialogue repeated eight times)

Mother: Now listen carefully, say 'Nobody likes me.'
Child: Oh! Nobody don't likes me.

(McNeill, 1966: 69)

In McNeill's example the mother attempts to correct the child's utterance but regardless of instruction the child continues to struggle with the grammaticality of the utterance.

Thus, formalists claim that children could not learn their target language from the input alone and thus must be genetically equipped with some form of linguistic knowledge. Within this framework then the child's task in acquiring their native tongue is to fine tune their innate linguistic knowledge in order to reflect the structural properties of their target language.

The no-negative evidence argument and the Poverty of the Stimulus argument are central to the formalist approach. However, not all researchers agree that children are bereft of feedback or indeed agree on what should be counted as feedback. A number of studies conducted in response to claims about no-negative evidence indicated that caregivers have a tendency to 'recast' their children's ungrammatical utterances as shown in (3) below:

3 Child: fix Lilly

Mother: Oh … Lilly will fix it.

(Sokolov and Snow, 1994: 47)

In (3) the child produces an ungrammatical utterance and the mother reformulates the gist of the utterance into a grammatical form. The process of recasting can be viewed as a form of feedback; first, the recast indicates to the child that their utterance was ill-formed in some way, and second, the target form is presented in quick succession to the error. This implicit feedback appears to have a positive effect on linguistic development (e.g. Demetras et al., 1986; Bohannon and Stanowicz, 1988). There have also been challenges regarding Chomsky's claims about the linguistic input available to young children (the Poverty of the Stimulus) as researchers investigate the characteristics of Child Directed Speech (CDS) at a fine-grained level. In order to present these arguments I will now move on to discuss a contrasting view of language development broadly referred to in this chapter as the constructivist approach.

THE CONSTRUCTIVIST APPROACH

While researchers working within the formalist tradition focused on the acquisition of linguistic structure and the form of underlying linguistic knowledge, a growing body of developmental linguists and psychologists were shifting attention towards more semantically orientated theories (for example, Bloom, 1970) and frameworks in which the social nature of language provided the backdrop to development (for example, Bates and MacWhinney, 1982; Bruner, 1983; Braine, 1994; Ninio and Snow, 1999). The constructivist approach as described below is an umbrella term for a range of theories (including social interactionist, usage-based and connectionist) which share a common belief that linguistic knowledge is constructed by the child as opposed to being pre-given at birth. Constructivist theories challenge the formalist representation of linguistic knowledge and suggest that adult linguistic knowledge is shaped by experience, that is the language addressed to and used by individual speakers (Hopper and Thompson, 1984; Langacker, 1987; Bybee and Scheibman, 1999; Tomasello, 2000; Croft, 2001). Rather than viewing language as an abstract system of categories and rules, researchers working within constructivist approaches typically view language in terms of linguistic constructions which are tied to specific functions. Thus, in the words of the cognitive linguist Langacker, the grammatical systems of natural languages consist of 'a structured inventory of conventional linguistic units' (1991: 548). This characterisation of language is reflected in the work of many linguists who believe that much of the speech we produce is not stored in terms of abstract linguistic units but instead as 'chunks' of speech with a specific purpose. Coulmas states:

> A great deal of communicative activity consists of enacting routines making use of prefabricated linguistic units in a well-known and generally accepted manner. We greet and bid farewell to one another, introduce ourselves and others, apologize and express gratitude, buy groceries and order meals, exchange wishes, make requests, ask for advice or information, report on what we did, and announce what we are about to do. As similar speech situations recur, speakers make use of similar and sometimes identical expressions, which have proved to be functionally appropriate. Thus competent language use is always characterized by an equilibrium between the novel and the familiar. (1981: 1)

This representation of language leads to very different claims regarding the type of knowledge the child has to learn and how they proceed in acquiring it. For example, Tomasello, Lieven and colleagues (see Tomasello, 1992; Lieven et al., 1997; Dabrowska, 2000; Theakston et al., 2001; Lieven et al., 2003) claim that children rely heavily on lexically based constructions in the early stages of language development (for example, *It's a X, want Y*). These units are stored, forming the basis of the child's knowledge of their target language. As more units are stored the child subconsciously extracts the underlying structural patterns that form the fabric of their target language.

Critiques have suggested that constructivist accounts bear a strong resemblance to old-fashioned behaviourism; that is, language develops through imitation of the input. However, the constructivist approach differs to behaviourism on two fundamental issues. First, although it is claimed that children are learning from the input, their learning is not straightforward imitation but rather a specific form of cultural learning. As Tomasello states:

> Human children differ from their nearest primate relatives not only in having language but also in being able to imitatively learn other types of social conventions, to communicate with others declaratively, to use material symbols such as pictures and maps, to make and use intentionally defined tools with a history, to collaborate using complementary roles, to teach one another, and to create social institutions such as governments and money. This suggests a fairly general human ability to interact with conspecifics culturally, that is, to create material, symbolic, and institutional artefacts historically and to acquire their use ontogenetically. No other species on the planet has this same propensity for things cultural. (2003: 290)

In the approach to development captured in the above quote Tomasello situates language and its development in children as an intrinsic part of cultural behaviour. Second, children are not limited to input forms but instead move beyond the input by constructing a more schematic representation of language. Therefore, a child learning English will gradually formulate a schema for plural formation which will result in the production of NOUN+s schema. By using this schema a child will produce both correct forms (*cars, bikes, cakes*) but also from time to time use the schema erroneously (*sheeps, feets*). Thus, unlike a behaviourist account, the child is not simply mimicking the input but instead working from the bottom up by learning lexically based constructions and then subconsciously working out the regularities between them.

Within the constructivist approach to language development the linguistic input that children receive is central to the developmental process. What then of the formalist claim that the input that children receive is 'impoverished'? Whether we believe that the language children hear is sufficient for language to develop or not very much depends on the nature of what we think it is that they are acquiring. If the child's task is to discover an abstract and highly rule governed system from the onset of language development then most researchers would agree that the language children typically hear does not contain the vast range of structure necessary for a child to know that '*he*' in (4a) could refer to Jay while in (4b) '*he*' could also refer to someone other than Jay:

4a When Jay entered the room, he was wearing a yellow shirt.

4b When he entered the room Jay was wearing a yellow shirt.

(Anderson and Lightfoot, 2002: 19)

However, if we claim that the child's task is to store units of speech and then use these as a basis to gradually extract the patterns of their language then research would indicate that the language children hear is well suited to the task. The specific nature of CDS has been well documented in language development literature. Typically the speech addressed to young children has a specific form of intonation, shorter sentence structure, restricted vocabulary and focuses on the here and now:

> The broad outlines of mothers' speech to children – that it is simple and redundant, that is contains many questions, many imperatives, few past tenses, few co- or sub-ordinations, and few dysfluencies, and that it is pitched higher and has an exaggerated intonation pattern – are quite well established. (Snow, 1977: 36)

All these adaptations appear well suited to gaining and maintaining the attention and understanding of young language learners. Studies also indicate that the structures used in CDS are highly repetitive and may thus facilitate the segmentation and abstraction of the lexically based frames which dominate young children's early linguistic systems. For example, Cameron-Faulkner et al. (2003) conducted a lexically based analysis of CDS from twelve mothers. The results demonstrated a high degree of lexical specificity in the speech of the mothers with over half of the CDS sample consisting of a very limited number of lexically based frames (e.g. *Are you ...? Look at ..., It's a ..., What's that?*). Thus, the study indicated that rather than being degenerate, the input addressed to nascent language learners may be well suited to the task at hand.

While studies of CDS indicate the adult may adapt their speech to young children, there are limitations as much of this work is based on a specific sample of the population, namely caregivers living in Western industrialised countries. As a number of researchers have pointed out, CDS is not attested in all cultures. In the next section child language development is discussed within a cross-cultural perspective.

LANGUAGE DEVELOPMENT ACROSS CULTURES

Cultural attitudes to language development differ worldwide. In the cultural context of Western, middle-class English-speaking communities, adults tend to employ some form of modified speech when talking to children, as mentioned in the previous section. However, as Lieven (1994) points out, this does not appear to be a universal phenomenon. In a number of cultures adults do not address children directly, for a variety of reasons. Heath (1983) presents an ethnographic study of two rural working-class communities ('Trackton' and 'Roadville') in South Carolina. Trackton is a black working-class area in which the older generations are engaged in farming, while Roadville (only a few miles down the road) is predominantly a white working-class area based around employment in the textile mills. Despite their close proximity, Heath's ethnographic study indicated clear differences within the cultures of the two communities and suggested that these differences are also manifested in caregivers' approach to language development.

In Roadville, Heath comments that: 'When the baby begins to respond verbally, to make sounds which adults can link to items in the environment, questions and statements are addressed to the baby, repeating or incorporating his "word"' (1983: 123), while Heath comments that in Trackton: '[caregivers] do not see babies or young children as suitable partners for regular conversations. For an adult to choose a preverbal infant over an adult as a conversational partner would be considered an affront and a strange behaviour as well' (1983: 86).

Heath claims that in the Roadville community language is viewed as a skill that should be fostered and nurtured by caregivers. Adults modify their speech when addressing young children in order to accommodate the linguistic knowledge of their conversational partners. In contrast, according to Heath, the prevailing ethos in Trackton is that children should discover how the world works for themselves and that this ethos also extends to the acquisition of language. Children are required to find their own way of breaking into the linguistic system of their speech community. However, it is important to note the social environment of the Trackton children:

> Infants are held during their waking hours, occasionally while they sleep, and they usually sleep in the bed with parents until they are about 2 years of age. They are held, their faces fondled, their cheeks pinched, and they eat and sleep in the midst of human talk and noise from the television, stereo, and radio. Encapsulated in an almost totally human world, they are in the midst of constant human communication, verbal and non-verbal. They literally feel the body signals of shifts in emotion of those who hold them almost continuously; they are talked about and kept in the midst of talk about topics that range over any subject. (Heath, 1986: 112)

Thus, while the Trackton children may not have been addressed directly, they were continually exposed to their target language and to the routines and daily activities encoded by it.

Schieffelin (1994) also presents an ethnographic account of language socialisation but this time among a very different population: the Kaluli community of Papua New Guinea. Schieffelin highlights the lack of CDS attested in the community, but further comments that:

> However, this does not mean that Kaluli children grow up in an impoverished verbal environment and do not learn how to speak. Quite the opposite is true. The verbal environment of the infant is rich and varied, and from the very beginning the infant is surrounded by adults and older children who spend a great deal of time talking to one another. (1994: 485)

The onset of language development is marked by the use of two key words by the child; 'mother' (no) and 'breast' (bo). After this point linguistic interaction between caregiver and child commences as the child is presented with eliciting 'elema' ('say like that') constructions such as (5) and (6). The elema are used to inform the child of the appropriate linguistic conventions required within a given context and provide direct instruction to the young language learning child.

5   ni nuwe suke! elema.

My grandmother picked! say like that

6   gi suwo?! elema.

Did you pick?! say like that

(Schieffelin, 1994: 486)

The ethnographic descriptions presented by Heath and Schieffelin are two of many studies which indicate that many children are exposed to language in an indirect way and thus 'tend to participate in communicative interactions in the role of overhearers of non-simplified conversations between others' (Ochs and Schieffelin, 1995: 78). There is a growing body of research that indicates children can and do learn aspects of language through overhearing speech as opposed to being addressed directly. For example, Akhtar et al. (2001) compared the ability of two-year-olds to acquire novel nouns and verbs when the items were presented directly and indirectly (i.e. with the children overhearing the words in question). The findings of the study indicated that children of around two-and-a-half years found it just as easy to acquire the words in both conditions and thus children can learn words which are not directly addressed to them. The results echoed the perceptions of the parents whose children were involved in the study:

> Many parents reported that their children knew many more words than they had been explicitly taught (including some words that parents would prefer their children had not learned). (2001: 428)

Nevertheless, children from these communities still acquire their native tongue and in addition there is evidence to suggest that children from CDS and non-CDS cultures actually develop language on the same timescale (Ochs, 1985). Such communities are still under-represented in the field of language development. However, it could be argued that in order to fully understand the process of language development it is not only the range of languages that needs to be widened with regard to analysis but also the cultural diversity in which children learn the language of their community.

BILINGUALISM AND MULTILINGUALISM

The current discussion has centred around children learning one language (i.e. monolingual language development). However, the reality for a large proportion of children and adults across the world is more complex. According to recent estimates more children are raised in bilingual or multilingual environments than monolingual contexts. Within this population the range of learning contexts is vast. For example, some children will be raised as balanced bilinguals with a relatively equal command of two languages; other children may display more advanced skills (or dominance) in one particular language. The social and political perspectives associated with bilingualism and multilingualism are far reaching; however, for the purposes of the current chapter the discussion will focus on aspects of language development within bilingual populations. This section begins with a discussion of some key distinctions made within the field of bilingual language development and then moves on to highlight trends regarding sound and lexical development in bilingual children.

Bilingual language learners are described as either simultaneous bilinguals or sequential bilinguals. Simultaneous bilinguals are exposed to two languages from birth. In cases where the child is brought up in a two-parent household it may be the case that they hear one language from their mother and one from their father (one parent, one language), or hear both spoken by both parents. However, as noted by de Houwer (1995) cases of total separation of the languages addressed to children are rare and in most cases children's input will be somewhere on a continuum between separate and mixed. A common question raised by bilingual parents is whether one approach is more effective than the other. Current research appears divided on the issue. For example, while some researchers suggest that the 'one parent, one language' approach facilitates native mastery of both languages (see Bain and Yu, 1980), others suggest that the linguistic development of bilingual children is not hindered by caregivers who address their children in more than one language (see García, 1983).

The impact of being raised bilingually on language development and cognitive development more generally is also a key area of debate. There is evidence to suggest the even before the age of twelve months bilingual infants possess different sensitivities to language than their monolingual counterparts. For example, infants around the age of six months are able to distinguish between a wide range of sounds (phonemes) found in both their native and non-native languages. However, over time this ability becomes confined to sounds associated with a speaker's target language only. For example, a Japanese-speaking adult learning English may find it difficult to distinguish the English sound 'r' from 'l' since the two sounds do not serve a meaningful contrast in Japanese. Research on bilingual infants indicates that seven- to eight-month-old Spanish-Catalan bilingual infants retain the ability to discriminate between particular vowel sounds, while their monolingual counterparts are no longer able to identify the sounds as different (Albareda-Castellot et al., 2011).

In terms of vocabulary development bilingual children display the same rate of word learning as monolingual peers. That is, when the lexical content associated with both languages is combined, bilingual children appear to acquire a comparable number of lexical items to monolingual children (Pearson et al., 1993). However the **lexicon** of a bilingual child tends to be smaller than age matched peers when considering each language individually (see Mahon and Crutchley, 2006). The grammatical development of bilingual children appears to follow similar trajectories to that of monolingual children. However, there is some evidence to suggest that there may be a lag with regard to some grammatical knowledge but that differences in rates of development reduce over time (see Hoff, 2008 for an accessible and informative overview). As with monolingual children the characteristics of the input play a central role in the language development of bilingual children though, due to the wide range of bilingual and multilingual contexts around the world, determining the role of the input provides unique challenges to child language researchers.

CONCLUSION

In this chapter, three approaches to language development have been presented. Each approach is informed by a different set of assumptions regarding the nature of linguistic knowledge and as a consequence results in markedly distinct theories of language acquisition. Cross-cultural differences with regard to linguistic input were also discussed with studies indicating that the characteristics of the linguistic environment reflect the cultural beliefs of the community with regard to the transmission of knowledge. The final section focused on language development in bilingual children and outlined some of the key issues of interest to bilingual researchers and parents alike.

Key points

- Theories of child language development vary in terms of the underlying mechanisms associated with the process.
- There is strong evidence to suggest that linguistic input and interaction play a crucial role in language development.
- Children can learn two or more languages successfully in childhood given appropriate levels of input; indeed bilingualism and multilingualism are actually the norm for many children and communities around the world.

Recommended reading

Brooks and Kempe (2012) and Clark (2016) provide good general introductions to language development (see references).

PLAY AND DEVELOPMENT
IN EARLY CHILDHOOD

JUSTINE HOWARD

CONTENTS

INTRODUCTION

The view that play is important, if not essential for children is something that is often assumed rather than demonstrated (Sutton-Smith, 1997). Play is 'all pervasive yet too vaguely acknowledged as a good thing' (Blenkin and Kelly, 1987: 37). Play scholars span many disciplines (including philosophy, psychology, sociology and anthropology) and their work highlights play's complexity from a historical, cultural and developmental perspective. It would be impractical to attempt an overarching review within an introductory chapter. The purpose here is to highlight the significance of play for development across domains in early childhood and the problems associated with its definition. In particular, the chapter will draw attention to the value of eliciting children's own perceptions of play and emphasise how play's fundamental qualities separate it from other modes of action.

WHY DO WE PLAY?

There have been many attempts to organise accounts of why we play. Strategies range from the popular classical versus dynamic distinction used by Saracho (1991) to the exotic, cross-disciplinary rhetorics of Sutton-Smith (1997). The well-used phrase derived from Greek philosophy that there is nothing new under the sun is almost certainly true for organising the literature surrounding play.

Hughes (1999) suggests play theories differ according to whether they emphasise physical, emotional or intellectual development. Earlier accounts focus on one of these domains, for example, philosophical ideas suggest physical reasons for play; psychoanalytic approaches see play as central to emotional health while constructivist theories consider social or intellectual development. More recently, however, there has been a move towards holistic theories that consider the underlying features of play and its significance across multiple developmental domains.

EARLY IDEAS ABOUT PLAY

Ellis (1973, cited in Saracho and Spodek, 1998) describes early accounts of play as armchair theories as they come from the philosophical tradition and are largely based on *ideas* about human existence rather than *supporting evidence*. Saracho (1991) presents these theories as competing pairs. Surplus energy versus relaxation, where play either consumes or creates energy, and recapitulation versus pre-exercise, where play either reflects evolutionary extinct behaviours or serves as practice for skills required in adult life (Howard, 2002). The regulatory function proposed by energy theorists is echoed in the arousal modulation of Berlyne (1969). Here children are motivated to play because it provides an optimum means of regulating environmental stimulation. An over-stimulating environment requires exploration (to reduce nervous activity) whereas an under-stimulating environment requires play (to increase nervous activity). The proposition that play allows children to practise essential social skills is an important feature of the bio-cultural approach. This suggests that increased anti-social behaviour in modern society may be a result of reduced free play opportunities and increased adult surveillance, disrupting the development of essential neural pathways and compromising social competence (Jarvis, 2007; Jarvis et al., 2014).

DEVELOPMENTAL THEORIES

Whereas philosophical accounts were primarily concerned with why play exists, developmental theories seek to detail the nature and function of this play.

The earliest developmental theories stem from the psychoanalysis of Sigmund Freud (1856–1939) and are concerned with the role of play for social and emotional development. While many of Freud's ideas have been discredited, it is important to recognise the significance of his work, in particular for our appreciation of the unconscious mind and the impact of early experiences. Anna Freud (1968) developed her father's theory further, and maintained that during play children resolved anxiety and developed coping strategies for future use. Play afforded the opportunity to explore feelings that it would be inappropriate to tackle in everyday life. Evidence of this can be seen in the content and language evident in children's spontaneous play following trauma (Bateman et al., 2013). These ideas were further developed by Erikson (1977) who, in addition to the resolution of trauma, suggested that play provided an opportunity for learning about the self and others. In play children learn about their personality characteristics and the complexity of human relationships (Pellegrini and Bohn-Gettler, 2013). Psychoanalysis continues to make an invaluable contribution to the growing professional fields of therapeutic play and playwork.

Constructivist accounts of play are embedded within broader theories of development and include the work of Piaget and Vygotsky (see Chapters 6 and 10). Piaget (1952) maintained that as a species we are motivated to learn in order to ensure that our mental representation of the world matches reality: this he described as equilibrium. To achieve equilibrium we are born with two mechanisms of change: assimilation and accommodation. Of significance is that Piaget saw play as largely assimilative, consolidating existing knowledge rather than being a principal mode of learning. His theory of play was strongly associated with his stage theory of development and he described play as reflecting increased cognitive ability. For Piaget, play was secondary to the business of learning and allowed children to perfect, rather than acquire, developing skills.

Vygotsky maintained that development was driven by our motivation towards social interaction. A central tenet of his work was the zone of proximal development and of significance was his proposition that play itself provides such a zone, where children are able to set their own challenges. Vygotsky argued that in play 'a child always behaves beyond his average age, above his daily behaviour' (1978: 102). This demonstrates his view of the child as both an independent and, critically, a social learner. He was particularly interested in symbolism during imaginative play and it is argued that, for Vygotsky, the ability to allow one thing to stand for something else represents children's first experience with symbolic systems, which they will later apply in numeracy and literacy (Whitebread and Jameson, 2005).

Alternative theories describe the holistic value of play rather than focusing on one particular developmental domain. These accounts propose that the value of play lies in its ability to promote adaptive and flexible patterns of behaviour. Bruner (1974) and Sutton-Smith (1979) suggest that play supports behavioural flexibility by freeing children from external goals and opens children's eyes to cognitive alternatives. During play children mix and match behaviours and being in control of the activity minimises the potential to fail and allows them to experiment with combinations fluidly. This theoretical proposition has been supported by recent research comparing children's behaviour when completing a jigsaw puzzle under playful or formal conditions. Under playful conditions, children demonstrated increased purposeful problem solving skills, persisting in their trials using new puzzle pieces and new rotations (McInnes et al., 2009). The power of play to facilitate adaptive and flexible thought is supported by animal analysis of Fagan (1984) who demonstrated that rats who were exposed to enriched, playful environments during infancy showed greater behavioural flexibility. Studies of their brain activity revealed that those who were reared in playful environments had increased **neural interconnectivity**, indicated by the complex branching and density of synapses. It is suggested that the increase in neural activity occurs because play activity stimulates the production of proteins that are responsible for the growth of important nerve cells (Siviy, 1998). Additional evidence from neuroscience, although again based on animal studies, suggests that playful experiences foster brain growth and in particular, nerve development in parts of the brain responsible for social and emotional functioning (Panksepp, 2003). Howard and Miles (2008, in Broadhead et al., 2010) suggest that play enhances children's learning and development because a 'playful state' leads to lower behavioural thresholds, enabling children to try out more complex and purposeful behaviours with minimal fear of failure. A further proposition about the holistic value of play is based on the notion of resilience. Fearn and Howard (2011) propose that playfulness has the power to reduce anxiety and to build and protect esteem which in turn maximises opportunities for learning and development across domains. There is strong empirical evidence to support the beneficial effects of 'playfulness', as is discussed later in the chapter.

WHAT IS PLAY?

Holistic theories are exciting as they remind us that there is something unique about play that requires investigation if we are to fully understand its contribution to development. A fundamental problem, however, is agreeing on an operational definition of what play actually is. Providing a definition is important as it ensures we are all talking about the same thing. Attempts to define play can be grouped into those that consider categories, criteria and continuum.

Concordant with his theory of cognition, Piaget (1951) identified three types of play that reflected children's thinking ability: practice play, symbolic play and games with rules (Howard and McInnes, 2013). These types of play are predominant at particular stages of development (such as practice play during the sensorimotor period) and are dependent on cognitive ability (for example, symbolic play emerging with symbolic thought). Piaget's identification of early sensory play resonates in Goldschmied's work on heuristic play that describes infants' absorption with objects chosen for their sensory and non-prescriptive qualities (see Goldschmied and Jackson, 2003). The proposition that early sensory experience is important for the development of future play skills is a pivotal feature of Jennings's (1999) Embodiment, Projection and

Role paradigm (EPR) in therapeutic play. Smilansky (1968) argued that Piaget's typology did not account for certain forms of play and added a category for construction, but for Piaget this represented accommodative rather than assimilative activity. This highlights the issue of subjectivity; what is considered play by one person may not be considered play by another (Howard, 2002). Even the fifteen-category typology of Hughes (1996) may defy this neat categorisation, and all-encompassing typologies, such as the **ludic/epistemic** distinction made by Hutt et al. (1989), may be too broad. In a review of the literature surrounding play behaviour, Whitebread et al. (2012) propose that play can be divided into five main types; these include: physical play, play with objects, symbolic play, pretence/socio-dramatic play and games with rules.

Criteria approaches suggest that for an activity to be defined as play it must demonstrate intrinsic motivation, positive affect, free-choice, non-literality and attention to means over ends (see Rubin et al., 1983). However, there is debate among scholars as to the relative importance of each of these characteristics. Smith and Vollstedt (1985) presented adult raters with video clips of children at play and found that the most common indicators used were non-literality, flexibility and positive affect. Interestingly, intrinsic motivation was not used by the raters despite it being a consistent feature of play within the literature. Smith and Vollstedt subsequently adopted these three principal criteria despite other theorists maintaining that play does not always appear enjoyable or involve pretence (Sutton-Smith and Kelly-Byrne, 1984). Research with children has found that absolute freedom of choice is not always a necessary characteristic of play. Children can still regard activities to be play even when they cede some elements of choice and control, negotiating with adults and peers when, where and with whom they play (Miller and Kuhaneck, 2008; King and Howard, 2012; Howard et al., 2017). The usefulness of the criteria approach is further reduced when we consider that Smith and Vollstedt's adult raters felt that at least two characteristics had to be present before a play judgement was made. Might an activity still be play even though only one characteristic is observed?

Rather than using criteria to make an absolute decision as to whether an activity is or is not play, Pellegrini (1991) suggests that the number of criteria present can be used to place an activity on a continuum from non-play to pure play. As with broad typologies, however, the ease by which this can be applied is questionable. Garvey (1991) presents a dynamic continuum and suggests that during an episode of play, children move in and out of the play frame using different modes of action. This movement in and out of the play frame highlights how difficult it is to make a decision as to whether or not activity is play regardless of whether we adopt a category, criteria or continuum approach as the situation is ever changing. Garvey's work is also interesting as it hints at the significance of play as an attitude or mode of action.

HOW DO CHILDREN DEFINE PLAY?

Animal studies aside, most play research relates to children and it is surprising that only a limited amount of time has been spent investigating their views. As Takhvar comments:

as play is mostly practiced during childhood, perhaps children themselves could provide a means to define this behaviour, or at least illuminate how far and to what extent they share adults' views. (1988: 238)

By focusing on theories and definitions of play that are the result of adult observations we have arguably been missing the affective elements that render it a powerful contributor to learning and development. Winnicott (1971) distinguishes the noun 'play' from the verb 'playing' and proposes that it is the noun, rather than the verb, that warrants investigation. This point is echoed by Lieberman (1977), who separates the behavioural elements of play from its quintessence: the quintessence of play being its essential and defining quality. Recently, there has been renewed interest in children's own perceptions of play in an effort to pinpoint what this elusive quality might be.

Interview studies have revealed that children categorise play according to activity type (including role play, construction activities and outdoor play rather than writing, drawing or reading books), the level of control they are afforded and whether or not an adult is present (see King, 1979; Karrby, 1989). Systematic procedures using the Activity Apperception Story Procedure (a photographic sorting game), have found that children use particular cues to categorise play based on who is involved (adult/no adult presence, interacting/not interacting with peers), the activity type (e.g., sand and water/writing and reading), whether or not they choose to participate and, in addition, where an activity takes place (Kayhaoglu, 2014). Children appear to develop these cues as a result of their experiences with both the physical and social environment (Howard et al., 2017).

PLAY AND DEVELOPMENT

The difficulties associated with defining play coupled with the need to isolate play as a **causal determinant** has meant that empirical support for the developmental potential of play has been limited. Research includes observational, longitudinal and experimental studies, each with its own strengths and limitations.

In the field of language acquisition (see Chapter 8), observational studies show how children play with sounds, nonsensical rhyming patterns and the grammatical construction of sentences and during play, adult interactions support the development of linguistic skills (Weisberg et al., 2015). During physical play we observe children running, jumping and riding bicycles. These children appear intrinsically motivated and seem to be having fun. There is no doubt that they are developing muscle control, co-ordination, balance and self-awareness but again this is not necessarily a result of the play. For instance, had the children been instructed to ride on the bicycles and in protest rode repetitively back and forth from one end of the yard to the other, the physicality of the activity would remain. While there appears to be a relationship between play and development, it is difficult to establish that this relationship is causal (Lillard et al., 2013).

The impressive longitudinal Effective Provision of Pre-school Education (**EPPE**) project reports that quality, play-based provision in the early years leads to superior social, emotional and cognitive development (Sylva et al., 2004). However, a quality environment is defined via indicators such as the nature of adult–child interaction, and so it is difficult to judge whether or not such superior development is a result of this or of play more fundamentally given that children, particularly in the early years, often categorise play as being something that does not involve adult participation. The difference between authentic play activities (ones which a child believes to be play) and contrived activities (those which a teacher designs to look like play) is documented by Walsh et al. (2011).

Experimental studies attempt to isolate play as a causal factor but even these do not escape criticism. The classic lure retrieval study by Sylva et al. (1976) is frequently cited as evidence for the relationship between play and problem solving. Children who were allowed to play with materials in a practice session performed better at retrieving an object with clamps and sticks than those who had not engaged in the play beforehand. This study (and others of a similar design) has been criticised, however, for failing to differentiate between play and children's initial exploration with objects and materials (Sutton-Smith, 1997).

Understanding children's own perceptions of their play has led to significant advances in demonstrating the relationship between playfulness and development. The cues used by children to define play (location, choice, adult involvement and interaction with peers) have been used to subtly change the conditions under which children complete some familiar activities so as to directly measure the impact of playfulness on behaviour. These have consistently shown that playful practice leads to significantly improved performance on problem solving tasks (Ramani, 2005; Thomas et al., 2006; McInnes et al., 2009), deeper concentration and involvement (McInnes et al., 2009; Howard et al., 2017) and higher levels of emotional wellbeing (Howard and McInnes, 2013). During play rather than formal classroom activities, children also demonstrate higher levels of **metacognition** and self-regulation (Whitebread and O'Sullivan, 2012).

PROFESSIONAL PLAY PRACTICE

Policy relating to children's health and social care, education and recreation emphasises the importance of wellbeing. Emotional health lies at the core of children's development and play is a key way to support this (Prendiville and Howard, 2014). Although educational, recreational and therapeutic professionals may encounter play in different settings and experience different pressures in relation to the experiences provided, they are unified by the qualities of play that render it powerful. Rather than seeing play as being qualitatively different across contexts (for example, play as pedagogy or play as therapy) it is more useful to see this as a spectrum of practice. There is developmental, educational and therapeutic value in all of children's play, although the emphasis placed on these values may differ according to context (Howard and McInnes, 2013). The benefits of playful experiences will vary depending on the depth and nature of the relationships that develop, the child's circumstances and the skills and judgement utilised by the practitioner.

THERAPEUTIC PLAY

The therapeutic power of play is rooted in the psychoanalytic tradition and since the 1920s play has been used to help children express themselves more readily (Landreth, 2002). *Play therapists* harness play to resolve psychosocial difficulties and to make clinical decisions about children's therapeutic needs. They are often, but not always, trained in psychotherapy and their emphasis is on the development of a therapeutic relationship. Other professionals trained in *hospital* or *developmental and therapeutic play* use play to enhance children's holistic development, working with individuals and groups, facilitating play skills to promote development, wellbeing and resilience (Howard and Prendiville, 2008). Approaches can be directive, non-directive or integrative. In a directive approach the therapist offers interpretation as to the meaning of the play and may plan specific interventions based on this interpretation. The early psychoanalytic approaches of Anna Freud and Melanie Klein were consistent with this tradition and saw play as an information gathering opportunity. Non-directive approaches are characterised by the active role of the child who essentially leads the session. Carl Rogers instigated a move towards client-led therapies and this is extended in the work of Virginia Axline (1969), whose approach draws attention to the value of both the therapeutic relationship and the play process. As well as using selected toys, therapeutic play also involves puppetry, storytelling, art, music, drama and dance. This range of media ensures opportunities for multi-sensory experiences, symbolism and role play, all of which are fundamental to the EPR paradigm. This developmental approach to therapeutic play emphasises the successful negotiation of progressive play stages. The process begins with embodied sensory experiences, progresses to symbolism in projective play and cumulates in children's ability to enact roles. Each stage is important, providing 'intrinsic learnings ... for life preparation' (Jennings, 1999: 55).

PLAYWORK

The importance of play as a child-directed process and the sensitive nature of adult–child interaction in play are principles shared by therapeutic play and playwork. The parallels between the two professions are particularly evident within the psycholudic approach that draws together the key features of play activity that facilitate healing and development and proposes that, regardless of professional status (e.g., teacher, therapist or playworker), being involved with children during play immerses both the player and adult attendant into a space where healing and development are negotiated (Sturrock, 2003). While playworkers are often associated with recreational play and out-of-school clubs, the range of employment is much wider than this, for example, playworkers may also work in social or health care contexts.

Playworkers adhere to a set of principles that are founded on children's right to play and the belief that opportunities for self-directed play are fundamental to development. In particular, they are very aware of the impact that adult presence can have on children's play and work hard to ensure that play opportunities remain child-directed. Playworkers understand and respond sensitively to children's play cues, creating stimulating and flexible opportunities that allow children to pursue their own agendas.

PLAY IN EARLY EDUCATION

Piaget (1951), Vygotsky (1978) and Bruner (1974) have played pivotal roles in the shaping and re-shaping of educational practices and we now acknowledge the importance of child-initiated activity and social interaction for learning and development. While play is embedded within current curriculum initiatives such as the EYFS (DfE, 2017) this is not entirely new. The **Plowden Report** clearly advocated the importance of play as a 'principal means of learning in early childhood' (CACE, 1967: 193). Despite this, observations of classroom practice demonstrated that play often tended to fulfil a subordinate role, secondary to principal classroom activity (Ofsted, 1993). The reasons for this have been researched widely. Bennett et al. (1997) propose that while teachers may advocate play, the uncertainty among scholars as to its value means that they lack the confidence to utilise it at classroom level. Other difficulties associated with implementing play-based curricula have included increased class size, pressure to account for and measure children's abilities, parental pressure towards the teaching of basic skills and a lack of understanding as to how to become involved in children's play (Howard and McInnes, 2013). Prendiville (2008) also found that some teachers were intolerant of the mess associated with some forms of play such as sand and water.

A re-conceptualisation of play that emphasises affective rather than behavioural qualities could ensure the success of curricula that centralise play. Research has shown that children's perceptions of play can be used diagnostically to plan a playful early years environment (Westcott and Howard, 2007). Understanding the cues children use to signal play as their mode of action allows teachers to create playful environments rather than activities that look like play and also to understand how they can become accepted as co-operative play partners (McInnes et al., 2010; 2011; Howard et al., 2017). These affective qualities empower practitioners and allow them to celebrate children's many ways of thinking, speaking and listening.

CULTURAL DIFFERENCES IN CHILDREN'S PLAY

Just as there are regional trends towards particular games *within* any given culture, there are also quantitative and qualitative differences in play *across* cultures. The unifying fact is children play in all different cultures. Hughes (1999) notes that the main conclusive evidence for cultural differences in children's play relates to competitive and co-operative play behaviour. Children within technologically advanced cultures are more likely to engage in competitive play and children from less affluent, underdeveloped countries are more likely to engage in co-operative games where the emphasis is on sharing and collectivity (see Chapter 4). From a social constructivist perspective these differences are unsurprising and even before this theoretical approach gained momentum within the social sciences, Lieberman talked of parents and teachers as 'cultural surrogates' (1977: 99) representing the environment at large in encouraging or inhibiting children's play behaviours. Research into children's perceptions of play has demonstrated that children develop an understanding of what it means to play, based on cues from their environment and social interaction (Howard et al., 2006).

For play professionals there are many reasons why understanding cultural difference is important. In some cultures, dolls are not regarded positively for religious reasons and the act of dressing up can bring bad luck (Lindon, 2001). Children's play can be influenced by immediate experiences such as parental separation, war or famine (Fearn and Howard, 2012) but also by culturally dependent myth and legend (Jennings, 1999). These differences have implications for practice in therapeutic, educational and recreational play contexts. While a common feature of good early years practice from a white Western view includes opportunities for children to engage in messy play (such as finger painting, clay, sand and water), David and Powell (2005) found that Chinese practitioners had great difficulty understanding the value of this, as it conflicted with their principles of orderliness and cleanliness. Children were afforded opportunities to be playful but these opportunities were different. Indeed, David and Powell noted how some Chinese practitioners frequently utilised children's natural propensity towards playfulness in their teaching.

While there are cultural differences in the nature of adult–child interaction during play, the types of play children engage in and the value placed on play for development (Roopnarine et al., 2014), there is little evidence that one particular practice is beneficial over another. Cross-cultural research into children's play warns us against the use of universal, observable behaviour as an indicator of developmental significance. Rather, we should seek to identify and explain the underlying qualities of this behaviour that render it important. It would seem that playfulness is the universal.

CONCLUSION

This chapter has considered theoretical perspectives as to why we play and the problems associated with defining this complex activity. It has shown how, in our quest to understand play and measure its developmental potential, we became distracted and lost sight of its unique qualities. Understanding children's perceptions draws us back to these qualities and reminds us that play is special. Play affords children the opportunity to learn and to heal and there is potential for these things to occur regardless of the context in which the play activity takes place. That is what makes play unique. Regardless of culture, when playful, children are afforded autonomy and control. Howard and McInnes (2013) propose that there are multiple, evidenced benefits associated with these characteristics: flexible and adaptive thinking, increased motivation and attention, the development and protection of confidence and esteem, effective communication, and the development of healthy attachments and social relationships.

Key points

- Philosophical accounts have guided our thinking about why children play.
- Developmental theories describe the way in which play both reflects and contributes to children's skills and abilities across domains.
- There are difficulties in defining play and historically, accounts have relied on adult inferences about children's behaviour.
- Play can be seen as a behaviour but also as a mode of action resulting from children's sense of autonomy and independence.
- When children perceive an activity to be play rather than not play (even when the task remains the same) they appear to demonstrate superior thinking and problem solving skills.
- The importance of children initiating, guiding and directing their own play activity unifies play professionals across contexts.

Recommended reading

Sheridan, M. with Howard, J. and Alderson, D. (2017) *Play in Early Childhood From Birth to Six Years* (Third Edition). London: Routledge.

CULTURAL-HISTORICAL THEORIES OF CHILD DEVELOPMENT

MARILYN FLEER

CONTENTS

INTRODUCTION

Previous chapters in this book have examined theories of child development in relation to thinking and cognition, social and emotional development, language development, and play. This chapter goes beyond these areas of development, and seeks to examine child development from a holistic perspective. To achieve this, it draws upon cultural-historical theory to conceptualise child development.

This chapter specifically foregrounds the cultural rather than the biological nature of children's development. Cultural does not mean ethnicity or race, but rather the higher forms of cultured development that are passed on from one generation to the next, such as values, ethics, morals, concepts, and specific ways of thinking about and doing things valued in a particular community (see also Chapter 4). In this conceptualisation, biology is not discounted, but rather the perspective put forward is that the child is shaped by, and shapes, the social and material world in which it exists. The child has agency in his/her own development. Child development is not biologically determined, or framed as an unfolding of a natural developmental trajectory (ages and stages), as has been shown in other theories of child development (such as that proposed by Piaget). Rather, child development is framed as a cultural process determined by the society in which the child lives and the child's active engagement in that society.

The chapter begins by illustrating what is meant by these two entangled lines of development – biological and cultural, followed by a discussion of the central concepts of a cultural-historical theory of child development. A model of child development is then presented that draws upon these concepts, illustrating through concrete examples how a cultural-historical theory of child development works in practice.

CULTURAL DEVELOPMENT

Shukla is sitting with her four-month-old infant on the grass in the local park. She sees a bird nearby and points to it, exclaiming 'Look Aarjaw. A beautiful bird'. Aarjaw initially looks at Shukla's face, then when Shukla becomes even more animated, waving her finger and saying 'Look, look, Aarjaw, quick or you will miss it!', Aarjaw looks at her finger. But he does not look to what Shukla is pointing at until Shukla picks him up and swings him towards the direction of the bird.

The pointing gesture, like many other forms of non-verbal communication, is learned within families and within cultural communities. As a symbolic tool in communication, pointing gestures and facial expressions are particularly important for orienting infants to what matters, and what one should pay attention to within a particular family and community. But the interaction cited above only focuses on communications of the adult towards the infant. It is only half of the picture. It gives no insight into how the pointing gesture itself becomes a tool for the infant to act upon their world. An example of Shukla and Aarjaw earlier in his life gives some clue about how this begins.

Shukla is watching her two-month-old infant Aarjaw lying on a soft mat on the floor of their living room. He is surrounded by rattles and soft toys, which are slightly out of reach, but are within view. Aarjaw swings his left arm across towards a toy rabbit. It is a physical movement often observed of young infants who are stretching their bodies without specific purpose. Shukla observes his arm movement, and immediately pushes the rabbit towards Aarjaw saying 'Oh you want the rabbit. Here it is.'

Vygotsky (1994a) famously wrote about a similar case to Aarjaw and Shukla, arguing that this is an example of an infant's actions being given social meaning, where the reflex action is named by the mother as a pointing gesture, allowing for objects in close proximity to be given to the infant. Over time and with repeated experiences such as that shown above, the infant learns that a movement of the arm, and later with more accuracy, the finger, will ensure that what it is directed at will be retrieved or at least noticed by the adult. Cultural development and biological development are intertwined. But this narrative of the pointing gesture is illustrative of more than just the development of eye-hand coordination or when or what stage an infant can crawl to retrieve an object. The child's development is viewed holistically within their family and community, where the infants' intentions and motives are considered alongside of what the adults in the infants' lives value and orient the infant towards. As noted by Vygotsky (1994b: 64, my emphasis) 'the organic maturation plays the part of a *condition* rather than a motive power for the process of cultural development'. A maturational view of development, which foregrounds ages and stages, often dissecting the child into the development of language, social skills, emotionality, and physically, is only part of the picture. A cultural-historical view of development explicitly foregrounds the cultural line of development of the child, where the family and societal values and needs frame what a child pays attention to, what they experience, and how they appropriate and use the cultural tools of their community to engage with, but also how they shape, their world.

As noted by Vgotsky (1997: 231):

> ... cultural development of the child represents a special type of development, in other words, the process of the child's growing into the culture cannot be equated, on the one hand, with the process of organic maturation and on the other hand, it cannot be reduced to simple mechanical assimilation of certain external habits ... cultural development, like all other development, is subject to its own patterns, its own stages ...

These patterns and complexities of cultural development of the child can be better understood when an analysis of the central concepts of Vygotsky's (1998) theory are examined. I now turn to a close study of the central concepts of a cultural-historical view of child development: 'leading activity' (see Chapter 13); 'social situation of development'; '*perezhivanie*'; and the 'ideal form'. Please note that these concepts are interrelated. One concept cannot be understood without considering it within a system of concepts about development.

THE CONCEPT OF LEADING ACTIVITY

Vygotsky (1966) introduced the concept of leading activity through the theoretical work he did in relation to play. He suggested that play was the leading activity of pre-school children. That is, pre-school children readily create imaginary situations when they change the meaning of objects and actions, such as turning a stick into a hobbyhorse, and then engaging in adventures.

Children also role-play what they have observed in real life (going to the markets with their family) or in fiction/media (e.g. TV, books, tablets) (see Chapter 5), orienting themselves to the rules and roles within society. Play is a special kind of motive that Vygotsky (1966) said leads pre-school children's development.

Leontiev (1978) further developed the concept of leading activity in relation to his theory of activity (see also Veresov, 2006), which Elkonin (1999) later conceptualised as a system of leading activities linked to particular periods in a child's life. The periods (infancy, early childhood, pre-school, early school, early adolescence, later adolescence), epochs (early childhood, childhood, adolescence) and phases within periods, each contain a motivational element that represents a unique characteristic of a person's life. Role-play is but one of these motivational elements. These periods, epochs and phases parallel Vygotsky's (1998) age periodisation of development. Hedegaard and Fleer (2013: 13–14) state that, 'A child's developmental age period is not the same as the child's biological age. A child's developmental age or age period reflects the child's quali-tative relation to his or her environment and depends on the child's motivational orientation.' Leading activities as a central motive in development are always conceptualised as the *relations between the child and the society* within which they live. For example, a child who begins school views him or herself as a *school child* engaged in *school type activities*, with both a motive for formal learning and with a display of certain competencies. The child expects to learn to read and write in this new societal institution of schooling where different kinds of activities take place to home (Hedegaard, 2012; Hedegaard and Fleer, 2013). Transition to school marks the child's leading activity for formal learning. But this does not mean that play is not present, rather a motive for learning becomes more pronounced in the child's hierarchy of motives because they expect to participate in a new type of activity at school that is different to pre-school and home.

In this reading of child development we see development clustered around particular leading activities, such as role-play or learning. These leading activities are shown below and should be read as non-linear, or as Elkonin (1999: 29) states as an, 'ascending spiral rather than linearly':

- Direct emotional communication
- Manipulation of objects
- Role-playing

- Learning activity
- Intimate personal communication
- Vocational or career-oriented activity

Elkonin (1999: 27) states that:

> child development is composed, on the one hand, of periods characterized chiefly by assimilation of the objectives, motives, and norms of human relations and, on that basis, by the development of the need-motivational sphere; and, on the other hand, of periods characterized chiefly by the acquisi-tion of socially evolved modes of action with objects and, on that basis, the formation of the child's intellectual and cognitive powers, his operational and technical capabilities.

What this means is that a child's wish for learning in school is different to their motive for play in pre-school. In this theorisation, moving institutions (from pre-school to school) represents a marked change in the child's life and influences their development. Transition from one period to another is marked as a *discrepancy in competence of the child* that realises itself as a *crisis or as a critical point in their life*. This happens in different ways when a child begins school. But also we see this later in adolescence, where an adolescent who feels him or herself to be responsible with much competence, and with a motive towards gaining employment, will come into conflict with the adults around him or her if s/he is treated as a child and not an adult. What matters here is: (1) the change in the child's life which results from how we organise the institutions or structures in society, and (2) how others around the child treat the child in their social relationships – their expectations in relation to the child's growing competencies and motives for doing different things (like being a school child or an adult).

For the early adolescent period, Elkonin (1999: 25) states:

> The formation of the adolescent personality is greatly influenced by the formation of relations within the peer group based on the code of friendship. Communicative activity, then, is the specific form in which adult relationships are reproduced among adolescents, and the means by which adolescents become more thoroughly versed in the norms that guide adult society. Thus, it is reasonable to assume that the dominant activity during this period is the activity of communication, the activity of building relations with friends on the basis of definite moral and ethical norms that mediate the actions of adolescents.

During this period a high level of self-reflection is evident and a level of social consciousness builds, allowing new motives and objectives to direct later activities towards a future career. But this also happens for the infant whose need for emotional communications with their carer is central for their development.

What is core in *direct emotional communications* in infancy and *intimate personal communications* in early adolescence is the *child–social adult relationship*. What is important here in the central lines of development within the above mentioned periodisation for both *child–social adult relationships* and *child–social object relationships?* The central lines of development that form the basis for this argument are:

1. *Child-social adult relationship:* Intimate personal communications of the adolescent, although different to the direct emotional communications evident between an infant and an adult, or the communications between play partners in pre-school, do *feature a common 'child-social adult' relationship.*

2. *Child-social object relationship:* The modes of action with objects displayed in early childhood, and again during play in the pre-school years, and learning for the school child, and vocational and career oriented actions of the later adolescent, all *represent a 'child-social object' relationship.* I explain this important line of development below using the words of Elkonin (1999).

Elkonin (1999: 26) states:

> ... what does mastering objective operations involving a spoon or glass have in common with mastering mathematics or grammar? Nonetheless, they have one common feature: they are all elements of human culture. They have a common origin and a common place in the life of society; they all represent the result of a product of history. Through this acquisition of the socially evolved modes of action with objects, the child becomes more fully oriented within the objective world; his [sic] intellectual powers are shaped; he becomes a part of society's productive forces.

In summary, a particular leading activity reflects a child's motive towards particular activities. A change from one leading activity to another, such as role-play to formal learning, is reflected as a relation between the ideal form found in society (for example what adults do) and the child's growing competence, needs and motives (what the child brings and is oriented towards). Transitions between leading activities as a form of development is explored further in the next section where we discuss the concept of the social situation of development.

THE CONCEPT OF THE SOCIAL SITUATION OF DEVELOPMENT

Vygotsky (1998) in his theory of child development stated that at the beginning of each period a unique relation between the child and social reality exits, which he termed the *social situation of development*. He argued that when 'the social becomes the individual' (Vygotsky, 1998: 198), that a qualitatively new child emerges. Bozhovich in describing this 'dialectical leap to a new quality' (2009: 61) suggests that Vygotsky wished to deliberately move away from an evolutionary view of child development (ages and stages) and to underscore his revolutionary view of development. Bozhovich (2009) argues that Vygotsky used the metaphor of the caterpillar transforming into a chrysalis, and the chrysalis transforming into a butterfly, to capture the qualitative change in children's development. That is, the child is completely transformed into something very different within different periods in childhood. This metaphor also illustrates the *new relationship that the qualitatively different child has to their environment* during different age periods. For instance, how a caterpillar relates to its environment is different to how a butterfly engages with its world – they have different competencies (such as mouths for biting or proboscis for drinking) and different needs (for example eating leaves or collecting nectar).

Vygotsky (1994b) illustrated the social situation of development by giving an example from clinical work of a mother and three children who are all in the same family situation. The mother when under the influence of alcohol behaves violently towards her children, and suffers with periods of psychological disorder which means that she is unable to adequately care for her children. Each of the three children present a very different case of disrupted development. The youngest child is overwhelmed by the horror of what is happening and is helpless. The second youngest child develops both ambivalence and a painful attachment to the mother, with the co-existence of terror and love. The third child, although exhibiting some delay in academic capacity, has taken on a very different role. As a ten-year-old child he understands the situation and feels pity for his mother. He in turn nurtures the younger children, taking on the role of the adult. Vygotsky (1994b: 340) asked, 'How can one explain why exactly the same environmental conditions exert three different types of influence on these three different children?' The same social situation is interpreted differently because of what each child brings to this specific situation. Vygotsky (1994b: 340–1) argued that in studying development and pedagogy we, 'ought to be capable of finding the prism through which the influence of the environment on the child is refracted, i.e. *it ought to be able to find the relationship which exists between the child and its environment, the child's emotional experience* [perezhivanie], in other words how a child becomes aware of, interprets, [and] emotionally relates to a certain event'. We now turn to the concept of *perezhivanie*.

THE CONCEPT OF *PEREZHIVANIE*

According to Vygotsky (1994b) the Russian word *perezhivanie* captures the emotional experience of the child in the course of the child's personal development. *Perezhivanie* represents the unity between the child and their engagement with their social and material environment. Vygotsky (1994b: 341) explained that:

> An emotional experience [perezhivanie] *is a unit where, on the one hand, in an indivisible state, the environment is represented, i.e.* that which is being experienced - an emotional experience [perezhivanie] is always related to something which is found outside the person - *and on the other hand, what is represented is how I, myself, am experiencing this,* i.e., all the personal characteristics and all the environmental characteristics are represented in an emotional experience [perezhivanie]; everything selected from the environment and all the factors which are related to our personality and are selected from the personality, all the features of its character, its constitutional elements, which are related to the event in question. So, *in an emotional experience [perezhivanie] we are always dealing with an indivisible unity of personal characteristics and situational characteristics, which are represented in the emotional experience* [perezhivanie].

What is important here is that child development must be viewed as the unity of the child (personal characteristics) and the situational characteristics. They cannot be separated from each other. What Vygotsky (1994b) also strived to capture with his concept of *perezhivanie* is that all aspects of a child's experience and therefore his/her development, are emotionally coloured or charged. He suggested too, that you cannot separate out cognitive development from emotional development. Educational experiences impact emotionally upon an individual. Social relations are framed as emotional exchanges. Physical activity occurs in relation to how one feels and acts in particular situations and environments. Vygotsky (1994b) argued strongly for the unity of all these dimensions of development, suggesting they could not be separated out from each other. He also suggested that the emotional-motivational dimensions of how a child engages with their social and material environment determines what kind of relationship they have with that environment. When there is a discrepancy, tension, critical point or crisis, then this creates the opportunity for development, as the child seeks to reconcile the new challenge. It is now possible to see why Vygotsky (1994b: 348) argued that the environment is the source of a child's development:

> ... the environment's role in the development of higher, specifically human characteristics and forms of activity is as a source of development. But for this to be successful a particular type of interaction between the ideal and rudimentary forms of development are necessary. We now turn our attention to this special type of interaction within the child's environment.

THE INTERACTION BETWEEN THE IDEAL AND THE RUDIMENTARY IN THE CHILD'S ENVIRONMENT

Vygotsky (1994b) stated that for the environment to be the source of a child's development then what is to be developed must already exist in the child's environment. Vygotsky gave the example of language, where children need to be in rich language environments specific to their society if they are to learn the dominant language of their community. Families engage infants by communicating with them verbally and non-verbally. Infants are not expected to begin speaking in an ideal form, but are surrounded by people who engage them socially and meaningfully by providing the ideal form of language to them. Having the ideal form in the child's environment affords development of exactly that which is valued and needed to success-fully interact. Vygotsky (1994b: 346) noted that, 'Something which is supposed to take shape at the very end of development, somehow influences the very first steps in this development'.

Having the ideal form within the child's environment is also important outside of the family context, such as pre-schools and schools, where different forms of the ideal may exist exerting new demands that have possibilities for further development (see Hedegaard and Fleer, 2013). For example, pre-school children participate in the everyday activities of eating and drinking to sus-tain life. This is of course a biological need. However, in some families mealtimes are also a source of social learning for particular social protocols, such as sitting still to eat around a kitchen table or bench, or sitting still eating in front of a TV, or as a mobile activity as family members gather food and eat it on the run as they head off for work in the morning, or take food to different areas within the house while playing. When children meet new situations and social protocols in other contexts, such as when attending childcare, this may cause tension for the child.

For instance, in a study of children's everyday lives and transition to school, Fleer (2010) has shown how JJ, a two-year-old child, begins childcare and meets the new demand of sitting at a table to eat. He comes from a home where family meals are served at the kitchen table, but the children are free to take their food and to move about the house to eat with no adult interaction or supervision. In childcare JJ avoids the routine of sitting at the clusters of tables where food is placed for all the children. He is observed hiding under a painting easel. When directed to sit, he places his feet on the table, and pushes his chair back, eventually moving the chair several meters from the table. The early childhood educators work hard to help him sit at the table. The ideal form that is valued in the childcare centre is ever present, as all the other children are seated eat-ing their meals. The expert skills acquired at home of eating while moving about are not valued or could not safely be allowed for within a centre where a group of fifteen toddlers have a hot lunch. The crisis for JJ of engaging in a new social protocol for eating places huge demands upon him to not only be together with other children to eat, but also to sit still while eating with his feet on the floor and not on the table. This affords the possibilities for development because although the demands are great, the ideal form is visibly present and the educators sensitively and carefully support JJ's transition and eventual development of new competencies and practices.

CULTURAL-HISTORICAL MODEL OF CHILD DEVELOPMENT

A holistic view of children's development as theorised through cultural-historical concepts of leading activity, social situation of development, *perezhevanie*, and the ideal form, are presented together as a model of child development in Figure 10.1. Although a number of models rel-evant to early childhood years have been empirically presented in the literature (see Fleer, 2010; Hedegaard and Fleer, 2013), only one example is possible within this short chapter. As such, we present a cultural-historical model of child development illustrated through an example from the findings of a study into children's development in everyday life (Fleer, 2010; Fleer and Hedegaard, 2010; Hedegaard and Fleer, 2013). We begin with the observations of Louise in her family over a twelve-month period, over three separate observation periods, followed by the child development model that draws upon conceptual work of Fleer and Hedegaard (2010), Hedegaard (2012), and Hedegaard and Fleer (2013).

Case example: Development in families

Walking to school and childcare: Louise at the beginning of the research was sixteen months old. She lives in a family that is very poor. Because the family does not own a car, the children walk each day for 10 kilometres in order to go to childcare, pre-school, school and home again. Louise is pushed in a stroller.

At home: Louise is usually placed in the highchair as dinner is prepared, is held while the adults perform late afternoon chores or supervise outside while the older children play with their bikes or with balls, etc. At sixteen months Louise is often placed in the highchair when the children are outside, or held and moved about as the mother moves about doing things inside or outside the house.

Community services: According to Louise's mother the government agency that supports families in caring for their children expressed concern that Louise was not walking.

Analysis: Louise did not need to walk. She observed all the activity from the vantage point of the stroller, the highchair or the arms of one of the adults – who were also highly mobile – thus affording a dynamic view of all the action occurring within the family (observation period 1). Three months later, a different kind of observation was noted when the children were given for Christmas a swing and slide set (see Fleer, 2010: 175–80 for further analysis).

Louise is seated on a swing. She is holding on to the metal bars that support the swing as her father gently moves the swing back and forth. The father explains to the researchers, who have not visited the house for three months, 'She won't go and walk by herself'. The father takes Louise from the swing and places her on her feet. He continues to hold one hand and walks with Louise saying, 'She will walk around everywhere doing this'. Louise looks to the researchers and smiles as they show appreciation of her walking. The father then explains that if he lets go of her hand, Louise immediately sits down and won't continue to walk (observation period 2, visit 1).

In observation period 3, visit 3 (3 months later), Louise is able to walk in the direction of the slide, even though she is unable to climb the ladder:

Louise slowly toddles over to the ladder of the slide. She attempts to lift one leg onto the rung of the ladder – she makes eye contact with an adult who is close by. The adult is visiting the family and notices Louise's repeated attempts to step onto the ladder. The adult lifts Louise to the top of the side. He then supports her body all the way down the slide. He steps back. Louise walks around from the slide to the ladder and again attempts to step onto the rung.

(Continued)

(Continued)

After two attempts she looks to the adult, who steps forward and lifts her to the top of the slide and, once again, supports her down the slide. This process continues, with the adult each time giving less support on the slide. Eventually, the adult invites the father to observe Louise going down the slide without adult support, saying 'She can now do it on her own' (observation period 2, visit 3).

In observation period 3, visit 5, Louise now has the competence to be able to climb up the ladder and slide unaided down the slide:

Louise has climbed to the top of the slide. She is seated on the slide holding onto the rails at the top. She calls to her mother. Her mother is inside and responds with a call, but does not come out to Louise. Louise pushes herself from the top of the slide, sliding down awkwardly, jolting from side to side. She arrives at the bottom of the slide and drops to the ground, knocking herself back as she falls. She rubs her back with her hand and cries. Both her siblings look to her as she cries (observation period 2, visit 5).

Analysis: What we see is a new self-awareness by Louise. The new equipment is enjoyed by her siblings and she too wishes to be on the swing, and later to go on the slide. Her growing strength, along with the need to be able to walk to use the equipment, develops a motive for walking. The introduction of the new slide and swing set was a critical point in Louise's development. The slide and swing set changed the concrete conditions of Louise's everyday world and thus generated an important moment in Louise's development.

We use this example of Louise to show a cultural-historical model of child development, where we specifically conceptualise development holistically, and not as the carving up of the child into social and emotional development, language development, physical development, as has been the case traditionally in early years education programmes and in psychology. As Veresov (2006: 9) notes, 'contemporary developmental psychology is moving away from linear (evolutionary-chronological) toward nonlinear (organic-functional) models of development' reflecting the limitations of the former, and venturing into Vygotsky's revolutionary view of development.

We are able to understand Louise's development by drawing upon a cultural-historical model of early years development shown in Figure 10.1. In using this model we determine that Louise is focused on the object of the slide and swing set. Her leading activity for engaging with objects (see centre of model for all leading activities), is supported by her new motive for wanting to walk so she can independently use the slide and swing set when she wishes to do so. The ideal form (box on right with the central concepts for development shown) of manipulating objects is evident as her siblings competently use the slide and swing set. The event is an emotional experience because over time she successfully challenges herself and gains physical competence in first walking, then sliding, and finally climbing. But her physical development could only be understood as a new relation with her environment that was an emotional experience (*perezhevanie*) where a crisis and a level of self awareness of her own physical competence emerged.

As is understood by the concept of the social situation of development, Louise in the same situation as her siblings engaged with the slide and swing set quite differently because of her

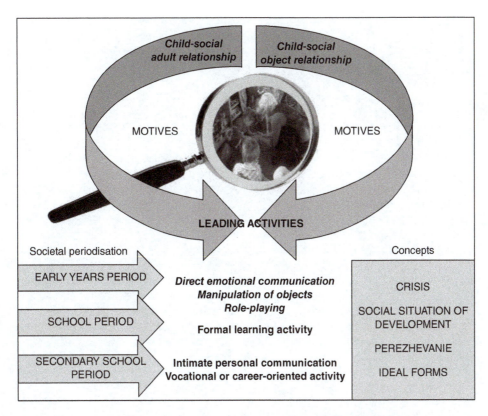

Figure 10.1 A cultural-historical model of child development for the early years

unique physical competence. While she observed the ideal forms, she was unable to do the same as her peers until she was able to walk. The model shown in Figure 10.1 allows for a deeper understanding of Louise's existing unique characteristics. Through using the concepts of the social situation of development, ideal forms, leading activity, and *perezhevanie*, it is possible to analyse and understand the cultural nature of Louise's development. Through identifying Louise's motive development, it is possible to go beyond a simple examination of Louise's physical development.

CONCLUSION

In this chapter we have taken a holistic view of children's development, drawing upon cultural-historical concepts to build a model of child development that allows for the cultural nature of development to be analysed and the outcomes used for supporting pedagogical practices in the early years.

--------- Key points ---------

- This chapter set out an holistic (rather than domain specific) perspective on child development and offered examples that show how actions acquire social meaning within a specific context in which cultural and biological development are intertwined.
- Societal values and needs orient a child towards what is given significance in their family and community. Children act upon these and create new patterns of cultural development.
- The 'cultural age' is different to 'biological age'. The 'cultural age' is clustered around particular leading activities and involves critical points or crises in a child's life. How others respond in these circumstances is important: the child–social adult relationship and the child–social object relationship feature.
- Leading activities change to reflect a relation between the ideal form found in society and the child's growing competence, needs and motives. Development is found in transitions between leading activities.
- As a child develops, s/he is transformed into someone qualitatively different with a new relationship to their environment. Social situations are interpreted differently by each child, bringing their own competencies and needs to particular situations. The dynamic relations between the child and the environment are captured in the concept of a social situation of development.
- The concept of *perezhevanie* concerns both the environment as a source of development, and the emotional experience by an individual, which together are considered as a unit of personal and situational characteristics.
- Crisis, or drama, is an important concept in a cultural-historical conception of development. Drama, tension or crisis acts as the force driving development. Discrepancies and crises create opportunities for development as a child seeks to reconcile the challenges.
- It is the relations between the ideal forms that surround the child, and their actual (rudimentary) development, that together afford (enable) development of valued cultural practices.
- A cultural-historical model of child development based on empirical (observational) research has been presented with an illustrative case example. This example demonstrates a crisis that brings together the concepts of the model: leading activity (and associated motives), ideal form and *perezhevanie* in the child's (Louise's) social situation of development.

--------- Recommended reading ---------

Fleer's (2010) *Early Learning and Development: Cultural-Historical Concepts in Play* (see reference list) shows practical examples of how a cultural-historical conception of child development can be drawn upon by educators in the birth to five years period to support learning through play.

PART 3

POLICY AND PROVISION
FOR YOUNG CHILDREN

EARLY CHILDHOOD POLICY AND SERVICES

SONIA JACKSON

CONTENTS

INTRODUCTION

This chapter discusses the development of policy on early childhood education and care (ECEC) in the UK and the influences that have shaped it and continue to do so. Comparisons with other Western European countries highlight the long-term effect of years of political neglect and under-funding (Jackson and Forbes, 2015; Rutter, 2016). The legacy of an historic split between care and education can still be felt throughout our early childhood services and in the thinking of policy makers and practitioners.

However, there has been some progress. Few people would now argue, as Margaret Thatcher did, that what happens to children in the years before compulsory schooling is a matter for their families alone. Mothers of young children are no longer criticised for working outside the home; indeed government policy is designed to encourage as many as possible to do so. The 1997–2010 Labour government transformed early childhood services with huge investment of public funding. Unfortunately, instead of establishing a comprehensive, properly thought-out service to meet the needs of all families with young children, new forms of provision were tacked on to a ramshackle structure that had evolved over half a century. This simply added to the existing confusion of day nurseries, playgroups, nursery schools, nursery and reception classes and childminders, 'all jostling for customers in a chaotic marketplace' (Moss, 2014).

ISSUES IN CHILDCARE AND EARLY EDUCATION

Five key policy issues in early years care and education have remained remarkably constant:

- Childcare and pre-school education have developed along separate lines, with differently qualified staff and different conditions of service.
- Because early education (three to five years) has never been integral to the free, statutory state education system, it is always at risk when there are cuts to local government funding.
- There is tension between cost and quality in childcare resulting in the children in most need receiving lower quality services and leaving many with no service at all.
- Childcare is mainly staffed by poorly paid women with low education levels and little prospect of career progression.
- The early age of school entry compared with other European countries raises questions about the suitability of the curriculum for such young children.

In addition, one group of especially vulnerable children, nought to four-year-olds in foster care, has been entirely overlooked, both by researchers and policy-makers.

INFLUENCES ON ECEC POLICY

Early years policy is shaped by a complex interaction of different factors. These include prevailing ideology, historical continuities, educational theories, cultural differences, economic and political conditions, and evidence from research (Baldock et al., 2013).

Events which might seem unrelated to early childhood policy, such as the 'Brexit' decision, may have a profound effect on what happens to young children in the four countries of the United Kingdom. The situation is highly volatile, with declared government policy often seeming to be in conflict with economic reality. This chapter goes on to consider major influences on early childhood policy and their effects on services for young children and their families.

HISTORY AND IDEOLOGY

A major shift in the debate on working mothers has seen the UK moving closer to the position in Nordic countries, where it is normal for women to return to work soon after maternity leave. Sweden, for example, took the opportunity in the 1960s and 1970s to build a fully integrated system of ECEC, available to all children from twelve months to six years, with a well-qualified workforce. The aim was to support women's right to participate in paid employment and to challenge stereotyped gender roles. The existing pattern of ECEC in Britain can be traced back to the Plowden Report, *Children and Their Primary Schools* (CACE, 1967). The Plowden Committee took the then orthodox position that women with young children should stay at home with them and was extremely hostile to working mothers. At the time, the Plowden recommendations were seen as an important advance by campaigners for the extension of nursery education but they set ECEC services on an unfortunate trajectory. In order to expand availability quickly at low cost, the report proposed making all provision part time and concentrating it in 'deprived' areas. Consequently, most full-time, local-authority-funded nursery education for three- to five-year-olds was reorganised on a sessional basis, as it still continues; and, secondly, it established the idea of publicly funded day care as a service primarily for children in social need or at risk of abuse or neglect, completely separate from nursery education (Jackson, 1993). The 1989 Children Act recognised the value of day nurseries and family centres, but failed to do anything to make them available. It was a lost opportunity to create integrated services and overturn the false dichotomy between education and care.

EDUCATIONAL THEORIES

Books about child development often begin by expounding the views of the philosophers John Locke and Jean-Jacques Rousseau, whose influence can be seen in many existing schools of pedagogical theory. Locke believed that a child's mind at birth was a 'tabula rasa', a blank slate, and that all human knowledge and abilities were acquired by learning through teaching and experience. Rousseau, on the other hand, thought that given the right environment, the child's innate capacity would simply unfold through exploration, discovery and imagination (Doddington and Hilton, 2007) (see Chapter 2). The Montessori and Steiner approaches both draw their inspiration from this view of childhood, in contrast, for example, to adult-directed learning broken up into pre-determined time periods (Nutbrown, 2011), with an emphasis on ever earlier attainment of the 'basic skills' of literacy and numeracy. Government policy in England, with its insistence on testing and setting standards to be met at fixed chronological ages, appears to have moved decisively away from a child-centred view of early education. This is less true in Scotland and Wales, which are increasingly pursuing their own different visions.

The belief that children's earliest experiences have a profound impact on their emotional and cognitive development is not in dispute. It is now firmly established that the early weeks and months of life are a time of rapid learning, which, in good conditions, accelerates as the child grows and lays the foundation for future experiences (Gray, 2010). However, the debate on how to create the best conditions for learning in the early years is very much alive, and especially how to counter the long-term effects of abusive and neglectful care in infancy.

CULTURAL INFLUENCES

Historical and cultural influences usually remain invisible but they are important in understanding why things are the way they are. For example, the Second World War had a different impact on countries that experienced it at first hand. One of the strengths of the much-admired Reggio Emilia early childhood service is the political support it enjoyed (Abbott and Nutbrown, 2001). The fascist experience had demonstrated that people who conformed and obeyed were dangerous. In building a new society in Italy, it was imperative to nurture and maintain a vision of children who could think and act for themselves (Dahlberg et al., 2007). English schools, on the other hand, tend to prefer compliant children who do as they are told and don't ask too many questions. The kinds of people we want children to be and become influences the nature of ECEC provision and the beliefs and behaviours of parents, professionals and policy makers towards young children (see Chapters 1 and 2). This can cause problems when strongly held beliefs and practices conflict with mainstream cultural norms (Jackson and Forbes, 2015).

EVIDENCE FROM RESEARCH

Analysis in the 1980s of data from the British Cohort Study (**CHES**) quantified the benefits of pre-school education, especially for disadvantaged children (Osborn et al., 1984). However, the first large-scale, systematic research to have a major influence on policy was the Effective Provision of Pre-school Education (EPPE) project, based at the London University Institute of Education (now UCL). Unlike any previous research, it looked in detail at the effect of attendance at different types of settings on children's cognitive and social-behavioural outcomes and the interaction between the home and pre-school environment. The findings provided a sound basis for the government's policy of expanding provision and justified the related expenditure (Sylva, 2010). They also provide strong evidence for the need to upgrade the workforce (see below). One of the most important findings is that settings with better qualified staff achieve markedly better outcomes for children. Other research suggests that the quality of the workforce is highly sensitive to the level of pay they receive (Family and Childcare Trust, 2016).

GOVERNMENT POLICY SINCE 1997

The election of a Labour government in 1997 was a significant turning point for early years policy and services. With the National Childcare Strategy (DfES, 1998), the state recognised a responsibility for the education and care of its youngest citizens for the first time. It also introduced an important change in terminology, with 'childcare' (one word) largely replacing 'day care' in official documents. Another change is the now general use of 'early years' to cover the period from birth to six years, or in some cases up to eight years. A series of government initiatives resulted in improved access to early years education over the next few years, supporting developments already in progress and stimulating new forms of provision. At the same time a falling child population created free places in infant schools, which in many areas were filled by admitting four-year-olds to full-time education. In fact four, rather than the statutory age of five, has become the usual age of entering primary school reception classes in England and Wales (though not in Scotland). There is considerable pressure on parents to send four-year-olds to full-time school regardless of their individual needs, as otherwise they risk losing the chance to gain a place in the primary school of their choice.

The Childcare Act 2006 was another landmark as the first ever piece of legislation to be exclusively concerned with early years and childcare. It was intended to take forward some of the key commitments from the Ten Year Childcare Strategy (HM Treasury, 2004) and was based on the five outcomes set out in *Every Child Matters* (see below) with special reference to early years care and education. The intention of the Act was to bring early years within the mainstream of local authority provision, but its provisions fell far short of the universal full-time nursery education with extended hours of subsidised childcare available to all children aged three to six years in Nordic countries and in many other parts of Europe. Because it failed to embed pre-school education as a free universal service on the same basis as school-age education, the important reforms introduced by the 1997–2010 Labour government remained highly vulnerable to political changes and budgetary factors.

SURE START AND CHILDREN'S CENTRES

The largest new component of the Childcare Strategy was 'Sure Start', the first government programme ever to be targeted at the birth to three age group. Sure Start was an area-based programme providing funds for a variety of different early education, childcare and family support services for children under four in the most disadvantaged areas. An important economic and political motive for the generous funding provided by the Treasury was to enable mothers and lone parents to work instead of being dependent on welfare payments. For this reason every Sure Start scheme originally had to include a day care component. Sure Start was generally regarded as one of the major successes of the Childcare Strategy. Evaluation was built in from the beginning and showed small but significant improvements in outcomes for children, for instance enhanced language development (Belsky et al., 2007). Equally important, the Centres were greatly appreciated by the parents who used them and the communities in which they were located (Eisenstadt, 2011).

Over the next few years, Children's Centres, built on the Early Excellence and family centre models (Whalley, 2000; Draper and Duffy, 2001), largely replaced Sure Start centres, although both names continue to be used. Many exemplified good and innovative practice, but they were still limited by the differing terms and conditions of employment for their staff and by the very low level of training and qualifications (**NVQ** Level 2) required of those who worked with young children. These issues were addressed by the review commissioned by the government in 2012 from Professor Cathy Nutbrown (see below).

Children's Centres might have become universal but for the change of government in 2010. At their height there were 3,500 throughout the country. Cuts in public services and local authority funding since then have put the process into reverse, with over 400 Centres closing in the first two years of the Coalition government. Even among those that remained open, the majority were obliged to discard the childcare element as unaffordable. Under the Conservative administration which followed after 2015, support for public services was sharply reduced and children's centres proved an easy target for local authority cuts.

CHILDCARE FOR WORKING PARENTS

A major weakness of all UK government policy on ECEC is the failure to differentiate between short-term sessional provision and full day care adapted to normal adult working hours. The Childcare Act 2006 lays a duty on local authorities in England and Wales to ensure that there are sufficient childcare places to 'meet the needs of working parents', but publicly provided childcare in England has almost disappeared. Care for children of working parents is found in the private sector, provided by childminders, voluntary bodies or in childcare settings run for profit, and increasingly by commercial chains. Private childcare centres largely serve families where both parents have professional jobs as the fees that they charge put them out of reach of families on average incomes (Rutter, 2016). Mothers with fewer educational qualifications are much more likely to work part time and turn to relatives, especially grandparents, for childcare. Informal care by relatives is extensively used to fill gaps in provision (Rutter and Evans, 2011).

The government funds part-time nursery places for all three- and four-year-olds whose parents want them, fifteen hours a week for thirty-eight weeks, extended to 'vulnerable' two-year-olds in England in September 2013, though only under stringent conditions. The government announced an intention to increase this entitlement to thirty hours a week by 2017. However, the policy has run into numerous problems, identified by Jill Rutter in her annual Childcare Survey (Family and Childcare Trust, 2016).

PLAYGROUPS

The playgroup movement originated in the 1960s as a response to the acute shortage of nursery places for three- to four-year-olds. It remained the major form of pre-school provision until schools began to admit four-year-olds and is still an important element in the patchwork of early years services, especially in rural areas. Although some pre-schools attain standards comparable to state nursery schools and classes, the majority have to operate in unsuitable and often shared premises, and staffing depends on the availability of people (usually women), prepared to work for token pay or none. Pre-schools have increasing difficulty in finding suitable staff and volunteers as the trend is for women to seek paid jobs at an earlier stage in their children's lives. The growth of the playgroup movement, which had no parallel in other European countries, and the strength of the Pre-school Playgroups Association, now called the Pre-school Learning Alliance, may have enabled the government to ignore the campaign for nursery education. The downward extension of the school starting age meant that pre-schools lost the older age group and were obliged to accept two-year-olds to remain viable. Welsh-medium playgroups (***Mudiad Ysgolion Meithrin***) were concerned that children might move into English-speaking primary schools before their speech was fully established. However, the opposite effect has occurred, with a growing demand for Welsh-medium primary schools (Siencyn and Thomas, 2007).

CHILDMINDING

For children under three the most common form of out-of-home care, apart from private day care centres, is childminding, known in other countries as family day care. Research during the 1970s uncovered some shocking conditions, especially among unregistered minders. In response, the BBC broadcast a series of programmes which led to the launch of the National Childminding Association. Renamed as **PACEY**, it is committed to raising standards of care through training and support as well as acting as an advocacy organisation for its members. The government introduced a new system of childminder agencies in 2014. These were intended to operate on a commercial rather than a co-operative model so they do not address the problem that childminders tend to work in isolation. The system has been note-ably unpopular with many childminders (Rutter, 2016).

The belated recognition by government that childminders are educators as well as carers has met with mixed reactions. All registered childminders in England who receive government fund-ing (for free places) must offer the Early Years Foundation Stage curriculum and are inspected by Ofsted. There continues to be a conflict, however, between standards and costs. Childminding is no longer a cheap service for poor parents, and the fees asked by registered childminders are at a similar level to those charged by private day nurseries. The average cost for twenty-five hours of childcare from a childminder is £104 a week (Rutter, 2016). Such costs lead many mothers to give up work when they have a second or third child (Abrams, 2001). In addition, many child-minders feel unable to cope with the paperwork required or to meet the requirements of EYFS: numbers of registered childminders have been declining steadily since 2000 and fell by another 13.3 per cent between 2013 and 2015 (Simon et al., 2015). This has resulted in a severe shortage of places in some areas.

The government's main interest in childcare is to reduce the cost of welfare payments by enabling mothers, especially those without partners, to return to work earlier. In practice most parents have to patch together a mixture of different forms of childcare to cover their working hours and travelling time. Childminders, along with relatives, play a vital role in filling the gaps.

There is a marked discrepancy between the Ofsted ratings of nurseries and childminders in more advantaged areas compared with others. Among childminders, 39 per cent working in the most disadvantaged areas failed to achieve a 'good' or 'outstanding' rating from Ofsted, compared with only 23 per cent in more prosperous areas (Ofsted, 2012).

WORKING TOWARDS MORE INTEGRATED SERVICES

The Laming report following on the death of Victoria Climbié (Laming, 2003), together with early findings from the EPPE project, initiated an innovative policy framework called *Every Child Matters* (ECM). The goals were not just to protect children from harm but to stress their entitlement to positive outcomes: being healthy, staying safe, enjoying and achieving, making a positive contribution and economic wellbeing. The focus on outcomes instead of services underpinned the ten-year strategy *Choice for Parents, the Best Start for Children* (HM Treasury, 2004). It led to a series of legislative and policy initiatives, some of which survived the 2010 change of government (although ECM was quietly allowed to fall into abeyance). These included the development of integrated education, health and social care provision, extended school hours and services targeted on the most disadvantaged children (see Chapters 15 and 19).

ESTABLISHING NATIONAL STANDARDS

The 2004 ten-year childcare strategy was an attempt to rationalise existing early years initiatives and create a coherent approach to improving the quality of services. The government had brought under one legislative umbrella all kinds of early years provision and was investing large sums of public money, so it needed to find a way of showing how the expenditure would benefit the nation. One answer was the introduction of a national curriculum for children under compulsory school age, the Early Years Foundation Stage.

EARLY YEARS FOUNDATION STAGE (EYFS)

In England, the **EYFS** became a statutory requirement from September 2008 for every type of 'early childhood service', to be enforced through inspections by Ofsted on a four-year cycle. A review two years after the EYFS was introduced concluded that it had raised standards but endorsed the widespread view that it was far too complicated and burdensome for practitioners (Tickell, 2011). A streamlined EYFS was therefore published in 2012. From a policy perspective, perhaps the most important part of the review was the section on the workforce, which noted that the majority of those attracted to work in the sector were young girls with poor academic qualifications or none. The report went on to state, 'the need to create a strong, resilient and experienced workforce has been a compelling message to this review' (Tickell, 2011: 42) and urged the government to 'maintain the ambition' for a graduate-led sector. The rapid expansion in the number of university degree courses in Early Childhood Studies, following the establishment of the first ones in Bristol and Swansea, would have made this a realistic aim if comprehensive changes to qualifications, pay and career routes had been implemented, as recommended by Professor Nutbrown's (2012) review of sector.

NEW DIRECTIONS IN WALES AND SCOTLAND

Proposals for the Welsh Foundation Phase Framework for children aged three to seven years were described by the then First Minister, Rhodri Morgan, as a break with 125 years of British educational practice. Drawing on approaches from, among others, Nordic countries and New Zealand, it adopted an active play-based approach to learning in both indoor and outdoor environments, balancing teacher-led and child-initiated activities (see Maynard et al., 2013). Early years settings are inspected by Estyn (equivalent to Ofsted), but, given the approach promoted in the Foundation Phase Framework, there is less incentive for services designed for three- and four-year-olds to institute formal teaching and achieve curriculum goals tied to age, instead of recognising that children's development does not follow a linear pathway. It is also worth noting that Wales was the first UK country to appoint a Children's Commissioner and to adopt a rights-based policy to ECEC. Although it has not followed England in joining up care and education formally, the Flying Start programme launched in 2005 lays a strong emphasis on integrating childcare, early learning, parenting and health services. A later initiative, *Building a Brighter Future: Early Years and Childcare Plan* (July 2013) preserved the ECM approach under a different name, and made it statutory in the Well-being of Future Generations (Wales) Act 2015. In relation to children aged nought to seven, it sets out seven areas with criteria for assessing progress, to be reviewed at specified intervals.

In October 2016 the First Minister of Scotland, Nicola Sturgeon, announced a plan to extend entitlement to free early education and childcare and make it more flexible and adapted to the varied needs of parents, with funding to follow the child rather then tied to particular providers. However, the underlying weaknesses in the structure of the workforce remain unresolved throughout the UK, as discussed in the next section.

PROFESSIONAL DEVELOPMENT AND TRAINING

Having accepted the main recommendations of the Tickell review, the (Labour) government commissioned a review of early years education and childcare qualifications from Professor Cathy Nutbrown. Her final report, *Foundations for Quality*, made nineteen recommendations designed to ensure that staff are 'as good as they can be' and have the skills, knowledge and understanding to make the most of the government's investment. Nutbrown argued that working in the early years sector should be 'a recognized and fulfilling career able to attract the very best staff, *both men and women*' (Nutbrown, 2012, emphasis added). The (new) government claimed that it had accepted most of the recommendations and incorporated them into *More Great Childcare* (DfE, 2013), but Nutbrown herself published an angry response accusing the government of 'Shaking the Foundations of Quality'. She claimed that the overall thrust of her report had been brushed aside and most of her recommendations rejected (Nutbrown, 2013). Almost the only change resulting from the Nutbrown report was the condition for early years apprentices and practitioners to have passed GCSE English and Maths in order to count in staffing ratios. It is a sad comment on the educational level of the workforce that this resulted in a crisis in recruitment, and was modified to become an exit rather than an entry requirement and later changed from GCSEs to functional skills. Unlike in other European countries, early years educators in Britain do not have qualified teacher status, and have pay and working conditions much inferior to teachers of older children. The unique opportunity to rationalise the creaking and outdated educational and career structure of early years work was lost.

BABIES AND YOUNG CHILDREN IN FOSTER CARE

Increased hours of free childcare are intended to benefit in particular disadvantaged children, but as noted earlier, one especially disadvantaged group, young children in local authority care, has been almost entirely overlooked. An extensive literature search found only one UK research report (Ward et al., 2012) on the subject and three journal papers, all from the US (Lipscomb and Pears, 2011). In contrast to the active debate on the qualifications and training of practitioners in early education and day care settings, little is known about foster carers who look after babies and toddlers full time and there is no specific research on the subject (Cameron et al., 2015). Official policy is that these children should all be reunited with relatives or placed for adoption. In practice, this does not happen for at least half of those concerned (Jackson and Hollingworth, 2017).

In addition two trends have led to many more young children being drawn into the care system and often remaining there for long periods. One is the fluctuation in adoption rates and the other is the increased number of babies removed from their mothers at birth (Broadhurst et al., 2016). This number rose from 802 in 2008 to over two thousand in 2013, an increase of 151 per cent over five years.

These children, who have usually suffered extreme adversity, need highly skilled care if they are to recover and achieve a good level of development (Jackson and Hollingworth, 2017). However, discussion on the subject with a senior civil servant revealed that there is no government policy relating to young children in foster care. Selection and training of foster carers is a matter for local authorities. There are no educational qualifications for applicants, not even basic literacy. Some carers specialise in short-term care for the youngest age group, but we have no evidence on the quality of the care they provide. Unlike childminders, they are not required to deliver the EYFS curriculum and most training focuses on older children, who are more likely to be overtly problematic. Cameron et al. (2015) suggest that many of the later problems of children who enter care in early childhood, such as attachment disorders and school failure, can be traced back to multiple placements and an unstimulating early environment.

Looked after children are one of the categories entitled to fifteen hours of free childcare from the age of two, but there is no available information on how many of these places are taken up or in what kinds of settings or, if they do attend, to what extent it contributes to their development. This is an area where research is urgently needed.

CONCLUSION

This chapter has briefly traced the political and policy developments relating to services for young children in the recent decades. It has highlighted the blurring of the boundaries between the public and private domains – largely linked to women's employment and child poverty levels – and the ideological basis for policy decisions, which have seen fluctuations in support and funding levels. These decisions have been shown to influence provision and practice and include the introduction of national curricular frameworks and professional education requirements and expectations. However, some areas remain less well developed in terms of political interest and intervention and these include foster care arrangements for babies and very young children.

Key points

- ECEC policy and services in Britain have been slow to adapt to changing economic and social conditions. The pattern of services set in the 1960s still underlies provision today. New Labour policies seemed to signal a great leap forward but policy and provision are again in decline.
- Children's Centres, once seen as the most successful element of the 1998 Childcare Strategy, are closing weekly. Childcare remains on the UK government's agenda principally as a means of reducing the cost of welfare payments by enabling more mothers to enter and stay in the workforce, and early education is supported in so far as it makes a contribution to this aim.
- The concept of childcare as a public service, never strong in the UK, has virtually disappeared. In England, most ECEC other than nursery education in schools, is only available from private providers charging high fees.
- The dilemma of how to reconcile quality and costs remains as insoluble as ever: huge inequalities persist in different parts of the country in the availability of high quality early education and between middle-class and low-income areas.
- The policy commitment to universally available educational provision for three- and four-year-olds looks more secure than in the past. National standards have been set for all forms of early years provision receiving state funding.
- There is growing recognition of the demand from working parents for flexible forms of childcare more closely matched to their hours of work.
- More early years settings are committed to the ethos of inclusion, taking account of ethnic and cultural differences and acknowledging the increasing diversity of family forms.

Recommended reading

Fitzgerald, D. and Kay, J. (2016) *Understanding Early Years Policy* (Fourth Edition). London: Sage, provides a useful timeline and an account of the way early childhood policy and provision of services are shaped by multiple external factors.

CHILDREN'S RIGHTS AND THE LAW

NIGEL THOMAS

CONTENTS

INTRODUCTION

The aims of this chapter are to introduce some key ideas about children's rights, to show how these are expressed in international instruments such as the United Nations Convention on the Rights of the Child, and then to use this as a foundation to explore the law relating to children, particularly in England and Wales, and how it expresses – or fails to express – children's rights. The chapter concludes with some reflections on the role of the Children's Commissioner.

THEORIES OF RIGHTS

According to *The Oxford English Dictionary*, a right is 'a justifiable claim, on legal or moral grounds, to have or obtain something, or to act in a certain way'. We can distinguish between legal rights, which are based in law and whose existence is therefore a question of fact, and moral rights, which are based in ethics and whose existence is a question of value.

A right is a claim, entitlement or demand. A right may be absolute – but is not necessarily so. Rights are not the same as wants or needs: they have a *fundamental* quality that justifies the force attaching to them. Cranston (1967) and Worsfold (1974) propose three essential criteria for rights – they should be practicable (consistent with conceptions of justice), universal (in that they apply to everyone) and paramount (i.e. important enough to override other considerations).

A distinction is often made between liberty rights, such as the right not to be imprisoned without good cause, and welfare rights, such as the right to a home or to a basic income. Justifications of rights may be based either on 'will', and so linked with membership of a *community of rational autonomous individuals*, or on 'interest', and so based on our membership of a *community who share needs and interests*. Those who favour a justification based on 'will' are likely to be more interested in liberty rights; those who accept a justification based on 'interest' may be prepared to consider welfare rights.

Whichever justification is favoured, rights always appear to be based on some idea of membership of a community. This raises questions about *who is included*. A conception of rights that emphasises rationality and 'will' may exclude adults with severe learning disabilities, or young children, while a conception that emphasises our common needs and interests may also be more inclusive.

THEORIES OF CHILDREN'S RIGHTS

Until the twentieth century, discussions of human rights made little if any reference to children, and the extent to which children can be bearers of rights has been much contested since then. Although campaigns to promote rights for children have gathered strength in the past hundred years, there has not always been agreement about what those rights are. A fundamental question is whether children are 'rights-bearers' in the same way as adults, or whether they are in need of special protection that justifies curtailing their freedom. One way to look at it is this:

1. Children have certain kinds of rights because they are fundamentally the same as adults. This includes rights to make decisions about their own lives.
2. Children have other kinds of rights because they are more vulnerable and dependent than adults. This includes care and protection, and it may include some restrictions on their freedom; but these restrictions must be justified and proportionate.

Children's rights are sometimes divided into 'participation' rights, which entitle children to take part in social and political life, and 'provision' and 'protection' rights, to ensure that children grow up safe and healthy.

Theoretical objections to the promotion of children's rights take two main forms. One line of argument objects to children having *welfare* and *protection* rights, on the grounds that children indeed ought to be looked after, but that it is misleading to express this in terms of 'rights', rather than adult *obligations* (O'Neill, 1992). Objections to *participation* rights are made on the basis that children are not competent to exercise these rights and must wait until they are adult (Purdy, 1992).

A strong statement of children's rights was made by Holt (1975), who argued 'that the rights, privileges, duties, responsibilities of adult citizens [should] be made available to any young person, of whatever age, who wants to make use of them'. This would include not only the right to vote, but 'the right to be legally responsible for one's life and acts', 'the right to direct and manage one's own education' and the right 'to choose or make one's own home'.

Others are less radical. Archard (2015) distinguishes between 'libertarian' and 'caretaker' interpretations of children's rights, with the former favouring maximum freedom and equality with adults, while the latter is more cautious and protective. Archard himself argues, while not accepting the libertarian case fully, that it is a good starting point as it challenges us to justify any restrictions on children's liberty rather than accepting all restrictions without question.

There is a growing consensus that children do have rights and that these include at least some rights that equate to the 'liberty' or 'participation' rights of adults. This consensus is forcefully expressed in a series of international agreements, of which the best known and most important is the United Nations Convention on the Rights of the Child.

DECLARATIONS OF CHILDREN'S RIGHTS

Among the foremost advocates of children's rights in the first half of the twentieth century were Eglantyne Jebb and Janusz Korczak. Korczak was a Polish paediatrician and pedagogue who ran child-centred orphanages, with children's parliaments and a children's newspaper (Lifton, 1988). Jebb was the founder of Save the Children, set up to assist child refugees after the First World War. In 1924 she persuaded the League of Nations to adopt a Declaration of the Rights of the Child, by which:

1. The child must be given the means needed for its normal development, both materially and spiritually.
2. The child that is hungry should be fed; the child that is sick should be helped; the erring child should be reclaimed; and the

orphan and the waif should be sheltered and succoured.
3. The child must be first to receive relief in times of distress.

4. The child must be put in a position to earn a livelihood and must be protected against every form of exploitation.
5. The child must be brought up in the consciousness that its best qualities are to be used in the service of its fellow men.

In 1948 the United Nations adopted an amended version of Jebb's Declaration, and then in 1959 a more extensive Declaration. In 1979 Poland, inspired by the memory of Korczak, proposed a Convention on the Rights of the Child, which would be a formal treaty and therefore binding on states that ratified it.

THE UNITED NATIONS CONVENTION ON THE RIGHTS OF THE CHILD (UNCRC)

The Convention adopted by the General Assembly of the United Nations in 1989 and over the next three years was ratified by almost every country in the world (the only exceptions now being South Sudan and the USA). States that have ratified the Convention (known as States Parties) have to report at regular intervals to the Committee on the Rights of the Child on their progress in implementing Convention rights. (The Committee also issues advice to States Parties on interpretation and implementation, through General Comments.)

The Convention requires States Parties to extend the rights in the Convention to every child without discrimination, and in all their actions concerning children to make their best interests a primary consideration (Articles 2 and 3). Forty-one articles set out in detail children's rights to an identity and a family life, to education and health care, to protection from abuse and harm and to participate fully in their cultures and communities. The remaining thirteen articles specify the duties of states to publicise and implement the Convention and the process for ratifying and amending it.

PARTICIPATION RIGHTS

Unlike earlier statements, the United Nations Convention on the Rights of the Child includes children's rights to participate in decision-making. Article 12 of the Convention says that:

> States Parties shall assure to the child who is capable of forming his or her own views the right to express those views freely in all matters affecting the child, the views of the child being given due weight in accordance with the age and maturity of the child.

The following five articles assert children's rights to freedom of expression, thought and assembly, privacy and access to information. In other words, children are seen as bearers of liberty rights as well as welfare rights.

In the period since 1989 there has been a dramatic increase in the attention paid to children's participation rights, especially by governments and non-governmental organisations. Laws and policies have been reframed to give expression to these rights, at least to some extent. The Committee has made it clear that Article 12 applies to children as a group, as well as to individual children. As organisations working for children and young people have shifted the emphasis of their programmes to a 'rights-based' rather than a 'needs-based' approach, participation has become an increasingly prominent feature of that work; and newer organisations have been set up whose primary purpose is to promote participation, some of them led by children and young people (see Thomas, 2007, 2011; Percy-Smith and Thomas, 2010). How much difference that participation has yet made to policies and services, or to the reality of children's lives, is not entirely clear. One limitation is that children themselves have not had access to a process that enables them to claim their rights or challenge governments, except in countries where the Convention is incorporated into national law. Since 2014 an Optional Protocol to the CRC has created such a route, but so far only a minority of countries (not including the United Kingdom) have signed or ratified the Optional Protocol.

YOUNG CHILDREN'S RIGHTS

So how do theories of children's rights apply to children in the earliest years? If one accepts that it makes sense to talk of 'rights' to care, health, education and welfare, then such rights apply regardless of age (and younger children's greater vulnerability may mean that their entitlement has greater urgency). If one takes the view that rights have to be claimed by 'rational autonomous beings', then the door opens to questions about who has sufficient rationality to be included and whether this is limited by age. If rights are something one grows into, when and how does this happen? If rights are something we have from birth, then how are those rights to be exercised by babies and toddlers, who may not know that they have them? A fundamental question is: are young children competent to exercise participation rights?

For a theoretical answer to that question, we can draw on arguments from psychology, and even more from sociology, about how competence is situated in context, achieved and negotiated (see Hutchby and Moran-Ellis, 1998). For a practical response, we should look at evidence from research which shows how very young children, even babies, can express views, preferences and wishes with subtlety, if they are communicated sensitively, respectfully and imaginatively (see Alderson, 1993; Clark, 2005; Clark and Moss, 2011). It is also valuable to consult the General Comment on implementing child rights in early childhood (UNCRC, 2006).

HOW RIGHTS ARE EXPRESSED IN LAW

It could be said that all laws have an impact on children directly or indirectly. Laws governing health, housing and welfare benefits have a major impact on children's lives, although they do not directly govern what children do or how their parents look after them. Education and employment laws have a more direct effect on children; they spell out who is expected to go to school and what kind of education they should receive, or at what age children may work for payment. Criminal justice law makes specific provision for children and how they should be treated if they are thought to have committed an offence.

However, the laws that have the most profound impact on individual children's lives, and that may affect all children including the very youngest, are the laws governing children's care and upbringing. It is these laws that will be the main focus of this chapter. The legislation of most concern to us will be the Children Act 1989, which is the main provision directly concerned with children's welfare in England and Wales. The Act sets out the framework for the relationship between children, parents and the state. It provides for resolution of disputes between family members and defines the circumstances in which the state may intervene in family life. It lays down the powers and duties of local authorities to provide for children's welfare, and provides safeguards against poor care, whether provided by private individuals and organisations or by state agencies (see Chapter 14). The equivalent laws in other parts of the UK are the Children (Scotland) Act 1995 and the Children (Northern Ireland) Order 1995, which are based on the same guiding principles but also incorporate significant differences.

THE DEVELOPMENT OF LEGAL PROVISION FOR CHILDREN

Laws to protect children developed in the mid-nineteenth century, beginning with factory legislation designed to prevent excesses of exploitation in the workplace, and leading to the novel idea that children should not be working at all. This was followed by laws prohibiting cruelty to children, an important development because it meant a breach in the principle of family privacy and parental (mainly paternal) authority. Laws to provide for children's welfare followed later, with the introduction of state elementary education, then compulsory health surveillance (following alarm at the poor condition of recruits to the army), and finally the extension of duties under the Poor Law to provide for destitute children.

On these foundations developed the modern law relating to children, through a series of landmark Acts of Parliament during the course of the twentieth century. The Children Act 1933 established a juvenile court system, introduced a 'fit person order' – where children could be removed from home without an offence being proved – and established a schedule of offences against children which is still in use today. The Children Act 1948 ended the Poor Law treatment of children, required local authorities to appoint Children's Officers, introduced the provision of care as a service to children and families rather than as a punishment, and improved the supervision of foster homes. The Children and Young Persons Act 1969 reformed the juvenile justice system on welfare principles (although it was never fully implemented) and established non-punitive grounds for children to be removed to local authority care.

It appears that the history of childcare legislation is characterised by an increasing emphasis on children's welfare and a shift away from 'cruelty' to 'care' as the key operating concept. It is also characterised by an increase in mutual accountability between families and the state; the first stage in this was the breaking of the barrier against any intrusion into family privacy or parental authority, while the second stage was bringing parents back into the picture as participants in the decision to provide 'care'.

What is missing up to this point is any real voice for children themselves, who are conceived of as *done to* rather than *doing*. Not until the Children Act 1975 did the law consider a child's wishes and feelings, and then only in a limited way. With the Children Act 1989 the law began to take children seriously as people with the right to a say in their own lives.

THE CHILDREN ACT 1989

The Children Act 1989 was more wide ranging than any previous legislation because it brought together the *public law*, governing state services to children and child protection, and the *private law*, governing family life and disputes over children's upbringing, in the same statutory framework. The Act reformed the way in which courts intervened in family disputes and the kind of decisions they could make. It reformed the duties and powers of local authorities and the way in which services were provided, especially when children are looked after away from home. Finally, it reformed the arrangements for regulation and inspection of childcare services.

Part One of the Act sets out over-arching principles (the 'welfare principles') for dealing with children's cases. These require that:

- When a court is making a decision about the upbringing of a child it should treat the child's interests as paramount.
- A court should assume that delay in resolving a case is against the child's interests.
- A court should not make any order in respect of a child unless satisfied that to do so is better for the child than making another order, or no order at all.
- In deciding what is in a child's interests the court must have regard to a set of eight factors often referred to as the 'welfare checklist' – the first of which is 'the ascertainable wishes and feelings of the child'.

Other important principles in the Act include:

- The concept of 'parental responsibility', which any legal parent has automatically and which others can acquire and which cannot be taken away except by the adoption of a child. Absent parents are expected to remain involved in their lives.
- The 'presumption of contact' – i.e. the presumption that contact is normally in the interests of children and should be positively promoted when they are separated from a parent or other significant person.

Part Two provides for disputes between parents and other relatives to be settled under the above principles. The starting assumption is that children's upbringing will be a matter of agreement between those involved, without the need for court intervention. The court only becomes involved if the parties cannot agree and someone applies for an order to be made. The most common orders are *residence* orders and *contact* orders, which decide whom a child will live with and who will have contact with the child.

Part Three of the Act, which governs services to children and families, defines when a child is 'in need' and the services to which they or their family are entitled (see Chapter 14). These services may include 'accommodation' if, for example, the child's parents are temporarily or permanently unable to provide appropriate care. This normally requires the agreement of a parent (or the child if he or she is over sixteen years). A child accommodated in this way is not 'in care' and the local authority does not have parental responsibility. They are, however, required to assess the child's needs and agree a plan with the parents and child.

Part Four of the Act relates to 'care and supervision' of children. It sets out the circumstances in which children may be removed from their families or the powers of parents restricted, and the process by which this is done. Applications may be made by the local authority or **NSPCC**.

Parents and children have the right to oppose the order and be represented. A 'children's guardian' is appointed to safeguard the child's interests and advise the court. Before making an order the court must be satisfied that: the child is suffering or likely to suffer 'significant harm' if action is not taken. Once this is established, cases are dealt with under the 'welfare principles' and the court is obliged to do what is best for the child. This can include making a care order, which means that the child is committed to the care of the local authority, which then has parental responsibility.

All children who are either accommodated or subject to care orders are 'looked after' within the terms of the Act. Agencies have a duty to safeguard and promote the child's welfare, to consult the child and family before making decisions, to review the child's case at regular intervals and to hear any complaints and representations.

Part Five of the Act deals with protection of children. It provides orders which courts may make in order to protect children from significant harm and sets out the duties of local authorities to investigate situations of risk. Other agencies have duties to assist the local authority with their enquiries. This provision is the basis for the 'child protection system', the apparatus of inter-agency work to protect children, including case conferences and child protection registers. This is a distinctively UK response to the problem of how to protect children from harm. Continental approaches tend to be based more on encouraging families to seek help on their own terms. In the UK, as in other English-speaking countries, the emphasis is on investigation, often leading to legal action. In the UK there also is a legal requirement on agencies to work together to investigate abuse and plan a response.

The Childcare Act 2006 has placed duties on English local authorities to improve the wellbeing of young children and reduce inequalities between them, in addition to a series of provisions requiring the provision of specific services (see Chapter 11).

THE CHILDREN ACT 1989 AND CHILDREN'S RIGHTS

The Children Act 1989 aims to strike a balance between the rights of children to autonomy and a voice, their right to care and protection and the rights of parents to bring up their children in the way they see fit. The Act puts into effect some of the key provisions of the UNCRC: the right of the child to live with his or her parents or at least to maintain contact with them; the right to protection from abuse and neglect; the right to suitable care if the child is not able to live with their family. Other legislation in the UK gives some effect to other Convention rights, such as the right to a good education and to participation in recreation and culture, the disabled child's right to care and education to help lead a full and active life, and the right to social security and an adequate standard of living. In each case there are limits on how fully the rights are implemented, which have been well scrutinised in reports such as *Righting the Wrongs* (Save the Children, 2006).

The Article of the UNCRC that has perhaps attracted most attention is Article 12, which gives the child the right to express an opinion and to have that opinion taken into account, in particular in any judicial and administrative proceedings affecting them. The Children Act 1989 made that right a reality at least for some children – those whose upbringing is being considered by a court and those who are looked after by a local authority (Thomas, 2000). It does not give the same right to children living in their own families. The Children (Scotland) Act 1995 does give parents a duty to take account of their children's wishes in making decisions affecting them, so that children in Scotland have more rights in this respect than those in England and Wales.

THE HUMAN RIGHTS ACT 1998

The European Convention on Human Rights was signed in 1950 by the Council of Europe (an organisation formed after the Second World War, which has nothing to do with the European Union and which now includes fifty-seven states). The Convention was intended to ensure that the atrocities of the Nazi era could not be repeated. It has become the basis of much European law, under the direction of the European Commission on Human Rights and the European Court of Human Rights in Strasbourg. Human rights under the Convention include the right to life, liberty, fair treatment at trial, privacy and respect for family life, freedom of thought, conscience and religion, freedom of expression, assembly and association, and the right to marry and found a family. The Convention prohibits torture, inhuman or degrading treatment, slavery, and also prohibits discrimination in enjoyment of all of the above rights.

By passing the Human Rights Act 1998, Parliament incorporated the European Convention into UK national law. The Act says that a court or tribunal determining any question in connection with a Convention right must take into account any judgment or decision of the European Court or Commission, and that as far as possible national law must be interpreted in a way which is compatible with the Convention. If national law is incompatible with the Convention, the court may make a 'declaration of incompatibility' and the government then has the power to amend the legislation by making an order.

The Human Rights Act also says that it is unlawful for a public authority to act in a way which is incompatible with a Convention right. A person may bring proceedings against a public authority which has acted unlawfully in this way; the court can order the authority to act differently and may also award damages.

Although the Human Rights Act and the European Convention do not mention children directly, they are clearly included. Article 14 prohibits discrimination 'on any ground such as sex, race, colour, language, religion, political or other opinion, national or social origin, association with a national minority, property, birth or other status'. It does not specifically mention age, but there is nothing in the Convention to suggest that all rights do not apply equally to children. Although the Human Rights Act is less comprehensive than the UNCRC, it has more 'teeth' because it can be enforced by the courts (Lyon, 2007).

THE CHILDREN ACT 2004 AND CHILDREN'S COMMISSIONERS

The Children Act 2004 contains a number of important reforms to provision for children. One of the key reforms is the establishment of the Children's Commissioner for England (following similar appointments in Wales, Northern Ireland and Scotland). Children's Commissioners are there to promote and safeguard the rights of children and young people and to be a voice and champion independent of government. All the Commissioners have slightly different powers and duties; the English Commissioner's duties were originally weaker, but were strengthened in 2014 following the Dunford Review in 2010 (see below).

It remains to be seen how successful the Children's Commissioners will be in advancing the rights and interests of children; however, their introduction arguably represents a major step forward in basing policy and services on children's rights and wishes, rather than simply on their needs as perceived by adults.

The European Union has now begun to take a serious interest in children's rights and across Europe Children's Commissioners and Ombudspersons are working together with the EU and the Council of Europe to promote rights-based approaches (Stalford et al., 2011).

THE CHILDREN AND YOUNG PERSONS ACT 2008

The Children and Young Persons Act 2008 further extended the statutory framework for children in care, aiming to improve the stability of placements and the educational experience and attainment of young people in local authority care. It also strengthened the role of Independent Reviewing Officers, who are expected to ensure that local authorities prioritise children's best interests and take account of their wishes and feelings. This reflects a growing emphasis on the importance of independent people such as visitors, advocates or inspectors in a child's life, particularly when they are in care (Thomas, 2008).

THE CHILDREN AND FAMILIES ACT 2014

The Children and Families Act 2014 introduced a range of important amendments to childcare law. Many of these relate to adoption, reflecting a government view (not universally shared) that more children could be adopted if artificial barriers were removed (see Chapter 14). The Act also made major reforms to the duties of local authorities in relation to disabled children and their families. In addition, there were changes to the court processes for care and protection, to fostering and adoption, to childcare and parental leave, and to the rules governing employment of children. As a result of the Dunford Review as mentioned above, the Act strengthened the role of the Children's Commissioner for England, for the first time stating that the Commissioner's 'primary function is promoting and protecting the rights of children', a move previously resisted by leading members of government. The Office of the Children's Rights Director for England was abolished and its function transferred to the Children's Commissioner.

RIGHTS OF CHILDREN AND YOUNG PERSONS (WALES) MEASURE 2011

Most of the changes in the Children and Families Act apply only to England, as Wales increasingly develops its own legal framework. The Rights of Children and Young Persons (Wales) Measure 2011 is a distinctively Welsh approach to children's rights. It requires that Welsh Ministers must, when exercising any of their functions, have due regard to the Convention on the Rights of the Child. They must publish a scheme setting out how they propose to do this, and report at intervals on this. They also have a duty to promote knowledge and understanding of the Convention amongst the public, including children.

CONCLUSION

This chapter has introduced the theoretical basis for children's rights, and some of the ways in which they are contested; and has shown how the adoption of the United Nations Convention on the Rights of the Child was a key moment in the development and implementation of these ideas. We have seen that even young children have rights, and how UK law attempts, in a rather uneven way, to give expression to children's rights, including the right to take part in decisions. In examining key provisions of the Children Act 1989, we have also learned something about the ways in which the law frames childcare policy, including the potential impact of the Human Rights Act 1998. Space has not permitted us to look in similar depth at other areas of law, or at the detailed provisions in Scotland and Northern Ireland, which in some respects are different from those in England and Wales.

Key points

- Children's rights are much debated. Who has rights, and what rights they have, depends on who is regarded as a full member of a community, and for children that is a contested issue.
- During the twentieth century claims for children's rights first emerged and became progressively more ambitious including the libertarian demands of the late 1960s.
- The first Declaration of the Rights of the Child in 1924 was succeeded by more extensive statements after the Second World War, culminating in the Convention on the Rights of the Child in 1989. This comprehensive statement included for the first time a child's right to take part in decisions.
- The application of children's rights to very young children is still very limited, but with the right approach they can be included in a variety of ways.
- The law relating to children has developed over the same period, from simple protection from cruelty to a broader concern with children's needs and rights. In England and Wales the Children Act 1989 is a key moment.
- The Human Rights Act of 1998, which incorporated the European Convention on Human Rights into UK law, is also relevant to children.
- The Children Act 2004 established a Children's Commissioner for England (following similar legislation in Wales, Scotland and Northern Ireland). The Children and Families Act 2014 further strengthened the role of the Children's Commissioner, for the first time stating that the Commissioner's 'primary function is promoting and protecting the rights of children'.

——————————— **Recommended reading** ———————————

Archard (2015) (see reference list) provides a very clear, well informed and balanced account of the arguments for and against different theories of children's rights, and the practical and ethical implications.

EARLY CHILDHOOD EDUCATION (ECE)

IRAM SIRAJ

CONTENTS

INTRODUCTION

The United Nations Convention on the Rights of the Child (Article 29, 1) agreed that all children have a right to education:

1. States Parties agree that the education of the child shall be directed to:

   a. The development of the child's personality, talents and mental and physical abilities to their fullest potential;

   b. The development of respect for human rights and fundamental freedoms, and for the principles enshrined in the Charter of the United Nations;

   c. The development of respect for the child's parents, his or her own cultural identity, language and values, for the national values of the country in which the child is living, the country from which he or she may originate, and for civilizations different from his or her own;

   d. The preparation of the child for responsible life in a free society, in the spirit of understanding, peace, tolerance, equality of sexes, and friendship among all peoples, ethnic, national and religious groups and persons of indigenous origin;

   e. The development of respect for the natural environment. (UN, 1989)

The educational component of early years provision has the potential to transform a child's life and set them on a positive learning trajectory for life. A child's education doesn't miraculously begin when they start 'school', it is therefore important to recognise that these principles should extend to all children regardless of age. For many children in their earliest years parents provide a rich educational as well as physical and social environment in the home. Unfortunately research shows us that this is not the case for all children. For many children from families disadvantaged by poverty and/or a lack of **cultural capital**, the quality of the home learning environment is poor and educational provisions of their nursery or playgroup can have a significant and long-term influence upon their abilities, learning and life chances (Schweinhart et al., 1993; Siraj-Blatchford and Sylva, 2004; Sylva et al., 2004; Schweinhart et al., 2005). Education begins at birth (some would argue, even earlier) and to understand the nature of education in the first five years of early childhood three concepts are particularly valuable: 'pedagogy', 'curriculum' and 'emergent development'. The first two of these originate in educational theory and the third is more often applied from developmental psychology. It is important for all those who work with young children to understand the transformative potential of good, early education.

AN EMERGENT CURRICULUM

While curriculum may be considered to define the content or product of teaching, the word 'pedagogy' is used by educationalists to describe the form that the teaching takes or the processes that are involved. Pedagogy is defined here, following Gage (1977, 1985), as 'the science of the art of teaching' and every capable early educator may certainly be considered to be a *practising artist*. The best early childhood educators creatively draw upon their knowledge of the interests and capabilities of the children in their care, and also upon a wide range of material,

cultural and intellectual resources to provide the children with the most effective and reward-
ing stimulation and hands-on learning experiences possible on a day-to-day basis. And, just as
a kind of scientific 'development' may be seen in the work of a great painter (Cezanne comes
to mind as a really good example), the performance of an effective early childhood educator
also develops as they continually reflect upon, critically evaluate and moderate their practice to
achieve excellence. This requires a very good understanding of how children learn, the content
of what they could learn – for example, including a good knowledge of the *Early Years Foundation
Stage* in England (DfE, 2017), the *Curriculum for Wales: Foundation Phase Framework (2015)* (DES,
2015) or the *Curriculum for Excellence* in Scotland (see Education Scotland, 2016) – and the ability to assess, plan and use the child's social and cultural experiences to help them 'access' the
curriculum.

In the context of early childhood education, the term curriculum may be defined broadly as
'all of those experiences, activities and events, whether direct or indirect, intended or otherwise,
that occur within an environment designed to foster children's learning and development'.[1]
Young children are actively observing and exploring all of the time, they learn from everything
that happens in the environment around them. However implicit or *hidden* **the curriculum**
may be in some childcare and education settings, the content of this learning (i.e., the 'curriculum') is thus always determined by the adults who care for them. The notion of a totally 'free'
play environment is really a myth. The material resources (toys, furniture, props) that are selected
and the activities, the social interactions, and the environments that we offer children, define
both the opportunities and the limitations for their learning. The linguistic and cultural context
in which children are immersed even more fundamentally influences what it is that they learn.

'Emergent development' is actually a philosophical notion that dates back to the very earliest writings in nineteenth-century psychology (Sawyer, 2003). In terms of child development,
emergence may be considered to involve processes that occur over time that result in the development of higher order structures of the mind. These may relate to particular intellectual, social
and cultural competencies and capabilities, and research has shown that in the early years they
are initially developed in social interaction with babies and pre-schoolers, as well as the acquisition of a range of communication and collaboration skills in play (see Siraj-Blatchford, 2008).

But it is important to recognise that there is much more than any simple process of accu-
mulation of skills involved in this. According to the principles of 'emergent development', the
developmental structures that finally emerge are *irreducible* to their component parts. In fact,
from the perspective of emergent development, it is considered impossible to deduce the child's
development as a *whole* from any observations of their previously learnt behaviour or behaviours (Sawyer, 2003). This does not mean that we should not learn from our observations of
children but that we accept there is a whole lot more going on than can be observed. Emergent
development requires an emergent curriculum, that is, content which is experienced but not in
the main directly or didactically taught.

'Emergent Literacy' was a term first applied in Marie Clay's doctoral dissertation (1966), and
Whitehurst and Lonigan (1998: 849) cite Sulzby (1989), Teale and Sulzby (1986) and Sulzby and
Teal (1991) in defining the concept as:

---

[1]Adapted from New Zealand Ministry of Education, 1996, p. 10.

the skills, knowledge, and attitudes that are presumed to be developmental precursors to conventional forms of reading and writing … [as well as] … the environments that support these developments.

Clearly this definition may be applied much more widely, with 'Emergent Curriculum' practices and resources being applied to support young children in learning and experiencing the skills, knowledge and attitudes identified as developmental precursors to a much wider range of curriculum subject areas and communities of practice:[2]

> Rather than individual development being influenced by (and influencing) culture, from my perspective, people develop as they participate in and contribute to cultural activities that themselves develop with the involvement of people in successive generations. People of each generation, as they engage in sociocultural endeavors with other people, make use of and extend cultural tools and practices inherited from previous generations. As people develop through their shared use of cultural tools and practices, they simultaneously contribute to the transformation of cultural tools, practices, and institutions. (Rogoff, 2003: 52)

Often this is how young children are learning in the home, in contingent, embedded contexts that they and their family share, often made more explicit through interactions and making meaning with the child.

PLAY AND EARLY CHILDHOOD EDUCATION

Rogoff and others (e.g., Maybin and Woodhead, 2003) have shown that a wide range of *playful activities* progressively engage children in the cultural life of adults and their communities (Rogoff et al., 1993; Rogoff, 2003). Play (see also Chapter 9) is also widely recognised as a leading context for the child's acquisition of communication and collaboration skills and if we apply our conception of 'emergence', then children's day-to-day learning through play may also be seen as contributing towards, but not itself constituting, the achievement of either a series, or continuous process, of irreducible restructurings of the young child's mind[3]:

> A child's play is not simply a reproduction of what (s)he has experienced, but a creative reworking of the impressions (s)he has acquired. (Vygotsky, 2004: 11)

For **neo-Vygotskians** (see Chapters 6 and 9) play is considered to be a 'leading activity' (Leontiev, 1981; Oerter, 1993) but it is important to recognise here that this doesn't mean that play should be considered to predominate in the life of young children, that play is the *only* way that young children learn (see Chapter 4), or that *all* kinds of play promote development or learning. Play provides an important *context* for learning and development, as Vygotsky put it:

---

[2]While the subject of science has been studied in depth as a community of practice (Kuhn, 1970), the concept may be applied much more widely to include schools of art and other scholarly communities.

[3]This may be seen as a 'renaissance' of the mind, and/or as a **gestalt** change.

Only theories maintaining that a child does not have to satisfy the basic requirements of life, but can live in search of pleasure, could possibly suggest that a child's world is a play world. (1933: 1)

But:

The child moves forward essentially through play activity. Only in this sense can play be termed a leading activity that determines the child's development. (1933: 1)

In terms of **empirical progression** we know from decades of research that play begins with solitary play and the child goes on to develop the capability to share, then to co-operate, and finally to collaborate in their play (Siraj-Blatchford, 2009). We also know that these developments open up much wider opportunities for learning. But solitary play, shared play, co-operative and collaborative play are not discrete 'stages' that the child works through.

Even solitary play serves us well at times throughout our adult learning lives! In most theoretical accounts describing the ways in which these different forms of play open up the possibility of learning, the notion of emergent development is often implicit. For example, when describing play as a 'leading activity', it is only being suggested that it should be seen as a driving force in the child's development of new forms of motivation and action.

Recent contributions from neuroscience have supported the idea that children's early experiences and interactions, including those during play, affect the way the brain develops and helps shape its structure (Bee and Boyd, 2013). Within this research, there is acknowledgement of the importance of play as a 'scaffold for development, a vehicle for increasing neural structures and a means by which all children practice skills they need in later life' (Isenberg and Quisenberry, 2002: 33).

Maude et al. (2006) make the connection between play and the physical environment and stress how play involves gross and fine motor skills as highly important in infants' movement development. Any physical education curriculum should be centred around that idea (see Archer and Siraj, 2017).

EFFECTIVE PEDAGOGY AND SUSTAINED SHARED THINKING

The Effective Provision of Pre-school Education (EPPE) research project (Siraj-Blatchford and Sylva, 2004) has provided a large-scale, longitudinal, mixed method research study that followed the progress of over 3,000 children, from age three to eleven (and subsequently through their secondary schools in the EPPSE project – see Sammons et al., 2015). The children started in 141 pre-schools and then entered 800 primary schools across England. The study applied **multi-level modelling** to investigate the separate effects of personal and social and family background, the quality of the learning support provided in the home, and the quality of the learning environment provided by the children's pre- and primary schools, as well as the effectiveness of the pre-/primary schools. The study showed that high quality pre-school education (as assessed by standardised instruments such as the *Early Childhood Environment Rating Scale [revised]*, Sylva, Siraj-Blatchford and Taggart, 2010) can ameliorate the effects of disadvantage by increasing children's learning attainment thereby reducing the effects of social exclusion. High quality early childhood education (ECE) can be a strong equaliser for the most disadvantaged children. While all children benefit from high quality ECE, some only get it through pre-school provision rather than in the home.

Sustained Shared Thinking (SST) was first identified in a qualitative analysis carried out in the *Researching Effective Pedagogy in the Early Years* (REPEY) project undertaken in association with the EPPE project (Siraj-Blatchford et al., 2002; 2003). The REPEY project was developed to identify the most effective pedagogical strategies that were applied in the early years settings to support the development of young children's skills, knowledge and attitudes, and ensure they made a good start at school. The qualitative case studies provided detailed accounts of the learning and teaching that was observed (400 hours of adult observations and 254 episodes of child observations) in 12 of the most effective settings identified by EPPE (from a national sample of 141 settings).

The transcriptions of episodes of SST were subsequently found to provide valuable (concrete) examples of the kind of effective pedagogy that were needed to develop practice. *Sustained Shared Thinking* thus featured in the *Key Elements of Effective Practice (KEEP)* (DfES, 2005) that was distributed to all English pre-school settings, and it has now been included in the national *Early Years Foundation Stage* (EYFS) (see also Chapters 11 and 17).

The REPEY findings may be summarised as follows:

1. **Adult initiated activity** - Effective pedagogues model appropriate language, values and practices. They also encourage socio-dramatic play, and praise, encourage, ask questions, and interact verbally with children. Excellent settings tended to achieve a good balance between teacher-led and child-initiated interactions, play and activities. Two-thirds of activities were child-led but in excellent settings half of these were extended with appropriate, guided, cognitive challenge by the adults.

2. **Child initiated but adult extended activities** - This is a particular form of teacher/practitioner initiation that may also be applied in cases where the child initiated. The most effective settings were found to provide both teacher-initiated group work and freely chosen, yet potentially instructive play activities. 'Extension' was included in the definition of 'sustained shared thinking' (see below), and one of the implications clearly identified in the research was that effective pedagogues require a good knowledge and understanding of the curriculum, and of how children learn.

3. **The provisions of differentiation and formative assessment** - Effective pedagogues assessed children's performance to ensure the provision of challenging yet achievable experiences (i.e., within the Zone of Proximal Development; Vygotsky, 1978) and provide formative feedback. The most effective settings seemed to have shared educational aims with parents supported by regular communication; weekly or monthly dialogues were more effective than termly or annual meetings.

4. **Attention to the relationships between children** - Effective settings viewed cognitive and social development as complementary and they supported children in rationalising and talking through their conflicts and resolving problems for themselves with the help of adults. This was not the case where the adults dominated and told the children what to do.

5. **Sustained shared thinking and open-ended questions** - Adults and children

in the excellent settings were more likely to engage at times in 'sustained shared thinking': episodes in which two or more individuals 'worked together' in an intellectual way to solve a problem, clarify a concept, evaluate activities or extend narratives, etc. During periods of sustained shared thinking (SST) both parties contributed to the thinking and developed and extended the discourse. Associated with SST was also the adult's skilled use of open-ended questioning. These are questions that could genuinely have more than one answer, e.g., 'What do you think?' 'What would you do?' (See Siraj-Blatchford and Manni, 2008b for the analysis of around 6,000 questions asked of children in 12 pre-schools.)

In the UK context, such findings also challenge entrenched beliefs about the value of exclusively encouraging free play, and promoting a solely non-interventionist role for early childhood practitioners (see also Meade, 2013).

INTERNATIONAL EARLY CHILDHOOD EDUCATION (ECE) MODELS

An 'ECE model' is an educational system that combines theory with practice. A number of such models may be identified in the UK and overseas that combine a theoretical knowledge base (that may reflect a particular philosophical orientation). The 'qualities' of several particularly popular and 'successful' international ECE models were identified in the first two *Starting Strong* reports (OECD, 2004, 2006) and as Pramling et al. (2004) observed, a number of interesting commonalities can be found between the most successful (widely replicated) ECE models developed in different countries. Indeed, the OECD drew together features of 'quality' ECE from various international contexts in its *Starting Strong III* 'Quality Toolbox' (OECD, 2012). Similarly, if we consider the accounts of the three ECE models most clearly identifying their pedagogy in the initial *Starting Strong* report, we can see that the particular strategies applied, according to these accounts of the models (by Ferre Laevers, David Weikart and Carla Rinaldi), match very closely with the REPEY findings and with additional evidence from the EPPE study (Siraj-Blatchford and Sylva, 2004). These show positive correlations, as can be seen in Table 13.1.

In the UK, the Effective Early Learning (EEL) project drew upon work carried out by Ferre Laevers (1995) in Belgium to provide a professional development programme that was intended to evaluate and develop quality in early childhood settings (Pascal and Bertram, 1995, 1997). In EEL, effective learning is considered to involve an essentially **symbiotic relationship** characterised by the 'involvement' of the child and the 'engagement' of the teacher. An involved child is one who has focused their attention and is persistent, is intrinsically motivated, rarely distracted, fascinated and absorbed by their activity. An engaged adult is one who shows sensitivity, stimulation and yet grants enough autonomy for the child to make their own judgements and express their ideas. These ideas continue to be influential in shaping high quality ECE practices internationally (see for example Kalliala, 2011).

Reggio Emilia is a district in Northern Italy where over the last forty years, the municipality has developed an extensive network of early childhood services for children from birth

Table 13.1 OECD Curriculum Outlines

	Teacher's initiating activities	Teacher's extending activities	Differentiation and Formative Assessment	Relationships and conflict between children	Sustained Shared Thinking
EEL*	Introducing new activities	Enriching interventions	Observe children	Work out sustaining relations	Engagement
High Scope	Sharing control	Participation as partners	Plan, do, review	Adopt a problem solving approach	Authentic dialogue
Reggio Emilia	Development of short- and long-term projects	Sustaining the cognitive and social dynamics	Teachers first listen don't talk	Warm reciprocal relationships	Reciprocity of interactions
EPPE/REPEY	Correlations found with effective practice	Correlations found with effective practice	Correlations found with effective practice	Correlations found with effective practice	Correlations found with effective practice

Note: 'Teacher' also refers to any other adult in early years settings

Source: OECD, 2004

*'Effective Early Learning' (EEL) (Pascal and Bertram, 1995), referred to as 'Experiential Education' (EXE) in Praming et al. (2004) taken from the work of Ferre Laevers.

to six, providing for over a third of children under three and nearly all children aged three to six. The city has become world famous for the pedagogical work in these services, attracting many visitors from all over the world (see Cagliari et al., 2016). The early childhood services in Reggio understand the young child to be a co-constructor of knowledge and identity, a unique, complex and individual subject, engaging with and making sense of the world from birth, but always doing this in relationship with others, both adults and other children. Reggio pre-schools employ specialist staff such as an *atelierista*, a person who runs the atelier, the school's art studio, and a *pedagogista*, who acts as a key worker providing support with documentation and individual planning for a group of children (often across a group of settings) and their families.

The High/Scope approach (Schweinhart et al., 2005), which has also gained considerable popularity in the UK, is based upon an approach originally developed from the practice of Sara Smilansky. The High/Scope daily routine consists of a cycle of 'planning', 'doing' and 'reviewing'. During planning, children decide what activity they will engage in for the session. Once the 'do' part of the routine is complete, the children recall what they have done during review time. A setting organised to provide the High/Scope experience is divided into interest areas to promote active learning and specific kinds of play and the materials are accessible to the children to allow independence. The adult's role is to participate as a partner in the children's activities and there is an emphasis on positive interaction strategies, allowing children to share control and form authentic relationships with other children. In addition, the adult must support children's learning and extend it by helping children to find solutions to problems they encounter.

There is strength to be found in variety and as each of these models are culturally specific it would be a mistake to make any judgement between them. But as suggested above, there are commonalities that may be identified to inform the development of all provisions. To take just one other significant example, the 'documentation' applied in Reggio Emilia and other ECE models provides a means by which children are encouraged to reflect upon their own work and that of their peers. They, therefore, 'become even more curious, interested, and confident as they contemplate the meaning of what they have achieved' (Malaguzzi, 1993: 63). When the children's efforts, intentions, and ideas are shown so clearly to be taken seriously by the adults this encourages the children to approach their work with greater responsibility, energy and commitment. Documentation also provides a basis for continuous planning based on the evaluation of work as it progresses; it provides a context for communicating with parents which often leads them to become more involved in their child's education. High/Scope takes the emphasis on continuous planning and review that is found in Reggio a stage further, providing a more structured and institutionalised approach in the daily plan-do-review routines.

OTHER COMMON PEDAGOGICAL MODELS OF ECE

A typology of the most commonly applied models of early childhood education has been adapted from a model first developed by Weikart (2000), and is shown in Figure 13.1.

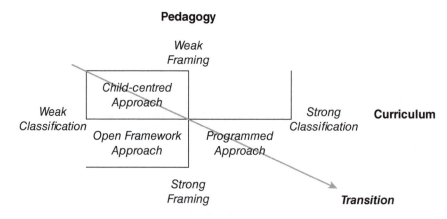

Figure 13.1 Pedagogy (Siraj-Blatchford, 2008)

The major organising principles applied in the typology are pedagogy and curriculum (Bernstein, 1981) and the different forms of early childhood practice are distinguished by applying Bernstein's formulation of classification and framing. 'Classification' refers to the strength of the boundaries placed between 'curriculum subjects'; in the early years we might refer to these as *domains of learning*. Where the curriculum content is clearly defined in terms of school subjects we refer to that as *strong* classification. Framing is about who is in control: who it is that selects, sequences or paces the learning. When framing is weak the child has more apparent control, and when it is strong it is the adult or educator who is most clearly in control. So for example, a collaborative, progressive and permissive classroom illustrates weak framing and a traditional didactic one strong framing.

In the most extreme applications of the child-centred approach in ECE, the teacher responds entirely to the individual child's interests and activities. More often, topic or project themes are adopted that have been chosen especially to appeal to the children's interests. The curriculum emphasis is on encouraging children's independence, their social and emotional growth, creativity and self-expression. The classroom or playroom environment is often rich in stimulus, permissive, and provides for open-ended exploration and discovery.

An open framework approach provides the educator with a strong pedagogic structure (or framework) that supports the child in their explorations and interactions with, and reflections upon, their learning environment. In this model, the curriculum classification is weaker as the child has a good deal of freedom to make choices between the various learning environments that are on offer. But the optional environments (e.g., sand, water, block play, puzzles) are often provided to achieve particular (usually cognitive or conceptual) curriculum aims, and these aims may be more or less acknowledged by the setting. In some settings children's choices are carefully monitored and a broad and balanced curriculum (including physical, creative, social and academic) is encouraged over the medium or long term.

The programmed approach is highly teacher directed providing for little initiative on the part of the child. The rationale for this method is drawn significantly from theories of learning. This pedagogy is usually applied where curriculum objectives may be clearly (and objectively) classified and is likely to be most effective where learning involves the development of simple skills or memorisation. The curriculum content in programmed approaches is often highly structured. This sort of programme has been shown to be detrimental to children's long-term development (Schweinhart and Weikart, 1997).

Some longitudinal studies have shown us that young children provided with programmed instruction sometimes do better than those provided with other forms of pedagogy in the short term (Camilli et al., 2010). But studies also suggest that even when these effects are apparent, the gains are short lived, with significant differences having 'washed out' soon after the provision has ended.

The England and Northern Ireland EPPE 3–11 has now identified some trends and patterns: children who attended medium and high quality pre-schools were found to have higher levels of 'self-regulation' in Year 6 (age eleven, end of primary school) than others. Children who attended high quality pre-schools were also found to display more 'pro-social' behaviour and were less likely to display 'hyperactivity' in Year 6 than children who had attended low and medium quality pre-schools (Sammons et al., 2015). EPPE also shows the importance of having professionals trained specifically in the teaching of young children: graduate teachers as managers of centres or higher proportions of graduate teachers were associated with better outcomes for children. Mixed teams of professionals which included teachers seem to work well (Sylva et al., 2004; Sammons, Sylva, Hall et al., 2017).

CONCLUSION

Of course, each of the approaches that are described here and in the *Starting Strong* reports remain 'ideal types', and the practices in many settings will involve a combination of all of them. The challenge for early childhood educators is to provide a gradual and supportive transition, as the children become more capable, that stimulates learning and development while avoiding any risk of regression or failure. This transition is often reflected in changes in the strength of the classification and framing offered to children as they get older (as shown by the arrow in Figure. 13.1).

The EYFS and the Curriculum for Wales promote a pedagogy which involves negotiating and co-constructing the curriculum through playful processes of 'sustained shared thinking' (SST) that may be initiated by either the adult or the child. The question of who initiates this SST is actually less relevant as long as both parties are committed to playing an equal part in determining its focus and direction (its co-construction) in 'collaborative free flow'. In a sense, 'initiation' is taken in turns as different material and symbolic resources are drawn upon, and each play is extended as a more or less unique improvisation. As children develop the capability and are motivated to play with peers, the curriculum guidance in the UK encourages us to continue to provide children with a rich range of experiences and resources to draw upon in collaborative play and to support them in developing a greater awareness of their development and learning. Ultimately, in school, young children take pleasure in learning for its own sake and restrict their play to scheduled playtimes, more disciplined creative activities, and their involvement in a variety of games with more formal rules.

Longitudinal studies from America provided early evidence of the effectiveness of pre-school education. The High/Scope Perry Pre-school evaluation showed the substantial benefits that were to be gained through pre-schooling for children brought up in low-income households and at high risk of school failure. Many studies have also shown that social and motivational elements of pre-school programmes are as important as academic outcomes. Early childhood education really matters.

—————————— Key points ——————————

This chapter has highlighted:

- The transformative potential of high quality ECE for children's abilities, learning and life chances.
- That pedagogy is both an art and a science and EC educators would do well to reflect on, evaluate and modify their pedagogical understandings and practices in a continuing quest for excellence.
- That curriculum consists of processes that are constantly evolving and is contingent upon context and people, including young children in social interaction. It is more than the sum of its constituent parts.
- Play is a 'leading activity', which may contribute towards, but does not constitute, the totality of children's learning experiences.
- Effective pedagogy is characterised by particular, identifiable approaches and features. One important feature is Sustained Shared Thinking (SST). Whether activities are adult-led or child-initiated, collaborative engagement in SST helps to develop and extend thinking and narratives.
- Commonalities can be found in some of the key pedagogic strategies across ECE models in many different countries.

—————————— Recommended reading ——————————

EPPE Technical Paper 10 (Siraj-Blatchford et al., 2003) provides case study illustrations of evidence based, pre-school pedagogy. Available online: http://dera.ioe.ac.uk/18189/14/EPPE_TechnicalPaper_10_2003.pdf [accessed 16.3.17].

CHILD WELFARE AND PROTECTION

DENDY PLATT

CONTENTS

INTRODUCTION

The majority of readers embarking on this chapter will approach it from a relatively informed perspective about the needs of children in general, their development and learning, their care and education, and policies aimed at addressing their needs. Many will be less familiar with the more specialist services that respond to children and young people with more significant needs, where sometimes very difficult decisions have to be taken to promote their welfare. This may include removing children from their families, prosecuting offences against children and providing alternative forms of care such as adoption and fostering.

Public awareness of this type of provision has been informed, in recent years, by high profile cases that have attracted press and media attention. Four such cases have been noteworthy and will be used as examples in this chapter. Peter Connelly's name has been well known in recent years. Originally identified as 'Baby P', he died in 2007 aged seventeen months, following abuse and neglect by his mother and her partner (Haringey Local Safeguarding Children Board, 2009). Daniel Pelka, perhaps less well-known than Peter Connelly, was the middle child of a Polish family who had immigrated to the UK in 2005. Daniel died aged four years eight months on 3 March 2012, following sustained physical and emotional abuse and neglect (Coventry Safeguarding Children Board, 2013). His mother and her partner were found guilty of his murder. In both these cases, considerable media criticism was directed against the various services involved, and, in the case of Peter Connelly, the social work profession was singled out for particular criticism.

The other two cases offer a contrast to these, with interesting insights that will be explored as this chapter unfolds. Shannon Matthews, at the age of nine years, was imprisoned, drugged and tethered by her mother and an accomplice in the accomplice's flat. The mother then presented the events to the world's media as an abduction, with the apparent intention of (fraudulently) obtaining financial donations to assist with finding Shannon. The case was subject to a **serious case review**, although the full findings were never published (BBC News, 2010). The last of the four cases is attracting considerable attention at the time of writing. Strictly speaking, it involves separate cases numbering well into the hundreds. They are the sexual crimes, mainly against children and young people, believed to have been committed by Jimmy Savile in his roles as television presenter and charity fundraiser (Smith, 2016). The allegations were the subject of police investigations and a number of inquiries by the BBC where Savile was employed for a number of years, most important of which was the inquiry by Dame Janet Smith cited above. This chapter will use these cases as material in exploring the work undertaken by child welfare services.

The concept of child welfare implies a relationship between the state and individual families, whereby the state is required to intervene if the care of the children is seen as unacceptable according to certain defined standards. The chapter will consider how child welfare problems come to light, how and when they receive a response and what is involved in those most serious of interventions: the removal of children from their families or compulsory placement for adoption. The difficulties that come to the attention of services include child abuse and neglect, severe financial problems, disability and learning difficulties, social and behavioural problems, and parents who have serious problems controlling their children's behaviour or managing basic care (e.g. provision of adequate food and clothing). The chapter will focus on *social* responses to these problems with only limited attention to health and educational services. It will analyse policy and service provision in a critical manner and will then consider the broader policy orientations underpinning that service provision. The reader is invited to consider ways in which the many policy dilemmas might be resolved.

THE EXTENT OF THE PROBLEM

To consider the prevalence of child welfare problems we can begin with poverty as a general indicator. Recent government statistics show that 3.9 million children[1] in the UK, or 29 per cent of the total child population, were living in poverty in 2015 (Department for Work and Pensions, 2016). The measures used to estimate poverty levels vary, but this figure is based on numbers of children in households earning below 60 per cent of the average (median) income after housing costs. Clearly, only a small minority of children in these circumstances will experience the welfare problems with which this chapter is concerned. However, it is well accepted that child welfare problems generally occur within the context of multiple difficulties, often involving or exacerbated by poverty (Parton, 1985; Cawson et al., 2000; Bywaters et al., 2016). In the cases of Peter Connelly, Daniel Pelka and Shannon Matthews, referred to earlier, it is highly likely that poverty contributed to the problems they faced, although it would have been a background factor rather than the immediate cause.

Regarding child abuse, the World Health Organization uses the term *child maltreatment* to cover all forms of abuse, and its definition of child maltreatment is:

> All forms of physical and/or emotional ill-treatment, sexual abuse, neglect or negligent treatment, or commercial or other exploitation, resulting in actual or potential harm to the child's health, survival, development or dignity in the context of a relationship of responsibility, trust or power. (Butchart et al., 2006: 59)

For the purposes of this chapter, we will focus on the first four of these forms of abuse, because they occur mainly in the family context – which in recent decades has been the predominant concern of child welfare services. Accurate figures regarding prevalence of child maltreatment are very difficult to identify, but a recent study suggested that as many as 14 per cent of adults in the UK may have been victims of severe maltreatment by a parent or guardian while under the age of eighteen years (Radford et al., 2011).

CHILD WELFARE PROBLEMS IN THE COMMUNITY

The ways in which cases of possible child maltreatment come to the attention of services are various. Neighbours may report possible abuse or concerns about poor parenting. Teachers, health visitors, child minders and others may observe children who appear to be having difficulties or may even be injured, and they may hear children's accounts of adverse experiences.

---

[1]A child is defined here as an individual under sixteen years of age, or an unmarried sixteen to nineteen-year-old in full-time non-advanced education.

The police and children's social work services are among the key organisations to which such reports are directed. The role of the police is to investigate crime and their involvement tends to be restricted to situations where the harm to the child has occurred as a result of a possible criminal offence. The role of social work services, generally part of the local authority, is to assess the needs of children referred to them and to take action where appropriate. Generally, the services prioritise the most serious cases, and the interpretation of seriousness is often related to current policy priorities and resource constraints (Platt and Turney, 2014). For example, with domestic violence referrals, a common pattern is to prioritise only children who are physically harmed during an incident of domestic violence (Stanley et al., 2011) – despite current awareness of the emotional damage to children from witnessing domestic abuse. Thus, in the case of Daniel Pelka, there were successive reported incidents of domestic abuse, but follow-up action by the services was limited. Successive governments in the UK have adopted an underlying policy position that child welfare and safeguarding children should be the responsibility of whole communities and not simply of specialist services. State intervention is thus seen as a last resort in dealing with child welfare problems.

Regarding Shannon Matthews, before the simulated abduction took place Shannon appears to have been experiencing neglectful parenting. Neglect involves an ongoing failure to provide the care needed to meet a child's most basic needs. It might become apparent through inadequate nutrition, severe lack of cleanliness, inadequate parental oversight of children, poor clothing and so on. The BBC report (BBC News, 2010) on the Shannon Matthews serious case review suggests that there was involvement by social workers with the family, but that the problems were never serious enough to warrant court action to remove the children. This finding is a good illustration of the difficulties of responding to neglect cases. Often there is a succession of low-level concerns that, individually, do not add up to a picture of actionable abuse. Services sometimes fail to examine the pattern over time (Daniel et al., 2011), although in Shannon's case, even with hindsight, the evidence prior to her abduction may not have been sufficient to warrant her removal. These limitations in responding to neglect cases affect adolescents as well as children (Hicks and Stein, 2009). In the case of Daniel Pelka, a key problem was a failure of communication between services, through which the pattern of neglect might have become clearer.

State provision regarding child welfare problems is governed mainly by the Children Act 1989 in England (see Chapter 12). Regarding the other countries of the UK, the arrangements are similar although each country has its own legislation (Stafford et al., 2012); the present chapter refers to England, but will draw only on provisions that are substantially equivalent, in general terms, to those in Scotland, Wales and Northern Ireland. There are two initial procedures used by children's social workers in responding to alleged child welfare concerns such as those faced by Daniel Pelka or Shannon Matthews. The first is an investigation of suspected child abuse, under s.47 of the Children Act 1989. The second (s.17), is a less formal response in which the family's difficulties are assessed and services such as family support may be offered. Such services are often referred to as 'preventive' (aiming to prevent further harm to the child) and were offered in the case of Daniel Pelka, but met with limited success. In both these responses, emphasis has grown in recent years regarding the importance of focusing on the child and hearing his or her voice; Daniel Pelka's situation would certainly have been helped if his voice had been sought more determinedly with a view to understanding his day-to-day experiences.

Another process might have been relevant to Shannon Matthews' situation prior to the abduction (although it was introduced after her case came to public attention), and it involves less specialist services. In 2008 the then Labour government introduced the Common Assessment Framework, now referred to generally as an **Early Help Assessment** (Ofsted, 2015c, 2015d). It is targeted on children who have additional needs beyond those of the majority population, and their difficulties are less likely to involve multiple family problems or severe allegations of abuse. The assessment can be undertaken by any professional involved with and concerned for the child, such as health visitor, school nurse, teacher, children's centre staff and so forth, and it emphasises preventive interventions. The professionals involved typically meet and co-ordinate the most appropriate form of help from within their own services, and social workers generally become involved only when the problems are more severe. The approach has had mixed success, with some positive experiences of improved support for families and some difficulties linked to inter-professional working and assessment skills (Holmes et al., 2012). As an approach, it is consistent with the viewpoint that the welfare of children is the concern of whole communities and not something that can be hived off as the responsibility solely of specialists such as social work, and child and adolescent mental health services.

In the case of Shannon Matthews, there was significant international press and media attention. Yet despite such close monitoring, the newspapers and TV news programmes failed to uncover her mother's lies. If armies of journalists, almost literally camped outside the family home, were so comprehensively deceived, it is illustrative of the very real problems facing child welfare services in assessing children's needs.

RESPONDING TO SERIOUS CASES

Moving on to serious allegations of maltreatment, two children where professionals failed adequately to recognise the problems were Peter Connelly and Daniel Pelka. Had their situations been understood more fully, the local authority in each case should have used the provisions of the Children Act 1989 to remove them from their parents' or guardians' care. In extreme circumstances, the Children Act enables local authorities to apply to the courts for an **Emergency Protection Order** (s.44) or to use police powers, to allow immediate removal of a child from his or her parents (the term 'parent' is used in this chapter to mean any legitimate carer). These are unusual measures, but may well have been applicable, particularly to Daniel Pelka's situation. Once immediate emergency issues have been resolved, local authorities can apply to the courts for a Care Order (s.31) or Interim Care Order, which will also allow removal of the child(ren), but there is more time and opportunity for assessment, for decision-making and for a full court hearing. There are also options to allow the perpetrator of abuse to be excluded from the family home, rather than the child having to be taken away. This course of action is most often used in cases of alleged sexual abuse.

Care Orders may be made in a wide range of situations, not simply those that come with the label 'child abuse'. Parents with severe cognitive or emotional limitations may have difficulties that become insurmountable in bringing up their children; other children may develop behavioural problems that their parents cannot cope with; problems such as parental drug use or criminality may add up to a picture of worsening childcare. Where the harm to the child is significant a Care Order may be the right answer for the child, although appropriate interventions and support may be offered to try to prevent this happening. The widespread image of the social worker walking in to a family's home and removing a child on their own authority is a long way from the truth. Unless a child has been abandoned by his or her parents, court involvement is always necessary. The test applied by the courts is whether the child has suffered (or is likely to suffer) *significant harm* (Children Act, s.31(2)), and whether that harm is attributable to the care given by the parents. Local authorities must present evidence to satisfy the courts on these particular points; legislation and legal precedent provide guidance regarding interpretation. In our examples, it is unlikely that a court would have turned down a Care Order application in respect of Peter Connelly or Daniel Pelka.

Despite the best efforts of child welfare agencies, many children with serious problems are not identified until well into their childhoods or teenage years, and sometimes not at all. Child sexual abuse is a particular case in point. The NSPCC study cited above showed that in 34 per cent of cases of contact sexual abuse by an adult, no one else knew about the abuse, and in 83 per cent of cases of contact sexual abuse by a peer, no one else knew about it (Radford et al., 2011). Even if someone knew about the abuse, the numbers that come to the attention of the authorities are small. In a previous NSPCC study, 90 per cent of the child sexual abuse identified by the researchers had never been reported (Cawson et al., 2000). The Jimmy Savile case described earlier is one illustration of this difficulty. The allegations only came to light fully after Savile's death, and involved at least 214 recorded crimes, from 1977 through to 2009 (Gray and Watt, 2013). The likelihood, in common with much sexual abuse, is that some of the individuals affected were too frightened to come forward, perhaps because of threats by the perpetrator, and if they had done so they may well not have been believed. For some, there was a lack of trust in the services or in the realistic possibility of successful prosecution. Savile clearly used his power as a celebrity to hide his activities (Gray and Watt, 2013) and possibly even to make some of his victims feel special at the time. Enabling victims of child sexual abuse to come forward, and ensuring that their voices are heard and adequate responses are made, are among the greatest unresolved policy challenges in this field.

Individual cases of physical abuse or neglect that lead to fatal consequences are more likely to get press and media coverage than child sexual abuse. Numbers are, thankfully, small. While the press and the media make great play of serious mistakes by child welfare professionals, the overall picture in the UK gives greater cause for optimism (although not complacency). During the thirty years to 2006, there is evidence that numbers of child abuse related deaths in England and Wales fell by 81 per cent. This constitutes a reduction that was significantly faster than that of child deaths in general (caused by ill health, accidents, etc.), an achievement that was matched only by a handful of other major, developed countries (Pritchard and Williams, 2010). Although it is difficult confidently to attribute these improvements to the success of services – and even a single child death from abuse is one too many – it may be that the work of child protection services made a contribution. A paradox of the child protection system is that professionals operate in a wide range of circumstances and outcomes are affected by a huge number of factors. It is not possible to say that the child protection system is wholly effective, but we can record that there are notable successes as well as notable failings.

CHILDREN IN THE CARE SYSTEM

Children may be placed in public care either as a result of a court order or at the request of their parent(s)/carer(s). Even in the case of a request from parents, the child would not be accommodated by the local authority unless the circumstances met the relevant Children Act criteria. Children in both types of situation are referred to collectively as *looked after children*. The older term, 'children in care' is also commonly used. A Care Order empowers the local authority to place a child with foster carers, in residential care, with relatives or in other suitable accommodation. In many cases, after a period in care, an attempt may be made to return a child to his or her family of origin, although where maltreatment of any type has occurred the success rates can be low (Farmer et al., 2011). If a young child cannot return home, adoption or some other means of achieving a permanent and secure future may be the preferred option.

The numbers of children who are looked after by the state have been increasing steadily in recent years (although significant peaks in numbers also occurred in earlier decades). There were 69,540 looked after children at 31 March 2015 in England, an increase of 6 per cent over the preceding five years.Of these, 75 per cent were in foster care (DfE, 2015b). A recent study by the Child and Family Court Advisory and Support Service, referring to children coming into care via Care Orders, suggests a number of possible explanations for the increase (CAFCASS, 2012). One explanation is the effect of the Peter Connelly case. In part, it seems that this case made local authorities and health workers more aware of the need to act in a timely fashion to protect children, and more cases have consequently been brought to court. There may also have been a reluctance to manage risk when supporting families in the community, although the report suggests that, in general, applications for Care Orders were of an appropriate degree of seriousness. The economic slowdown since 2008 may be relevant, in that services to support families in the community, reduced as part of austerity measures, might otherwise have prevented removal to care. And a court judgment has placed an expectation on local authorities to accommodate homeless older teenagers in the care system where previously they might simply have been offered housing (G versus the London Borough of Southwark [2009]).

Had Peter Connelly or Daniel Pelka been placed in care, their paths would have differed somewhat. In the case of Peter Connelly, if no suitable family carer had been found, given his young age, it is very likely he would have been placed in foster care with a view to eventual adoption. Daniel Pelka would also have been placed in foster care, but adoption would have been more difficult to achieve (see below).

It is important to recognise, therefore, that the placement of children in a new family situation is not the end of their story. Children looked after by local authorities will be affected psychologically for the remainder of their lives, by the harm they have experienced and in some cases by both the trauma associated with being removed and their experiences in care. Some overcome these difficulties better than others, and the stability and consistency of the care they receive is crucially important. Attention has been drawn, in the last decade or so, to the alleged failings of the looked after system. Some politicians, for example, have spoken about poor outcomes affecting such children, particularly regarding educational achievement. However, we now know that the picture is more positive than it is often portrayed. A recent study showed that looked after children do better, educationally, than children who have comparable needs but are not in care (Sebba et al., 2015). Additional educational support was introduced approximately ten years ago for children in care, and is likely to lead to improved outcomes in future years (Berridge, 2012). More broadly, research indicating that children, on balance, do well in the care system is increasingly available (Bullock et al., 2006).

ADOPTION

A key aspiration of those responsible for looked after children is to see them placed on a secure and permanent basis with a single family who can care for them for the remainder of their childhoods. An obvious way to achieve this is to have such children adopted. In the case of Peter Connelly, he might well have been placed in care by the age of twelve months or so, subject to relevant applications to court. Delays – which are detrimental to the children involved – can occur in legal and administrative processes, but it is likely that time savings would be made by what is known as concurrent planning. In other words, the social workers would *at the same time* have worked on the possibilities of both a return home to Peter's birth parents and placement for adoption. If assessment demonstrated that a return home would not meet Peter's needs, then the plans for adoption would all be in place and legal and practical arrangements could be concluded as swiftly as possible.

Unfortunately, the processes outlined here typically can take at least nine months to resolve and for many children cases can go on for more than two years (Sinclair, 2005). Peter Connelly would have been very young if he had been placed for adoption – which, optimistically, might have occurred by the age of eighteen to twenty-four months. A considerable body of research suggests that the chances of successful adoption are reduced incrementally with each additional year of a child's age (Selwyn et al., 2006), and Daniel Pelka might have been affected in this way. The importance of timely placement is well supported by child development theory and research, particularly in relation to infants achieving secure attachments with key caregivers (see Chapter 7). A wide range of research suggests that the best opportunities to support a child's development occur between birth and approximately the age of four years, and that the earlier intervention occurs to establish a permanent home for a child, the better the outcomes (Brown and Ward, 2012).

The difficulty of achieving adoption at an early stage is compounded by the fact that many child welfare problems do not come to light during the first few years of the child's life, and fewer prospective adopters want to adopt older children, large sibling groups or those with complex needs. It would have been much more difficult for Shannon Matthews to be adopted since she would have been nine or even ten years by the time decisions of this kind were being addressed. Furthermore, the prospects of adoption for a minority ethnic child, such as Daniel Pelka, would have been worse. There is evidence, for example, of poorer quality information being collected for black children and of delays caused by attempts to obtain the best possible ethnic match for the child (Selwyn et al., 2010).

INTER-PROFESSIONAL WORKING

This chapter has reviewed the main activities of child welfare services in the UK and has analysed both the potential of these services and the difficulties they face. One area that deserves particular attention is the fundamental role of inter-professional working. Where professionals work together, they can be more effective in co-ordinating a timely response to the child; in building a shared understanding of the child's situation; identifying patterns of care (or lack of care) given to the child; ensuring there is sufficient knowledge of the child to form the basis of a proportionate intervention; and making good decisions by sharing the thinking and the responsibility to do so (see Chapter 19).

Successive inquiries and serious case reviews into child abuse tragedies have endorsed this position. Where things go well, the public don't often hear about it. But where things go wrong, typically there has been a catalogue of major misunderstandings between different professionals, lost documentation, failures to include important people in key meetings and delayed responses to new information. In the case of Daniel Pelka there were significant instances, for example, of information (about possible abuse of Daniel) not being treated with urgency; of concerns not being picked up clearly by senior colleagues or other relevant agencies; of failures to talk to Daniel about his home life; and so on. However, there were also a number of features of Daniel's situation, such as plausible and manipulative behaviour by his mother, that made it more difficult for professionals to uncover the truth. It is important to be aware that failings of professionals often occur in a context of under-resourced, demoralised teams of staff, with difficulties of staff recruitment and retention, and inadequate management (Reder and Duncan, 2004). Successive commentators have identified these as systemic, organisational problems, and that blaming individual professionals for difficulties outside their control is unlikely to be productive (Munro, 2010).

POLICY ORIENTATIONS

In all four of the situations explored in this chapter, many would argue that if key people had listened to the *voices of the children* involved, and sought to understand the child's lived experience, there would have been a much greater chance of preventing further harm from occurring. One way of addressing this and other shortcomings in child welfare services, arguably, is to re-examine the nature of the whole system of provision for vulnerable children. In the past, there has been an often quite polarised debate between a *child protection orientation* and a *family service orientation* (Gilbert et al., 2011). The child protection policy orientation is characterised by a strong focus on responding, often in a legalistic and adversarial way, to reports of child abuse, and a focusing of resources on removing children into the care system when they need to be protected. Systems of this kind are found particularly in English-speaking countries such as the UK, USA and Australia. The family service orientation, by contrast, places greater emphasis on supporting families to retain the care of their children; and services such as family support, parenting education and so on are offered before removal of the children is contemplated. This orientation is more characteristic of continental European and Scandinavian child welfare systems. Arguably, the child protection orientation may emphasise the child's right to protection at the expense of his or her right to a family life. On the other hand the family service orientation may prioritise that right to a family life and indeed the desire to ensure the parents have the best possible chance to bring up their children themselves, but it risks neglecting the safety of the child in the process.

More recently, it has been suggested that a third policy orientation is emerging, the *child-focused orientation*, which acknowledges recent policy developments in a number of countries that have attempted to achieve a middle way between the other two approaches

(Gilbert et al., 2011). The child-focused orientation, it is suggested, maintains a clearer focus on the child's needs, promotes the benefits of early interventions to help support the family, but has a clarity in terms of the importance of balancing the rights of the parents with the rights of the child by acting decisively where to do so is warranted. It remains to be seen whether this new orientation will offer greater benefits than the other two.

CONCLUSION

Child welfare and protection is an emotive topic. This chapter has attempted to describe key aspects of the system in the UK, and at the same time to explore a range of commonplace perceptions of how that system operates. It argued that many of the public criticisms of child welfare services are at best misperceptions and often have been over-exaggerated. There is considerable evidence of good practice, but this occurs alongside significant scope for improvement in the ways in which services operate. If there is one thing I hope the reader will take from this chapter, it is the need for a balanced perspective in a context where personal and political positions often become polarised. In particular, in responding to the needs of the individual child, there is no substitute for clear and careful analytical thinking about how best to deal with the problems. As to whether it is individual practitioners, organisational systems, management, the economic context, government policies or the intractability of child welfare problems that are the causes of the difficulties described, the reader must form his or her own judgement.

Key points

- Child welfare systems in the UK provide for early help for children with significant needs, for investigation of alleged maltreatment, and where necessary for placement in alternative accommodation.
- Professionals working in the child welfare and child maltreatment fields encounter public and political criticism when things go wrong.
- The child welfare system, nevertheless, has considerable positive achievements that are often overlooked.
- The key to policy development in the future may be a balanced child-focused orientation.

Recommended reading

Corby et al. (2012) covers child protection from a variety of perspectives; and a good source of information about children in the child welfare system is Fahlberg (2012).

CHILDREN'S HEALTH AND WELLBEING

SALLY ROBINSON

CONTENTS

INTRODUCTION

How we improve the health and wellbeing of children cannot be divorced from how we improve the health and wellbeing of the population. This chapter, focusing on England within an international context, shows how the prevention of illness and death first became the business of the state, then of doctors and then a matter for everyone. It explains how the World Health Organization facilitated an understanding of health as an entity in its own right, separate from that of illness. Their holistic and positive definition of health embraces wellbeing and includes all aspects of people's lives. The World Health Organization has simultaneously influenced the methods we use to bring about health improvement, from authoritarian propaganda to education and community empowerment. The chapter introduces health education, health promotion and public health, all of which aim to improve the health and wellbeing of individuals and communities through communication, education and economic, political, social and environmental change. It is through this type of work that the early years workforce has the potential to make a significant impact on children's health and wellbeing, which can influence the rest of their lives.

THE STATE TAKES AN INTEREST IN HEALTH

Understandings about what makes us healthy or ill vary across history, place and culture. In early nineteenth century England most people believed that illness was both God's will and caused by the foul smelling air. The 1848 Public Health Act aimed to improve the environment, particularly sanitation, and in so doing clean the air. It heralded the first state intervention in the population's health and formally marked the beginning of the public health movement, not only in England, but also around the world (Lupton, 1995). By 1900, the idea of cleanliness being next to Godliness emerged and the state had turned its attention away from the environment towards modifying individuals' behaviour. Children, and their poor physical health, had become more visible to the state thanks to the introduction of universal schooling. School physical education, domestic science, hygiene, the provision of some school meals and medical inspections were introduced (Sutherland, 1987). The state turned its attention to mothers' behaviour because they were seen as the guardians of the next generation's health. It was their duty to produce healthy workers and soldiers for the empire. As science evolved, mothers were positioned at the forefront of fighting the new enemy, germs. The state instructed the volunteer health missioners, the forerunners of health visitors, to provide training to mothers about correct infant care and hygiene (Holdsworth, 1988). In this way formalised health education, in the form of state-led propaganda, began in schools and homes. In a period of fifty years the state's attention to the causes of ill health had moved away from the environment to individuals' behaviour and the germ. The perceived solution had moved away from the provision of long-term, expensive, environmental change paid for by the state to blaming the individual for becoming ill and exhorting them to behave in ways that would prevent illness.

THE MEDICAL MODEL

Doctors became the masters of both mothers and germs. The scientific study of the human body had been quietly in ascendance for more than two centuries (Mosley, 2010). Jenner's vaccination for small pox in 1796 raised the prospect that an entire population could be immunised against infectious diseases. By the second half of the nineteenth century Robert Koch and Louis Pasteur proved that germs caused disease (bacteriology); John Snow showed how diseases spread through populations (epidemiology); and Florence Nightingale showed how to communicate complex epidemiological data in easy to understand diagrams. Public health medicine (disease prevention and the monitoring and control of disease in populations by doctors) attracted greater attention than traditional/environmental public health (social and environmental change). The law compelled mothers to vaccinate their babies until 1898 when the anti-vaccinationist movement successfully introduced the concept of 'conscientious objector' into English law (Wolfe and Sharp, 2002). The arrival of penicillin, the 'magic bullet', in the late 1920s created a belief that if disease could not be entirely prevented through immunisation, it could be cured through antibiotics.

The medical model dominated health for most of the twentieth century. It is characterised by a mechanistic understanding of the physical body, an emphasis on objectivity, science, experts and pathology. The model rests on the idea that health is achieved through attaining the 'absence of illness', which is a 'negative definition of health' (Aggleton, 1990). An individual cannot be held responsible for contracting a germ or for a malfunction such as a break or an internal blockage, but he is responsible for complying with the advice of the experts in order to make himself better. One of the legacies of the medical model has been to create an automatic association, in people's minds, that 'health' is synonymous with 'illness'. For example, in 1948, medical science and medical power were perceived as being unimpeachable, and so these understandings about health and illness led to the creation of a national service to prevent and treat illness: a National 'Health' Service (NHS). Through the NHS the state continued to expect mothers to take responsibility for the health of their families as well as the nation, and to do so without upsetting their husbands. If mothers did not comply with medical advice, and their child became ill, it was their fault (Amos, 1993) regardless of the wider socio-economic environment and poor living conditions over which they usually had no control (Holdsworth, 1988).

HOLISTIC HEALTH AND WELLBEING

The physical and mental trauma of the soldiers who fought in the two World Wars forced a recognition that a person's health was not reflected in their physical body alone, and that if cure was not possible ('absence of illness'), rehabilitation was. The rise of the allied health professionals, such as occupational therapists and speech and language therapists (Wilcox, 2006), along with the contribution of the Quakers (Abbott et al., 2011), were pivotal in helping to bring about the recognition that someone's mental, emotional, social and spiritual state influenced their physical state and vice versa. These advances culminated in a holistic understanding of health as a separate entity to illness, a view which the World Health Organization (WHO) was keen to emphasise when setting out its own definition of health as, not simply about 'attaining the absence of illness', but 'physical, mental and social wellbeing' at its inception in 1946 (WHO, 1946). This is a 'positive definition of health' (Aggleton, 1990), and the inclusion of the word 'wellbeing' was significant. Aristotle, the ancient Greek philosopher, referred to 'wellbeing' as flourishing, happiness, blessedness or prosperity from the Greek term *eudemonia* (Mehmet, 2011). The creation of the World Health Organization marked the moment that health was formally and internationally recognised as being positive, holistic and incorporating wellbeing.

COMMUNITY EMPOWERMENT

By the late 1970s, the limitations of medicine, and the medical model, were becoming apparent. Improvements in population health were found to owe more to improved sanitation and other environmental interventions than to medical care, which most of the world could not afford (Stewart et al., 2003). There was an international imperative to prevent disease, promote health and reduce costs. The World Health Organization endorsed the point that health care professionals, while experts in illness, injury and disease, were not, and could not be, the exclusive experts in something as broad as health. The Declaration of Alma Ata (WHO, 1978) made clear that people have the right and duty to participate individually and collectively in their health. The prevention of illness and the promotion of health should be in the community, by the community and for the community. In contrast to the *outcomes*-led medical model, the declaration was saying that the *process* of people's engagement was, in itself, health promoting.

In England, *The Black Report* (Black et al., 1980) provided ground-breaking evidence that people's health, their length of life and quality of life, was more significantly influenced by the social and environmental factors around them than health care, and these factors were causing inequalities in health across social classes. If a child was born into a lower socio-economic environment, they would have more ill health and die earlier than a child born into a better socio-economic environment. Poverty was the most significant barrier to achieving health. Health was now a matter for the health, social and economic sectors of society (WHO, 1978).

Studies began to ask what health meant to 'lay' people who were not health professionals. Noreen Wetton and her colleagues asked children, aged four to eleven, 'What makes you healthy and keeps you healthy?' (Williams et al., 1989). Nearly every child's picture of a healthy person featured a smile. For many, health was, and still is, happiness (The Children's Society, 2011). The children's labelled drawings were positive and holistic including 'I am work[ing] to make me healthy', 'I am tap dancing', 'God', 'I am playing with my friend', 'fresh air keeps me cool', 'milk' and 'sunshine'. In this era understandings about health were focused on lifestyles and the environment. The physical and social environment needed to be made healthy for the people, and people needed to be given information and skills to articulate what they need and want, and to get it. Health became a matter for all government departments. The health care services were now an important part of, rather than the whole of, the Department of Health. They needed to give higher priority to people in the community, rather than hospitals, and to disease prevention (Great Britain NHS and Community Care Act, 1990).

Health education became communication to empower people. This was characterised by a two-way dialogue with an emphasis on understanding people's own aspirations for health, skills development and recognition of the wider social determinants of health (Weare, 1992; Green, 2012). *Our Bodies Ourselves*, a seminal publication about women's health first published in 1971, by women and for women, epitomised how health education changed through the 1970s and 1980s. Women were no longer prepared to be simply the recipients of others' instructions nor were they prepared to shoulder all the responsibility for family health. Women's own lives and experiences, which included their children's experiences, began to shape their own health education. *The New Pregnancy Book* and *Birth to Five*, published at this time, included women's own words (Amos, 1993). At a professional level, health education became part of the job role of the multidisciplinary workforce, led by health education specialists who up-skilled the teachers, health care and local authority professionals (see Chapter 19).

THE OTTAWA CHARTER FOR HEALTH PROMOTION: A NEW PUBLIC HEALTH

The international community recognised a need to combine health education with the best of traditional/environmental public health with the best of public health medicine. The Ottawa Charter for Health Promotion (WHO, 1986) was a call for a 'new public health' for the world, and it became the bedrock on which all WHO health improvement policy and action has been based, from then until now. Most governments today have national health policies that reflect much of the Ottawa Charter, which defines health promotion as:

> The process of enabling people to increase control over, and to improve, their health. To reach a state of complete physical, mental and social wellbeing, an individual or group must be able to identify and to realize aspirations, to satisfy needs, and to change or cope with the environment. Health is, therefore, seen as a resource for everyday life, not the objective of living. Health is a positive concept emphasizing social and personal resources, as well as physical capacities. Therefore, health promotion is not just the responsibility of the health sector, but goes beyond healthy life-styles to wellbeing. (WHO, 1986)

It explains that in order to promote health we need to be advocates for health, we need to enable people to achieve their full health potential through equal opportunities and resources. We need to encourage mediation across health, social, economic, non-governmental and voluntary sectors, industry and the media because health cannot be achieved by the health sector alone. Its six priorities were:

1. Build public policies, which support health. When public policy is being created, be that financial, educational or social, it should automatically be a health promoting policy. If it is not, then the obstacles need to be identified and removed. Healthy choices should be easy choices.

2. Create supportive environments. Protect and conserve our natural and built environments in ways that are conducive to our health and wellbeing.

3. Strengthen community action. Give power to the people, strengthen their voices, encourage local community

development by giving community projects information, learning opportunities and support.

4. Develop personal skills.
   Enable people to access life-long learning including the skills to cope with personal health changes and maximise health potential. This needs to be facilitated by schools, home and community settings.

5. Re-orientate the health services.

Health services need to move beyond clinical care and cure, and give greater attention to promoting health, and support health professional education in this direction.

6. Moving into the future.
   The planning, implementation and evaluation of health promotion are activities for everyone to work on together. Caring, holism and ecology are essential ingredients.

HEALTH EDUCATION, HEALTH PROMOTION, PUBLIC HEALTH

Although much of the world has adopted the principles of the Ottawa Charter, there has been much less consensus about what to call the work: health education, health promotion or public health. Here are three straightforward definitions.

> Health education is any planned activity designed to produce health – or illness – related learning. (Green et al., 2015: 25)

> Health promotion is a range of activities and interventions to enable people to take greater control over their health. Activities may be directed at individuals, families, communities or whole populations. (Naidoo and Wills, 2016: 57)

> Public health comprises preventing disease, prolonging life and promoting health through work focused on the population as a whole. (Scriven, 2010: 239)

Public health always has a clear *population* focus. Health promotion and health education are terms used for individuals, groups and populations. Health promotion always includes health education. Neither health promotion, health education nor public health includes 'hands on' personal care such as giving injections, dressing and feeding.

England is not typical amongst the rest of the world. While Europe uses the term health promotion (Speller et al., 2012), current English government policy prefers to use public health as an umbrella term containing four domains:

- Improving the wider determinants of health (social contributors to health inequalities);
- Health improvement (healthy lifestyles and choices);
- Health protection (environmental and medical protection e.g. vaccinations);
- Health care, public health and preventing premature mortality (preventable illness and death).

In 2013, Public Health England was created as an equal sibling to the National Health Service, to 'protect and promote the nation's health and wellbeing and reduce health inequalities'. It leads a national movement to embed the responsibility for the public's health within local government

(LGA, 2014), the National Health Service (NHS England, 2014; NHS England/PHE/HEE, 2016), health care professional practice (DH/PHE, 2014; AHPF/PHE, 2015), workplaces (Liverpool City Council, 2016), the voluntary sector, professional bodies, universities, industry and members of the public (PHE, 2014a). The *core* public health workforce comprises those who identify public health as being the primary part of their role such as health visitors (CfWI, 2016). The *wider* public health workforce describes those whose work provides opportunities to make a positive impact on people's health and wellbeing (CfWI, 2015). It comprises fifteen million workers in England, and includes every member of the early years' workforce.

MEASURING AND PREVENTING CHILDREN'S ILLNESS

The medical model continues to provide a highly valued approach to treating and preventing illness. Early years practitioners working only with a medical model will measure the health of children by referring to the number who are ill and the range of illnesses. Measuring the amount of illness in a population, what epidemiologists call the morbidity rate, is straightforward. Many disease prevention activities such as raising awareness about the importance of vaccinations to prevent measles, and pictures to remind children to wash their hands to prevent the spread of germs, can be clearly linked to reduced numbers of sick children (Goldhaber-Fiebert et al., 2010; Burton et al., 2011). This makes this model popular in cases where a practitioner needs to produce clear, measurable outcomes.

PROMOTING CHILDREN'S HEALTH AND WELLBEING

Promoting a child's health means working with a holistic and 'positive definition' which means not only attaining the 'absence of illness', but also 'physical, mental and social wellbeing'. It is a holistic model that combines the biological, social and psychological determinants of health. Scriven (2010) breaks health into six dimensions. She explains that physical health is concerned with the body, functioning as a well-oiled machine; mental health comprises thinking clearly and coherently; emotional health is about feelings, expressing these appropriately and coping with difficult feelings such as stress or anxiety; social health is our ability to make and maintain relationships with people; and spiritual health concerns personal creeds, morals and may, or may not, be linked to religious beliefs. These five are interrelated (Weare, 2007; Stacey, 2011) in that physical activity is known to help with emotional health due to changes in brain chemicals. Mental and emotional health are often conflated as psychological health. Being stressed blocks the **neuronal pathways** that facilitate learning and thus someone's mental health. People with social health problems often have associated emotional health difficulties, and health inequalities across the British population are recognised to be the result of, and caused by, poor mental health. The holistic and positive approach recognises that the individual aspects of a child's health, which are influenced by genetics and personal lifestyles are, in turn, shaped by wider social and environmental determinants (WHO, 2009; Stewart and Bushell, 2011). Scriven (2010) calls her sixth dimension 'societal health'. This is visually

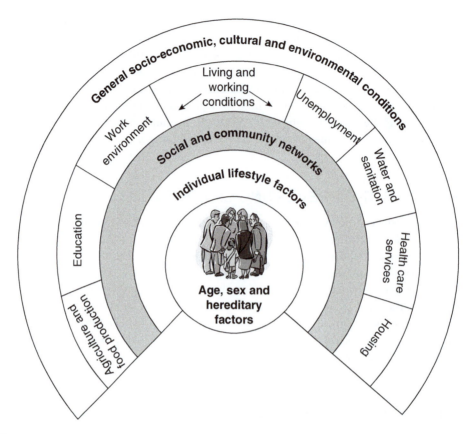

Figure 15.1 A social model of health (Dahlgren and Whitehead, 1991)

Dahlgren, G. and Whitehead, M. (1991) *Policies and Strategies to Promote Social Equity in Health.* Stockholm, Sweden: Institute for Futures Studies.

represented in social models (Dahlgren and Whitehead, 1991; Barton and Grant, 2006) as illustrated in Figures 15.1 and 15.2.

Over the last thirty years, the 'wellbeing' aspect of health has been given more prominence. Wellbeing focuses on the mental, emotional and social aspects of health. Research has shown that children and families benefit from connecting with people around them, being active, being curious and taking notice, continuing learning and giving to others (Aked et al., 2008; Abdallah et al., 2014). The word 'health' has expanded to 'health and wellness' or 'health and wellbeing' to shake off entrenched and popular perceptions from the medical model (that health equals illness with a particular emphasis on the physical body and medical care). The wider concept communicates the broader and current understanding of health so that local authorities, voluntary agencies, community groups, children's centres, the public and others can all play their part (DH, 2010; Walker, 2012). A pragmatic approach informed by the WHO,

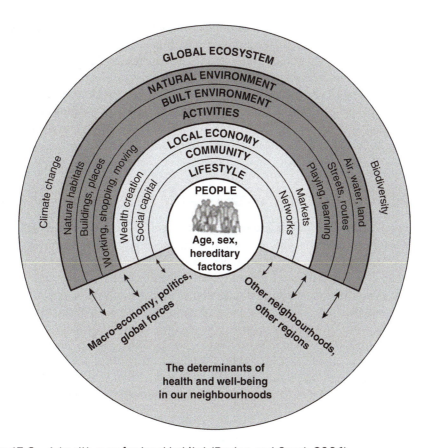

Figure 15.2 A health map for local habitat (Barton and Grant, 2006)

which defines 'wellness' as the optimal state of health (Smith et al., 2006: 5), is that 'health' and 'health and wellbeing' reflect the same positive and holistic goals, and in that sense they are the same.

MEASURING CHILDREN'S HEALTH AND WELLBEING

Early years practitioners working with a positive, holistic model of health will quickly find that, unlike working with the medical model, there is no universally agreed way of measuring health because it is a dynamic, and ultimately individual, concept. Practitioners and research-ers select a range of subjective and objective measures of physical, mental, social, emotional, spiritual, socio-economic and environmental status, in addition to measures of illness. Quantitative and qualitative research, often used in combination, tries to capture the whole. This can include epidemiological research on illnesses and causes of death; psycho-social research about children's self-concept, emotional literacy, social skills, family relationships and their health-related knowledge, attitudes and behaviours; clinical research such as measuring height and weight or blood tests; socio-economic research measuring housing conditions, community resources and deprivation. Research often tries to capture children's and families' assets, strengths and protective factors, such as esteem, life skills, resilience, healthy behaviours, a safe home and access to play and education, as well as focusing on the deficits, needs and problems. For example, Public Health England has selected thirty-two indicators for measuring child health and wellbeing for its annual Child Health Profiles.

THE LIFE COURSE APPROACH TO HEALTH AND WELLBEING

The life course approach to health and wellbeing (Marmot, 2010) rests on the wealth of evidence that places the antenatal and early years of childhood as the most important period to invest in health because this is when our bodies, including our brains, are at their most vulnerable to be shaped by social, physical and emotional influences. Socio-economic and emotional surroundings cumulatively reduce or enhance the chances of children developing common health problems in later life. These can include: physical ill health, such as circulatory diseases, obesity, diabetes, drug and alcohol misuse; poor mental, emotional and social health concerns such as the inability to empathise, to form happy relationships with others or anti-social behaviour; and involvement in criminal actions (Marmot, 2010; Allen, 2011; SACN, 2011).

> What a child experiences during the early years lays down a foundation for the whole of their life.
> (Marmot, 2010: 60)

Promoting the health and wellbeing of children means focusing on children who seem to be fully healthy and well, children who have symptoms of illness or poor health, sick children and dying children. The priorities for young children in England today include:

- early years nutrition (SACN, 2011) and child obesity (Robinson et al., 2012; Parliament, 2015; RCPCH, 2015);
- mental, emotional health and social health (DH, 2015);
- bullying (Ofsted/Children's Services and Skills, 2012);
- the sexualisation of childhood (Bailey, 2011);
- abuse and neglect (Anda et al., 2010; Radford, 2011);

- intentional and unintentional injury, accident or trauma (PHE, 2014b; DfE, 2015a);
- improving standards of health care for all children (Lewis and Lenehan, 2012), in particular for those in care, with disabilities, mental health needs and life-limiting illnesses (Foyle and Nathanson, 2013; Paget and Cadywould, 2015).

Many argue that the most pressing priorities are child poverty and the political will to give greater priority to children's health and wellbeing (DWP/DfE, 2011; Foyle and Nathanson, 2013). The evidence is overwhelmingly strong; universal early intervention, that is promoting the holistic health and wellbeing of all babies and young children, plus more intense targeted early intervention for those with greater needs, can reap more benefits for individuals and the population, than at any other point of their lives (Marmot, 2010; Davies, 2013).

CONCLUSION

Children's health is a holistic and positive concept influenced by social, political, cultural, historical, financial and commercial factors as well as genetics, emotional and other personal experiences. In order to communicate this understanding of health to others, it is acceptable, and perhaps desirable, to use the term children's 'health and wellbeing' or just 'wellbeing'. These influences are at their most potent during the early years as they can have life-long health outcomes. Improving the health and wellbeing of children requires multi-professional, multi-layered approaches which include the views and actions of children, their families and their communities. Early years practitioners are well placed to use communication, education and economic, political, social and environmental change to promote the health and wellbeing

—————————— **Key points** ——————————

- Health policy advocates well being as part of a healthy life-style.
- Promoting children's health requires a holistic model which contains biological, social and psychological determinants.
- A holistic approach to children's health recognises that it is dynamic and individual and does not always lend itself to universal measurements.

—————————— **Recommended reading** ——————————

A comprehensive introduction to the subject can be found in Foyle and Nathanson (2013) (see references).

INCLUSIVE POLICY AND PRACTICE

SIOBHAN O'CONNOR AND POLLY BOLSHAW

CONTENTS

On 25 September 2015, my sister moved into her own home. It was a significant day in her life and for my family. It had taken four years of planning, countless set-backs and many difficult decisions to make, all without knowing whether we were making the right choices for her. Nor were we in a position to make the decisions we wanted to. We were dependent on the support and funding from a variety of services who ultimately had the final say on where my sister could live and with whom.

Having lived in residential care homes since the age of thirteen, my sister had always shared her home with children and then adults who were considered similar to her. Her life had been regulated by the policies and procedures of each care home; each providing an institutionalised way of living that determined times for eating, sleeping and recreation, which parts of her home she was excluded from, and when she was allowed to leave the fortified walls that were designed to keep her in and others out.

It was the death of our father and my sister's grief that became the catalyst for change. We were unable to support her to understand death and its finality. Her dad just stopped coming to her home on Sundays. He was no longer at my parents' home when she came to visit, and despite searching for him, he just couldn't be found. Her dad no longer played her favourite songs, he didn't sit with her holding her hand and he wasn't even there anymore to tell her off for the behaviour she knew provoked a cross reaction from him. It was heartbreaking to experience, but this was the way in which she was experiencing his death and her loss. She was diagnosed with depression, she lost considerable weight and her behaviour could no longer be controlled. However good her care home was, they couldn't provide the care and support she needed any longer. Change was needed, not only for my sister, but also in how we as a family and the professionals in her life conceptualized her multiple cognitive and physical impairments and the barriers to inclusion and participation experienced throughout her life.

As my sister approaches her fiftieth year, she is cared for in her own home by a team of professionals on a 24 hour basis. Supported by their love and professionalism, her transformation has been remarkable to watch; she is learning how to communicate more than ever before, she has become a valued member of her community and continuously challenges the expectations we have always held with regards to what is, and what isn't, possible for her.

Siobhan O'Connor

INTRODUCTION

In the previous edition of this chapter, the extract chosen to mark the beginning of a dialogue about the concept of inclusion was written from the perspective of loving a sister with profound learning difficulties and multiple impairments during our shared childhood experiences. In this new edition, we have chosen a new extract that explores how discourses of inclusion are allied closely with social justice, challenging inequality and reducing exclusion by non-discriminatory responses to diversity and removing barriers to participation. There are multiple perspectives on inclusion and attempts to capture its meaning can remain elusive, as Booth (2010: 2) argues, 'inclusion is a complex notion and its definition cannot be settled in a single sentence with a few well-chosen words'. At its heart, the concept of inclusion involves a commitment to the values of equality and participation; to reducing exclusion; and to non-discriminatory responses to diversity that respect and value difference within our shared humanity. Rather than seeking a definitive answer to the question, 'what does inclusion mean?', literature commonly refers to a range of ideas associated with the word 'inclusion' and the principles that are characteristic of an inclusive approach. The meaning of inclusion can only be fully understood as these principles or underpinning values are 'played out in particular contexts' (Ainscow et al., 2006: 27). For example, Booth and Dyssegaard (2008: 42) recognise inclusion to be concerned with:

- Increasing the participation of all and reducing the exclusion of all;
- Increasing the capacity of settings and systems to respond to diversity in ways that value everyone equally;
- Putting into action inclusive values.

Our chapter is framed around these three principles. First, we examine discourses of inclusion concerned with increasing participation and reducing exclusion for all, exploring in particular the possibilities for early childhood education and care (ECEC) to contribute to combating social exclusion and ameliorating the effects of disadvantage. Second, we examine the capacity to respond to diversity in ways that value everyone equally. We consider how taking steps to promote social justice may empower every individual 'to pursue a self-determined course of life, and to engage in broad social participation' (Schraad-Tischer, 2011: 11). For example, how the provision of community-based ECEC services can address social inequalities that limit the participation of individuals within society and produce unfair outcomes. Finally we consider a principled approach to inclusive development, associated with putting into action inclusive values. We explore how 'values literacy' can support a process of negotiating a values framework in which actions towards inclusive development can be taken to identify and reduce the 'exclusionary pressures that impede participation' (Booth and Ainscow, 2011: 11).

INCREASING PARTICIPATION AND REDUCING EXCLUSION

The first element of Booth and Dyssegaard's (2008) definition of inclusion concerns a need to increase participation and decrease exclusion for all. Clough and Clough propose that, by their very nature, there is exclusivity of cultures, communities and curricula (2013, cited in Nutbrown et al., 2013). Therefore, effective inclusive practices and policies must seek to promote participation for all whilst still responding to and valuing the diversity of cultural, community and curricula characteristics (see Chapters 1 and 4). Levitas et al. (2007: 9) define social exclusion as:

> ... a complex and multi-dimensional process. It involves the lack or denial of resources, rights, goods and services, and the inability to participate in the normal relationships and activities, available to the majority of people in a society, whether in economic, social, cultural or political arenas. It affects both the quality of life of individuals and the equity and cohesion of society as a whole.

In relation to early childhood, within the European Union (EU), children are more likely to be at risk of poverty or social exclusion if they live in single parent families or families with three or more dependent children, live in monetary poverty, have parents with a low level of education, or are from migrant backgrounds (López Vilaplana, 2013). Thus, when considering participation for all, it is particularly important to mitigate against social exclusion for children with these risk factors. Within England, it has been recognised that one way to combat social exclusion and promote participation is by ensuring all children have access to high quality ECEC. This is one of the findings of the Effective Provision of Preschool Education (EPPE) Project (Sylva et al., 2008), which aimed, amongst other things, to consider the link between ECEC and social exclusion. The research found that by attending ECEC, children categorised as being disadvantaged may have a better start when they begin primary school as they will be less likely to struggle. In addition, high quality ECEC helped to narrow the achievement gap between the most able and the least able children and thus may boost the successful participation of children in primary education. This suggests that enhancing uptake of ECEC is a positive method of increasing the participation of all children and decreasing social exclusion in their primary school experiences and beyond, both in terms of access to education and of academic success.

Drawing upon the results of the EPPE Project, the UK government recognised the importance of ECEC for promoting social inclusion. The Childcare Act 2006 (see Chapter 11) requires Local Authorities to provide free early years education. Currently this provision takes the form of 570 hours per year for all children from the term following their third birthday as well as for the least advantaged two-year-olds, which constitute approximately 40 per cent of all two-year-old children (DfE, 2016: 32). Two-year-olds can access free ECEC if their parents are entitled to particular welfare benefits.

ECEC has been conceptualized as a form of early intervention, and has become fundamental to strengthening the concept and goals of social inclusion, particularly in relation to three key areas (Friendly, 2007). The first is associated with the potential contribution of ECEC to enhance children's development, learning and wellbeing, particularly for children 'with diverse learning rights, whether these stem from physical, mental or sensory disabilities or from socio-economic disadvantage' (OECD, 2006: 17). Secondly, according to UNICEF (2011) the challenges to social inclusion as it relates to child poverty and social exclusion 'cannot be overestimated'. Save the Children (2012: 14) argues that 'poverty blights children's lives and their futures' and yet, in England, it is predicted that absolute and relative child poverty levels will rise sharply by 2020 (Browne and Hood, 2016). Affordable and flexible early childhood programmes that are universally available can support families to overcome disadvantage and social exclusion associated with poverty, unemployment and isolation and can strengthen issues of social justice in relation to gender equality. Finally, social inclusion and respect for diversity are critical in responding to increasing diversification within societies. Early childhood is considered a critical period for attitude formation and developing positive responses to diversity. Challenging discriminatory attitudes and negative stereotypes on the basis of perceived differences associated with multiple identities are therefore fundamental to early childhood programmes, pedagogy and practice and the content of curriculum frameworks.

Rather than a perspective that considers all inclusion and exclusion as socially constructed, the term 'social inclusion' implies that there is an understanding of inclusion that is non-social.

In England, this has encouraged the term 'inclusion' to refer specifically to the education of children categorised as having special educational needs and disabilities (SEND). It is a perspective that remains embedded within a medical model of disability, where 'there exists some non-social exclusion which befalls people with impairments which arises naturally as a direct result of their impairment' (Booth, 2010: 2). In the same way early intervention policies segregate children according to criteria of advantage, two-year-olds are also entitled to free ECEC if they have 'a current statement of special education needs or an education health and care plan' (DfE, 2016: 32). Thus rather than ECEC being considered democratically as a public good for all children and communities (Moss, 2011), a focus on disadvantage, deficiency and additional or special needs not only enforces categorisation and labelling towards perceived difference, but also 'forms the basis for segregated and exclusionary provision' (Roberts-Holmes, 2009: 191). The concept of inclusion does not therefore refer to particular groups of people; it is about everybody and the lens through which we choose to see children and adults who 'may be subjected to a range of exclusionary pressures' (Booth and Ainscow, 2011: 40).

VALUING EVERYONE'S DIVERSITY EQUALLY

If we acknowledge that inclusion within the early years is seen as promoting participation for all and, most simply, as the '*unified drive* towards maximal participation in, and minimal exclusion from, early years settings, from schools and from society' (Nutbrown et al., 2013), then one way in which this can be supported is by 'increasing the capacity of settings and systems to respond to diversity in ways that value everyone equally' (Booth and Dyssegaard, 2008: 42). This suggests that to promote inclusion, it is necessary to consider social justice. Some may understand social justice as concerning the fair distribution of resources, whilst others may focus on its role in eliminating discriminatory and oppressive conduct (Newman and Yeates, 2008: 3). Yet, what is more important is seeing social justice as a means by which to value diversity and achieve 'genuinely equal opportunities for self-realization' for everyone – with a focus on investing in inclusive policy, practice and processes rather than applying compensatory measures against exclusion (Schraad-Tischer, 2015: 69). In this way, the focus of Nutbrown et al.'s (2013) maximal participation is maintained.

In order to identify key areas for the development of social justice on a global scale, Schraad-Tischer (2015) outlines six dimensions, which make up the Social Justice Index. This index is used to consider the extent to which the countries of the European Union are achieving social justice, based around six areas:

1. Poverty prevention
2. Equitable education
3. Labour market access
4. Social cohesion and non-discrimination
5. Health
6. Intergenerational justice

A strength of breaking down social justice into these specific elements, measured by twenty-seven qualitative and quantitative indictors, is that it can support policymakers in identifying what particular actions may be worth focusing on in their particular region. For instance, one of the three ways in which social justice in regard to *Equitable Education* is measured across EU countries by the Social Justice Index is government expenditure in ECEC. Whilst Denmark, ranked first by this measure, invested 1.6 per cent of their total GDP in ECEC in 2015, only 0.3 per cent of the UK's GDP is spent on this – a figure that has remained unchanged since 2008. This may explain why the UK stands below the EU average for equitable education overall (Schraad-Tischer, 2015: 26), and could suggest to the UK government that this low expenditure may need to be reflected upon.

There is evidence to suggest that England is acting upon the comparatively lower investment in ECEC. It could be said that the introduction in 2013 of 'free' (i.e. government subsidised, no cost to parents) 15-hours early years provision for two-year-olds from disadvantaged backgrounds may be a response to the call to consider the role of ECEC for promoting equitable education. By 2015 around 58 per cent of eligible two-year-olds had taken advantage of the entitlement (Huskinson et al., 2016). However, there was no evidence that children who took part in the early years education pilot at the age of two had better outcomes at the age of five than their counterparts who did not take part in the pilot (DfE, 2013). This suggests that to achieve equitable education in terms of educational outcomes, there is perhaps the need to invest in developing settings so that they offer high quality provision, rather than focusing on increasing the enrolment of children into early years settings that are not providing high quality ECEC. As other authors have indicated, this is a challenge and a paradox (see Chapters 11 and 13).

ECEC may be advantageous not only for furthering social justice in terms of promoting educational outcomes; there may also be benefits in access to the labour market, particularly for women who may face barriers when combining motherhood with employment. Family policies such as free or subsidised ECEC, or parental leave entitlements, which seek to enable both mothers and fathers to successfully combine working and parenting may also boost intergenerational justice. As generous paid parental leave may also foster higher rates of breastfeeding (Cooklin et al., 2012), health-related inequalities may also be countered by developing family policy. This may ensure that there is not a pronounced gap in the extent to which children throughout their lives are valued, treated and are able to participate as a result of their earliest experiences. In this way, it is possible to see the role of ECEC in impacting on multiple areas of Schraad-Tischer's (2015) six dimensions of social justice.

The UN (2015) have also identified that ECEC leads not only to educational benefits for children, but also to positive societal impacts, particularly in less advantaged communities and specifically in poorer countries. Whilst Schraad-Tischer (2015) focuses on actions that policymakers within the EU should consider on a worldwide scale, the significance of ECEC is also stressed within the United Nations' *Sustainable Development Goals* (UN, 2015), which were adopted in 2015. Goal 4 states that governments should, 'ensure inclusive and equitable quality education and promote lifelong learning opportunities' and within it, Target 4.2 aims to secure access to ECEC for all children by 2030, in order to ensure children are ready for primary education. This shows a commendable global commitment to ECEC, which will play a role in supporting social justice, albeit within the framework of a global 'school readiness' agenda (see Chapter 4). Yet, the 2015 target must be considered in relation to its forerunner, UNESCO's (2000) *Education for All* goals, which were set out at the turn of the millennium with the intention of being achieved by 2015. Goal 1 sought to expand and improve 'comprehensive early childhood care and education, especially for the most vulnerable and disadvantaged children', and between 1999 and 2015 the number of children accessing ECEC increased by almost two-thirds – 40 countries now have compulsory pre-primary education (UN, 2015). However, statistics from 2013 show that globally only 54 per cent of children were enrolled in ECEC (The World Bank, 2016). Schraad-Tischer (2015: 13) notes that it is important that policymakers consider the role of early childhood education in furthering social justice and in particular as a way to limit the socio-economic impact on educational outcomes for children living in economically disadvantaged circumstances. The World Bank's statistics may imply that policymakers need to heed Schraad-Tischer's suggestions if ECEC is to be used as a policy mechanism for developing social justice, and also for combating poverty and disadvantage.

Consequently, in relation to Booth and Dyssegaard's (2008) principled approach to inclusive development as focusing on developing capacity to value everyone equally, this may be achieved by taking steps to promote social justice through improving both quality and access to ECEC and developing effective family policy. Promoting the importance of ECEC as a method of combating educational and social disadvantage is important not only in England but across the rest of the world too. However, it must also be noted that as well as considering strategies to increase participation, reduce exclusion and increase the capacity for settings to value everyone equally, we must also think about how inclusive values can be put into action.

ENACTING INCLUSIVE VALUES

Values are fundamental guides and prompts to action. They spur us forward, give us a sense of direction and define a destination. We cannot know that we are doing or have done the right thing without understanding the relationship between our actions and our values. For all actions affecting others are underpinned by values: every such action becomes a moral argument whether or not we are aware of it (Booth, 2010: 2).

The final principle that contributes to our dialogue about inclusion is associated with putting inclusive values into action. We have identified throughout this chapter a number of values associated with the concept of inclusion including: care, love, participation, community, equality, respect for diversity, justice and compassion. Yet we have assumed a shared agreement on what each of these values may mean and how they are put into action. However, it can be extremely difficult to locate and make explicit the values that lie behind constructions of children and childhoods and the policies and pedagogies within ECEC and education, or indeed the meanings behind the values. As Lee and Walsh argue, 'values are deeply embedded in cultural beliefs and practices [and as such are] too transparent for people to easily recognise and voice' (2004: 370). However, a values-infused philosophy offers a particular vantage point from which to engage in inclusive development. For example, ECEC as a form of early intervention has been recognised throughout this chapter as a powerful way in which the values of participation, equality and respect for diversity can be put into action, with particular emphasis placed on how these values may contribute towards children's readiness for compulsory education. And yet, within the English context of ECEC, the concept of school readiness remains highly contested

(Whitebread and Bingham, 2011; Evans, 2013; Moss, 2013). Akin to the deficit model of inclusion and social inclusion that may exacerbate inequality and exclusionary processes on the basis of categories of SEND and/or disadvantage, reductionist approaches to readiness limit the extent to which the values of participation, equality and respect for diversity can be put into action. An alternative set of values are prioritised, including the reduction of complexity, normativity, performativity and conformity that reduce the complexity of children's learning and development to predetermined outcomes for all children, and constrain how we think about children and their childhoods and of the ECEC environments that are possible for our communities (Evans, 2013). Being explicit about values can therefore offer a possible way forward for contesting the dominant discourses associated with ECEC that may promote exclusion rather than the inclusion of all children and communities. Putting inclusive values into action is therefore an 'invitation to dialogue' about values. In creating space in which to make values explicit, or as Booth and Dyssegaard explain, 'developing literacy in thinking about, discussing and acting on values' (2008: 38), the process of inclusive development can take place from within a framework of values negotiated through the process of values literacy.

The *Index for Inclusion* (Booth and Ainscow, 2011) adopts a particular perspective on inclusive development as 'systematic change according to inclusive values' (Booth and O'Connor, 2012: 1). It sets out in considerable detail the implications for the way adults and children live and learn together. Responses to the diversity of adults and children in society and education value all equally and encourage everyone's participation. Development takes place along three dimensions: 'creating inclusive cultures, producing inclusive policies and evolving inclusive practices' (Booth and O'Connor, 2012: 1). The *Index* can support the development of a negotiated framework of values in which sustained inclusive development is embedded. A model values-framework is set out which is concerned with: 'equality, rights, participation, community, respect for diversity, sustainability, non-violence, trust, compassion, honesty, courage, joy, love, hope/optimism and beauty' (Booth, 2011: 33). While not intended as a prescriptive or an exhaustive list, each value heading and accompanying description signifies the beginning of an investigation into what the value may mean for those negotiating a values framework in which actions towards inclusive development can be taken. The *Index* is organised according to a series of headings that contribute towards inclusive development. Each heading is related to a series of questions to support reflection, dialogue and for the meaning of inclusion to become clearer by connecting both theory and practice, for example:

Dimension A2: Creating Inclusive Cultures: Establishing Inclusive Values: The school counters all forms of discrimination

Examples of questions:

1. Is it recognised that everyone absorbs prejudices against others which take effort to identify and reduce?
2. Do adults consider their own attitudes to diversity and identify their prejudices so as to better support children to identify and reduce theirs?

3.   Is it recognised that institutional discrimination can stem from cultures and policies which devalue the identities of, or otherwise discriminate against, some groups of people?

4.   Are legal requirements to reduce 'inequalities' in relation to ethnicity, disability, gender, sexual orientation, sexual identity, religion, belief and age part of comprehensive plans to counter all forms of discrimination? (Booth and Ainscow, 2011: 93)

The process inherent within the *Index* is intended to engage with the ideas behind each of the questions explored. Reflection and dialogue may encourage acknowledgement of discriminatory attitudes held by adults and children on the basis of negative responses to diversity and help deepen understanding about the ways that such views generate the dimensions of disadvantage, barriers to participation and oppression. It may lead to explicit guidance in how negative attitudes to difference can be challenged within the context of children's peer cultures and to understand and comply with the requirements of the Equality Act (2010) to extend inclusive practice.

The *Index* has been used variously throughout the world, ranging from whole setting development, to the examination of one aspect of inclusive development from particular aspects of cultures, policies and practices. Its use has been documented in Australia and South Africa as a framework for supporting the professional development of educators (Carrington and Robinson, 2004; Duke, 2009; Oswald, 2010).

CONCLUSION

Using Booth and Dyssegaard's (2008) three principles may be a useful way to think about what steps need to be taken in children's earliest experiences to reduce exclusion and to promote social justice for all. Firstly, developing access to ECEC may be a valuable way of removing barriers to learning and development, enabling as strong a start as possible to compulsory education for all children. Secondly, we can consider what strategies may be effective in encouraging processes and practice to value everyone equally, for instance in ensuring greater degrees of equity in terms of both access to, and outcomes of, ECEC. Finally, it is important to think about the ways in which children and the communities to which they belong can be encouraged to think about what their beliefs and values are, so that inclusive development may be put into practice. Yet we must bear in mind that inclusion is a never-ending process because values and beliefs of individuals and groups adapt, alter and change and so inclusive practice 'involves us in taking responsibility for processes of exclusion experienced by others, and requires our continuous reflection of the values that underlie our actions' (Plate, 2012: 60). Just as Schraad-Tischer (2015) has re-assessed the efforts of OECD countries in achieving social justice, individuals must also re-assess and reflect upon the success and implementation of inclusive practices and how these may need to be developed to reduce exclusion and to remove the barriers to participation and learning that children and adults may experience.

'It is a natural, and surely a proper, feeling that individuals or groups of individuals should not be written off, marginalised, left out of things, cut off from their fellows or sidelined; and that feeling goes along with, or is constituted by, both a sense of justice and a sense of compassion.' (Wilson, 2000: 297).

Promoting inclusive development within early childhood is key to ensuring that individuals do not feel 'written off' or 'sidelined'. It becomes more urgent to do so when we return to the extract at the beginning of this chapter. Siobhan's sister experienced responses to diversity that discriminated against her, that limited her participation through exclusion and which segregated her to different ways of living on the basis of her impairments and learning difficulties. It is only now and through the continuous and at times challenging process of inclusion, that in her fiftieth year she can experience opportunities for self fulfilment that many of us take for granted.

Key points

- The concept of inclusion in early childhood can be considered as a process, linked to three principles.
- The first principle focuses on the need to promote participation and combat social exclusion for all children.
- The second principle concerns developing the capacity to respond to diversity in ways that value everyone equally, through promoting social justice.
- The third principle focuses on putting into action inclusive values, using 'values literacy' to support the development of a values framework.

Recommended reading

Tony Booth's *Index for Inclusion Network* provides a framework on how to develop inclusive values in schools and early years settings and is available online: http://www.indexforinclusion.org/.

PART 4

DEVELOPING EFFECTIVE PRACTICE

OBSERVING CHILDREN TO IMPROVE PRACTICE

HELEN MOYLETT

CONTENTS

INTRODUCTION: THINKING ABOUT OBSERVATION

A teacher asks a five-year-old girl what she is doing.

'I'm drawing God', she says.

'But nobody knows what God looks like', retorts the teacher.

'They will in a minute', replies the child.

If that story amuses you, you are not alone. I have been told various versions of it – and told it myself and it is always met with laughter. It seems to have originated in the United States. Sir Ken Robinson told it during a TED (Technology, Entertainment, Design) talk in 2006, introducing it as, 'I heard a great story recently'. His is the most viewed TED talk of all time, so perhaps that's why the story has gained popularity. Adults laugh when they hear it in recognition of the way in which we can be caught out by a child's creative thinking – the child does not share the fixed mindset of the practitioner, who takes it as a given that nobody knows what God looks like. Some of the adults who laugh at this tale may also be laughing at the child's ignorance – but that only means that they share the belief of the teacher that nobody knows what God looks like. In fact, in seeking to represent God to her own satisfaction, the girl is following the artistic, creative and cultural traditions of many centuries and her belief in her power to make such a representation is a 'taken for granted' powerful enough to challenge the teacher's.

The story starts this chapter because it is essentially a story about thinking and captures some important issues involved in observing children.

- Observation is never value free – you bring who you are, your beliefs and your habits of mind to it, even when you stand back.
- An adult observer who is standing back (non-participant) only uses their brain and therefore perceptions – not the child's.
- Adult brains work differently from those of young children – your brain is about half as active as theirs.
- Never assume you know what the child's purpose is – your 'taken for granted' may not be theirs.
- Even the most experienced practitioner will sometimes be surprised by young children's thinking if they maintain an open mind and pay attention!

In the story about the child drawing God, the teacher is not engaging in formal observation of the child; it is an everyday interaction. So what is the difference between this sort of interaction and observation in an early years setting? The short answer is – sometimes not a lot.

Early years practitioners are not experimenters and do not observe children in laboratory conditions but use **naturalistic observation** methods which include everyday activities. Sometimes, for instance, if they use a particular approach to pedagogy such as the Effective Early Learning (EEL) programme (Pascal et al., 2001), are taking part in a research project, are hosting students undertaking a degree in early childhood studies or are closely observing a particular child or group about whom they are concerned, settings may use non-participant observation methods. Both participant and non-participant observers may use informal conversations as well as more structured methods such as time sampling, photos, video recording, sticky notes, record sheets and profiles. The rest of this chapter looks at why observation is so important in the early years as well as how observations may be recorded and used to assess children's progress and plan next steps in learning.

THE IMPORTANCE OF OBSERVATION IN THE EARLY YEARS

'Observation is important because it provides adults with a lens through which to study the child's world' (Langston, 2011). It is this perceived need to observe children that has informed early years education and care for centuries. Linda Pound (2011), introducing a book on learning theories ranging from the seventeenth century to the present day, points out observation's pivotal importance:

> Theories can be rooted in research and experimentation or they may be philosophical and hypothetical. Whatever their basis, the importance of observation is a common strand in the work of many theorists who were interested in finding out how children learn. Some were academics who became interested in children - others were experienced in working with children and developed theories to help them understand their experience. What is interesting is how often ideas which were based purely on observation are now supported by developmental theory. (Pound, 2011: 2)

So it is not surprising that all current curriculum models stress the importance of observation; this is often seen as an essential part of adopting a 'child-centred' approach.

THE ROLE OF CONTEXT

Learning and development from birth to five years are not context free. They occur as the result of a complex interaction between children and their experiences within relationships and within particular environments. This process is described in the literature as occurring within the interactionist tradition. One such approach conceives of development as located within nested social contexts (Bronfenbrenner in Evangelou et al., 2009). In England the Bronfenbrenner model (see Chapter 5) is reflected in the themes of the Early Years Foundation Stage (EYFS) (DfE, 2017) which positions the unique child at the centre of the framework enabled by positive relationships and enabling environments which support the child's learning and development. It is represented thus (see Figure 17.1) in the EYFS non-statutory guidance *Development Matters* (Early Education, 2012).

All these themes emerge from the ideas underpinning Bronfenbrenner's early model of three ecological domains: the family, the settings attended, and the community in which the child lives. Bronfenbrenner's theory has been extended and developed (Bronfenbrenner, 2005; Swick and Williams, 2006) but the simpler model, as modified by Myers, was used by Evangelou et al. (2009). This helpfully identifies how value systems and beliefs mediate these ecological domains. These factors come together in the social context and impact on the child's learning. Evangelou et al. (2009) represent this interplay in the diagram below with the arrows operating in all three domains (see Figure 17.2).

The importance of context explains why the statutory framework for the EYFS makes it clear that observations are not the sole preserve of setting-based practitioners: 'In their interactions with children, practitioners should respond to their own day-to-day observations about children's progress, and observations that parents and carers share' (*EYFS Statutory Framework 2.1*; DfE, 2017).

So observation is important in helping practitioners to understand children. When carried out in collaboration with parents it may set the child's learning not just in the context of the setting but of their family, cultural, social and community background. How effectively or authentically this happens will depend on a range of factors – not least the relationship established between staff and parents.

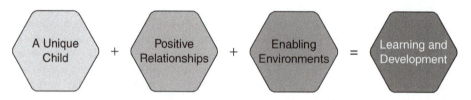

Figure 17.1 The four themes of the EYFS

Source: Early Education (2012) *Development Matters in the Early Years Foundation Stage*

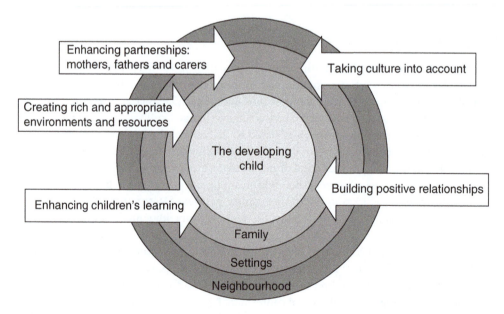

Figure 17.2 The contexts of children's development

Source: Evangelou, M. et al. (2009) *Early Years Learning and Development Literature Review*

THE PURPOSES OF OBSERVATION

The diagram (Figure 17.3) from *Development Matters* (Early Education, 2012) demonstrates how observation does not stand alone but is the starting point in the 'observation, assessment and planning' cycle. The main purpose of observation in most early years settings is to enable practitioners to begin to get to know the children and what they can do, assess children's progress and plan accordingly for their next steps in learning. It also helps them to assess whether their practice and provision is appropriate. Putting together observation evidence from the setting with evidence from parents (and sometimes other professionals involved with the child) also aims to help practitioners and parents develop a rounded, holistic picture of the child.

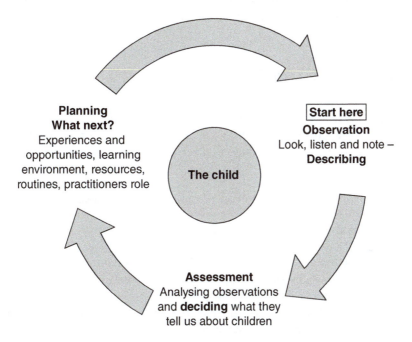

Figure 17.3   Observation, assessment and planning

Source: Early Education (2012) *Development Matters in the Early Years Foundation Stage*

Langston (2011: 16) illustrates the importance of this sharing with parents.

> A practitioner watched as a boy selected block after block, creating a 3m by 0.5m structure, until finally he ran out of floor space when his construction reached a wall.
>
> The practitioner was amazed to note the care with which the boy fitted smaller blocks against the wall so that no gaps were left between the wall and what she assumed was his 'path'. He then began to walk carefully along the 'path', stopping from time to time to stamp his heels firmly on certain blocks. Interested in the boy's imagination and concentration, the practitioner discussed his 'path' with him, photographed the construction and made a note about his precision and attention to detail.

Some time later she showed her photographs and observations to the boy's father who revealed, to her amazement, that the boy's construction was not a path but a parquet floor! It turned out that the boy had seen his father, a floor-layer, at work and had been imitating his actions, building a floor and compressing the tightly fitting blocks by stamping his heels on them.

This is also an example of how adult conversations with children are not always democratic dialogues in that children may want to please or be reluctant or unable to reveal the true extent of their thinking. If we think back to the story which started this chapter, the child showed great, possibly, unusual, belief in her idea and confidence in challenging the teacher's certainty about the impossibility of the task. (It is also worth considering, in relation to Langston's example above, how you might have approached the conversation with the boy making the 'path', in order to find out more about his thinking and what he was actually doing.)

OBSERVATION METHODS

If practitioners are following the cycle illustrated in Figure 17.3 it is important that observations are not just random or repetitive, but capture significant moments in children's thinking, learning or development because these observations are used as the first step in this important cyclical process. So what are the best ways to observe? The EYFS statutory framework is very clear that:

> Assessment should not entail prolonged breaks from interaction with children, nor require excessive paperwork. Paperwork should be limited to that which is absolutely necessary to promote children's successful learning and development (*EYFS Statutory Framework*, *2.2*; DfE, 2017: 13).

It appears that several things underpin successful observation: real interest in noticing what the child says and does; knowledge of child development; and observers' willingness to be aware of their own pre-conceptions. These are much more important than getting the right format – although that can help! There are some useful methods which minimise paperwork and support effective observation and which are utilised in many settings.

PARTICIPANT OBSERVATIONS

STICKY NOTES

For most of the time practitioners should be interacting with children but as we have seen, that does not stop them from observing learning. Many settings use sticky notes or labels for these incidental observations which can be dated and then stuck in a child's folder and/or shared with other staff. Practitioners only record things which are different or new for the child and which they regard as significant. In the example below (Figure 17.4), although this is an informal note, the practitioner has included the child's name, date, where the observation took place and added his or her initials at the end. This note was given to Connor's key person who added it to

> Connor M
>
> 17.10.12
>
> Craft area
>
> Connor tried again to make cuts in the edge of paper unaided and succeeded for the first time. He said 'Look, Look' to everyone as he repeated his success several times. DH

Figure 17.4 **Sticky note observation**

his folder, thought about how she could encourage his interest and new-found skill in future, and shared the information with his mother when she collected him.

DIGITAL PHOTOGRAPHY AND VIDEO RECORDING

The use of photographs and video has reduced the need for writing copious notes. Photographs can capture some of the process of children's learning as well as the product. For instance, a series of photographs can show Jessica, aged three, carefully placing beads and twigs on a piece of paper, her careful outlining of her structure with a purple felt pen and then her proud smile when she declares, 'It is finished!'. Video could enrich the observation even further by enabling her verbal communication and body language to be recorded.

Many settings now have access to small cameras and smartphones with excellent recording capacity. In some settings young children are used to being photographed and filmed – and taking their own photographs and making their own films – as well as watching the results on the whiteboard or laptop. Digital cameras and videos will date photographs and film and they can easily be shared with parents and other professionals. Settings often upload photos, film and other observations to secure sites for this purpose. All settings should have policies and procedures for seeking parental permission to take photographs and film footage of their children as well as policies on the safe use of the internet. You might want to reflect on how practitioners might obtain informed consent from children to use or share video and photographic images and why this may be important.

NON-PARTICIPANT OBSERVATIONS

The types of observation methods discussed above are very useful but often happen 'as and when' rather than having a specific focus. The result may be that practitioners have more information about some children than others. Many settings try to ensure that all children are observed in a more formal and focused way at regular intervals. Where there are concerns about a child's learning and development this may occur every week or even every day.

These observations may take various forms. It may be that each key person observes each child in their group as a non-participant observer on a rolling programme and as the term or the year progresses chooses different foci to ensure that the child has been observed across a wide variety of activities or contexts. It is important to observe play or a freely chosen activity as it is in these that the child will best demonstrate what they can do and how they think (see Chapter 13).

Sometimes practitioners will be using particular observation frameworks with all the children to inform them about aspects of their provision and/or children's wellbeing and involvement. This combination of wellbeing and involvement as an important indicator of children's learning has been developed by Ferre Laevers at Leuven University in Belgium and extensively used in the UK as part of the EEL and Baby Effective Early Learning (BEEL) programmes (Pascal et al., 2001; Bertram and Pascal, 2006).

The Leuven Involvement Scale uses five levels as a framework for observing children's involvement. Table 17.1 is a brief version adapted from Laevers (1994) and Robson (2006).

Table 17.1 Adapted Leuven Scale

Level	Activity
1	No activity. The child may appear to be mentally absent.
2	Actions with many interruptions for approximately half the time of the observation.
3	More or less continuous activity. The child is doing something but lacks concentration, motivation and pleasure in the activity. In many cases the child is functioning at a routine level.
4	Activity with intense moments. The activity matters to the child and involvement is expressed for as much as half the observation time.
5	Sustained intense activity. The child's eyes are more or less uninterruptedly focused on the activity. Surrounding stimuli barely reach the child and actions require mental effort.

Any scale that attempts to categorise another person's involvement will be open to many layers of interpretation. You may be interested in the case studies around this in Moylett (2013). A child may not appear to be engaged in the task that the practitioner has asked him or her to do but is very involved in some other learning. Think, for example, about the child who is not engaging with the adult-set task because he or she and a friend are negotiating and planning a course of action for when they go outside.

TARGET CHILD OBSERVATION

If practitioners have concerns about a particular child's development or behaviour they may want to carry out a series of **structured observations**. An example is the Antecedents, Behaviour, Consequences (ABC) approach (see, for example, Drifte, 2004). In this a non-participant observer spends some time focusing on what triggers the behaviour causing concern (the antecedents) then what actually happens and the consequences. Below and in Table 17.2, readers will find an example of a format for this form of observation.

Table 17.2 Example of format for ABCs of behaviour observation

ABCs of Behaviour					
Child's Name:		**Group/Key Person:**		**Recorded by:**	
Date	**Time**	**Antecedents**	**Behaviours**	**Consequences**	
		Who was the child with? Activity? What were adults doing/saying? Resources available? What happened immediately before the behaviour?	What exactly does the child do that causes concern?	What does the practitioner do/say? What does the child do/say? What do other children do/say? What do other adults do/say?	

After carrying out a series of these observations, practitioners and parents may reflect on the following questions to make an assessment:

- What do you think the child is communicating?
- How do you think the child might be feeling?
- What usually happens next?
- What do you think the child might be getting out of behaving this way?
- What do you think the other children might be getting out of him or her behaving in this way?

It is always important to bear in mind the fact that we are all biased observers, and this can be particularly significant when reflecting on children's behaviour. Many of the children, for instance, will have been brought up in a different culture than the observer's and their family and community may have different expectations regarding behaviour. Politeness rituals such as saying please and thank you, for example, are not universal. Some children may have been positively discouraged from making eye contact with adults as it is seen as disrespectful (Lane, 2008: 134).

TIME SAMPLING

Time sampling involves watching a child for a specific period of time, e.g. ten minutes at regular intervals throughout the day. Ideally this would be repeated at least once more in the same week. As well as giving information about a child, this form of observation can be helpful in finding out more about provision.

During their work on the *Every Child a Talker* programme (DCSF, 2009a), for instance, a nursery school in a very disadvantaged area had become increasingly concerned about language delay among the afternoon group of boys. In order to begin to understand their needs two types of observation were undertaken over a period of about one week. The observation methods included: (1) recording how the boys were using the environment, and where and when they interacted with adults; and (2) language observations recording the purposes of language children were using. The results are represented in Figure 17.5. The staff realised that the observations were telling them as much about their own provision and practice as about the children and they responded by making pedagogical changes in four main areas:

- Organisation
- Physical environment

- Interactions
- Experiences (DCSF, 2009a: 15–8).

FROM OBSERVATION TO ASSESSMENT

The next part of the cycle according to the diagram from Early Education (2012) (Figure 17.3) is assessment. There are two types of assessment:

- **Formative assessment**
- **Summative assessment**

In the assessment part of the cycle, practitioners reflect on what they have observed the child doing and/or saying. As well as standing back and observing, practitioners will usually have been interacting with the children, and these interactions will also have contributed to the picture. This stage can be described as a process of 'putting the clues together' to understand more about who the child is. These clues may reveal something about the child's:

- Feelings – pleasures, fears, excitements, security and so on.
- Preferences.
- Interests and current pre-occupations in what they are learning.

- Ways of approaching the world around them.
- Ways of thinking and learning.
- Skills and knowledge.

Deciding what the observation might say about a child is the practitioner's assessment. In order to make this assessment the practitioner draws on many aspects of professional knowledge and skill, including knowledge of child development and knowledge of likely learning pathways within and across different areas of learning. Moylett and Stewart (2012: 43) note:

> A good assessment also depends on using emotional intelligence, as well as awareness of the context, the culture, family and home experiences. What parents and carers share about the child outside of the setting provides crucial information to help practitioners and parents together to understand and interpret what they observe.

Effective assessment is never drawn from just one observation but is grounded in a growing awareness of the whole child. Formative assessment is ongoing because new observations often link to earlier ones and children's interests shift, sometimes in unpredictable ways. Observations need to be thought about and analysed in order to make decisions about both 'how' and 'what' the child is learning.

Sometimes observation, assessment and planning happen 'in the moment' and may only be 'recorded' in the practitioner's mind: babies and young children, however, are experiencing and learning in the here and now, not storing up their questions until tomorrow or next week. It is in that moment of curiosity, puzzlement, effort or interest – the 'teachable moment' – that the skilful adult makes a difference. By using this cycle on a moment-by-moment basis, the adult will be always alert to individual children (observation), always thinking about what it tells us about the child's thinking (assessment), and always ready to respond by using appropriate strategies at the right moment to support children's wellbeing and learning (planning for the next moment) (DCSF, 2009b).

Observations	Conclusions
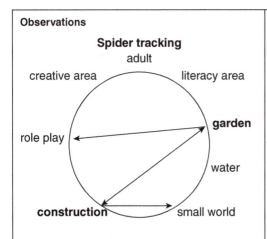 **Spider tracking**	• The boys' activities centred in a few areas, with a main pathway between the construction area and garden. • Boys rarely chose to access the literacy and creative areas. • Adults were deployed at planned activities but boys usually opted out of these and joined in only with encouragement. • Boys rarely approached adults – fewer than one interaction with an adult per boy each session. Where this did take place it was usually with their group leader (key person). • Boys therefore had limited exposure to skilled adult support for developing language.

Language observations		Conclusions
Communicate preferences, choice, wants or needs	✓(22)	• The boys used little language, for a limited range of purposes. • Little language was used to join play activities – the boys would first watch, then play alongside, then join without words. • A leader organised the play, and was the only one to plan the activity and assign roles. • Play was divided between girls and boys – conflict arose if groups of girls and boys were accessing the same activity.
Enter play or join an activity	✓(16)	
Plan, develop, or maintain play or group activity	✓(5)	
Resolve or avoid conflict	–	
Entertain, describe past events, tell or retell story	–	
Find things out, wonder, hypothesise	–	

Figure 17.5 Observations and assessment

Source: DCSF (2009a)

AN EXAMPLE OF THE OBSERVATION, ASSESSMENT AND PLANNING CYCLE

Figure 17.6 illustrates an example of a practitioner observing and assessing the learning of a group of children.

A group of four three- and four-year-olds are engaged in discussion about making a whale to go with some other sea creatures they have talked about and made. The practitioner's process is important but not recorded until after the event when she makes a brief note about her planning for later.

FROM ASSESSMENT TO PLANNING

The next stage in the cycle is planning and we saw the practitioner both assessing and planning 'in the moment'. Planning involves deciding how best to respond to, support and extend the children's wellbeing, interests, ways of learning, current competence and confidence, or their progress in skills

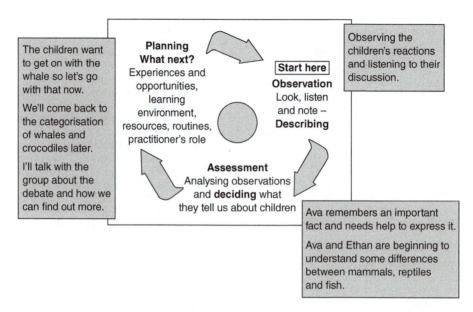

Figure 17.6 The observation, assessment and planning cycle in action – what the practitioner is thinking about and noting at each stage

Source: Moylett, 2013. Adapted from Early Education, *Development Matters in the Early Years Foundation Stage* (2012).

and knowledge. Settings will have their own approaches to short-term planning. Some arrange regular planning sessions where team members share observations and assessment and discuss ways forward for individuals and groups – sometimes knows as PLODs – Possible Lines of Direction.

RECORDING ASSESSMENT

As we saw in the discussion about making the whale, not all assessment is recorded but some of it must be in order to help children learn and provide evidence of progress which can be discussed and thought about with the children, their parents and other professionals. Many settings create learning journeys, learning stories, learning diaries and/or other forms of documentation. The purpose of these varies depending on the setting. Some settings develop learning stories with and for the children that become a significant part of the child's life, with contributions from children, staff and parents. These are often based on the ideas of Margaret Carr (see the further reading section at the end of this chapter). Other settings develop learning journeys or portfolios that are available for parents to see if they wish and are not regularly discussed with the children. Others illustrate and display the processes of learning and assessment on the wall as a public celebration of learning and development. Often these settings are influenced by the Reggio Emilia pre-schools approach to documentation. Rinaldi (Project Zero and Reggio Children, 2001: 83) describes their documentation as 'visible listening, the construction of traces (through notes, slides, videos and so on) that not only testify to the children's learning paths and processes, but also make them possible because they are visible' (see Chapter 13).

LIMITATIONS OF OBSERVATION – LINKS TO EFFECTIVE PRACTICE AND PROVISION

Although Ofsted is often cited as the reason for excessive paperwork, both the inspection handbooks introduced under the new Common Inspection Framework emphasise learning and teaching rather than administration (Ofsted, 2015a, 2015b). Ofsted's 2013 report on the features of strong early years leadership reported that in outstanding settings staff were routinely expected to ask themselves:

- What is it like for a child here?
- What difference are we making, and how do we know?

This becomes part of a self-improvement cycle of observation, reflection, improvement, further observation and evaluation. Effective staff always make links between what they observe the children doing, saying, thinking and feeling and the quality of their practice and provision. So the EYFS observation, assessment and planning cycle is replicated in the setting's professional development cycle.

Even in an outstanding setting the potential benefits of observation, assessment and planning can be limited by the approach to pedagogy that is employed. Stevens (2013) explores an interesting example:

> The practitioner plans an activity, based on observations of the children, identifying a learning intention of 'Counts up to three or four objects by saying one number name for each item.' Building on the children's interests in rhymes, the practitioner provides five green speckled frogs, a log and some crepe paper 'lily pad' leaves. The children engage in counting the frogs, some counting three or four frogs, saying one number name for each. The children are engaged, the practitioner makes observations and assesses their achievement in that particular aspect of learning and development.

Reading this you may think it sounds perfectly acceptable, but Stevens points out the limitations of the activity and how they can be avoided:

> If the children are fascinated by the number rhyme 'Five Little Speckled Frogs', then make a collection of all sorts of frogs – wooden, fabric, plastic, in different shapes, sizes and colours. Introduce these in wicker baskets, alongside logs and natural objects. Observe how the children investigate and explore the resources.
>
> Sabiha: Notice the descriptive and comparative language Sabiha uses as she sorts the frogs. Notice the words she uses to compare the size of the sets she creates – 'there are more green frogs, there's millions. No, not millions, one, two, three … eleven.' Notice also, how she puts the frogs into sets, starting with materials, then realizing this is too complex, debates size and moves on to colour – green, and 'not green'. She plans, makes decisions about how to approach her self identified task, solves the problem and reaches her goal. (Stevens, 2013)

Stevens brings us back to where this chapter started with a story about thinking that illustrates the fact that while observation can be informal it is never value free. It is also very dependent on what we notice or attend to. We are all biased observers who will interpret children's actions through the lens of our own experience and perspectives. Stevens shows us that it is not just these 'in observer' factors that influence what we observe but also what we provide for children because that influences the children's learning and behaviour. Remember the observations in the nursery school cited previously where concerns about boys' under-achievement led to changes in practitioner practice. If you want to explore what we notice (and don't notice) in more depth try reading Chabris and Simons (2011) and/or watching 'The Monkey Business Illusion' (Simons, 2010) which is both amusing and challenging!

CONCLUSION

Observation is about watching and listening to make learning visible. Children need adults beside them who are fascinated by their 'thinking in action' and use their observations to support and extend children's learning. Kline (1999) links the quality of our attention-giving skills to the creation of space to think. She states: 'The quality of your attention determines the quality of other people's thinking ... Attention, the act of listening with palpable respect and fascination, is the key to a Thinking Environment' (1999: 36 and 37). When adults pay that sort of attention to children they not only support children, but open themselves up to becoming what Bruce (1999) has called 'long-term-forever-learner' kinds of practitioners.

—————— Key points ——————

- Observation involves listening to and watching children in order to understand more about their development and learning.
- Practitioners can observe children while engaged in conversation and/or activity with them. They can also stand back as non-participant observers.
- Effective practitioners use observation as the basis for making assessments of children's interests, skills and knowledge. These assessments inform planning for possible next steps in learning and for improving practice.

—————— Recommended reading ——————

Margaret Carr's (2001) *Assessment in Early Childhood Settings: Learning Stories* is a useful guide to the philosophy and practice of observing and documenting children's learning through learning stories. Carr and Lee's *Learning Stories* (2012) is a more recent take on this approach.

18

UNDERTAKING RESEARCH WITH YOUNG CHILDREN

ALISON CLARK

CONTENTS

INTRODUCTION

This chapter sets out to provide an introduction to undertaking research with children and, in particular, with young children under five years old. The focus will be on qualitative research methods. The chapter will discuss some of the characteristics of research 'with' rather than 'on' children. This will be followed by a brief exploration of a number of challenges and possibilities of carrying out research with young children. A chapter of this length cannot give a comprehensive investigation of this important subject but is intended as a pointer to a number of key issues which can be followed up in volumes dedicated to research with children (for example, Greene and Hogan, 2005; Christensen and James, 2008a; Harcourt et al., 2011) and to individual research studies referred to in the text.

RESEARCH 'WITH' NOT 'ON' CHILDREN

Continuing interest in the sociology of childhood (see Chapter 3) has led to an increasing number of research studies which seek to understand children's own experiences of their everyday lives (for example, Davis et al., 2008; Clark et al., 2014). This research paradigm focuses on research 'with' rather than 'on' children (Fraser et al., 2014). The differences are rooted in how children are viewed in the research process. Do researchers view children as passive research objects on whom research is carried out or do researchers view children as active participants in the research process, sharing, for example, in what is being studied, the control of research tools and in what happens next as a result of the research?

Woodhead and Faulkner (2008) in their discussion of children and research within developmental psychology investigate a range of views about children which have been adopted within this influential discipline. They identify two of the approaches as the 'closely observed child' and the 'test tube child' (2008: 17–19). The 'closely observed child' might be the focus of intense observation in the same way as a wildlife documenter might observe animals from a hide:

> Observers may be found backed up against the corner of a classroom or playground trying to ignore children's invitations to join in the game, kidding themselves they can appear as a metaphoric fly on the wall. (Woodhead and Faulkner, 2008: 17)

A researcher setting out to observe three- and four-year-olds would probably encounter particular difficulties in trying to convince an enquiring group of young children that the researcher was in fact 'not there'. This particular form of **non-participant observation** is only one of a number of ways in which to undertake observations of children. Different approaches to observation will be discussed later in this chapter.

Woodhead and Faulkner illustrate their second category, the 'test-tube child' in which children are placed under a research 'spotlight' under laboratory conditions. They encapsulate this way of viewing children in research by referring to a photograph of the developmental psychologist Arnold Gessell undertaking research on a baby. The young child is seated within a glass dome. Gessell is standing in front of the child, dressed in his white laboratory coat. The photograph shows two other adults within the frame: a note taker and a cameraman (in addition to the photographer who captured this image). Two of the questions to be asked in interpreting such a scene might be: whose world is being explored here? Who is on strange territory, the researcher or the child?

Research which sets out to undertake research 'with' rather than 'on' children might be identified as research in which the researcher sets out to understand more about children's worlds by entering unfamiliar territory. This can involve learning directly from children on their own 'home ground' which may include a range of environments including a nursery (for example, Clark and Moss, 2011; Clark, 2010), a residential children's home (Emond, 2005) or a local neighbourhood (for example, Hart, 1979; Percy-Smith, 2002).

RESEARCH WITH YOUNG CHILDREN

There are particular challenges for those who are setting out to involve young children in research. This section will examine some of these challenges. The issues discussed are not unique concerns to the field of early childhood research. There are many other research groups whose ways of communicating challenge research strategies based on written communication. One such example is non-literate communities in the majority world (for example, Holland and Blackburn, 1998). However, the factors discussed below can be accentuated in the case of young children, particularly if the research participants are pre-verbal or with limited apparent verbal skills.

LANGUAGES

Establishing modes of communication between the researcher and the research participant is central to many qualitative research studies (Christensen and James, 2008b; Fraser, et al., 2014). Carrying out an interview, for example, relies on the researcher being able to express her or his questions in a way which conveys their meaning clearly without forcing a hoped-for response (Hatch, 1990). Misunderstandings can abound whatever the age group of the participant but there are particular complexities related to the thinking and language skills of young children.

The following is an example of misunderstanding taken from a research study with a group of three-to five-year-olds about their outdoor play space (Clark, 2005; Clark and Moss, 2005). The researcher was interviewing a group of children while they were all sitting outside in a play house:

> The question was: 'What is missing outside at [your pre-school]?' Some of the children's responses were more literal than anticipated. Children … answered 'the window'. The perspex was missing because a vandal had broken the pane and it had been removed. (Clark and Moss, 2005: 102)

This was a sensible answer in the context in which the researcher had asked the question but was a very different response than was anticipated. The research question appeared simple but was in fact asking the children to understand the term 'missing' in a particular way: 'In view of your experience of this and other play spaces what resources or opportunities should be added to this preschool's outdoor space?' (Clark and Moss, 2005: 102).

This last example illustrates the link between language and context in establishing meaningful communication between young children and researchers. A child who appears to be 'non-verbal' or using few words in the research environment may in fact be talkative at home or in another setting (see, for example, Wells, 1986). This may especially be the case for children for whom English is an additional language (see, for example, Brooker, 2002). Cousins (1999), in her research which focused on listening to four-year-olds, discusses several examples where the children's spoken contributions to the research were influenced by where the conversations took place. She describes a four-year-old boy, Dean, who had not talked to anybody during his first two weeks in his reception class:

> By chance, I watched him in the playground and saw Dean bend down and peep through the railings to look longingly at his old nursery. The children were just going out for a walk and I could see big tears rolling silently down his cheeks. (1999: 25)

Cousins asked Dean if he would like to visit his old nursery and with the permission of his teacher the researcher and child made a visit together:

> The change in Dean when we stepped through the nursery door was instantaneous and I captured it all on my mini-tape recorder.

> The children were still out having their walk, so Dean rushed round and round the nursery touching familiar toys and looking in cupboards and on shelves. He talked non-stop and when he spotted the indoor pond full of fish and tadpoles he remembered all the details of going to collect them and building the pond with his nursery nurse. (1999: 25)

These examples highlight the importance of how language is used and in what context to enable young children to be involved in research (see Alderson and Morrow, 2011 for a discussion of the importance of context when conducting research with older children). This leads to the question of whether babies and older non-verbal children can be active participants in research rather than passive research objects. An important starting point in such cases is to begin by establishing the modes of communication used by each individual child, whether this is a baby or an older child with disabilities. This tuning in to each child's preferred ways of communicating may require considerable effort, patience and imagination on the part of the researcher (see, for example, Davis et al., 2008).

These concerns draw attention to the importance of respect within the research relationship between the researcher and the research participant. This notion of respect is one of the characteristics of research which sets out to work 'with' rather than 'on' children.

POWER

Research can be understood in many ways. One interpretation is to see research as being about the revealing and handling of knowledge which in turn has an impact on the creators, gatherers and distributors of that knowledge. Research involving young children has the added complication of involving a generational imbalance of power between adult and child (Greene and Hill, 2005). When a researcher walks into a setting to begin a study he or she carries the twin advantage of being an adult and also a 'knowledge collector', the bearer perhaps of a notebook or laptop and audio recorder. This impression can be heightened, the younger the age group of the research participants. Awareness of the power divide can be the starting point for efforts to attempt to lessen these gaps in order for more honest communication to take place (see below). However, adult researchers still remain the most powerful players in the research process. This highlights the importance of considering the ethical implications of undertaking research with young children. Alderson and Morrow (2011) stress how this reflection on ethics applies throughout the research process from an early planning stage to dissemination.

CASE STUDIES

This next section draws on examples of two research studies with young children. The studies illustrate different ways of engaging with the challenges of language and power posed by undertaking research with young children. Both studies seek to listen to young children's perspectives about their everyday lives. The first, carried out by a Danish researcher, Hanne Warming, explores **participant observation** as a means of listening to young children (Warming, 2005). The second study involving the Mosaic approach uses participatory, visual methods to involve young children in the process of reviewing and changing early childhood provision.

Case study one: participant observation

Observation can cover a range of different approaches to research ranging from a detached 'invisible' observer described earlier to a 'total immersion' strategy whereby the observer seeks to join in or participate in the lives of those being observed. Warming describes the aim of 'participant observation' as to 'learn about "the other" by participating in their everyday life' (2005: 51). This is one of a number of interpretations of 'participant observation' (Atkinson and Hammersley, 1998; Montgomery, 2014).

The aim of Warming's study was to find out from young children about what an ideal life in early childhood provision would look like. She decided in this study to choose participant observation as the research method which fitted her research aims:

> Participant observation would allow me to study children's interactions with each other, with pedagogues and with the physical surroundings, whereas interviews would only allow me to study narratives about these interactions, producing a construction of children's cognitive perceptions of *det gode børneliv* contextualised by the interview process itself. (2005: 54)

The study carried out in a *bornehave* or kindergarten in Denmark involved Warming joining in the children's everyday lives. Warming explains:

(Continued)

(Continued)

> This participant role means the researcher makes an effort to participate in the children's everyday life in the kindergarten, and as far as possible in a way like the children do: play with the children, submit to the authority of the adult carers, abdicating from one's own adult authority as well as from one's own adult privileges. (2005: 59)

This approach can been seen as choosing to take a 'least adult' role (Corsaro, 1985; Mandell, 1991; Thorne, 1993; Mayall, 2000). This is one way of engaging with the question of power in relation to undertaking research with young children. However, as Warming states, the differences between adults and children cannot be removed but perhaps reconsidered and renegotiated through this research approach.

Spending time in the research setting immersed in the everyday routines of the young children's lives revealed several different sources of information for piecing together what were the significant ingredients of a 'good life' for the children in the setting. These pieces relied on different languages or modes of communication. Several sources of research material emerged from listening to children's talk with each other and their pedagogues together with conversations with the researcher. However, how children moved around the space and expressed their feelings through a range of non-verbal communication also formed a rich source of information. Warming describes this as 'listening with all the senses' (2005: 55). Participant observation thus provided more than one method for engaging with the research question.

Listening to young children through participant observation can be seen as one way of addressing the questions of power and language discussed. Warming presents the case for listening through participant observation as a form of giving voice to young children's perspectives in contrast to listening as a way of understanding:

> Giving voice involves listening, whereas listening does not necessarily involve giving voice. Listening as a tool requires hearing and interpreting what you hear, whereas giving voice further requires 'loyal' facilitation and representation, making common cause with children. (Warming, 2005: 53)

Case study two: the Mosaic approach

This second case study illustrates another possible research strategy for undertaking research with young children. The Mosaic approach is a framework for viewing young children as competent, active explorers of their environment. It has been developed by Alison Clark and Peter Moss as a research tool for listening to young children's perspectives (see, for example, Clark and Moss, 2005; Clark, 2010). The approach has since been adopted by other researchers and practitioners in the UK and abroad (for example, see Einarsdóttir, 2005). There are links between this approach and the idea of 'documentation' promoted in the pre-schools of Reggio Emilia in Northern Italy (Clark and Moss, 2005: 29–49).

The Mosaic approach is based on the following view or understanding of children and childhood:

- Young children as 'experts in their own lives' (Langsted, 1994);
- Young children as skilful communicators;
- Young children as rights holders;
- Young children as meaning-makers. (Clark and Moss, 2005: 5-8)

The Mosaic approach uses several different ways of listening to young children – the tools of observation and interviewing together with participatory tools. These are tools in which the children are actively involved in expressing their perspectives. These include taking their own photographs, making books of their images, taking adults on tours and recording the tours themselves, making maps and responding to images of other spaces (the magic carpet). The approach is designed to be flexible to allow for other methods to be used according to individual children's strengths or needs. The emphasis is placed on the researcher adjusting to the modes of communication preferred by the children rather than those in which the researcher is most comfortable. The listening is not designed as a one-off activity but as giving the research participants many different opportunities to think what they think, through using different modes of expression but also through revisiting and reviewing views and experiences expressed.

The adoption of digital photography as one of the research tools controlled by the children is one example of how young children have been 'placed in the driving seat'. During the first study in which the Mosaic approach was developed during 1999 and 2000, children took their photographs using single-use cameras. However, by the third study which began in 2004 many of the young children involved became more confident in using the digital camera and photo printer than the researcher. The introduction of visual methods, using both types of camera, opened up different possibilities for young children to document their experiences. Part of the value appears to relate to the cultural status of photographs:

> Cameras offer young children the opportunity to produce a product in which they can take pride. Children who have seen members of their family taking photographs, poured over family albums or looked at photographs in books and comics, know that photographs have a value in the 'adult world'. This is not always the case for children's own drawings and paintings. (Clark and Moss, 2011: 28)

One of the research tools in the Mosaic approach is map-making using children's own photographs and drawings (see, for example, Clark and Moss, 2005: 39–43; Clark, 2011a). This documentation can make children's perspectives visible in a way which can open up conversations with peers, practitioners, researchers and parents. The following example is taken from the Spaces to Play project, the second study undertaken by the authors of the Mosaic approach to involve young children in the redesign of an outdoor play space (Clark, 2005; Clark and Moss, 2005). Two three-year-olds, Ruth and Jim, had been engaged in leading the researcher on a tour of their play space while they recorded the tour with photographs. Ruth and Jim met shortly after the tour to make a map using their chosen images and drawings.

(Continued)

(Continued)

During this activity a visitor came to see the study in action:

Ruth: This is a very pretty map.

Researcher: It's a very pretty map. You know, it tells me such a lot about outside. Shall we see what Gina can see on our map? Gina, what do you think about our outside …

Gina: I can see that Ruth and Jim have very special things outside. I can see that you chose the prams and the buggies, and I can even see you in the picture so I know you like playing with those things, maybe. And, Jim, your favourite thing … I think your favourite thing outside might be the train. Yes? And can we have a picture of you outside with the train.

Ruth: What do I like?

Gina: You tell me what you like. Do you like Heather [member of staff] with the climbing frame?

Ruth: No, I like going on …

Gina: Oh, you like going on the climbing frame.

(Extract from Clark, 2005: 43–4)

Ruth relished the opportunity to be in control of the conversation and the meaning-making. She had been the one to ask the visitor for her interpretation of what she saw and took delight in contradicting the adult's interpretation. The power differences between adults and children are not removed by conducting research with children in this way but spaces are created within the research encounters which enable children to demonstrate their expertise.

Observation	Child interviews	Cameras and book-making
Tours	Map-making	Parent's views
Practitioners' views		Magic Carpet

Figure 18.1   An example of methods brought together in the Mosaic approach

Source: Clark, 2005

ROLES IN RESEARCH

This final section raises some questions about the roles of children and adults when research is undertaken with children. If the roles which children play within research are expanded there is a subsequent impact on the role of the researcher, other adults and, at times, the research audience.

THE ROLES OF CHILDREN IN RESEARCH

The case studies above have raised some possible ways in which children can be active participants during fieldwork. Alderson and Morrow (2011) have been among those to raise the question of how children – including young children – can be actively involved before and after fieldwork takes place – in setting the research agenda and in the analysis, writing up and dissemination. Kellett's work on children as researchers (for example, Kellett, 2005, 2010) has raised new possibilities for how children can take responsibility throughout the research process. When the research participants are under five years the term 'children as co-researchers' may be interpreted differently. The aim would not be to make young children into mini-adult researchers but to reinterpret the role in ways which demonstrated young children's competencies. In terms of setting research agendas it is far easier for young children to influence the topic explored in an action research model of research in which the local knowledge of adults and children is valued (see, for example, Reason and Bradbury, 2006).

There needs to be a note of caution here in assuming that every child will want to be engaged with research. As Roberts remarks:

> It cannot be taken for granted that more listening means more hearing or that the cost benefits to children of participating in research on questions in which they may or may not have a stake is worth the candle. (2008: 264)

This warning applies whatever the age of children involved. A research study may not be of particular interest to individual children or may be seen as an invasion of their time. Roberts continues:

> we need to be clear when it is appropriate for us to ask young people to donate time – one of their few resources – to researchers and when it is not. (2008: 271)

The question of children's voluntary engagement in research is an ethical one and sensitivity to the demands research may place on children's free time continues to be an important one at a time when the educational policy places more demands on children from a younger age.

ROLE OF THE RESEARCHER

Undertaking research with young children can release researchers from some responsibilities but at the same time can add new dimensions to their role. A researcher who shares power with children is relinquishing the need to 'know all the answers'. This can be a relief, realising that research seen in this way is not about gathering further evidence of what is known but expecting new ways of understanding to emerge. This role as 'adult as enquirer' may be at odds with the role children expect of adults. If the research context is one which highlights the role of adults as experts then this contrast may be marked. This may be the case for many children who take part in research in educational and health settings if the adults in these institutions are seen as the 'experts'.

A further freedom for researchers may emerge through the use of a wider range of 'languages' within the research process. Visual methods, for example, described in the second case study above, may open up new modes for communication for the researcher as well as for the research participants (see, for example, Thomson, 2008; Mitchell, 2011). This may lead to alternative approaches for researchers to record their research experience and to disseminate their findings.

However, undertaking research with young children places different ethical responsibilities on researchers (for example, see Harcourt et al., 2011). One particular concern with working with young children rests on how research findings are disseminated. Sharing conference platforms with young children may not be an appropriate use of their skills and time. However, this increases the importance of the researcher's role as mediator of the children's experiences.

ROLE OF PRACTITIONERS AND PARENTS

Research with young children needs to be viewed in context. Young children spend the majority of their time with adults and therefore research which seeks to understand their lives will also encounter adults, whether they are family members, practitioners or friends. There is a particular advantage of involving parents and practitioners in research with the youngest children, those under three years, as their knowledge of the fine details of children's lives will add important perspectives to research undertaken (for example, see the case study of Toni, age twenty-two months, in Clark and Moss, 2011: 38–41).

Research into the everyday lives of young children in early childhood environments raises questions about the experiences of practitioners. These spaces are shared spaces in which adults and children spend many hours together each week. One possibility is that the principles which can be applied for engaging with young children in participatory research can also be explored with practitioners. Such ideas have been investigated in a three-year study, Living Spaces, which set out to involve young children and adults in the design and review of a nursery and Children's Centre (Clark, 2010, 2011b). Here the visual, participatory methods have supported teachers, early years professionals, health workers and students to explore the question, 'What does it mean to be in this place?' This perhaps indicates that rather than discussing the need for child-friendly methods it is more a question of seeking 'participant-friendly methods' which enable participants of different ages and abilities to communicate their perspectives (Fraser et al., 2014).

CONCLUSION

This chapter has considered some of the ways in which children, particularly young children, can be involved in research. It has highlighted two areas in particular which need to be addressed in undertaking research with young children, those of language and power. The case has been made for developing research methods that play to the strengths of young children by drawing on different modes of expression, not limited to the spoken or written word. The question of power is an inevitable part of a research process between adults and children. There can be a freedom for the researcher as well as children involved if research is not viewed as a process of extracting the 'right' answer but as creating opportunities for the co-construction of knowledge. This in turn, raises issues concerning the ethics of research. Once children are involved in research the roles of adults are changed in some way, whether they are acting as researchers, practitioners or as a research audience. Reflecting on these issues is part of the ethical awareness necessary for embarking on research with rather than on research participants, whether those engaged are young children or adults. This is one indication of why developments in early childhood research over the past two decades may have wide implications for the undertaking of social research in general. Early childhood researchers, practitioners and students have important contributions to make to these debates.

Key points

- Engaging young children in research highlights issues of language and power.
- Research methods are discussed that play to the strengths of young children, involving modes of expression not limited to the spoken word.
- Research methods involving co-constructing meanings can relieve children and adults from the need to produce 'the right answers'.
- Research with young children always involves ethical questions.

Recommended reading

Clark (2011a) focuses on the process of map-making within the Mosaic approach as a site of multi-modal communication. It 'dissects' the research process to reveal the different modes of expression that young children adopt in co-constructing maps. This is followed by an investigation of how completed maps can facilitate the exchange of meanings within learning communities and professionals beyond educational contexts.

IS WORKING TOGETHER
WORKING?

ANGELA ANNING AND
MARTIN NEEDHAM

CONTENTS

INTRODUCTION

Over the last two decades Labour, Coalition and Conservative governments' policies have promoted integrated services delivered by multi-agency teams for families with young children. As Sonia Jackson outlined in Chapter 11, early years services have often been at the cutting edge of innovation in implementing the policies. It has been both the 'best and worst of times' to be a professional who works with young children and their families as services expanded and then adapted to fewer financial resources.

There are significant ideological differences between the different governments' approaches to public services. The New Labour vision was encapsulated in the famous 'onion' diagram (see Figure 19.1).

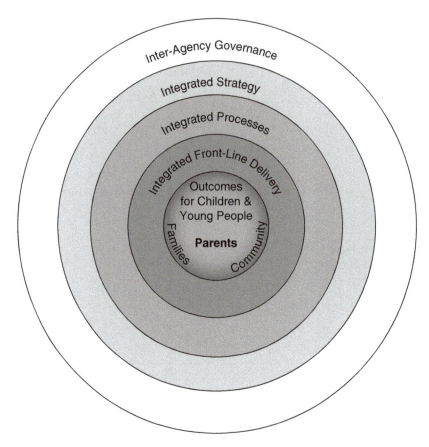

Figure 19.1   The New Labour model of integrated services

Source: DfES, 2004: 6

The Labour government invested massively in early years services (e.g. extending the hours of universal free education for all three- and four-year-olds), intervention programmes (such as Sure Start), workforce reform (e.g. Early Years Professionals) and the expansion of childcare (e.g. Neighbourhood Nurseries). The role of the state was central to addressing social exclusion, cycles of deprivation and poverty through universal services. Local authorities and settings charged with delivering services were audited by government regulation, targets and inspections (Anning et al., 2010).

The Coalition and Conservative governments have operated in a climate of economic austerity; sometimes it is hard to disentangle ideological from economic imperatives in their policies. The policy of Results Based Accountability produces performance related measures for all settings and agencies delivering services. Payment by results systems were introduced into Children's Centres in 2012. Results are linked to value for money and renewed funding and to ensure services reach the 'most troubled families'. This system, though draconian, may result in the analysis of data being fed back into revised practices. At the same time, the Coalition and current Conservative government's visions have been to decentralise and deregulate. The focus of government policy overall continues to reduce directly managed government jobs and seek to increase local solutions and diversity in services with a greater role for the voluntary and private sector. Prime Minister David Cameron's 2011 vision to achieve social justice in a Big Society (BBC, 2010), where volunteer and community based groups work alongside paid professionals to deliver services continued to be visible in his 2016 Life Chances speech. Subsequently, in 2017 Prime Minister May's approach has been to shift attention away from rights and towards shared responsibilities to address inequalities.

Local authorities are responsible for strategic thinking and commissioning and for delivering statutory services. However, conservative policy has emphasised that the 'nanny' state is to be rolled back from the private space of family life. Unless families are identified as 'at risk' or in need of authoritarian treatment, families were to take responsibility for their own futures (Cameron, 2016: Harold et al., 2016). It remains to be seen whether the new administration's attention to 'everyday injustices' and shared responsibilities will effect change in this respect.

Despite different ideologies, Labour, Coalition and Conservative governments are united by a strong commitment to early intervention and partnerships with parents, to address poverty by tackling parental unemployment, to increase efficiency by systemic changes, to rely on evidence-based practice and to continue with 'joined up thinking' in the design and delivery of services. The 2015 Conservative government continues to develop multi-agency policy in this context in the form of the Life Chances strategy wider services plan, although central government guidance is currently focused on core safeguarding responsibilities in the form of Multi-Agency Safeguarding-Hubs (MASH) (Home Office, 2014) and looking more broadly across the life course to tackle 'troubled families'.

MULTI-AGENCY WORKING

The agreed core functions of a multi-agency safeguarding hub (MASH) were listed as:

1. Acting as a single point of entry - gather all notifications related to safeguarding in one place.

2. Enabling thorough research of each case to identify potential risk (and therefore the opportunity to address that risk).

3. Sharing information between agencies, supported by a joint information sharing protocol.
4. Triaging referrals, exemplified in the use of agreed risk ratings.

5. Facilitating early intervention to prevent the need for more intensive interventions at a later stage. Managing cases through co-ordinated interventions. (Home Office, 2014)

At a time of more limited funding, this is a more reactive and targeted working model focused on those in most need as compared to previous more proactive, preventative and universal government definitions of multi-agency working. Local authorities continue to refer to multi-agency support as Team around the Child or Family meetings (TAC/TAF). These services may work together within a single unit, either co-located or virtual through regular meetings across services and with families. Multi-agency working could involve anyone whose job or voluntary work puts them in contact with children, young people and their families and is likely to include professionals from social work, health, education, 'Early Years', youth work, playwork, guidance and counselling, police and youth justice.

The benefits are intended to include:

- early identification and intervention;
- easier or quicker access to services or expertise;
- improved achievement in education and better engagement in education;
- better support for parents;

- children, young people and family's needs addressed more appropriately;
- better quality services;
- reduced need for more specialist services. (DfE, 2012)

One can read into these statements the underpinning vision that built on the theme of prevention which was central to New Labour's social exclusion task force policy and continues to underpin the importance of early intervention in improving young children's life chances and trajectories.

THEORETICAL PERSPECTIVES

Government policies all over the world have shifted from considering the child in isolation from societal, community and familial contexts to a clear understanding that all these features of a child's life are inter-related. The application of socio-cultural theory to this construct of childhood has informed our thinking on how changes in social policy impact on those who both deliver and receive integrated services.

In the United Kingdom, integrated services have developed from the distinct and separate histories and traditions of social services, the National Health Service and education. Of particular relevance to inform our understanding of the impact of policy changes are two socio-cultural-historical theoretical frameworks (see Chapter 10). We have found these helpful in trying to understand how the policy of multi-agency working has impacted on early years practitioners and service users.

First, Wenger's (1998) seminal work on *communities of practice* explores how knowledge is generated and shared in the world of work. Some knowledge is conceptual, learned in training or from propositional knowledge, e.g. psychology or sociology. Some is experiential, learned in the daily routines of working, often embedded in actions. Knowledge gained from experience is mostly tacit. We are rarely required to make it explicit or justify it to clients. Wenger argues that new members of a community are introduced to this kind of knowledge through *legitimate peripheral participation* alongside more experienced practitioners. This kind of knowledge may generate habits or rituals which are seen as 'normal' within a community of practice. Practitioners from different agencies are trained and experienced in distinct practices – e.g. working as a family support worker or as a teacher – and use different languages or styles of discourse to exchange information in their daily work. These ways of acting and talking within a particular community can exclude others, including service users, and may be problematic when groups of professionals are required to work together in multi-agency teams.

Wenger's model of how knowledge is created in communities of practice defines two complementary processes: *participation* and *reification*. Participation involves the daily, situated interactions and shared experiences of members of the community working towards a common goal. Staff in a Children's Centre bring together the previous histories, cultures and activities of nursery education and day care to an integrated setting where they are required to work together delivering seamless services. Reification involves the explication of these versions of knowledge into representations. These may be embodied in the artefacts in a centre (for example, alphabet friezes and floor cushions), documents (for example, children's profiles on the Early Years Foundation Stage Curriculum and daily notes on young children's diets for their parents) and rules and rituals (for example, all children must 'do' an educational activity each day and key workers must always 'hand' the child to the person who collects them at the end of the day). The problem is that workers from day care settings may have made very different uses of artefacts than workers from educational settings. A book or paper and pencil may be used in informal, play-based activities by day care staff – storying and drawing. In educational settings they may be used in formal, didactic activities – learning about letters and practising writing one's name – in preparation for 'school readiness' (DfE, 2013), which continues to be advocated by government. Rules and rituals around eating and toilets may be dominated by health and safety concerns by care workers, but by the exigencies of 'the school day' by teachers. New members of the communities, such as trainees or children, are encultured into the activities, acquiring the relevant discourse and habits as they learn how to be professionals or pupils. It is unlikely that staff from either agency would have been expected to justify their rites and rituals to anybody. It is just what they do.

A second theoretical perspective we have found useful is Engeström's *activity theory*. In activity theory (Engeström, 1999) a key concept is that new knowledge is created within work organisations through collaborative activities each of which may form *parallel activity systems*. The *subject* of an activity system is the agent from whose point of view an analysis of the work activity is perceived. The *object* is the raw material (overweight children) or problem space (poor educational standards) at which the activity system is directed. The *outcomes* may be intentional – improvements in children's health or educational outcomes – or unintentional – dissatisfaction of parents with clinical services 'telling them' how to feed their children or three-year-olds becoming alienated from 'school' learning. The *instruments* utilised to work towards outcomes include powerful tools such as health visitor records, immunisations procedures or the developmental assessments of two-year-olds, 'school readiness' equipment and training, or informal notes on children's interests and achievements. The *community* comprises the many individuals and groups who share the common aim of servicing the welfare, health and educational needs of a locality. Their *division of labour* is premised on both horizontal division of tasks across services and vertical division of tasks through power and status of individuals within services. Finally, *rules* underpin all activity systems and regulate the way members of the community allocate time to tasks, record their actions, are appraised for their efficiency and are allocated rewards and promotions.

An activity will look very different to a health visitor, family support worker or an early years professional, though they may share the same intended outcomes of the health, development and wellbeing of a child. An important premise in Engeström's model is that since subjects within a team construct objects in an activity system differently, conflict is likely to arise as tasks are redefined, reassigned and divided differently within changing organisations. Different perspectives or 'voices' meet, collide and eventually merge into new versions of knowledge. His premise is that these conflicts must be brought out into the open and articulated in debates if any progress is to be made towards creating new forms of knowledge appropriate for new social/political/historical situations and contexts. Through contradictions within and between activity systems being articulated and evidenced, connections can be used creatively to create strategies for managing change. Engeström describes how these connections should be anchored up to a vision for the future and down to actions that are 'real'. His research methods for eliciting understandings of knowledge creation in working organisations include taking evidence of work activities (photographs, films or written descriptions) to meetings to confront subjects with different perspectives (for example, those of doctors, nurses and patients), recording their dialogues and transcribing their interactions for subsequent analysis and reflection. In turn these analyses of what has been said are fed back to the members of organisations or communities to support them in articulating and refining an extended, shared knowledge base. They are then able to design and 'own' new activities which exemplify or represent the team's extended, shared knowledge.

EXAMPLES FROM THE REAL WORLD

Throughout the last two decades we have observed professionals grappling with the realities of multi-agency working. Between us we have evaluated Centres of Excellence, Sure Start Local Programmes (SSLPs), Children's Centres and vulnerable/at risk two-year-olds in day care programmes. Within these different socio-cultural-political contexts we have observed common dilemmas and have grouped a discussion of these dilemmas into three sections: *Who I am*, *What I know* and *What I do*.

WHO I AM

Some early years practitioners were recruited into multi-agency teams such as those who applied for jobs in **SSLPs** (many of which morphed into Children's Centres in 2005). These early adopters were 'volunteers'. They had seen for themselves the limitations of children's services operating in silos and welcomed the opportunity to develop new ways of working. Others found that their workplace settings were transformed by government/local authority edicts into integrated service settings. These workers were 'conscripts' to the vision of integrated services, grouped into multi-agency teams at a discomforting rate, often with little preparation or training.

Individuals brought to the teams the baggage of their own 'tribal' affiliations to a particular agency such as social services, education, health or welfare. They brought their personal histories of the status and hierarchies of particular disciplines within agencies – teachers and nursery officers, speech therapists and health visitors, social workers and family support workers, psychologists and doctors. Their identities, values and beliefs were different. An example was the way they explained the causes of family dysfunctions or attributed 'blame' for problems. A social worker might blame a family crisis on the inequalities inherent in a divided society; a teacher might blame parents' lack of aspirations and education; a health visitor might blame poor parenting and children 'failing to thrive'. Each 'tribe' had its own language and preferred ways of 'treating' problems. It is no surprise that, as Engeström's theory predicts, the 'voices' of these disparate groups of practitioners collided.

Often members of multi-agency teams found their professional identities destabilised by these collisions (Frost and Robinson, 2016). Most had excellent track records in their jobs; that is why they were appointed to innovative services. They were anxious when they saw responsibilities at which they had traditionally excelled being handed to, as they saw it, 'less well qualified' professionals. For example, a health visitor said of outreach work in a SSLP, 'Sometimes I get anxious when family support workers seem to be taking on work that I see is my role in families'. A speech therapist in a nursery for children with disabilities expressed concern that she was asked to 'train' nursery officers to work with children with language delay in the 'classrooms' rather than delivering the specialist treatment herself in clinics (though appointments were often missed).

Blurring of professional roles was confounded by labels assigned to them in revised staffing structures. A teacher in a Children's Centre told us that being rebranded as a generic 'nursery worker' and expected to take on routine care work with under-three-year-olds had made her feel under-valued: 'I don't know if I'm a nursery nurse or a teacher any more'. A care worker expressed unease at being expected 'to act like a teacher and deliver a curriculum these days – I'm not a teacher'. A worker in a child mental health team said: 'First of all we called ourselves project workers, which I absolutely hated, because it says that we could be someone who had been employed as a volunteer you know, off the streets, without any qualifications ... Now we've got this new ghastly generic label and I can never say it without stumbling over it and people have no idea what it means'.

The complications of differing pay and conditions of work exacerbated tensions. A teacher in a Children's Centre, working 'traditional' school hours and with school holiday entitlements is likely to earn more than their manager who works under less generous social services day care conditions, pay structures and holiday entitlements. An early years professional, trained to graduate level, with responsibility for early learning within a setting, is paid far less than a teacher. It takes determined leadership and skilful management to disentangle these inequalities, anxieties and resentments about professional identities and changing roles and responsibilities. A key imperative is that team members support both the emergent team as a unit and at the same time individuals who are struggling with new working practices that make them feel insecure or uncomfortable. Leaders in settings who understood this imperative were much more likely to translate a vision of integrated services into practices that 'worked' (Ang, 2011).

WHAT I KNOW

Sharing knowledge is critical to making multi-agency team work effective. But it takes time and infinite patience to listen to and learn about what colleagues from other agencies know, and time is a precious commodity. Making time for meetings is problematic; as one practitioner said, 'Who looks after the children while we sit and talk to each other?'. A further complication is that many peripheral but essential members of multi-agency teams are seconded or employed on a part-time basis. Time for attending meetings is not costed into their hourly contracts. Managers struggle to find times when all staff members are able to attend.

As we observed teams struggling to understand other professionals' perspectives, values, language and knowledge it became clear that some strategies *are* productive in sharing and redistributing knowledge. Managers and leaders need to set up robust and reliable systems for sharing core knowledge and current information. Strategic information and policy-based knowledge/updates can be shared electronically. But deep knowledge exchange requires a different approach. When staff join the team, annual dates and times for regular, well-chaired, whole team meetings (monthly) and more reflective away days (when the settings are closed on dates to which parents are alerted well in advance) need to be mandatory and costed into hourly contracts. For groups within settings, the most effective way of sharing knowledge is for sub-groups to meet to share evidence of their daily activities (what Wenger called 'participation'). Participants bring to the meetings work schedules, notes of encounters with parents, children's work or records or specific case studies to use as the stimulus for exchange of ideas (Anning and Edwards, 2006). For individuals within teams, work shadowing or delivering services with colleagues from different agencies, observing their 'reifications' of practice, are productive. Implicit knowledge is made explicit as professionals work alongside each other. However, time needs to be set aside in staff/team meetings to tease out, discuss and make explicit this kind of knowledge. This is best done by openly sharing examples of critical incidents or observations of practice from the team's workplaces. This kind of collaboration provides fertile ground for teams to work together to co-construct 'expanded' versions of their professional knowledge.

A further challenge is sharing professional knowledge with volunteers. Parent Champions were developed and funded in response to evidence from evaluations of early intervention programmes of low take up of services by many of the most vulnerable families. In Parent Champions projects parent volunteers from local communities are trained to reach out to other parents to support children's participation in early learning. Value is placed on the parents' own local knowledge and sharing knowledge between professionals and parent champions is a two-way process. Partnership with parents requires new ways of redistributing and co-constructing knowledge. Evidence from the National Evaluation of Sure Start (National Evaluation of Sure Start, 2011) and The Effective Pre-School and Primary Education 3–11 Project (EPPE) (Sylva et al., 2008) reinforced the importance of actively involving families in the development, health and wellbeing of children. The quality of the home learning environment – measures such as access to books, amount of story reading, paper and pencils, use of libraries, everyday opportunities for learning about numbers, shapes and sizes – predicted better than expected cognitive outcomes for children, regardless of the socio-economic status of their family. It is more important what parents do with their children than who they are. This kind of evidence sits uneasily with systems based on socio-economic indicators as predictors of children's potential attainments.

For professionals to work in true partnership with parents requires courage and new skills. The most radical SSLPs had a vision of *empowering parents* and redistributing knowledge to the local community. They encouraged local parents to volunteer, train, then gain employment in local services. For these programmes, the redistribution of professional knowledge was a democratic aim, crucial to capacity building in the local community and in common with a 'funds of knowledge' orientation to community engagement (e.g. Moll et al., 1992). An evaluation officer said:

> Our early years, speech and language and occupational specialists are willing to share expertise, because they acknowledge that so much of what they do is not rocket science. It is the ethos of this Sure Start that those things can be shared. It's encouraging people to come from the community to be trained.

Such a radical approach to the redistribution of knowledge brings with it the challenges of maintaining quality and the threat of deskilling professionals. It is hard to get the balance right. A speech and language therapist expressed this dilemma:

> We are cascading information down, because this is our model. We like to get the community and parents working on the programme. We can teach them practically how you do it, we can teach them the words to say, but there are all the other things, like the professionalism, that isn't there. We are now trying to make sure that these people have the right kind of training, that they've got confidence in their own skills, but they're not over confident and they don't think, I know everything there is to know about speech and language. I've found that quite difficult. (Anning et al., 2005: 45-6)

A final challenge is how professionals from different agencies, volunteers and parents as partners share information about families and children. The Common Assessment Framework (CAF) was designed to collate information about families with additional or complex needs. A team of professionals who are in contact with the family, including family members themselves, meet to contribute perspectives on the family's needs. The administration and responsibility for enacting the CAF is co-ordinated by a Lead Professional (a Special Educational Needs Co-ordinator (SENCO), teacher, health visitor or family support worker) who acts as the single point of contact for the team around the family (TAF). The policy of the Coalition government is that such protocols and systems enable multi-agency teams to *develop outcomes-focused plans for time-limited interventions that are owned by the families themselves*. These aspirations sound neat and efficient; but in the real world of communities with complex needs, issues of confidentiality trouble practitioners. Volunteers have to be trained in how to deal with confidential information. Health professionals and social workers have anxieties about handling sensitive information inherited from the disciplines of their own agencies. In one SSLP the manager's attempt to get her team to share administrative space and work stations to promote better communications and more efficient use of space was thwarted when the health visitor moved her files into a locked cabinet and her work station into a cupboard. She refused to budge.

WHAT I DO

Without a shared vision and good leadership multi-agency teams retreat back into their preferred, single agency ways of working. Engeström calls them *'parallel activity systems'*.

The ways in which professionals and parents use spaces is a metaphor for how people are able to change what they do. During the decades when SSLPs and Children's Centres were flagship exemplars of 'joined up' thinking and practice, costly, new buildings were designed and built with single, non-stigmatised reception areas, multi-purpose service delivery suites and shared staffrooms. Yet we observed spaces designed for generic purposes re-shaped into separate zones, cupboards and shelving used to screen off sections of shared areas and doors shut. A popular 'Stay and Play' area for children and parents attending pre- and postnatal clinics was closed down during clinic hours because health staff complained that it was too noisy. Community cafés where parents and young children met to socialise in a relaxed and safe space were converted into offices by managers on 'health and safety' grounds. A parent said: 'They shut our café down because they said it was too risky to have hot drinks where there were kids around'.

Some services did offer genuinely new ways of working. As the speech therapist quoted above said, these activities were not 'rocket science'; but they were informed by a different kind of understanding. One example is given next.

Example 1

A teacher was seconded to an intervention project designed to promote early literacy and language in an area where many children started school with poor communication skills and little experience of books/reading. She worked in a range of settings such as pre-school playgroups in church halls, sessional care for children whose parents attended literacy and numeracy training and Children's Centres. She was used to working in the ethos of a nursery school and found the 'chaotic' nature of the sessions in her new peripatetic role unsettling. She found herself retreating into 'teacherly' behaviours – sitting with groups of children in the corner focusing on books/storying and emergent writing activities. She was polite to the parents; but they tended to sit around the edges of the rooms talking and drinking coffee, enjoying rare opportunities to talk with like-minded adults. The teacher saw the children and their development as her prime responsibility and the parents were equally preoccupied with their own priorities.

During a particularly 'chaotic' stay and play session, the teacher made a quick decision to staple onto a parents' notice board drawings of their families that the children had done with her that day. Parents crowded around the board to look at the drawings. The teacher stood with them and chatted informally. She used the 'object' of the display to anchor down to realities of their own children's drawings and anchor up to general talk about the development of children's mark-making, drawing and writing.

She recalled later that this intuitive action marked a turning point in what she did in all her subsequent work. Having gained a way of talking with parents, she was able to build up a rapport with them. She encouraged them to make and enjoy scrap books of their own child's mark-making at home and in setting sessions. A group of parents recreated the local Post Office in the role play area to encourage their children to talk and 'write'. Two fathers made scrap books with the children from magazines about football and cars. Parents began taking a real interest in story books they borrowed from the setting, making puppets with the children to act out the stories and enjoying reading to their children. The pivotal moment for this professional was when she connected with the parents. It turned her relationship with the parents into one of mutual co-operation for the benefit of the children's development as eager learners of early literacy.

CONCLUSION

What evidence is there that working together works? NESS reported that SSLPs improved some parent outcomes, but results for child outcomes, particularly cognitive measures, were disappointing. Where health workers worked closely with SSLPs, their well-tried systems for home interventions and record keeping enhanced the effectiveness of services for young children. These results encouraged the adoption in the UK of Family Nurse Partnerships (NHS, 2016) to work with young teenage parents.

It was disappointing that the educational outcomes of the target SSLP children were not 'better than expected'. It is likely that the emphasis on universal free early education for all three- and four-year-olds in the control groups accounted partly for this finding. The good news was that most young children in the UK were benefiting from free early education. However, the influential EPPE project reported that educational outcomes were better when children had access to high quality teaching. Qualified teachers are too expensive for many settings; many employ graduate level Early Years Teachers (EYTs) instead who are less well paid. Evaluation of the impact of EYTs' forerunners – Early Years Professionals (EYPs) – suggested that, especially if they were managers, they could improve the quality of provision for over-three-year-olds. However, both studies suggested further development of the pedagogy for two-year-olds was required (Mathers et al., 2011; Hadfield et al., 2012). This is particularly significant since many of the most disadvantaged two-year-olds are offered fifteen or thirty hours a week of free 'education and childcare'. The need to provide appropriate pedagogical training for staff and funding for places continue to raise concerns.

Children's Centres, though less well funded, continue to be expected to coordinate services to improve outcomes for young children and their families, with an increased focus on the most disadvantaged families. Multi-agency teamwork, though in many respects still unproven and more difficult to implement with fewer resources, continues to be a key idea within early intervention. Each centre has linked health visitors to provide advice and run services, plus linked social workers to help build confidence in child protection. Outreach staff continue to manage home-based interventions but these are increasing targeting services for 'troubled families'. However, no matter what central government policy changes for integrating early years services are introduced, without a serious commitment to developing in the workforce the knowledge, skills and attitudes to make working together work, the kinds of dilemmas outlined in this chapter will not go away.

Key points

This chapter has:

- Summarised successive governments' ideologies and approaches to policymaking to support families with young children, especially those in poorer localities. Despite their different ideological positions, successive governments have promoted inter-agency and multi-professional working but these practices have had different emphases and structures as a result of changing government priorities.
- Highlighted some of the tension, challenges, opportunities and benefits that can be involved when different professionals are tasked with working together and developing partnerships with parents.
- Demonstrated how theories can help to identify, illuminate and unravel some of the complexities that characterise multi-agency working. So while working together across professional boundaries can be notoriously difficult, theories such as Wenger's 'Communities of Practice' and Engeström's 'Activity Theory' can help professionals to understand and resolve some of the challenges of multi-professional teamwork.

Recommended reading

For information on research methods and the theory underpinning this chapter read Frost and Robinson (2016) *Developing Multi-Professional Teamwork for Integrated Children's Services* (see reference list).

EFFECTIVE EARLY CHILDHOOD LEADERSHIP

CAROL AUBREY

CONTENTS

INTRODUCTION

This chapter focuses on effective early childhood (EC) leadership. It will consider the role that EC leaders play in the improvement of outcomes for very young children, particularly those growing up in circumstances of poverty. It will not linger on generic leadership and management skills but will attempt to identify ways in which EC leaders may have an impact on worthwhile outcomes for children. It will examine what existing policy requires and what EC leadership literature reveals. It will also draw upon EC leadership research carried out by the writer and colleagues with EC leaders who are willing to explore their own leadership and interrogate their own leadership practice. The chapter will end with an exploration of emergent themes that may shed further light on effective EC leadership practice.

CHANGING POLICY CONTEXT

When the British Coalition Government came into office in May, 2010 it inherited three strands of early childhood policy: social-welfare services for children and their families living in poverty, delivered by Sure Start children's centres; universal state-funded early childhood education for three- and four-year-olds of fifteen hours a week, delivered in schools and by private-sector providers; and childcare for children with employed parents, delivered by the private sector (Lloyd, 2015). At the time, a number of reports were commissioned and published, with a particular focus on addressing the needs of the most disadvantaged families and young children; ensuring that all children were 'ready for school'; and providing affordable and accessible childcare for working families. As noted by Eisenstadt (2011), a theme of recent years has been early intervention. The Frank Field review of poverty and life chances (Field, 2010) considered in particular the effect of the home environment on school readiness and strongly recommended further investment in the early years. Meanwhile, the Graham Allen review of early intervention (Allen, 2011) endorsed the need to break the cycles of family deprivation to ensure children were school-ready but also went on to emphasise evidence-based parenting programmes to improve the outcomes for children. In line with this focus on early intervention, the Coalition Government (2010–2015) committed to expand free universal early education to the poorest one-fifth of two-year-olds. This came at a time of severe economic recession between 2011 and 2012 that, combined with public funding cutbacks, had repercussions on the provision of the government's financial support and services to families.

At the same time, the Clare Tickell review of the Early Years Foundation Stage (EYFS) statutory guidance on the curriculum for birth to five years and the EYFS Profile (Tickell, 2011) proposed simplification of the EYFS, with a focus on three areas of learning: personal social and emotional development; communication and language; and physical development. As with the reviews of Field, Allen and Tickell, the Eileen Munro review of child protection (Munro, 2011: 10) emphasised the growing body of evidence of the effectiveness of early intervention with children and families and shared their view on the importance of providing early help.

Tickell (2011:7) also stressed the importance of a 'strong, well-qualified early years workforce' throughout her review. Accordingly, Professor Cathy Nutbrown's review of early education and childcare qualifications (Nutbrown, 2012) considered the overall qualifications system and its fitness to provide EC practitioners with the knowledge, skills and experience necessary for their role. In terms of leadership, the Nutbrown review focused most attention on pedagogic leaders who work directly with children, leading by example and supporting other staff in the setting with their practice, and their reflection on this and its refinement. Brief reference was made to the National Professional Qualification in Integrated Centre Leadership (NPQICL) introduced for children's centre leaders that has since been discontinued. The government's response to this report was to announce two new early years qualifications: the Early Years Teacher, with training and assessment suitable for children from birth to five years to work in reception classes, and the Early Years Educator at level 3 National Vocational Qualifications (NVQ) (DfE, 2013).

More recently, under a Conservative Government since 2015, these developments have been honoured despite a period of austerity and cuts to local authority budgets. Overall, there have been extensions to the number of early learning places for the most disadvantaged two-year-olds, the introduction of training for the Early Years Teacher and Early Years Educator, a tax-free childcare scheme for working families and early years pupil premium to provide extra funding for providers to support disadvantaged three- and four-year-olds, an updated EYFS framework (DfE, 2017) and profile and a new early years inspection framework (Ofsted, 2015a). Meanwhile there is no recognised leadership training and development for EC leaders unless they undertake the National Qualification for Headship in primary schools.

RESEARCH EVIDENCE ON EFFECTIVE EARLY CHILDHOOD LEADERSHIP

Over a past decade of strong policy and public attention to EC education, many OECD countries have focused on expanding access, improving quality, and developing more coherent and co-ordinated policies (Neuman, 2005). Countries have followed different models for organising EC systems, with potential implications for quality regulations and staffing (including leadership), access and funding, and coherence of services. A small but increasing number of countries have developed integrated care and administrative arrangements under the auspices of education, resulting in more centralised and prescriptive approaches to decision-making, regulation, monitoring and evaluation of learning and achievement. Consequently, a contextual analysis of EC leadership has been proposed based on Bronfenbrenner's ecological theory (see Chapters 5 and 7) (Nivala, 2002; Hujala, 2013). This draws attention to all the operating environments of leadership, from the micro-level closest to the leader, to the institutional structures and wider macro-level societal influences that define leadership. EC leadership is thus seen to operate within a broader social structural system that recognises the effect of external structural as well as internal organisational factors. An EC social systems perspective has also been associated with the concept of a self-improving system in education, by Siraj-Blatchford and Sum (2013).

While research into effective educational leadership is abundant in the compulsory-education sector, it remains under-investigated in EC research (Muijs et al., 2004; Robinson et al., 2009). Bush (2014: 543) identified many models of educational leadership,

distributed leadership being 'most favoured'. He also noted that instructional or ped-agogical leadership was regaining significance. Whilst distributed leadership approaches have been advocated, theorising and researching is relatively recent and much is focused on school leadership (Heikka et al., 2012). Moreover, it is an evolving concept that marks a shift from leadership as an individual to a collective enterprise that operates at differ-ent organisational structures and levels, through situations, relationships and processes. Heikka and Waniganayake (2011) also noted the overlap between distributed leadership and pedagogical leadership, connecting effective leadership with both children's learning and capacity-building.

Bush (2014: 3) suggested that 'leadership for learning' models may be located more often in decentralised contexts that are less hierarchical and where principals have more scope to deter-mine leading and managing. Scrivens' (2002) exploratory study in New Zealand identified a desired leadership style emphasising consultation, communication and empowerment that did not sit easily with an increasingly neo-liberal climate of competitiveness and control. Woodrow and Busch (2008: 83) in Australia also noted that EC practitioners did not readily identify with leadership in a situation of 'increasing control … through mandated curriculum and auditing, the rise of corporate childcare and commodified children's services'.

Chan (2014) explored EC principals' more centralised leadership styles in Hong Kong, noting that they were expected to be autocratic. This finding aligned with Ho's (2010) report of centralised approaches to EC leadership in Hong Kong in which she concluded that characteristics of leadership practice as perceived by various school stakeholders were different from the concepts of distributed leadership prevalent in Western literature. At the same time, Tan and Dimmock (2014) found that more direct government control in the Singapore context was being replaced by 'a more subtle centre–periphery relationship'. Singaporean pre-school teachers however have reported cultures where principals' and senior teachers' unwillingness to share status was a factor in their reluctance to take on leadership roles (Ebbeck et al., 2014).

Whilst the issue of children's attainment (and how to raise this) remains central to effective EC leadership, this area remains largely unexamined. In order to identify the contribution of leadership to English EC settings identified as effective by the *Effective Provision of Pre-school Education* project (Sylva et al., 2004), Siraj-Blatchford and Manni (2008a) drew on demographic information, policies, documents, observations and interviews with managers, to link leader-ship behaviours to the improvement of children's learning outcomes.

English Sure Start children's centres, launched to offer disadvantaged children and families integrated services, including childcare and early education, health and social welfare services, have provided a distinctive multi-agency model of EC leadership (see Chapters 11 and 19). Sharp et al. (2012) identified different models of service delivery:

- clusters of centres working together on strategic goals;
- a cluster model with a locality man-ager responsible to the local authority;
- a hub-and-spoke model, where the hub centre leader was responsible for work of satellite or 'spoke' centres – as well as cen-tres subsumed within other organisations and agencies.

The recent evaluation of children's centres in England by Sylva et al. (2015) reported a service evolving away from a traditional 'stand-alone' model towards a clustering organisation in the face of funding cuts, reduction of services and even closure for some. Higher ratings for leadership and management appeared to be associated with:

- an older leader;
- a 'stand-alone' rather than cluster model of delivery;
- aspects of multi-agency working;
- offering a higher number of services; and
- achieving higher Ofsted ratings for overall effectiveness.

It was also noted that cluster managers tended to have lower qualifications than single-centre managers with more senior staff working external to the site. Overall, effective leadership training and qualifications of staff received the highest rating from managers and staff.

The lack of leadership development programmes remains an unresolved issue. Studies of programme effectiveness (Bloom and Sheerer, 1992; Bella and Bloom, 2003; Talan et al., 2014) have given way to professional learning and leaders' capacity-building, where leaders are encouraged to develop themselves and their staff teams through coaching and mentoring, and ultimately to engage children and families (John, 2008; Ang, 2011; Ord et al., 2013).

Globally, the importance of high-quality EC education is now recognised, particularly for young children growing up in circumstances of poverty (see Chapter 16). Effective leadership is also recognised to be at the heart of improvement and the challenge must now be to encourage leaders themselves to take more responsibility for developing themselves and their staff, a point that will be revisited later.

A CASE STUDY OF EARLY CHILDHOOD LEADERSHIP

In the interests of linking reported views and experiences of English EC leaders to observed practice, the author and colleagues decided to plan an investigation of EC leadership through an initial seminar with twenty-five local leaders that led to an in-depth study of twelve leaders and colleagues through a survey, interviews and 'day-in-the-life' observations (Aubrey, 2011; Aubrey et al., 2013).

THE SEMINAR

Leaders were selected on the basis of their effective practice, identified by the local adviser and confirmed by Ofsted reports. They were asked to answer five key questions:

1. What does leadership mean in your setting? Here the leaders stressed having a clear vision and working towards it. To them, this meant having an awareness of the wider social, political and educational context. It entailed raising the profile of early education and care and developing a shared philosophy. Fundamental to this was a recognition of its multidisciplinary nature, valuing learning and having a commitment to ongoing professional development.

2. What factors contributed to the effectiveness of this role? Promoting early years across a range of agencies was regarded as prerequisite, with a firm commitment to working towards specific outcomes. Again, commitment to ongoing professional development and support for staff was thought to contribute to effective leadership.

3. What factors hindered effectiveness in this role? It was felt that the state of change and development over a number of years had created a real lack of clarity about EC care and education. This was coupled with a general lack of knowledge about childhood at all levels, a lack of status, a lack of resources in terms of staffing, time and materials and a lack of professional development. In turn, it could lead to a sense of isolation and low levels of responsibility.

4. What were the training needs? The need for more general accreditation of EC leadership and management at varying levels and with appropriate funding was emphasised.

5. How could capacity be built in the field? It was felt there were distinct training and development needs in the sector. This sentiment resonated through their responses. Valuing learning was at the core, with a commitment to working towards specific outcomes and promoting EY across a range of agencies.

THE SURVEY

Twelve leaders and exemplar settings continued to work with us in investigating the full range of EC provision that included three private nursery and day care settings; two voluntary family centres; four nursery and reception classes in infant and primary schools (foundation stage units for children aged three to five years); and three children's centres (providing a range of services for children from birth to four years, their families and community).

One hundred and ninety-four practitioners responded to our survey of views on EC leadership that included the majority of leaders and middle leaders and a range of practitioners working in and around the centres concerned. In terms of demographics, the workforce was mainly female (four males responded), aged between twenty and forty-eight years old. The majority who responded had at least a diploma in nursery nursing or NVQ Level 3 or equivalent. Respondents in foundation stage units and children's centres predominantly had a first degree or postgraduate qualification, while private and voluntary day care workers were more likely to have on-the-job NVQs at Levels 2 and 3. Two-thirds had original training that covered the period from birth upwards while, disproportionately, respondents from foundation units had not trained to work with very young children.

In terms of roles and responsibilities, there was high agreement that the most important aspect of the leader's role was to deliver a quality service. By contrast, nobody ranked first an 'entrepreneurial approach, mindful of competition with others'.

With respect to personal characteristics of effective leaders, a more sophisticated analysis of responses suggested that respondents with postgraduate qualifications tended to favour warmth, rationality, knowledgeability, assertiveness, goal orientation, coaching, mentoring and guiding, which we described as *leaders as guides*. Those with NVQs tended to favour vision, warmth, professional confidence, systematic planning, proactivity and empowerment, which we described as *leaders as motivators*. Those with so-called 'other qualifications' who had been trained for professions other than education, such as the library service, health-related professions, play leadership or social work, tended to favour systematic planning, risk-taking, influence, proactivity, vision and empowerment, which we described as *leaders as strategists*. Finally, those with postgraduate qualifications were also likely to favour influence, authority, economic competitiveness, business awareness and risk-taking, which we described as *business oriented*.

While there was some overlap between these categories there was at least some indication that leaders with different qualifications, coming from different professional heritages and working in different types of setting, regarded a different set of characteristics and emphases as important to effective EC leadership. Given different job descriptions and role specifications among the range of leaders, this was scarcely surprising. It does, however, indicate the existence of many different types of EC leader and the need for a 'best fit' approach that is derived from organisational development theory and that takes account of leader, followers, task and environment. It may also go some way to understanding participants' response to the question – who makes the decisions? Many differences were found in the weight given to 'all staff', 'appropriate individuals', 'children' and 'parents'. Middle and senior management were regarded as unimportant and the child was reported overall as having least input. Given the current emphasis on children's participation and voice, this finding was surprising, though private and voluntary providers were more likely to say decisions were made by children 'all the time', which might reflect a stronger emphasis on 'client' expectations. Children's centre leaders were more likely to say that parents made decisions 'all the time', in line with original programme practice that they should be locally driven and responsive to the needs of families.

INTERVIEWS WITH LEADERS AND STAFF GROUPS

Perceptions and definitions of EC leadership were wide-ranging and diverse when probed in more depth through interview. The role of previous experience, role models and academic study were all identified by leaders as important and a variety of training models were considered that included peer-mentoring, developing critical friends and paired visits to peers' settings. Staff groups collectively reported no experience of leadership training but mentioned the influence on them of role models and the more *ad hoc* picking up of 'nuggets of what people said'. Leaders acknowledged that general leadership theory and principles were common across sectors but what was distinctive about EC leadership was its being female-led, its emotional involvement and its caring. That is not to say that males make ineffective leaders but rather, as Blackmore (1989) emphasised, organisational theorists have characterised leadership by masculine traits of aggression, competition and independence, while Shakeshaft (1989) in the US revealed women's leadership as focused on collaboration, power-sharing, caring and relationships. Shakeshaft also noted women leaders were consultative, creating a nurturing and non-hierarchical culture that reflected Gilligan's (1982) 'ethic of caring'. Court (1994) in the New Zealand context described women in leadership positions who 'empowered' or shared power with others and created organisational cultures based on collaboration, communication and shared decision-making.

In England, Hall (1996) identified an organisational culture created by women school leaders as one of trust, openness and commitment. In terms of our own respondents, staff inevitably stressed the leadership qualities that impacted on them as followers, and leaders commented on the role of followers in shaping their practice.

In terms of roles and responsibilities, high-quality education and care and children's achievements were emphasised by leaders and staff alike. Views of leaders and staff on business and entrepreneurial skills were again mixed but interviews uncovered a deep unease about 'for-profit motives in a sector so poorly paid'. One respondent stated: 'I came from the private sector because I did not like the idea of making a profit … exploiting those on low wages'. In terms of decision-making, there was recognition of 'top-down' LA decision-making but nevertheless retention of a collaborative culture within the organisation. Overall, respondents felt that their organisations were hierarchically organised at the strategic level but collaborative at the operational level.

A TYPICAL 'DAY-IN-THE-LIFE' OR EC LEADERSHIP IN ACTION

A typical 'day-in-the-life' was consistent with leaders' previous reports and included rich and varied activities. Leaders working in foundation stage units had very demanding roles, balancing teaching, administration and pedagogical leadership. Leaders observed in private and voluntary organisations were more likely to lack administrative support and to be preoccupied with low-level administrative tasks. Leaders in children's centres were seen working on complex and large-scale projects that might entail substantial financial and administrative responsibility for new buildings, developing new policy through consultation with the public, private and voluntary sector that represented a variety of professional groups. At the same time, there was a blurring of distinctions between private, voluntary and state, as new children's centres were being formed and extended schooling developed. This meant that leaders were finding themselves taking on new major operational tasks, calling for financial and administrative or technical expertise that they must learn 'on-the-job'.

Robinson's earlier advice to employ backward mapping that involved working backwards from positive impacts on children to tease out leader influence provided a useful frame for examining observed practice. This revealed the high intensity of foundation stage leaders' roles in working both directly with children and with other professionals and **para-professionals** that they worked alongside. The same intensity of focus on high-quality learning and teaching was observed in those children's centres, state, voluntary and private provision. Here, the leaders were coaching staff in planning, teaching and profiling of young children's work thereby supporting and challenging their practice in order to raise the quality of provision provided. A strong focus of attention was observed to be on play, learning and childcare experiences with a range of other indirect activities being carried out around core services of support for families and communities.

There was laughter when leaders shared their own video highlights with one another. They exclaimed at their evident tiredness, the long hours and the intensity of their work, what Evans et al. (1994) first termed the 'culture of over-conscientiousness' of EC practitioners. They applauded their capacity to deliver the new childcare strategy. They celebrated their ability to 'hold focus' in spite of underlying emotions and uncertainties and indeed, were willing to articulate their own feelings of inadequacy at times as well as their outstripping of their LA line managers in expertise.

The need for and celebration of 'upskilling' in the workforce was very apparent in the displays of newly acquired NVQs and welcoming, greeting and supporting of new staff. These all marked the new pathways into the EC workforce. Leaders bemoaned the lack of leadership training available, accentuating the gap in training opportunity between those least and most qualified. Indeed, the need for new skills, knowledge and understanding across the sector was a feature of the video footage. The scale of workforce reorganisation highlighted the reported low status accorded to EC work and the variability of qualifications across the sector identified by the survey. This threw into relief the lack of opportunity for EC leadership training.

CONCLUSION

Similar conditions have been described in the Australia and New Zealand context where low priority has been given to leadership development programmes (Nuttall, 2013). At the same time, there has been a growing awareness of the need for EC professional development opportunities. Ord et al. (2013) have emphasised that the most effective EC leaders are those who promote the learning of their teams thereby having a direct relationship on positive outcomes for children. Typically, leaders are more experienced at working with children and families but less so in fostering adult learning. Thornton et al. (2009) identified a range of strategies for leadership learning to occur:

- Problem-solving in real-life situations;
- Reflection on experience based on appropriate feedback;
- Coaching to raise performance;
- Creating a community of practice to mobilise the centre team.

Central to achievement of this is the leader's own continued learning and development whereby leadership workshops can be complemented by coaching and mentoring of staff in the centre. Hence, leader-learning will comprise: leadership development (pedagogic, contextual and distributed); professional development that takes account of the needs of adult learners and knows how to bring together the organisation around common goals; deployment of specific skills of coaching and mentoring. Traditional, 'one-off' professional development events led by external consultants are unsuitable here since changes in professional knowledge and development of collaborative working with colleagues, children and communities take time.

Thornton et al. (2009) have argued that this approach requires a reconceptualisation of leadership and professional learning that is focused on relevant, everyday problems, involves coaching in large, centre-wide as well as small-group work, with follow-up mentoring for individuals and pairs to analyse, apply and review problem-solving in real settings. The leader's role is to assist in the development of professional learning thus, *pedagogic leadership* is required that relates to learning of staff, children and community. The pedagogic leader and learner foster a collective and collaborative learning community. The contextual leader, however, is alert to internal and external influences, hence *contextual leadership* is required to interpret the centre's internal and external environments. But leadership is also located within the networks of interacting individuals and groups who bring collective expertise from both within and beyond the community so *distributed leadership* is required to cultivate processes and structures that encourage professional learning in a nurturing environment. By such means, the effective leader continues to learn, develop and assist in complex problem-solving that serves to achieve centre goals, as a coach (or co-thinker and co-learner) and as a mentor (or co-constructor of new knowledge).

Key points

- The importance of high-quality early childhood care and education is now recognised globally and effective leadership is at the heart of the improvement process.
- Effective early childhood leadership is still an under-researched area and lack of opportunities for leadership training and development remains unresolved.
- The leader has a central role and responsibility for her own professional development and the development of staff.
- There is a need to consider all the operating environments of leadership from macro- to micro-level, hence pedagogic, contextual and distributed leadership will be required.

Recommended reading

A state-of-the-art summary can be found in Aubrey, C. (2016) Early childhood leadership. In D. Couchenour and K. Chrisman (Eds) *The SAGE Encyclopedia of Contemporary Childhood Education*. Thousand Oaks, CA: Sage.

EARLY CHILDHOOD EDUCATION
FOR SUSTAINABILITY

NICOLA KEMP

CONTENTS

INTRODUCTION

Early Childhood Education for Sustainability (ECEfS) is an emerging field and one that is growing in both national and international importance. This chapter will introduce the concept of sustainability and consider how it relates to education, and specifically early childhood education (ECE). It argues that sustainability demands a radical questioning of the nature, purpose and practice of early childhood education rather than a simple accommodation of new knowledge. This chapter will explore the philosophical roots of ECE and consider more recent conceptual developments in the field to demonstrate how ECE aligns with sustainability. It will argue that understandings within early childhood might usefully inform other educational phases seeking to develop more sustainable education and will conclude with a consideration of implications for practice.

WHAT IS SUSTAINABILITY?

Sustainability must be one of the most widely used buzzwords of the past two decades. There is nothing, it seems, that cannot be described as 'sustainable': apparently everything can be either hyphenated or paired with it. (Scoones, 2007: 589)

The concept of sustainability can be difficult to grasp and to explain. As Scoones (2007) highlights, sustainability is a concept which is applied to multiple contexts but whose nature is both complex and contested. What follows is a brief introduction to some commonly used definitions and models to support an understanding of what it might mean within the context of early childhood education.

MODELS OF SUSTAINABILITY

Sustainability is often associated with 'green' or 'environmental' issues and its roots are in the environmental concerns of the post-war period, particularly those emanating from the United States. In 1962, American Rachel Carson wrote a book entitled *Silent Spring* in which she highlighted the negative effects of pesticide use on birdlife. As well as influencing national policy, the book contributed to a more general global awareness of the importance of the environment and its conservation. During the 1970s and 1980s the debate developed and the inter-relationship between the state of the environment, economic growth and the wellbeing of the human population started to be acknowledged. Contemporary understandings of sustainability now recognise these three dimensions in the terms environmental protection, social justice and economic development. The relationships between these dimensions are represented in a number of well-accepted models.

In the 'three pillars' model, society, economy and environment are shown as physical pillars on which sustainability is balanced rather like the colonnades of a Greek temple (Figure 21.1). However, this implies that each of the dimensions is independent when in fact there are often complex interconnections and interdependencies between them. The figure also implies that each pillar is of equal significance and valued in the same way. However, there is evidence to suggest that economic profit, environmental protection and social justice are valued in different ways.

An alternative approach is the 'over-lapping circles' model in which the environmental, economic and the social are visualised as a Venn diagram with sustainability at the centre point

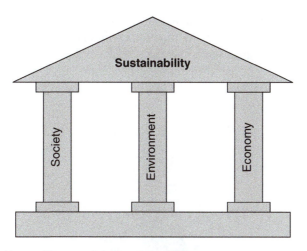

Figure 21.1 The three pillars model of sustainability

Adapted from Ashton, P. and Kubik, M. 2014 Beyond sustainability. *E-Journal of Public Affairs,* 3(2).

where all three circles overlap. This highlights the interaction between the three dimensions and the different ways in which there can be synergy (Figure 21.2).

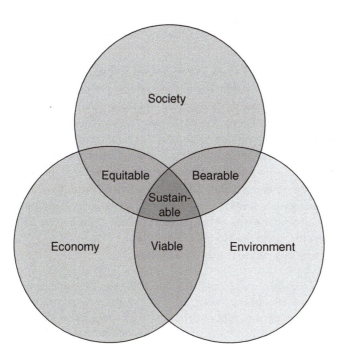

Figure 21.2 The overlapping circles model of sustainability

Adapted from Pezzoli, K. (1997) Sustainable development: a transdisciplinary overview of the literature. *Journal of Environmental Planning and Management,* 40(5): 549–74.

A further adaptation of this is the 'ecological' or nested dependencies model in which society and economy are nested within the physical environment, emphasising environmental limits (Figure 21.3). The diagram shows that the economy is dependent on society (which surrounds it) and then both of these elements are dependent on the environment. This is often referred to as a deep green position.

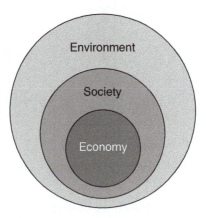

Figure 21.3 The ecological or nested dependencies model

Based on Giddings, B., Hopwood, B. and O'Brien, G. (2002) Environment, economy and society: fitting them together into sustainable development. *Sustainable Development*, 10(4): 187–96.

All these models fail to account adequately for the complexity of real-life and as such can be difficult to apply in practice. One criticism relates to their over-simplification; particularly when other aspects such as culture, politics, geography and history may be significant to understanding the issue. Another criticism derives from the fact that sustainability itself is a rather abstract notion and what one person considers to be sustainable may be quite different to another. The concept of sustainable development attempts to ground sustainability by linking it explicitly to development decisions. In 1987 the World Commission on Environment and Development (WCED) published *Our Common Future* (also known as the Brundtland report). It contained what is now an established definition of sustainable development: 'Sustainable development is development that meets the needs of the present without compromising the ability of future generations to meet their own needs' (WCED, 1987: 43).

The definition contains within it two key concepts:

- the concept of 'needs', in particular the essential needs of the world's poor, to which over-riding priority should be given; and

- the idea of limitations imposed by the state of technology and social organization on the environment's ability to meet present and future needs (WCED, 1987: 43).

Although nearly 30 years old, this definition is now an established way of understanding how sustainability might be put into practice. Its recognition of a temporal dimension to sustainability has particular resonance within the context of early childhood which understands the child as simultaneously **being** (in the present) and **becoming** (in the future). As Uprichard (2008: 313) argues, 'children ... are always being and becoming ... the onus of agency is present and future'. There is inter-dependency between the present and the future which means that the temporal focus of childhood must be flexible. This, it could be suggested, is also true for sustainable development.

Both sustainability and sustainable development are conceptualised as 'universal' concepts that can be applied in any place, at any time. However, their universality and generality mean that they are also concepts that are inherently 'ambiguous and open to multiple interpretations' (Stables, 2013: 177). To address this problem, it can be helpful to explore unsustainability within the context of real world issues.

UNSUSTAINABILITY

You know about water scarcity, dwindling forests, extinctions, acid oceans, overfishing, hunger, poverty and that cross-roads of all challenges: climate change ... Before 2050 the world population will increase by 2 or 3 billion ... (Edwards and Timberlake, 2012: 10)

Engaging with real-world issues is one way of exploring what (un)sustainability might mean in practice. As Pearson and Degotari (2009: 99) argue, 'the identification of examples of non-sustainable practices is more straightforward than the promotion of sustainable approaches'. Recognising this, photographer Mark Edwards and journalist Lloyd Timberlake have collaborated to raise awareness of global challenges in a meaningful and provocative way through two international projects and exhibitions: *Hard Rain* and *Whole Earth?* These offer a unique way to connect to issues facing the world in the twenty-first century and provide numerous examples of unsustainable practices relating to children and childhood. The headlines at the time of writing focus on migration and war; both are issues which provide what Stables (2013: 180) refers to as '**human purchase**'; that is an emotional connection, particularly in terms of the implications of current practices for young children and their families. Both also highlight the complexity and inter-related nature of the global challenges.

Learning about unsustainable practices can be challenging and unsettling. Hicks (2014: 106) noted the different responses students expressed when faced with information about the state of the world, '[s]ome feel excited or challenged ... others feel worried or even overwhelmed. Some ... challenge the veracity of the information they are exploring; others feel it is exaggerated and go into denial.' Duhn (2012) argues that this can be a particular concern in relation to young children since childhood is often associated with innocence and a need for protection. Hicks (2014) argues for the need for 'deep hope'. Likewise, Orr (2009: 173) refers to 'radical hope'. Hope, in this sense, derives from the possibility of action and change. It is grounded in the fact that rather than being fixed, the future is subject to change and that individual and collective actions can contribute to change. Education becomes important here both in creating an awareness of the need for change and in building capacity to make the change.

SUSTAINABILITY AND EDUCATION

> I want to argue that we, humankind, are in a period of such crisis and peril ... that we must review fundamentally the purposes of all education and, therefore, the values, qualities and practices needed of all educators. (Moss, 2010: 9)

Education has long been seen as a powerful force for change. It is unsurprising then that education should be seen as central to meeting the sustainability challenges of the contemporary world in the form of Education for Sustainable Development (ESD). The need for 'a vast campaign of education' was highlighted in *Our Common Future* (WCED, 1987: 23), and education's role has continued to be emphasised in international policy initiatives such as the UN Decade of Education for Sustainable Development 2005–2014 and its successor the Global Action Programme on Education for Sustainable Development (UNESCO, 2015).

Different relationships can exist between sustainability and education, the type of learning involved and the pedagogical approach, as illustrated in Figure 21.4.

Form of ESD	Learning	Pedagogy
Education about sustainability	First order learning (cognition)	Transmissive
Education for sustainability	Second order learning (meta-cognition)	Transactional
Education as sustainability	Third order learning (epistemic change)	Transformative

Figure 21.4 Forms of ESD (after Sterling, 2001)

ESD is often understood as involving teaching and learning about sustainability based on the assumption that a lack of information is the problem. However, this is a rather weak understanding that fails to generate change since new knowledge can simply be accommodated into existing ways of thinking and acting. In order to create the types of transformational change Hicks (2014) envisages, a much more radical process is required in which educational systems and structures are themselves transformed. Sterling (2001: 15) explains that, '... educational systems need to engage in deep change in order to facilitate deep change – that is, need to transform in order to be transformative'. He uses the term 'sustainable education' to describe this 'double learning' of society and the individual. Understood in this way, education and sustainability are in a symbiotic relationship in which changes to the one influence the other and vice versa. An implication of this is that education should challenge understandings of sustainability and sustainability should in turn demand that the nature, purpose and practice of education are questioned. There is a need to move beyond simplistic understandings that see education and/or sustainability uncritically as 'good things' without any exploration of the values and assumptions that lie beneath.

EARLY CHILDHOOD EDUCATION FOR SUSTAINABILITY

Early Childhood Education for Sustainability (ECEfS) is an emerging field and one that is growing in both national and international importance. In many ways, the early years are a logical place to start when considering the challenge of education for sustainability. We know that experiences in the earliest period of childhood influence the way people think and act for the rest of their lives. As Froebel (1826: 24) recognised 'often the whole life of man is not sufficient to efface what he has absorbed in childhood … for this reason the care of the infant is so important'. During the 1990s, there was a move within early childhood to respond to environmental concerns and environmental education in early childhood has generated some important understandings. Work by Tilbury (1994), for example, made the connection between early childhood experiences of the natural environment with the development of pro-environmental attitudes. Hacking and Barratt (2007) also emphasise the importance of the early years and later care for the environment. This recognition of the importance of the early years in relation to future attitudes and action has provided a solid foundation for the incorporation of broader sustainability concerns.

Research interest in sustainability from within the field of early childhood is relatively new and still developing. In 2009, Davis identified a research 'hole' based on a comprehensive literature search of international research journals over a twelve-year period. Since then, sustainability has been a major focus for The World Organisation for Early Childhood Education (OMEP) and was the theme for their World Congress in 2010 (see Siraj-Blatchford et al., 2010). This and other international developments have arguably helped to put sustainability on the ECE agenda although none of the current ECE policy documents in England makes reference to sustainability. The work of Australian academics Julie Davis and Sue Elliott has been particularly important in developing research and practice in the field and their understanding of ECEfS is articulated below:

> The approach to ECEfS that we promote is one of children working authentically in the exploration of topics and issues of interest to them. This means working alongside their teachers, families and communities in solving problems, seeking solutions and taking action to 'make a difference', mostly within their local context but occasionally on a bigger stage. (Davis and Elliott, 2014: 1-2)

In order to understand what ECEfS is and if or how it might differ from ECE more generally, three key dimensions of Davis and Elliott's definition will be explored:

1. The purpose of early childhood education
2. Conceptualisations of the child within early childhood education
3. The pedagogy of early childhood education

These can be understood as the questions that sustainability demands of early childhood education (Moss, 2010). Research, theory and policy will be employed to address these important questions.

THE PURPOSE OF ECE: MAKING A DIFFERENCE

From a policy perspective at least, early childhood education is increasingly positioned as preparation for compulsory schooling – implicit within the use of the term 'school readiness' (see Chapter 16). The Early Years Foundation Stage, for example, explicitly 'promotes teaching and learning to ensure children's "school readiness"' (DfE, 2017: 5). In this sense, ECE is simply a stage that prepares young children to achieve in school. As Moss (2010: 9) argues, 'existing in self-imposed isolation, [ECE] is at growing risk of being taken for granted and, worse, subsumed into school education – "schoolification" as some call it'. Understood in this way, early childhood education is both limited and limiting for young children and educators and assumes that the future is fixed and that the role of ECE is simply a reproduction of existing social, economic and environmental structures. Sustainability demands a radical questioning of such understandings of educational purpose and intent.

A brief review of its philosophical roots reveals that ECE has always demanded this type of radical thinking and demonstrates a clear sense of transformational purpose on an ambitious scale. For Froebel the purpose of education went beyond the individual to humankind as a whole. In his book *The Education of Man* (1826: 9) he likens the child to a plant and calls upon parents to let their child 'unfold in beauty and develop all-sided harmony'. For Froebel's many successors, there was often a social reformist agenda evident in their writings. Rachel and Margaret McMillan set up their open-air nursery in 1911 to improve the life chances of the growing number of children living in London's slums in response to the industrial revolution. Rudolph Steiner's (1919) writings on education were part of a much larger concern to create peaceable society following the destruction and devastation of the First World War. He writes of bringing into harmony 'the development of the pupil and the development of the civilized world' and is explicitly idealistic in his writing. Loris Malaguzzi's grassroots post-war movement of pre-schools in the Reggio-Emilia district of Italy derived from the understanding 'that Reggio has the potential to confront political and ethical problems that are ruining our world and its peoples' (Hall et al., 2010: 129). The roots of ECE are in transformation and change rather than stasis and reproduction. Many of the writers who continue to influence early childhood education today were writing at times of immense social change and upheaval. They recognised the importance of the early years not just for individual children but to society as a whole (see Chapters 2, 4 and 16).

Today, when policies and political aims are directed towards an increasingly narrow agenda these early childhood pioneers offer a way of reimagining the nature and purpose of early childhood education as transformational. This is evident within Davis and Elliott's (2014: 2) definition, where the purpose of ECE is to 'make a difference' and aligns with Sterling's (2001) concept of sustainable education.

CONCEPTUALISATIONS OF THE CHILD: AN EXPANDED FRAMEWORK OF CHILDREN'S RIGHTS

Another question raised by sustainability relates to understandings of the child and their associated agency. Researchers agree that 'children' and 'childhood' are not absolutes or universal concepts but are constructed by societies at a particular time and in a particular place (Corsaro, 2017; James et al., 1998) (see Chapters 1–4). These constructions tend to be based around a series of dualisms. One such dualism relates to young children as vulnerable and in need of adult protection versus the strong capable child who can participate in matters affecting them (see Chapter 12). Contemporary media representations of young children often position them as victims in need of help, particularly within the context of environmental or social crisis. Recent sociological perspectives have challenged early childhood educators to view young children as 'active social agents with rights'. This is increasingly reflected in national policy documents such as the EYFS where it is recognised that 'every child is a unique child, who is constantly learning and can be resilient, capable, confident and self-assured' (DfE, 2017: 6). Internationally, the United Nations Convention on the Rights of the Child (UN, 1989) identifies the right of the child to participate in matters which affect them and early childhood researchers continue to explore ways of encouraging active and meaningful participation by very young children (see Chapter 18).

Sustainable education is explicitly participative in character and it is in this regard that researchers in ECE continue to lead. As an example, Figure 21.5 shows Davis' (2014) Expanded Rights Framework for Early Childhood.

Here the child's rights are represented as five distinct components/layers:

1. **Foundational rights** - the UNCRC's survival and development rights; protection rights and participation rights lie at the core of the framework.
2. **Agentic participation rights** - aims to build upon the UNCRC by developing and extending the understanding of participation where young children are agents of change.
3. **Collective rights** - this directly challenges the overtly individualistic framing of the UNCRC. Davis refers here to Hardin's (1968: 27) tragedy of the commons in which 'a tragedy arises when individual consumers of an otherwise sustainable resource bring about its collapse. If rights are understood only on an individual basis rather than collectively, this tends to result in unsustainable practices.'
4. **Intergenerational rights** - considers the challenge of balancing present and future needs and is particularly significant in relation to children.
5. **Biocentric/ecocentric rights** - finally the framework recognises that human and non-human (bio)diversity are mutually inter-connected. It seeks to situate the concept of 'rights' spatially within geographical environments which have particular characteristics and physical limits.

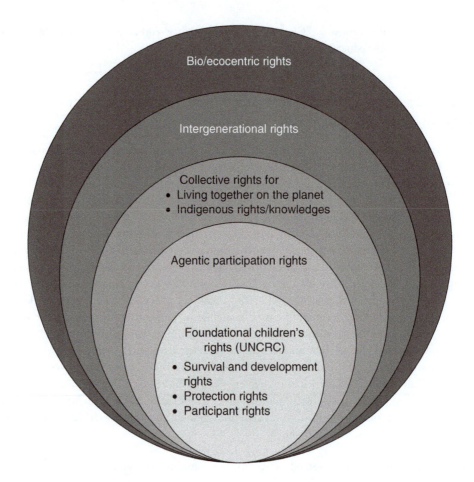

Figure 21.5 Davis' Expanded Rights Framework for Early Childhood Education

Davis, E., *Research in Early Childhood Education for Sustainability* (1st Edition) Copyright © 2014, Routledge. Reproduced by permission of Taylor & Francis Books UK.

Davis's work exemplifies the importance of early childhood education in developing understandings of the child that align with the transformational purpose of sustainable education.

PEDAGOGY OF EARLY CHILDHOOD EDUCATION: RELATIONAL PEDAGOGY

Sustainability also raises questions about ECE pedagogical practices. Relationships are at the heart of ECE and the notion of 'relational pedagogy' is gaining currency as a way of defining and understanding this pedagogical approach (Papatheodorou and Moyles, 2009). Relational pedagogy explicitly recognises the role of emotion within educational practice. As Farquhar and

White (2014: 825) explain, 'pedagogy can be interpreted as a relational experience that locates emotionality as a co-requisite to learning'. This understanding offers a significant challenge to 'privileged approaches that situate learning merely as participation in activity or in isolated cognitive domains'. In Davis and Elliott's definition there are two important aspects to the relational pedagogy: relations to others, and relations to places.

a.   Relations with others

Understanding about the importance of social relationships for the child is not new. Early Childhood pioneers such as Froebel (1826: 15) recognised their importance. He refers to '... higher common feeling at first between mother and child, then with the father and other members of the family, later between brothers and sisters, all human beings and the child'. He also emphasised the importance of peer relationships where 'several children unite skills and energy for common purpose' (107). These values continue to be reflected in contemporary policy documents such as the EYFS. Ritchie (2013) argues that relationality is central to the notion of sustainability since living sustainably depends upon positive reciprocal relationships between ourselves, others and the environment; it is a collaborative rather than individual challenge. Early childhood philosophy and pedagogy might have important insights for other educational phases, which may not prioritise relationality in the same way.

b.   Relations with places

It is not just social relations that Davis and Elliott (2014: 1–2) emphasise in their definition; they also acknowledge the importance of children developing relationships with places 'mostly within their local context'. Griffiths (2013: vii) agrees that connecting with their 'local acre' is important both to the development of identity and attitudes in young children. The phrase 'kith and kin' illustrates the historical importance of both social and physical connections; kith to physical place and kin to extended family (see Chapter 1 on socio-genealogical theory). This understanding is present within the writings of many early childhood pioneers. Froebel (1826), for example, understood the importance of young children building connections with the physical environment starting with the nearest and most familiar surroundings before moving to the more remote. This is now recognised as being important in the development of pro-environmental attitudes (Gill, 2011). There is some recognition of the importance of place in the EYFS (DfE, 2017: 8) where 'understanding the world' is one of seven areas of learning and development. However, globalisation requires an understanding of place that goes beyond the simple binary of the local and the global. Duhn (2012: 27) suggests that, 'ECE is in a powerful position to critically and respectfully explore diverse notions of place as a complex assemblage of materiality and discourse, of human and non-human'.

ECEᶠS: IMPLICATIONS FOR PRACTICE

The previous discussion has made connections between the essential characteristics of early childhood education and sustainability. It has revealed areas of alignment between existing policy and practice and Davis and Elliott's (2014) approach to ECEfS. However, there are also some areas where current policy and practice falls short of the transformational intentions of the early childhood pioneers. This suggests that in order to look to the future and to develop understanding of ECEfS, it may be appropriate to engage more fully with the historical legacy of ECE. An historical perspective reminds us that, 'it is not necessary to invent "new" pedagogies in order to "do" education for sustainability in the early years – one can build on its pedagogical traditions to do so' (UNESCO, 2008: 13). Importantly, the discussion has revealed dimensions of ECE, which could be adapted and transferred to other ESD contexts; in particular, the work on children's rights and participation. As Tilbury argues (in Davis and Elliott, 2014: xvi), 'early childhood education, through the education for sustainability lens, provides an interesting set of perspectives that have implications for mainstream educators'.

CONCLUSION

> The world of 'older childhood' education pays little attention to the innovative theory and practice to be found in the world of early childhood education. (Moss, 2010: 9)

Sustainability is an abstract concept that can be difficult to understand. Real-world examples of unsustainable practices can provide a connection from which to explore. Education provides a way of challenging unsustainable practices and of building a different future. Education for Sustainable Development (ESD) is now a global priority although it may take different forms. In its weakest form it may simply involve the transmission of knowledge about sustainability. However, the relationship between education and sustainability can be symbiotic. This means that sustainability is able to challenge the purpose and practices of education in an interactive and dynamic manner.

Early childhood is the logical place to start when considering the challenge of sustainability. Its philosophical roots in transformation and societal reform mean that from the outset its purpose and practice has been experimental and risk-taking – exactly the type of creative pedagogy called for in periods of global crisis. More recently, research within the field of early childhood has been instrumental in challenging passive and powerless conceptions of young children and empowering children with agency to participate in matters that affect their lives. However, early childhood education is more than just a logical place to start thinking about sustainability. Instead, it is a place where, as Moss (2010: 9) acknowledges above, 'innovative theory and practice are found'. The new approaches which are being pioneered in ECE have the potential to provide inspiration for those involved in other stages and phases of education. This might include:

- Expanding understanding of children's rights beyond UNCRC;
- Rethinking participation;
- Extending relational pedagogy which recognises the importance of children's connections with people and place (particularly the natural environment).

At a time when war, poverty, environmental disasters and famine continue to dominate the human experience, there is a growing recognition that 'we cannot continue as we are'

(Moss, 2010: 8). Early childhood education has a vital role to play in developing the capabilities, capacities and resilience of young children to make a difference now and in the future.

Key points

Early Childhood Education for Sustainability can be understood in the following way:

- Its purpose is to make a difference not just to individuals but also more widely within society.
- It values participation and the right of young children to be active social agents.
- Its pedagogy is explicitly relational and recognises the importance of connections with people and places. Existing practice may already align to some degree with these principles and in these cases ECEfS may be synonymous with good early childhood education.
- Conceptual understandings within the field of ECE may be important to apply to ESD in other contexts.

Recommended reading

Davis and Elliott (2014) is a must-read for those interested in developing their knowledge and understanding of sustainability within the context of early childhood.

OPENING PANDORA'S BOX: POSTMODERNIST PERSPECTIVES OF CHILDHOOD

JAYNE OSGOOD

CONTENTS

'The Unknown That Scares Us' © Paulo Sérgio Zerbato. Reprinted with permission.

INTRODUCTION

From ancient Greek mythology comes the tale of Pandora's Box. While there are many variations on the tale, depending upon the translation, the interpretation and the intended audience for which it has been re-crafted, the myth might be useful for thinking-with when considering postmodernist perspectives in early childhood education. Our everyday, commonsense reference to 'Pandora's box' is typically in relation to warning against allowing curiosity to get the better of us for fear of unleashing some source of endless trouble.

The tale of Pandora can be traced back to the poetry of Hesiod (*Theogony* and *Works and Days*) from the seventh century BC (Encyclopaedia Britannica, 2012). The poems recount the creation of Pandora, the first mortal woman to live amongst the gods, and 'the box'; a gift bestowed upon her by Zeus – which ultimately unleashes all manner of evil and destruction on the world.

The myth, in brief, proclaims that at Zeus' command, Hephaestus crafted a beautiful woman from clay, the first of her kind and a gift to Epimetheus. The woman, unnamed in the *Theogony* but referred to as Pandora ('all gifted') in *Works and Days*, is showered with gifts by the Olympians. Athena teaches her to weave, Aphrodite sheds grace upon her head, and Hermes gifts her speech. Zeus also bestows Pandora a jar, or pithos (which over time has been mistranslated to box).

She was instructed never to open the jar, but Pandora's curiosity was too great and eventually she lifted the lid. Although she opened the jar only fleetingly it was enough for endless troubles to escape: conflict, disease, drudgery and myriad other disasters were set loose. In horror, Pandora snapped the lid shut and managed to trap the last spirit; a nymph named Elpis, typically translated as 'hope' (although other translations offer 'expectation').

There has long been debate about what meanings might be made of this myth. Trapping 'hope' has been variously interpreted. Nietzsche claimed that Pandora was denying access to hope and so doomed humanity to eternal suffering. Of course, Pandora is not the only female protagonist in myths and legends to be responsible for apparently destroying an all-male paradise and unleashing intolerable suffering. Harrison (1903) asserts that 'Pandora is not a genuine myth, but an anti-feminist fable, probably of Hesiod's own invention'. Critique of the myth reveals it to be a social construction of the time which, on account of its ancestry and grandiose association to an ancient Greek poet it gains unquestioning authority. This gives a sense of how certain accounts come to hold greater currency than others and highlights some of the political machinations at play.

SO WHAT DOES PANDORA'S BOX HAVE TO DO WITH POSTMODERNIST APPROACHES TO EARLY CHILDHOOD EDUCATION?

As suggested, Pandora's Box might be considered something to think-with (Barad, 2007): whether as myth or metaphor what we are given to think-with has altered over time, place and context. Taking the author of the poem, Hesiod, as something else to think-with, we find that the authorship has been disputed over the centuries and the original works are now thought to have been added to and embellished so that details and interpretations have come to mean very different things to different people at different times (so how accounts of the world, and people's place within the world are firstly constructed, then taken up) (see Encyclopaedia Britannica, 2015).' Ultimately, how persuasive those accounts are is what gets recorded in history and what comes to shape dominant ways of thinking at any given sociopolitical historical moment.

Postmodernism is concerned to acknowledge that there are diverse worldviews, knowledges and ways of being. It challenges dominant regimes of truth and grand narratives and instead recognises that how we come to understand the world in which we are located is contextually and discursively fashioned. Early childhood education is shaped and defined by particular regimes of truth and grand narratives. Postmodernist perspectives seek to find ways to make these known and to recognise children, and how we engage with them, as inherently political and subject to constant change.

Postmodernist theorists understand early childhood education to be framed in particular ways. The dominant discourses that come to shape early childhood practice privilege certain interpretations, versions of reality and truth claims. We can accept the dominant narratives we are offered about early childhood (for example, about developmentalism, individualism, and objective measures of cognition) and ensure that our work with children is shaped by these imperatives and that 'evidence' is generated to prove their validity. Alternatively, we can unsettle, challenge and wrestle with where these 'truths' have come from and what they might mean for different children in various social, political and geographical locations. We might question the likely repercussions of a standardised, one-size fits all approach to early childhood practice, pedagogy and policy. One example of such a standardised and dominant approach to current thinking in early childhood is the preoccupation with 'school readiness'.

OPENING THE BOX/LIFTING THE LID …

Postmodernism asks a different set of questions about children than those concerned with measurement and evidence of effectiveness that have typified 'positivist' research. Postmodernist questioning takes us beyond a 'know and fix' preoccupation that many philosophies and approaches in early childhood promote (Burman, 2008; Blaise, 2010).

Fundamental to a postmodernist agenda are the following questions adapted from Dahlberg and Moss (2005):

- What knowledge counts?
- Whose knowledge is
  - represented;
  - privileged;
  - excluded?

- Who decides what knowledge is valuable?
- What are the implications of working with only certain knowledges?

Beginning to grapple with these questions opens a Pandora's Box for the early childhood researcher and educator and invites curiosity about how particular theories and philosophies find expression (e.g. developmental psychology) while others are marginalised (e.g. play-based) or silenced altogether (e.g. **indigenous cosmologies**). Postmodernist approaches make explicit the political motivations underpinning research, policy and practice with young children. So again, we might think-with Pandora's Box and the poet Hesiod to ask the questions outlined above, and by applying one of many critical postmodernists' lenses (for example **feminist poststructuralism**, **postcolonialism** or **queer theory**) a different emphasis will be placed upon the questions posed. There is undoubtedly a privileging of powerful white men in ancient Greek mythology, both as authors and characters, which has not gone unnoticed by feminist scholars (Holland, 2006; Zeitlin, 1995). Therefore, a postmodernist examination of Pandora's Box would question and challenge the subjugated position of women within the narrative; the **heteronormativity** informing the romantic plot; issues about social class privilege; the whiteness of the cast and so on. Moving beyond the content of the narrative alone, postmodernism would also encourage critical questions about the actors, motivations and processes involved in crafting and refashioning it throughout history and the uses to which it has been put.

This same questioning opens up ways to view early childhood practice more expansively and to expose the power and politics that are at play in the formation of policies, imposition of curriculum, and regulation of the workforce. So we could ask: Why is developmental psychology privileged? Why must children be assessed against standardised (Western, Anglo/Euro-centric) milestones? Why is the workforce predominantly female? Why is the sector underpaid? Why does this matter? These sorts of trouble-making questions are uncomfortable to ask and open up ever more questions but working in a postmodernist paradigm insists that we must ask the difficult questions. In the spirit of Pandora, early childhood practitioners must exercise their curiosity and unleash difficult questions to gain deeper insights into how and why practice is the way it is and crucially to pursue social justice for themselves, the communities in which they are located, and the children they educate (Robinson and Jones-Diaz, 2016).

Despite the multiple approaches (cultural studies, postcolonialism, poststructuralism, queer theory) that fall within the postmodernist paradigm, what unites them is a commitment to unearth and make known power asymmetries as they play out in everyday encounters within early childhood contexts. For early childhood researchers influenced by postmodernist thought the aim becomes to find ways to learn from children, in contrast with learning about how they function/develop so that they can be known (through assessment) and fixed (through extra or remedial provision) (see Burman, 2008). Postmodernist approaches to work with children understands them as key actors in the world rather than recipients of adult, expert knowledge. Increasingly early childhood educators and researchers are prepared to view children as competent beings but often this is undermined by prevailing discourses of childhood innocence that shape commonsense views of the child (Robinson, 2013).

It is important to put aside saccharine notions of romanticised childhoods that are somehow separate from the world. As I have argued elsewhere (Osgood, 2015; Osgood and Scarlet, 2016; Osgood et al., 2016) children's engagements with power, politics, inequity are everywhere and are constantly being reworked through routine everyday interactions with people, places, events and matter. By attending to the ways in which children and childhood are socially constructed through discourses, within institutions, laws and policies, media portrayals and everyday relational interactions, and by focusing attention on children beyond narrow prescriptions (i.e. developmental milestones, learning outcomes) our view of children can broaden out so that we recognise them as interconnected to the worlds of which they form part. So in a postmodernist tradition researchers are encouraged to discard many dominant and entrenched ideas about what children are (e.g. unformed, innocent, developing), how they learn (e.g. through imitation, social learning), and what they should become (e.g. worthy, productive citizens of the future).

Influential philosophers shaping postmodernist approaches to research in early childhood education include, but are not limited to: Foucault (1972), Derrida (1978), Lyotard (1984), Harding (1986), Anzaldua (1987), Haraway (1991; 2008), Spivak (1988), Butler (2006), Fraser (1989) and Davies (1989; 2014) and while these philosophers have developed a range of theoretical tools, to help understand a whole raft of social inequalities and injustices, what unites their work is a shared commitment to challenge grand narratives and urge that we question, unsettle, resist and work to reconceptualise taken-for-granted and commonsense ideas that at first glance might appear benign.

Not all postmodernist approaches to research and practice in early childhood challenge power relations *directly* but in various ways they attend to the privileges afforded by modernism (related to social class, race, gender, able-bodiedness) that are deeply embedded in all aspects of our lives but not always immediately visible. These privileges claim supremacy for certain ways of being, thinking and doing as well as granting the right to intervene in the lives of those deemed to fall short of normalised expectations. Here we might think of the taken-for-granted-ness of child development in early childhood. Thinking of children's linear progression from one developmental milestone to another is so deeply entrenched in curriculum frameworks, pedagogical practices and routine engagements with children, and since it is claimed to be based upon incontestable scientific evidence of the ways that children are or should be, too often we fail to recognize that there are alternative ways to view the child (Charlton et al., 2012). Furthermore, we fail to recognise that developmentalism serves to disadvantage children in multiple ways. Children falling outside normative expectations for child development are marked as other, and pathologised as lacking against a set of expectations for standardised progress (Cannella and Viruru, 2004; Burman, 2008). Another example of the hegemony of particular ways of being is evident in the approaches taken to engage and support so-called 'hard to reach' communities (Osgood et al., 2013) marked by differences in language, culture and ethnicity (Robertson and Drury, 2014). Ideas about children and their families in early childhood contexts continue to be shaped by normative expectations for traditional family formations, heteronormativity and the privileging of white, middle-class cultures and ways of being in the world (Robinson and Jones-Diaz, 2016).

Postmodernist thought has resided in the margins; the trouble-making agenda has not always been appreciated and therefore found itself routinely side-lined, silenced and obscured from mainstream approaches to educational research and policy-making (Lather, 1991). Yet philosophers and theorists have worked tirelessly for decades to pursue criticality in their conceptualisations of the world, and researchers have taken up their theories and put them to work in multiple ways that consistently recognise the interdependence of researcher and knowledge production.

There has been persistent critique and deconstruction of grand narratives by a range of scholars who have informed the work of early childhood research in the postmodernist paradigm, from feminists such as bell hooks, Judith Butler and Patricia Hill-Collins to critical, postcolonialist, subaltern and indigenous studies (e.g. Gayatri Chakravorty Spivak, Edward Said, Stuart Hall), to more recent post-humanist and new materialist engagements with the world in which we are entangled (e.g. Karen Barad, Rosi Braidotti and Donna Haraway). This extensive and continually evolving body of work has generated diverse ways of perceiving, conceptualising, and acting upon/with the world. Critical postmodernist approaches hold the potential to create ways to view the world as multiple and to resist shutting down, and instead be constantly open to transformation. Underlining this postmodernist literary canon though is a desire to avoid displacing one totalising way of viewing the world with another – so multiplicity, diversity, creativity, experimentation and the creation of new and unanticipated ways of viewing the world are what broadly holds it together.

EXAMPLES OF PANDORA'S CURIOSITY IN ACTION ...

Over the past thirty or so years postmodernist perspectives have made important contributions to childhood studies in their refusal to unquestioningly accept ideas that are claimed to be founded upon scientific fact; researchers and educators working with postmodernist ideas are ready to contest dominant modernist universal 'truths' such as predetermined outcomes and linear progress. There are numerous examples of postmodernist approaches to research in early childhood that have made important contributions to calling into question the ways in which children are viewed and the ways in which they are constructed (through policy, curriculum and pedagogy).

An excellent introductory text that illustrates the potential of postmodernist approaches to thinking and doing in early childhood contexts is *Deconstructing Early Childhood Education: Social Justice and Revolution* by Gaile Cannella (1997). Although written some time ago, Cannella's text can be regarded as having made a crucial impact to encouraging the take up of postmodernist approaches to early childhood research and practice. The book continues to be highly relevant and its traces can be identified in many contemporary early childhood studies. In the book Cannella refuses to accept traditional notions of child development, customary research methods used to study childhood, the portrayal of childhood as fixed, or the dominant educational approaches used to teach young children. Working principally with Foucauldian and Butlerian theories she undertakes critical deconstruction of historical, societal and policy discourses to offer a sensitive account of how and why these ideas and practices have emerged and hold such currency in early childhood contexts. The intention of the book is to stimulate a critical conversation about discourses of early childhood and question perspectives that, while well-intentioned, are often oppressive.

Throughout the 2000s a growing number of early childhood researchers drew on a broad range of poststructural and postcolonial thinkers to pay attention to the intersections of race, class and gender and their implications for practice and community engagement. Amongst them was Glenda MacNaughton (2005) in *Doing Foucault in Early Childhood Studies*; as the title suggests, she put key post-structuralist theorists to work in research and practice in early childhood. MacNaughton (2005) worked with a small number of practitioners located in different geopolitical contexts to generate action-research case studies. These cases demonstrate the practical ways in which work with poststructuralist theories in the classroom can be used strategically to reconstruct knowledge-power relationships in early childhood practices and relationships. The book illustrates ways to create points of resistance to traditional early childhood discourses and to reconstruct pedagogical knowledges, practices and relationships. Furthermore, the book attempted to breakdown some perceived and sometimes real barriers to produce new forms of collaboration between practitioners, children, the academy, parents and local communities.

Bronwyn Davies has made, and continues to make, a major contribution to postmodernist approaches to the study of early childhood. Her work spans more than thirty years and in that time she has illuminated the potential for critical, feminist poststructuralist perspectives to challenge the hegemony of modernist approaches in early childhood practice. *Frogs and Snails and Feminist Tales* published in 1989 was a vital new departure from research that had come before; Davies introduced a whole generation of early childhood educators and researchers to a more critical and nuanced approach to understanding children and early childhood contexts. She continues to work within the postmodernist paradigm, most recently in *Listening to Children* Davies (2014) works with post-humanist and feminist new materialist theories to explore more expansive ways to work with and learn from children. There is a burgeoning trend in early childhood research to work with post-humanist and new materialist ideas (e.g. Olsson, 2009; Pacini-Ketchabaw, 2010; Taylor, 2013; Blaise, 2016) which open up aspects of poststructuralist theorising to explore new ways of thinking about and intra-acting with children. Davies (2014) defines her most recent research as '**diffractive**'. She works with patterns of diffraction to offer new ways to think about children, communities, listening as emergent, and the importance of being open to the not-yet-known. Davies provides diffractive accounts of co-experimentation she undertakes with early childhood educators in Sweden, from collective biography in her own community in Australia, and through memory-work, art-making and Buddhist thought she illustrates new ways of making sense of 'data' that we routinely encounter in the seeming minutiae of everydayness in early childhood contexts. Davies brings together a series of new ideas about agency, meaning-making, ethics, community, listening to children and experimenting that retains a place broadly in the postmodernist paradigm but offers up expansive possibilities for early childhood pedagogy and research.

What these selected examples, from the past thirty or so years, demonstrate is that while postmodernist scholars take very different approaches in their research they all ask specific onto-logical and epistemological questions through their research that question reality and researcher subjectivity; by recognising that the production of knowledge is always partial and subjective; and by challenging scientific 'truths' they promote diverse and more encompassing approaches to research (and practice). Working in a postmodernist vein means putting forward new ideas, arguing for a range of possibilities and facilitating critical enquiry into all aspects of childhood. This body of scholarship has involved questioning beliefs and practices concerning reality and the dominance of scientific thought. There has been a steady but important reconceptualisa-tion of early childhood, research and knowledge about children that recognises each is socially constructed and, if left untroubled, has serious implications for the wellbeing of children and entire communities.

CONCLUSION

Postmodernist writers argue against the existence of universal truths and remind us that domi-nant views of truth and reality are fabrications formed from a school of thought that is white and male oriented and furthermore privileges particular socio-economic groups and world-views. So postmodernism can be thought of broadly as a movement informed by key theorists offering alternative worldviews to those firmly established within the Enlightenment period of the mid-twentieth century. What is significant about postmodernism, and continues to shape our understandings of the child, is the means it has provided to reconceptualise iden-tity, subjecthood, power and diversity. Through critiquing modernist perspectives, the everyday, commonsense-ness of entrenched ideas (such as developmental stages and ages in childhood, or that gender is biologically determined) are dismantled, problematised and re-imagined. Postmodernist perspectives are multifarious but nevertheless united by a distrust of humanist and positivist principles. For those working within the postmodernist paradigm there is general recognition that knowledge and knowledge production is never objective, there are no univer-sal truths; rather all knowledge is socially constructed and based upon partial and subjective interpretations. Crucially, it is the interpretations of powerful groups and individuals (i.e. white, middle-class, able-bodied, heterosexual men) that have become unquestioningly embedded in many prevailing ideas about education and childhood and these in turn have become reinforced by hegemonic discourses that present ideas as unequivocal truths.

Returning to Pandora's 'box', postmodernist thinkers are invested in an **ethico-onto-epistemological** (Barad, 2007) obligation to lift the lid on what might appear obvious and reasonable in early childhood at first glance. Whilst this chapter has outlined the vast array of postmodernist approaches to the study of children and childhood there remains a shared, underpinning commitment to the pursuit of social (or worldly) justice (Osgood et al., 2016). This means that researchers working in this tradition, despite different theoretical influences, are compelled to ask the difficult, unsettling and provocative questions – not to wreak havoc on the planet or humanity – but rather to be curious, to wonder, to question, to expose, to explore and to experiment in the hope of reaching a future with generative possibilities for kaleidoscopic childhoods and for us (adults: educators, researchers, parents, policy-makers) to be open to uncertainty, serendipity and the not-known and the not-yet-known.

Key points

- Postmodernist approaches ask difficult questions about seemingly commonsense ideas that have come to shape early childhood.
- Postmodernist research is concerned to explore and expose power asymmetries (shaped by gender, social class, race and ablity).
- Postmodernists understand children as key actors in the world rather than recipients of adult, expert knowledge.
- Postmodernist approaches pay attention to the routine everyday lives of young children and so invite curiosity about the reasons why commonsense ideas (such as developmental stages and ages in childhood, or that gender is biologically determined) are so entrenched, and the (detrimental) effects that such ideas can have for different groups of children.

Recommended reading

Davies, B. (2014) *Listening to Children: Being and Becoming.* London: Routledge.

REFERENCES

Abbott, L. and Nutbrown, C. (Eds) (2001) *Experiencing Reggio Emilia*. Buckingham: Open University Press.

Abbott, M.P., Chijioke, M.E., Dandelion, P. and Oliver, J.W. (2011) *Historical Dictionary of the Friends (Quakers)*. Maryland: Scarecrow Press.

Abdallah, S., Main, G., Popple, L. and Rees, G. (2014) *Ways to Well-being: Exploring the Links between Children's Activities and their Subjective Well-being*. London: The Children's Society.

Abebe, T. and Aase, A. (2007) Children, AIDS and the politics of orphan care in Ethiopia: the extended family revisited. *Social Science and Medicine*, 64: 2058–69.

Abrams, R. (2001) *Three Shoes, One Sock and No Hairbrush: Everything You Need to Know About Having Your Second Child*. London: Cassell.

African Commission on Human and Peoples' Rights (ACHPR) (1990) *African Charter on the Rights and Welfare of the Child*. OAU Doc. CAB/LEG/ 24.9/49 [online]. Available: http://www.achpr.org/instruments/child/ [accessed 16.3.17].

Aggleton, P. (1990) *Health*. London: Routledge.

Ainscow, M., Booth, T. and Dyson, A. (2006) *Improving Schools, Developing Inclusion*. London: Routledge.

Aked, J., Marks, N., Cordon, C. and Thompson, S. (2008) *Five Ways to Wellbeing: A Report Presented to the Foresight Project on Communicating the Evidence Base for Improving People's Well-Being*. London: New Economics Foundation.

Akhtar, N., Jipson, J. and Callanan, M. (2001) Learning words through overhearing. *Child Development*, 72: 416–30.

Alanen, L. and Mayall, B. (2001) *Conceptualising Child–Adult Relations*. London: Routledge Falmer.

Albareda-Castellot, B., Pons, F., and Sebastian-Galles, N. (2011) The acquisition of phonetic categories in bilingual infants: new data from an anticipatory eye movement paradigm. *Developmental Science*, 14: 395–401.

Alderson, P. (1993) *Children's Consent to Surgery*. Buckingham: Open University Press.

Alderson, P. and Morrow, V. (2011) *Ethics of Research with Children and Young People: A Practical Handbook*. London: Sage.

Allen, G. (2011) *The Report of the Independent Review of Poverty and Life Chances. Early Intervention the Next Steps*. London: HMSO.

Allied Health Professionals Federation (AHPF)/Public Health England (PHE) (2015) *A Strategy to Develop the Capacity, Impact and Profile of Allied Health Professionals in Public Health 2015–2018*. London: PHE.

Amos, A. (1993) In her own best interests? Women and health education: a review of the last fifty years. *Health Education Journal*, 52(3): 141–50.

Anda, R.F., Butchart, A., Felitti, V.J. and Brown, D.W. (2010) Building a framework for global surveillance of the public health implications of adverse childhood experiences. *American Journal of Preventive Medicine*, 39(1): 93–8.

Anderson, A.M. (1996) Factors influencing the father–infant relationship. *Journal of Family Nursing*, 2(3): 306–24.

Anderson, S. and Lightfoot, D. (2002) *The Language Organ: Linguistics as Cognitive Psychology*. Cambridge: Cambridge University Press.

Ang, L. (2011) Leading and managing in the early years: a study of the impact of NCSL programme on children's centre leaders' perceptions of leadership and practice. *Educational Management Administration and Leadership*, 40(3): 289–304.

Anning, A. and Edwards, A. (2006) *Promoting Young Children's Learning from Birth to Five: Developing the New Early Years Professional (Second Edition)*. Maidenhead: Open University Press.

Anning, A., Chesworth, E. and Spurling, L. (2005) *The Quality of Early Learning, Play and Childcare Services in Sure Start Local Programmes*. Research Report 09. Nottingham: DfES publications.

Anning, A., Cottrell, D., Frost, N., Green, J. and Robinson, M. (2010) *Developing Multi-Professional Teamwork for Integrated Children's Services: Research, Policy and Practice* (Second Edition). Maidenhead: Open University Press.

Anzaldua, G. (1987) *Borderlands/La Frontera*. San Fransciso: Spinsters/Aunt Lute.

Archard, D. (2015) *Children: Rights and Childhood* (Third Edition). London: Routledge.

Archer, C. and Siraj, I. (2017) *Encouraging Physical Development Through Movement-Play*. London: Sage.

Ariès, P. (1962) *Centuries of Childhood*. London: Jonathan Cape.

Arnett Jensen, L. (Ed.) (2015) *The Oxford Handbook of Human Development and Culture: An Interdisciplinary Perspective*. Oxford: Oxford University Press.

Atkinson, M., Wilkin, A., Stott, A., Doherty, P. and Kinder, K. (2002) *Multi-agency Working: A Detailed Study*. Slough: NFER.

Atkinson, P. and Hammersley, M. (1998) Ethnography and participant observation and interviewing. In N. Denzin and Y. Lincoln (Eds), *Strategies of Qualitative Inquiry* (pp. 110–13). Thousand Oaks, CA: Sage.

Aubrey, C. (2011) *Leading and Managing in the Early Years* (Second Edition). London: Sage.

Aubrey, C., Godfrey, R. and Harris, A. (2013) How do they manage? An investigation of early childhood leadership. *Educational Management, Administration and Leadership*, 41(1): 5–29.

Aubrey, C. (2016) Early childhood leadership. In D. Couchenour and K. Chrisman (Eds), *The SAGE Encyclopedia of Contemporary Childhood Education*. Thousand Oaks, CA: Sage.

Austin, M. (2003) Children of childhood: nostalgia and the romantic legacy. *Studies in Romanticism*, 42 (1): 75–98.

Axline, V. (1969) *Play Therapy*. New York: Ballentine Books.

Baggerman, A. and Dekker, R.M. (2009) *Child of the Enlightenment: Revolutionary Europe Reflected in a Boyhood Diary. Vol. 1*. Leiden, Netherlands: Brill Academic Publishers.

Bailey, R. (2011) *Letting Children be Children. Report of an Independent Review of the Commercialisation and Sexualisation of Children*. London: DfE.

Bain, B. and Yu, A. (1980) Cognitive consequences of raising children bilingually: 'One Parent, One lauguage'. *Canadian Journal of Psychology*, 34, 304–313.

Baldock, P., Fitzgerald, D. and Kay, J. (2013) *Understanding Early Years Policy* (Third Edition). London: Paul Chapman.

Barad, K. (2007) *Meeting the Universe Halfway: Quantum Physics and the Entanglement of Matter and Meaning*. London: Duke University Press.

Baron-Cohen, S. (2011) *Zero Degrees of Empathy: A New Theory of Human Cruelty*. London: Allen Lane.

Barton, H. and Grant, M. (2006) A healthy map for the local human habitat. *The Journal of the Royal Society for the Promotion of Health*, 126(6): 252–3.

Bateman, A., Danby, S. and Howard, J. (2013) Living in a broken world: how young children's well being is supported through playing out their earthquake experiences. *International Journal of Play*, 2(3): 202–19.

Bates, E. and MacWhinney, B. (1982) A functionalist approach to grammatical development. In E. Wanner and L. Gleitman (Eds), *Language Acquisition: The State of the Art*. Cambridge: Cambridge University Press.

BBC News (2010) *Shannon Matthews: Kirklees Social Services Cleared* [online]. Available: http://www.bbc.co.uk/news/10323906 [accessed 28.10.12].

Beaty, B., Cahan, D. and Grant, J. (2006) *When Science Encounters the Child: Education, Parenting, and Child Welfare in 20th-Century America*. New York: Teachers College Press.

Bee, H. and Boyd, H. (2013) *The Developing Child*. London: Pearson.

Bella, J. and Bloom, P.J. (2003) *ZOOM: The Impact of Early Childhood Leadership Training on Role Perception, Job Performance and Career Decisions*. Wheeling, IL: Centre for Early Childhood Leadership.

Belsky, J. (1996) Parent, infant and social-contextual antecedents of father–son attachment security. *Developmental Psychology*, 32(5): 905–13.

Belsky, J., Barnes, J. and Melhuish, E. (Eds) (2007) *The National Evaluation of Sure Start: Does Area-Based Early Intervention Work?* Bristol: The Policy Press.

Bennett, N., Wood, E. and Rogers, S. (1997) *Teaching through Play: Teachers' Thinking and Classroom Practice*. Buckingham: Open University Press.

Berlyne, D.E. (1969) Laughter, humour and play. In G. Lindzey and E. Aronson (Eds), *Handbook of Social Psychology*. Reading, MA: Addison-Wesley.

Bernier, A., Carlson, S.M. and Whipple, N. (2010) From external regulation to self-regulation: early parenting precursors of young children's executive functioning. *Child Development*, 81: 326–39.

Bernstein, B. (1981) Codes, modalities and the process of cultural reproduction: a model. *Language and Society*, 10: 327–63.

Berridge, D. (2012) Educating young people in care: what have we learned? *Children and Youth Services Review*, 34(6): 1171–5.

Bertram, T. and Pascal, C. (2006) *The Baby Effective Early Learning Programme* (BEEL). Birmingham: Amber Publishing.

Bjorklund, D.F. (2011) *Children's Thinking: Cognitive Development and Individual Differences* (Fifth Edition). Belmont, CA: Wadsworth.

Black, D., Morris, J.N., Smith, C. and Townsend, P. (1980) *The Black Report*. Edited and with an introduction by P. Townsend and N. Davidson. In P. Townsend and N. Davidson (1982), *Inequalities in Health*. London: Penguin.

Black, K. and Lobo, M. (2008) A conceptual review of family resilience factors. *Journal of Family Nursing*, 14(1): 33–55.

Blackmore, J. (1989) Educational leadership: a feminist critique and reconstruction. In J. Smyth (Ed.), *Critical Perspectives on Educational Leadership*. London: Falmer Press.

Blair, C. (2002) School readiness: integrating cognition and emotion in a neurobiological conceptualization of children's functioning at school entry. *American Psychologist*, 57: 111–27.

Blair, C. (2010) Stress and the development of self regulation in context. *Child Development Perspectives*, 4(3): 181–8.

Blair, C. and Razza, R.P. (2007) Relating effortful control, executive function, and false-belief understanding to emerging math and literacy ability in kindergarten. *Child Development*, 78: 647–63.

Blaise, M. (2016) Fabricated childhoods: uncanny encounters with the more-than-human. *Discourse: Studies in the Cultural Politics of Education*, 37(5): 617–26.

Blaise, M. (2010) Creating postdevelopmental logic for mapping gender and sexuality in early childhood. In S. Edwards and L. Brooker (Eds), *Engaging Play*. Maidenhead: Open University Press.

Blenkin, G. and Kelly, A. (1987) *The Primary Curriculum*. London: Harper & Row.

Bloch, C. (2007) Foreign language learning in South Africa early childhood education. In M. Cochran and R. New (Eds), *Encyclopedia of Early Childhood Education*, 4, 1224–6. Westport, CT: Praeger.

Bloom, L. (1970) *Language Development: Form and Function in Emerging Grammars*. Cambridge, MA: MIT Press.

Bloom, P.J. and Sheerer, M. (1992) The effect of leadership training on childcare program quality. *Early Childhood Research Quarterly*, 7(4): 579–94.

Boag-Munroe, G. (2012) Engaging 'hard-to-reach' families: a view from the literature. In T. Papatheodorou (Ed.), *Debates on Early Childhood Policies and Practices* (pp. 183–92). London: Routledge.

Bohannon, N. and Stanowicz, L. (1988) The issue of negative evidence: adult responses to children's language errors. *Developmental Psychology*, 24: 684–9.

Boland, A.M., Haden, C.A. and Ornstein, P.A. (2003) Boosting children's memory by training mothers in the use of an elaborative conversational style as an event unfolds. *Journal of Cognition and Development*, 4: 39–65.

Booth, T. (2000) Reflection. In P. Clough and J. Corbett (Eds), *Theories of Inclusive Education*. London: PCP/Sage.

Booth, T. (2010) *How should we live together? Inclusion as a framework of values for educational development*. Unpublished.

Booth, T. (2011) Curricula for the Common School: What shall we tell our children? *FORUM*, 53(1): 31–48.

Booth, T. and Ainscow, M. (2011) *Index for Inclusion: Developing Learning and Participation in Schools*. Bristol: CSIE.

Booth, T. and Dyssegaard, B. (2008) *Quality is Not Enough: A Discussion Paper*. Copenhagen: Ministry of Foreign Affairs of Denmark, Danida.

Booth, T. and O'Connor, S. (2012) *Lessons from the Index for Inclusion: Developing Learning and Participation in Early Years and Childcare* [online]. Available: https://heimatkunde.boell.de/2012/08/01/lessons-index-inclusion-developing-learning-and-participation-early-years-and-childcare [accessed 28.3.17].

Bornstein, M.H. and Bruner, J.S. (Eds) (1989) *Interaction in Human Development*. Hillsdale, NJ: Erlbaum.

Bossard, J. and Boll, E. (1966) *The Sociology of Child Development*. New York: Harper & Row.

Bourdieu, P. (1992) *The Logic of Practice*. Cambridge: Polity.

Bowlby, J. (1951) *Maternal Care and Mental Health* (Report to the World Health Organisation). Geneva: WHO.

Bowlby, J. (1965[1953]) *Child Care and the Growth of Love*. Harmondsworth: Penguin.

Bowlby, J. (1988) Developmental psychiatry comes of age. *American Journal of Psychiatry*, 145: 1–10.

Bozhovich, L.I. (2009) The social situation of child development. *Journal of Russian and East European Psychology*, 47: 59–86.

Braidotti, R. (2013) *The Posthuman*. London: Polity Press.

Braine, M. (1994) Is nativism sufficient? *Journal of Child Language*, 21: 9–31.

Braungart-Rieker, J.M., Garwood, M.M., Powers, B.P. and Wang, X. (2001) Parental sensitivity, infant affect, and affect regulation: predictors of later attachment. *Child Development*, 72(1): 252–70.

Brehony, K. (2000) Montessori, individual work and individuality in the elementary school classroom. *History of Education*, 29(2): 115–28.

Briggs, A. and Burke, P. (2000) *Social history of the media: From Gutenberg to the Internet*. London: Polity.

Britten, B. and Savill, R. (2008) Police fear Internet cult inspires teen suicides. *Daily Telegraph*, 24 January, 2008 [online]. Available: http://www.telegraph.co.uk/news/main.jhtml?xml=/news/2008/01/23/nsuicide123.xml [accessed 16.3.17].

Broadhead, P., Howard, J. and Wood, E. (2010) (Eds) *Play and Learning in the Early Years*. London: Sage.

Broadhurst, K., Alrouh, B., Mason, C.S. with Yeend, E., Kershaw, S., Shaw, M. and Harwin, J. (2016) Women and infants in care proceedings in England: new insights from research on recurrent care proceedings. *Family Law*, 46(2): 2008–114.

Bronfenbrenner, U. (1979) *The Ecology of Human Development: Experiments by Nature and Design*. Cambridge, MA: Harvard University Press.

Bronfenbrenner, U. (1986) Ecology of the family as a context for human development: research perspectives. *Developmental Psychology*, 22: 723–42.

Bronfenbrenner, U. (2005) *Making Human Beings Human: Bioecological Perspectives on Human Development*. Thousand Oaks, CA: Sage.

Bronfenbrenner, U. and Morris, P.A. (1998) The ecology of developmental processes. In W. Damon (Series Ed.) and R.M. Lerner (Vol. Ed.), *Handbook of Child Psychology: Vol.1. Theoretical Models of Human Development* (Fifth Edition) (pp. 993–1028). New York: Wiley.

Brooker, L. (2002) *Starting School – Young Children's Learning Cultures*. Buckingham: Open University Press.

Brooks, P. and Kempe, V. (2012) *Language Development*. Sussex: John Wiley & Sons.

Brown, R. and Ward, H. (2012) *Decision-making within a Child's Timeframe: An Overview of Current Research Evidence for Family Justice Professionals Concerning Child Development and the Impact of Maltreatment*. London: Childhood Wellbeing Research Centre.

Browne, J. and Hood, A. (2016) *Living Standards, Poverty and Inequality in the UK: 2015–16 to 2020–21*. London: Institute for Fiscal Studies [online]. Available: http://www.ifs.org.uk/uploads/publications/comms/R114.pdf [accessed 1.7.16].

Bruce, T. (1999) In praise of inspired and inspiring teachers. In L. Abbott and H. Moylett (Eds), *Early Education Transformed*. London: Falmer Press.

Brumbaugh, C.C. and Fraley, R.C. (2006) Transference and attachment: how do attachment patterns get carried forward from one relationship to the next? *Personality and Social Psychology Bulletin*, 32(4): 552–60.

Bruner, J. (1974) Child's play. *New Scientist*, 62: 126–8.

Bruner, J. (1983) *Child's Talk: Learning to Use Language*. Oxford: Oxford University Press.

Bruner, J. (2000) Foreword. In J. DeLoache and A. Gottlieb (Eds), *A World of Babies: Imagined Childcare Guides for Seven Societies*. Cambridge: Cambridge University Press.

Bruns, A. (2006) Towards produsage: futures for user-led content production. In F. Sudweeks, H. Hrachovec, and C. Ess (Eds), *Proceedings: Cultural Attitudes towards Communication and Technology 2006* (pp. 275–84). Perth: Murdoch University.

Buckingham, D. (2007) Childhood in the age of global media. *Children's Geographies*, 5(1–2): 43–54.

Bullock, R., Courtney, M., Parker, R., Sinclair, I. and Thoburn, J. (2006) Can the corporate state parent? *Children and Youth Services Review*, 28(11): 1344–58.

Burke, A. and Marsh, J. (Eds) (2013) *Children's Virtual Play Worlds: Culture, Learning and Participation*. New York: Peter Lang.

Burman, E. (2001) Beyond the baby and the bathwater: postdualistic developmental psychologies for diverse childhoods. *European Early Childhood Education Research Journal*, 9(1): 5–22.

Burman, E. (2008) *Developments: Child, Image, Nation*. London: Routledge.

Burton, M., Cobb, E., Donachie, P., Judah, G., Curtis, V. and Schmidt, W.P. (2011) The effect of handwashing with water or soap on bacterial contamination of hands. *International Journal, of Environmental Research and Public Health*, 8(1): 97–104.

Bush, T. (2014) Instructional leadership in centralized context: rhetoric or reality? *Educational Management Administration and Leadership,* 41(1): 3–5.

Busza, J., Castle, S. and Diarra, A. (2004) Trafficking and health. *British Medical Journal*, 328: 1369–71.

Butchart, A., Putney, H. and Kahane, T. (2006) *Preventing Child Maltreatment: A Guide to Taking Action and Generating Evidence*. Geneva: WHO.

Butler, J. (2006) *Gender Trouble*. London: Routledge.

Bybee, J. and Scheibman, J. (1999) The effect of usage on degrees of constituency: the reduction of don't in English. *Linguistics*, 37: 575–96.

Bywaters, P., Bunting, L., Davidson, G., Hanratty, J., Mason, W., McCartan, C. and Steils, N. (2016) *The Relationship between Poverty, Child Abuse and Neglect: An Evidence Review*. London: Joseph Rowntree Foundation.

Cagliari, P., Castagnetti, M., Giudici, C. and Rinaldi, C. (2016) *Loris Malaguzzi and the Schools of Reggio Emilia*. London: Routledge.

CAFCASS (2012) *Three Weeks in November... Three Years On ... Cafcass Care Application Study 2012*. London: CAFCASS.

Cameron, C., Connelly, G. and Jackson, S. (2015) *Educating Children and Young People in Care: Learning Placements and Caring Schools* (Chapter 7). London and Philadelphia: Jessica Kingsley.

Cameron, D. (2016) Prime Minister's speech on life chances [online]. Available: https://www.gov.uk/government/speeches/prime-ministers-speech-on-life-chances [accessed 2.5.15].

Cameron-Faulkner, T., Lieven, E. and Tomasello, M. (2003) A construction based analysis of child directed speech. *Cognitive Science*, 27: 843–73.

Camilli, G., Vargas, S., Ryan, S., and Barnett, W.S. (2010) Meta-analysis of the effects of early education interventions on cognitive and social development. *The Teachers College Record*, 112(3): 579–620.

Cannella, G.S. (1997) *Deconstructing Early Childhood Education: Social Justice and Revolution*. New York: Peter Lang.

Cannella, G.S. and Viruru, R. (2004) *Childhood & Postcolonization: Power, Education and Contemporary Practice*. New York: Routledge.

Carlson, S. and Moses, L. (2001) In differences in inhibitory control and children's theory of mind. *Child Development*, 72: 1032–53.

Carr, M. (2001) *Assessment in Early Childhood Settings: Learning Stories*. London: Paul Chapman Publishing.

Carr, M. and Lee, W. (2012) *Learning Stories: Constructing Learner Identities in Early Education*. London: Sage.

Carrington, S. and Robinson, R. (2004) A case study of inclusive school development: a journey of learning. *The International Journal of Inclusive Education*, 8(2): 141–53.

Carson, R. (1962) *Silent Spring*. London: Penguin.

Cawson, P., Wattam, C., Brooker, S. and Kelly, G. (2000) *Child Maltreatment in the United Kingdom*. London: NSPCC.

Central Advisory Council for Education (CACE) (1967) *Children and Their Primary Schools* (The Plowden Report). London: Stationery Office.

Centre for Workforce Intelligence (CfWI) (2015) *Understanding the Wider Public Health Workforce*. London: Centre for Workforce Intelligence.

Centre for Workforce Intelligence (CfWI) (2016) *Understanding the Public Health Practitioner Workforce: A CfWI Study*. London: Centre for Workforce Intelligence.

Chabat, A. (Originator) and Balmes, T. (Director) (2009) *Babies*. France: StudioCanal.

Chabris, C. and Simons, D. (2011) *The Invisible Gorilla: And Other Ways Our Intuition Deceives Us*. London: HarperCollins.

Chan, C.W. (2014) The leadership styles of Hong Kong kindergarten principals in a context of managerial change. *Educational Management Administration and Leadership*, 42(1): 30–9.

Charlton, M., Giugni, M., Hooper-Hansen., G., House, R., Osgood, J., Palmer, S. and Simpson, K. (Eds) (2012) *Unhurried Pathways: A New Framework for Early Childhood*. Winchester: Early Childhood Action.

Chaudron, S. (2015) *Young Children (0–8) and Digital Technology: A Qualitative Exploratory Study Across Seven Countries* [online]. Available: http://publications.jrc.ec.europa.eu/repository/handle/JRC93239 [accessed 20.5.16].

Chomsky, N. (1959) A review of B.F. Skinner's 'Verbal Behavior'. *Language*, 35: 26–58.

Chomsky, N. (1965) *Aspects of the Theory of Syntax*. Cambridge, MA: MIT Press.

Chomsky, N. (1995) *The Minimalist Program*. Cambridge, MA: MIT Press.

Christensen, P. and James, A. (Eds) (2008a) *Research with Children: Perspectives and Practices* (Second Edition). London: Routledge Falmer.

Christensen, P. and James, A. (2008b) Introduction: researching children and childhood cultures of communication. In Christensen, P. and James, A. (Eds), *Research with Children: Perspectives and Practices* (Second Edition) (pp. 1–9). London: Routledge Falmer.

Clark, A. (2005) Ways of seeing: using the Mosaic approach to listen to young children's perspectives. In A. Clark, A.T. Kjørholt and P. Moss (Eds), *Beyond Listening: Children's Perspectives on Early Childhood Services* (pp. 29–49). Bristol: Policy Press.

Clark, A. (2010) *Transforming Children's Spaces: Children's and Adults' Participation in Designing Learning Environments*. London: Routledge.

Clark, A. (2011a) Multimodal map making with young children: exploring ethnographic and participatory methods. *Qualitative Research*, 11(3): 311–33.

Clark, A. (2011b) Breaking methodological boundaries? Exploring visual, participatory methods with adults and young children. *European Early Childhood Education Research Journal*, 19(3): 321–30.

Clark, E.V. (2016) *First Language Acquisition* (Third Edition). Cambridge: Cambridge University Press.

Clark, A. and Moss, P. (2005) *Spaces to Play: More Listening to Young Children Using the Mosaic Approach*. London: National Children's Bureau.

Clark, A. and Moss, P. (2011) *Listening to Young Children: The Mosaic Approach* (Second Edition). London: National Children's Bureau.

Clark, A., Flewitt, R., Hammersley, M. and Robb, M. (Eds) (2014) *Understanding Research with Children and Young People*. London: Sage/The Open University.

Clark, A., Kjørholt, A.T. and Moss, P. (2005) *Beyond Listening: Children's Perspectives on Early Childhood Services*. Bristol: Policy Press.

Clay, M.M. (1966) *Emergent Reading Behavior*. Unpublished Doctoral Dissertation, New Zealand: University of Auckland.

Cockburn, T. (2013) *Rethinking Children's Citizenship*. Basingstoke: Palgrave Macmillan.

Cohen, S. (1987) *Folk Devils and Moral Panics: The Creation of the Mods and Rockers* (Second Edition). Oxford: Blackwell.

Collins, P.H. (2000) *Black Feminist Thought: Knowledge, Consciousness and the Politics of Empowerment*. New York: Routledge.

Cooklin, A., Rowe, H., and Fisher, J. (2012) Paid parental leave supports breastfeeding and mother-infant relationship: a prospective investigation of maternal postpartum employment. *Australian and New Zealand Journal of Public Health,* 36(3): 249–56.

Corby, B., Shemmings, D. and Wilkins, D. (2012) *Child Abuse: An Evidence Base for Confident Practice* (Fourth Edition). Maidenhead: Open University Press.

Correa-Chavez, M.R., Mejia-Arauziteso, R. and Rogoff, B. (Eds) (2015) *Children Learn by Observing and Contributing to Family and Community Endeavors: A Cultural Paradigm* (*Advances in Child Development and Behaviour, Volume 49*). Amsterdam, NL: Academic Press.

Corsaro, W. (1985) *Friendship and Peer Culture in the Early Years*. Norwood, NJ: Ablex.

Corsaro, W. (2017) *The Sociology of Childhood* (Fifth Edition). USA, CA: Sage.

Coulmas, F. (Ed.) (1981) *Conversational Routine*. The Hague: Mouton.

Court, M. (1994) *Women Transforming Leadership*. Palmerston North, New Zealand: ERDC Press.

Cousins, J. (1999) *Listening to Four-year-olds*. London: National Early Years Network.

Coventry Safeguarding Children Board (2013) *Serious Case Review re Daniel Pelka: Overview Report*. Coventry.

Cranston, M. (1967) Human rights, real and supposed. In D.D. Raphael (Ed.), *Political Theory and the Rights of Man*. Bloomington, IN: Indiana University Press.

Croft, W. (2001) *Radical Construction Grammar: Syntactic Theory in Typological Perspective*. Oxford: Oxford University Press.

Cunningham, H. (2005) *Children and Childhood in Western Society since 1500*. Harlow: Longman.

Dabrowska, E. (2000) From formula to schema: the acquisition of English questions. *Cognitive Linguistics*, 11–20.

Dahlberg, G. and Moss, P. (2005) *Ethics & Politics in Early Childhood Education*. London: Routledge.

Dahlberg, G., Moss, P. and Pence, A. (2007) *Beyond Quality in Early Childhood Education and Care: Languages of Evaluation* (Second Edition). London: Routledge.

Dahlgren, G. and Whitehead, M. (1991) *Policies and Strategies to Promote Social Equity in Health*. Stockholm: Institute for Futures Studies.

Daniel, B., Taylor, J., Scott, J., Derbyshire, D. and Neilson, D. (2011) *Recognizing and Helping the Neglected Child: Evidence-Based Practice for Assessment and Intervention*. London: Jessica Kingsley.

David, T. and Powell, S. (2005) Play in the early years; the influence of cultural difference. In J. Moyles (Ed.), *The Excellence of Play*. Buckingham: Open University Press.

David, T., Goouch, K., Powell, S. and Abbott, L. (2003) *Birth to Three Matters: A Review of the Literature* (DFES Research Report No. 444). London: DfES.

Davidson, C., Danby, S., Given, L.M. and Thorpe, K. (2014) Talk about a YouTube video in preschool: the mutual production of shared understanding for learning with digital technology. *Australasian Journal of Early Childhood*, 39(3): 76–83.

Davies, B. (1989) *Frogs and Snails and Feminist Tales: Preschool Children and Gender*. Sydney: Allen & Unwin.

Davies, B. (2014) *Listening to Children: Being and Becoming*. London: Routledge.

Davies, D. (1999) *Child Development: A Practitioner's Guide*. New York: Guilford Press.

Davies, S. (2013) *Annual Report of the Chief Medical Officer 2012. Our Children Deserve Better: Prevention Pays*. London: Department of Health.

Davis, J. (2009) Revealing the research 'hole' of early childhood education for sustainability: a preliminary survey of the literature. *Environmental Education Research*, 15(2): 227–41.

Davis, J. (2014) Examining early childhood education through the lens of education for sustainability: revisioning rights. In J. Davis and S. Elliott (Eds), *Research in Early Childhood Education for Sustainability: International Perspectives and Provocations* (pp. 21–37). London: Routledge.

Davis, J. and Elliott, S. (Eds) (2014) *Research in Early Childhood Education for Sustainability: International Perspectives and Provocations*. London: Routledge.

Davis, J., Watson, N. and Cunningham-Burley, S. (2008) Learning the lives of disabled children: developing a reflexive approach. In P. Christensen and A. James (Eds), *Research with Children: Perspectives and Practices* (Second Edition) (pp. 220–38). London: Falmer Press.

de Houwer, A. (1995) Bilingual language acquisition. In P. Fletcher and B. MacWhinney (Eds.), *Handbook of Child Language*. London: Blackwell.

De Lange, A. (2005) *Observations on Burkina Faso*. Unpublished paper presented at Childhoods in Emerging and Transforming Societies. 29 June–3 July 2005, University of Oslo.

Degotardi, S. and Sweller, N. (2012) Mind-mindedness in infant child-care. *Early Childhood Research Quarterly*, 27: 253–65.

Demetras, M., Post, K. and Snow, C. (1986) Feedback to first language learners. *Journal of Child Language*, 13: 275–92.

Denham, S.A., Bassett, H.H., Brown, C., Way, E. and Steed, J. (2015) 'I know how you feel': preschoolers' emotion knowledge contributes to early school success. *Journal of Early Childhood Research*, 13(3): 252–62.

Department for Children, Schools and Families (DCSF) (2008a) *Social and Emotional Aspects of Development*. Nottingham: DCSF.

Department for Children, Schools and Families (DCSF) (2009a) *Every Child A Talker: Guidance for Consultants and Early Language Lead Practitioners, Third Instalment, Destination: Every Child A Talker*, 00971-2009DOM-EN (London: DCSF: Crown copyright 2009a) [online]. Available: http://www.foundationyears.org.uk/2011/10/every-child-a-talker-guidance-for-consultants-and-early-language-lead-practitioners-third-instalment/ [accessed 13.3.17]. Reprinted under the Open Government Licence http://www.nationalarchives.gov.uk/doc/open-government-licence/version/3/

Department for Children, Schools and Families (DCSF) (2009b) *Learning, Playing and Interacting – Good Practice in the Early Years Foundation Stage*, 00775-2009BKT-EN. London: DCSF: Crown copyright [online]. Available: http://www.foundationyears.org.uk/wp-content/uploads/2011/10/Learning_Playing_Interacting.pdf [accessed 13.3.16].

Department for Education (DfE) (2012) *Early Years Qualification List* [online]. Available: http://www.education.gov.uk/eypqd/qualifications.shtml [accessed 14.3.17].

Department for Education (DfE) (2013) *More Great Childcare: Raising Quality and Giving Parents More Choice*. London: DfE.

Department for Education (DfE) (2015a) *Child Death Reviews – Year Ending March 2015*. London: DfE.

Department for Education (DfE) (2015b) *Statistical First Release: Children Looked After in England*. SFR 34/2015. DfE [online]. Available: https://www.gov.uk/government/statistics/children-looked-after-in-england-including-adoption-2014-to-2015 [accessed 06.7.2016].

Department for Education (DfE) (2016) *Take-up of Government Funded Childcare by Two-Year-Olds* [online]. Available: https://www.gov.uk/government/uploads/system/uploads/attachment_data/file/504568/take-up_of_government-funded_childcare_by_2-year-olds.pdf [accessed 1.6.16].

Department for Education (DfE) (2017) *Statutory Framework for the Early Years Foundation Stage. Setting the Standards for Learning, Development and Care for Children from Birth to Five*. Published March 2017. Effective April 2017 [online]. Available: https://www.foundationyears.org.uk/files/2017/03/EYFS_STATUTORY_FRAMEWORK_2017.pdf [accessed 19.9.17]

Department for Education (DfE) and Department of Health (DH) (2011) *Supporting Families in the Foundation Years*. London: DfE.

Department for Education and Skills (DfES) (1998) *National Childcare Strategy*. London: HMSO.

Department for Education and Skills (DfES) (2003) *Birth to Three Matters*. London: DfES.

Department for Education and Skills (DfES) (2004) *What Works in Promoting Children's Mental Health*. Nottingham: DfES. Reprinted under the Open Government Licence http://www.nationalarchives.gov.uk/doc/open-government-licence/version/3/

Department for Education and Skills (DfES) (2005) *Primary National Strategy Key Elements of Effective Practice (KEEP)*. London: DfES/Sure Start.

Department for Work and Pensions (DWP)/Department for Education (DfE) (2011) *A New Approach to Child Poverty: Tackling the Causes of Disadvantage and Transforming Families' Lives*. London: The Stationery Office.

Department for Work and Pensions (2016) *Households Below Average Income*. London: DWP.

Department of Health (DH) (2010) *Healthy Lives, Healthy People. Our Strategy for Public Health in England*. London: Department of Health.

Department of Health (DH) (2011b) *No Health without Mental Health*. London: HM Government.

Department of Health (DH) (2015) *Future in Mind*. London: Department of Health.

Department of Health (DH)/Public Health England (PHE) (2014) *A Framework for Personalised Care and Population Health for Nurses, Midwives, Health Visitors and Allied Health Professionals. Caring for Populations across the Lifecourse*. London: Public Health England.

Derrida, J. (1978) *Writing & Difference*. Chicago: University of Chicago Press.

DES (2015) *Curriculum for Wales: Foundation Phase Framework* (revised 2015). Cardiff: DES.

Diamond, A., Barnett, W.S., Thomas, J. and Munro, S. (2007) Preschool program improves cognitive control. *Science*, 318: 1387–8.

Doddington, C. and Hilton, M. (2007) *Child-Centred Education: Reviving the Creative Tradition*. London: Sage.

Douglas, M. (1966; 2006) *Purity and Danger: An Analysis of Concept of Pollution and Taboo*. Routledge Classics.

Dominici, G.(1927[1401]) *On the Education of Children*. Washington DC: Catholic University of America.

Draper, L. and Duffy, B. (2001) Working with parents. In G. Pugh (Ed.), *Contemporary Issues in the Early Years* (pp. 151–62). London: Paul Chapman.

Drifte, C. (2004) *Encouraging Positive Behaviour in the Early Years*. London: Paul Chapman Publishing.

Duckworth, A.L. and Carlson, S.M. (2013) Self-regulation and school success. In B.W. Sokol, F.M.E. Grouzet and U. Müller (Eds), *Self-Regulation and Autonomy: Social and Developmental Dimensions of Human Conduct* (pp. 208–30). New York, NY: Cambridge University Press.

Duhn, I. (2012) Making 'place' for ecological sustainability in early childhood education. *Environmental Education Research*, 18(1): 19–29.

Duke, J. (2009) *The Use of the Index for Inclusion in a Regional Educational Learning Community* (unpublished) [online]. Available: http://eprints.qut.edu.au/29400/1/c29400.pdf [accessed 16.3.17].

Duncan, G.J., Dowsett, C.J. and Claessens, A. (2007) School readiness and later achievement. *Developmental Psychology*, 43: 1428–46.

Dunford, J. (2010) *Review of the Office of the Children's Commissioner (England)*. London: HMSO.

Dunn, J. (1984) *Sisters and Brothers*. London: Fontana.

Dunn, J. (1993) *Young Children's Close Relationships: Beyond Attachment*. Newbury Park, CA: Sage.

Dunn, J. (1999) Mind-reading and social relationships. In M. Bennett (Ed.), *Developmental Psychology*. London: Taylor and Francis.

Early Education (2012) *Development Matters in the Early Years Foundation Stage*. London: Early Education, © Crown copyright 2012 [online]. Available: http://www.foundationyears.org.uk/files/2012/03/Development-Matters-FINAL-PRINT-AMENDED.pdf [accessed 13.3.17]. Reprinted under the Open Government Licence http://www.nationalarchives.gov.uk/doc/open-government-licence/version/3/

Ebrahim, H. (2017) *Muslim Early Childhood in South Africa*. London: Routledge.

Ebbeck, M., Saidon, S., Soh, S. and Goh, M. (2014) Readiness of early childhood professionals in Singapore to take on a leadership role. *Asia-Pacific Journal of Research in Early Childhood Education*, 8(1): 79–98.

Ebrahim, H. (2017) *Muslim Early Childhood in South Africa*. London: Routledge.

Education Scotland (2016) *Curriculum for Excellence*. Livingstone: Education Scotland.

Edwards, M. and Timberlake, L. (2012) *Whole Earth? Aligning Human Systems and Natural Systems*. London: Still Pictures Moving Words Ltd.

Einarsdóttir, J. (2005) Playschool in pictures: children's photographs as a research method. *Early Childhood Development and Care*, 175(6): 523–42.

Eisenstadt, N. (2011) *Providing a Sure Start: How Government Discovered Early Childhood*. Bristol: Polity.

Elfer, P. (2016) Psychoanalytic theory, emotion and early years practice. In T. David, K. Goouch and S. Powell (Eds), *The Routledge International Handbook of Philosophies and Theories of Early Education and Care* (pp. 69–79). London: Routledge.

Elfer, P., Goldschmied, E. and Selleck, D. (2011) *Key Persons in the Early Years: Building Relationships for Quality Provision in Early Years Settings and Primary Schools*. London: David Fulton.

Elkin, F. (1960) *The Child and Society: The Process of Socialisation*. New York: Random House.

Elkonin, D.B. (1999) Toward the problem of stages in the mental development of children. *Journal of Russian and East European Psychology*, 37(6): 11–30.

Elman, J.L. (2005) Connectionist models of cognitive development: where next? *TRENDS in Cognitive Sciences*, 9: 111–17.

Emond, R. (2005) Ethnographic research methods with children and young people. In S. Greene and D. Hogan (Eds), *Researching Children's Experience: Approaches and Methods* (pp. 123–40). London: Sage.

Encyclopaedia Britannica (2012) [online]. Available: http://www.britannica.com/EBchecked/topic/441113/Pandora [accessed 20.3.17].

Encyclopaedia Britannica (2015) *Pandora*.

Engeström, E. (1999) (Eds) *Perspectives on Activity Theory*. New York: Cambridge University Press.

Erikson, E. (1977) *Toys and Reasons: Stages in the Ritualisation of Experience*. New York: Norton.

Erikson, E.H. (1995) *Childhood and Society*. Vintage Books.

European Commission (2014) *Key Data on Early Childhood Education and Care in Europe. 2014 Edition*. Eurydice and Eurostat Report. Luxembourg: European Union.

Evangelou, M., Sylva, K., Kyriacou, M., Wild, M. and Glenny, G. (2009) *Early Years Learning and Development Literature Review*, DCSF Research Report No. DCSF-RR176, copyright © Oxford University 2009. Published under the Open Government Licence https://www.nationalarchives.gov.uk/doc/open-government-licence/version/3

Evans, J. (2013) *Philosophy for Life and Other Dangerous Situations*. London: Rider/ Random House.

Evans, L., Packwood, A., Neill, S.R. St.J. and Campbell, J. (1994) *The Meaning of Infant Teachers' Work*. London: Routledge.

EveryChild (2012) *Making Social Work Work: Improving Social Work for Vulnerable Families and Children Without Parental Care Around the World*. London: EveryChild.

Fagan, R.M. (1984) Play and behavioural flexibility. In P.K. Smith (Ed.), *Play in Animals and Humans*. Oxford: Basil Blackwell.

Fahlberg, V. (2012) *A Child's Journey through Placement*. London: Jessica Kingsley.

Family and Childcare Trust (2016) *In for a Pound: The Relationship Between Staff Wages and Ofsted Grades in Group-Based Childcare Provision*. London: FCT.

Farah, M. J., Shera, D.M., Savage, J.H., Betancourt, L., Giannetta, J.M., Brodsky, N.L., Malmud, E.K. and Hurt, H. (2006) Childhood poverty: specific associations with neurocognitive development. *Brain Research*, 1110: 166–74.

Farmer, E., Sturgess, W., O'Neill, T. and Wijedasa, D. (2011) *Achieving Successful Returns from Care: What Makes Reunification Work?* London: BAAF.

Farquhar, S. and White, E. (2014) Philosophy and pedagogy of early childhood. *Educational Philosophy and Theory*, 46(8): 821–32.

Fearn, M. and Howard, J. (2011) Play as a resource for children facing adversity: an exploration of indicative case studies. *Children & Society*, 26(6): 1–13.

Ferguson, J. (1994) *The Anti-Politics Machine: Development, Depoliticization and Bureaucratic Power in Lesotho*. Minneapolis, MN: University of Minnesota Press.

Ferguson, J. (2015) *Give a Man a Fish: Reflections on the New Politics of Distribution*. Durham, NC: Duke University Press.

Field, F. (2010) *The Foundation Years: Preventing Poor Children becoming Poor Adults. The Report of the Independent Review on Poverty and Life Chances*. London: HMSO.

Fildes, V. (1995) The culture and biology of breastfeeding: an historical review of Western Europe. In P. Stuart-Macadam and K.A. Dettwyler (Eds.) *Breastfeeding: Biocultural Perspectives* (pp. 101–26). New York: Aldine De Gruyter.

Fitzgerald, D. and Kay, J. (2016) *Understanding Early Years Policy* (Fourth Edition). London: Sage.

Fleer, M. (2010) *Early Learning and Development: Cultural-Historical Concepts in Play*. Cambridge: Cambridge University Press.

Fleer, M. and Hedegaard, M. (2010) Children's development as participation in everyday practices across different institutions. *Mind Culture and Activity*, 17: 149–68.

Ford, R.M., McDougall, S.P. and Evans, D. (2009) Parent-delivered compensatory education for children at risk of educational failure: improving the academic and self-regulatory skills of a Sure Start pre-school sample. *British Journal of Psychology*, 100: 773–97.

Foucault, M. (1972) *The Archaeology of Knowledge*. New York: Pantheon.

Fox, J.L., Diezmann, C.M. and Grieshaber, S.J. (2011) Teachers' and parents perspectives of digital technology in the lives of young children. In S. Howard (Ed.), *AARE Annual Conference 2010*, 28 November to 2 December 2010, Melbourne, Australia [online]. Available: http://eprints.qut.edu.au/41179/ [accessed 16.3.17].

Foyle, G. and Nathanson, V. (Eds) (2013) *Growing Up in the UK. Ensuring a Healthy Future for our Children*. London: BMA board of Science.

Fraser, N. (1989) *Unruly Practices*. Minneapolis: University of Minnesota Press.

Fraser, S., Flewitt, R. and Hammersley, M. (2014) What is research with children and young people? In A. Clark, R. Flewitt, M. Hammersley and M. Robb (Eds), *Understanding Research with Children and Young People* (pp. 34–50). London: Sage/The Open University.

Freud, A. (1968) *The Psychoanalytic Treatment of Children*. New York: International Universities Press.

Freud, S. (1924) The loss of reality in neurosis and psychosis. *Standard Edition*, 19: 183–7.

Friendly, M. (2007) How ECEC programmes contribute to social inclusion in diverse societies. *Early Childhood Matters*, June: 11–14.

Frith, U. and Frith, C. (2001) The biological basis of social interaction. *Current Directions in Psychological Science*, 10: 151–5.

Froebel, F. (1826) *The Education of Man*. Translated by W.N Hailmann (2005). New York: Dover Publications.

Frost, N. and Robinson, M. (Eds.) (2016) *Developing Multi-Professional Teamwork for Integrated Children's Services*. McGraw-Hill Maidenhead: Open University Press.

García, E. (1983) Becoming bilingual in early childhood. *International Journal of Behavioral Development*, 6: 375–404.

Garcia, M., Pence, A. and Evans, E. (Eds) (2008) *Africa's Future, Africa's Challenge: Early Childhood Care and Development in Sub-Saharan Africa*. Washington: World Bank.

Gage, N. (1977, 1985) *The Scientific Basis for the Art of Teaching*. New York: Teachers College Press.

Garon, N., Bryson, S.E. and Smith, I.M. (2008) Executive function in preschoolers: a review using an integrative framework. *Psychological Bulletin*, 134: 31–60.

Garvey, C. (1991) *Play* (Second Edition). London: Fontana.

Gauvain, M. (2005) With eyes to the future: a brief history of cognitive development. *New Directions for Child and Adolescent Development*, 109: 119–26.

Geary, D.C. and Bjorklund, D.F. (2000) Evolutionary developmental psychology. *Child Development*, 71: 57–65.

Giddens, A. (1976) *New Rules in Sociological Method: A Positive Critique of Interpretive Sociologies*. London: Hutchinson.

Gilbert, N., Parton, N. and Skivenes, M. (2011) Changing patterns of response and emerging orientations. In N. Gilbert, N. Parton and M. Skivenes (Eds), *Child Protection Systems: International Trends and Orientations*. New York: Oxford University Press.

Gill, T. (2011) *Children and Nature: A Quasisystematic Review of the Empirical Evidence*. London: London Sustainable Development Commission, Greater London Authority [online]. Available: www.londonsdc.org/documents/Children%20and%20Nature%20-%20Literature%20Review.pdf [accessed 15.4.16].

Gilligan, C. (1982) *In a Different Voice: Psychological Theory in Women's Development*. Cambridge, MA: Harvard University Press.

Goldhaber-Fiebert, J.D., Lipsitch, M., Mahal, A., Zaslavsky, A.M. and Salomon, J.A. (2010) Quantifying child mortality reductions related to measles vaccination. *PLoS ONE* 5:11 [online]. Available: http://journals.plos.org/plosone/article?id=10.1371/journal.pone.0013842 [accessed 15.3.17].

Goldschmied, E. and Jackson, S. (2003) *People under Three: Young Children in Day Care*. London: Routledge.

Goleman, D. (2004) *Emotional Intelligence and Working with Emotional Intelligence*. London: Bloomsbury.

Goleman, D. (2007) *Social Intelligence: The New Science of Human Relationships*. London: Arrow Books.

Goody, J. (1982) *Cooking, Cuisine and Class*. Cambridge: Cambridge University Press.

Goouch, K. and Powell, S. (2013) Orchestrating professional development for baby room practitioners: raising the stakes in new dialogic encounters. *Journal of Early Childhood Research*, 11(1): 78–92.

Gopnik, A. and Wellman, H. (1992) Why the child's theory of mind is really a theory. *Mind and Language*, 7: 145–71.

Graves, R. (1960) *The Greek Myths. Vol. 1*. London: Penguin.

Gray, C. (2010) Understanding cognitive development: automaticity and the early years child. *Child Care in Practice*, 10(1): 39–47.

Gray, D. and Watt, P. (2013) *Giving Victims a Voice: Joint Report into Sexual Allegations Made Against Jimmy Savile*. London: NSPCC and Metropolitan Police.

Great Britain National Health Service and Community Care Act 1990: Elizabeth II. Chapter 19 (1990). London: The Stationery Office.

Green, J. (2012) Educating for health. In L. Jones and J. Douglas (Eds), *Public Health: Building Innovative Practice* (pp. 277–314). Milton Keynes: Sage/The Open University.

Green, J., Tones, K., Cross, R. and Woodall, J. (2015) *Health Promotion: Planning and Strategies* (Third Edition). London: Sage.

Greene, S. and Hill, M. (2005) Researching children's experience: methods and methodological issues. In S. Greene and D. Hogan (Eds), *Researching Children's Experience: Approaches and Methods* (pp. 1–21). London: Sage.

Greene, S. and Hogan, D. (Eds) (2005) *Researching Children's Experience: Approaches and Methods*. London: Sage.

Griffiths, J. (2013) *Kith: The Riddle of the Childscape*. London: Penguin.

Guo, Y. (2000) Food and family relations: the generation gap at the table. In Jun Jing (Ed.), *Feeding China's Little Emperors. Food, Children and Social Change* (pp. 94–113). Stanford, CA: Stanford University Press.

Hacking, E. and Barratt, R. (2007) Editorial: childhood and environment. *Environmental Education Research*, 13(4): 419–23.

Hadfield, M., Jopling, M., Needham, M. and Waller, T. (2012) *The Final Report of the Longitudinal Study of Early Years Professional Status*. London: DfE.

Hagekull, B., Stenberg, G. and Bohlin, G. (1993) Infant–mother social-referencing interactions: description and antecedents in maternal sensitivity and infant irritability. *Early Development and Parenting*, 2(3): 183–91.

Halford, G.S. and Andrews, G. (2010) Information-processing models of cognitive development. In U. Goswami (Ed.), *Wiley-Blackwell Handbook of Childhood Cognitive Development* (Second Edition). Oxford: Wiley-Blackwell.

Hall, K., Horgan, M., Ridgway, A., Murphy, R., Cunneen, M. and Cunningham, D. (2010) *Loris Malaguzzi and the Reggio Emilia Experience*. London: Continuum International.

Hall, V. (1996) *Dancing on the Glass Ceiling: A Study of Women Managers in Education*. London: Paul Chapman.

Haraway, D.J. (1991) *Simians, Cyborgs and Women*. London: Routledge.

Haraway, D.J. (2008) *When Species Meet*. Minneapolis: University of Minnesota Press.

Harcourt, D., Perry, B. and Waller, T. (Eds) (2011) *Researching Young Children's Perspectives: Debating Ethics and Dilemmas of Educational Research with Children*. London: Routledge.

Hardin, G. (1968) The Tragedy of the Commons. *Science*, 162(3859): 1243–8.

Harding, D. (1986) *The Science Question in Feminism*. New York: Cornell University Press.

Hardman, C. (1978) Can there be an anthropology of children? *Journal of the Anthropological Society Oxford*, 4(1): 85–99.

Haringey Local Safeguarding Children Board (2009) *Serious Case Review: Baby Peter. Executive Summary*. London, Haringey Children's Services Department.

Harold, G., Acquah, D., Sellers, R. and Chowdry, H. (2016) *What Works to Enhance Inter-parental Relationships and Improve Outcomes for Children*. London: Department for Work and Pensions.

Harris, P. (1989) *Children and Emotion: The Development of Psychological Understanding*. Oxford: Blackwell.

Harrison, J.E. (1903) *Prolegomena to the Study of Greek Religion* 1922, 283–85 quoted in Graves *The Greek Myths* (1955,1960) sect. 39:8, 148.

Hart, R. (1979) *Children's Experience of Place*. New York: Irvington Publishers.

Hashim, I. M. (2006) *The Positives and Negatives of Children's Independent Migration: Assessing the Evidence and the Debates*. Sussex Centre for Migration Research Working Paper T16 [online]. Available: http://www.migrationdrc.org/publications/working_papers/WP-T16.pdf [accessed 15.3.17].

Hatch, J. (1990) Young children as informants in classroom studies. *Early Childhood Research Quarterly*, 5: 251–64.

Heath, S.B. (1983) *Ways with Words*. Cambridge: Cambridge University Press.

Heath, S.B. (1986) What no bedtime story means: narrative skills at home and school. In B. Schieffelin and E. Ochs (Eds), *Language Socialization Across Cultures*. Cambridge: Cambridge University Press.

Hedegaard, M. (2012) Analyzing children's learning and development in everyday settings from a cultural-historical wholeness approach. *Mind Culture and Activity*, 19: 1–12.

Hedegaard, M. and Fleer, M. (2013) *Play, Leaning and Children's Development: Everyday Life in Families and Transition to School*. Cambridge University Press: New York.

Heikka, J. and Waniganayake, M. (2011) Pedagogical leadership from a distributed perspective within the context of early childhood education. *International Journal of Leadership in Education*, 14(4): 499–512.

Heikka, J., Waniganayake, M. and Hujala, E. (2012) Contextualising distributed leadership within early childhood education: current understandings, research evidence and future challenges. *Educational Management Administration and Leadership*, 41(3): 30–44.

Hendrick, H. (2003) *Child Welfare: Historical Dimensions, Contemporary Debates*. Bristol: Policy Press.

Hendry, J. (2008) *An Introduction to Social Anthropology: Sharing Our Worlds* (Second Edition). London: Palgrave MacMillan.

Heywood, C. (2001) *A History of Childhood: Children and Childhood in the West from Medieval to Modern Times*. Cambridge: Polity Press.

Hicks, D. (2014) *Educating for Hope in Troubled Times*. Stoke on Trent: Trentham Books Ltd.

Hicks, L. and Stein, M. (2009) *Neglect Matters: A Multi-Agency Guide for Professionals Working Together on Behalf of Teenagers*. London: DCSF.

HM Government (1989; 2004) *The Children Act*. London: HMSO.

HM Treasury (2004) *Choice for Parents: The Best Start for Children: A Ten Year Strategy for Childcare*. London: The Stationery Office.

Ho, D.C.W. (2010) Leadership for school improvement: exploring factors and practices in the press of curriculum change. *Early Education and Development*, 21(2): 263–84.

Hoff, E. (2008) *Language Development* (Fourth Edition). Belmont, CA: Wadsworth Publishing.

Holdsworth, A. (1988) *Out of the Dolls House*. London: BBC Books.

Holland, J. (2006) *Misogyny: The World's Oldest Prejudice*. New York: Avalon Publishing Group.

Holland, J. and Blackburn, J. (Eds) (1998) *Whose Voice? Participatory Research and Policy Change*. London: Intermediate Technology Publications.

Holloway, D., Green, L. and Livingstone, S. (2013) *Zero to Eight. Young Children and their Internet Use*. London: London School of Economics and EU Kids Online.

Holloway, S. and Valentine, G. (2000) *Children's Geographies: Playing, Living, Learning*. London: Routledge.

Holmes, L., McDermid, S., Padly, M. and Soper, J. (2012) *Exploration of the Costs and Impact of the Common Assessment Framework*. London: DfE.

Holt, J. (1975) *Escape from Childhood: The Needs and Rights of Children*. New York: Penguin.

Home Office (2014) *Multi Agency Working and Information Sharing Project Final Report* [online]. Available: https://www.gov.uk/government/uploads/system/uploads/attachment_data/file/338875/MASH.pdf [accessed 2.5.16].

Hooks, b. (2000) *Feminism is for Everybody: Passionate Politics*. Cambridge: South End Press.

Hopper, P. and Thompson, S. (1984) The discourse basis for lexical categories in universal grammar. *Language*, 60: 703–52.

Hornstein, D. and Lightfoot, N. (1981) *Explanations in Linguistics*. London: Longman.

Howard, J. (2002) Eliciting young children's perceptions of play, work and learning using the activity apperception story procedure. *Early Child Development and Care*, 127: 489–502.

Howard, J. and McInnes, K. (2013) *The Essence of Play: A Practice Companion for Professionals Working with Children and Young People*. London: Routledge.

Howard, J. and Prendiville, E. (2008) Developmental and therapeutic play. *Ip-Dip: For Professionals in Play*, 5: 16–7.

Howard, J., Jenvey, V. and Hill, C. (2006) Children's categorisation of play and learning based on social context. *Early Child Development and Care*, 176: 379–93.

Howard, J., Miles, G.E., Rees-Davies, L. and Bertenshaw, E.J. (2017) Play in middle childhood: everyday play behaviour and associated emotions. *Children and Society.* doi:10.1111/chso.12208.

Howes, C., Hamilton, C.E. and Matheson, C.C. (1994) Maternal, teacher and child care history correlates of children's relationships with peers. *Child Development,* 65: 1, 264–73.

Hughes, B. (1996) *A Playworker's Taxonomy of Play Types.* London: Playlink.

Hughes, C., Jaffee, S., Happe, F., Taylor, A., Caspi, A. and Moffitt, T. (2005) Origins of individual differences in theory of mind: from nature to nurture? *Child Development*, 76: 356–70.

Hughes, F. (1999) *Children, Play and Development.* Boston, MA: Allyn and Bacon.

Hujala, E. (2013) Contextually defined leadership. In E. Hujala, M. Waniganayake and J. Rodd (Eds), *Researching Leadership in Early Childhood Education* (pp. 47–60). Tampere, Finland: University of Tampere.

Hummel, S., Chilcott, J. Rawdin, A. and Strong, M. (2011) *Economic Outcomes of Early Years Programmes and Interventions Designed to Promote Cognitive, Social and Emotional Development Among Vulnerable Children and Families. Part 2. Economic Model.* School of Health and Related Research, University of Sheffield.

Huskinson, T., Hobden, S., Oliver, D., Keyes, J., Littlewood, M., Pye, J. and Tipping, S. (2016) *Childcare and Early Years Survey of Parents 2014 to 2015* [online]. Available: https://www.gov.uk/government/uploads/system/uploads/attachment_data/file/516924/SFR09-2016_Childcare_and_Early_Years_Parents_Survey_2014-15_report.pdf.pdf [accessed 10.6.16].

Hutchby, I. and Moran-Ellis, J. (Eds) (1998) *Children and Social Competence: Arenas of Action.* London: Falmer.

Hutt, S.J., Tyler, S., Hutt, C. and Christopherson, H. (1989) *Play, Exploration and Learning.* London: Routledge.

Immel, A. and Whitmore, M. (Eds.) (2013) *Childhood and Children's Books in Early Modern Europe, 1550–1800.* London: Routledge.

Isenberg, J. and Quisenberry, N. (2002) Play: essential for all children. A position paper of the Association for Childhood Education International. *Childhood Education*, 79(1): 33–9.

Jackson, S. (1993) Under fives: thirty years of no progress? *Children & Society*, 7(1): 64–81.

Jackson, S. and Forbes, R. (2015) *People Under Three: Play, Work and Learning in a Childcare Setting.* London: Routledge.

Jackson, S. and Hollingworth, K. (2017) Children in care in early childhood. In L. Miller, C. Cameron, C. Dalli and N. Barbour (Eds), *The SAGE Handbook of Early Childhood Policy* (pp. 298–301). London: Sage.

Jagger, G. and Wright, C. (Eds) (1999) *Changing Family Values.* London: Routledge.

James, A. (2013) *Socialising Children.* London: Palgrave Macmillan.

James, P. (2006) *Globalism, Nationalism, Tribalism: Bringing Theory Back In.* London: Sage.

James, A. and James, A. (2012) *Key Concepts in Childhood Studies.* London: Sage.

James, A. and Prout, A. (1996) Strategies and structures: towards a new perspective on children's experiences of family life. In J. Brannen and M. O'Brien (Eds), *Children in Families: Research and Policy.* London: Falmer.

James, A. and Prout, A. (Eds) (1990, 1997) *Constructing and Reconstructing Childhood: Contemporary Issues in the Sociological Study of Childhood.* London: Falmer Press.

James, A., Chris, J. and Prout, A. (1998) *Theorizing Childhood*. Vermont: Teachers College Press.

Jarvis, P. (2007) Monsters, magic and Mr Psycho: rough and tumble play in the early years of a primary school, a biocultural approach. *Early Years*, 27: 171–88.

Jarvis, P., Newman, S. and Swiniarski, L. (2014) On 'becoming social': the importance of collaborative free play in childhood. *International Journal of Play*, 3: 53–68.

Jennings, S. (1999) *Introduction to Developmental Play Therapy*. London: Jessica Kingsley.

John, K. (2008) Sustaining the leaders of children's centres: the role of leadership mentoring. *European Early Childhood Research Journal*, 16(1): 53–66.

Johnson, G.M. (2010) Young children's internet use at home and school: patterns and profiles. *Journal of Early Childhood Research*, 8: 282–93.

Johnson, M.H. and de Haan, M. (2011) *Developmental Cognitive Neuroscience* (Third Edition). Oxford: Wiley-Blackwell.

Jones, N. with Vilar, E. (2008) Situating children in international development policy: challenges involved in successful evidence-informed policy making. *Evidence and Policy*, 4(1): 31–51.

Joshi, L.H. (2016) How to unplug your iPad-addicted child. *The Telegraph*. 20 January, 2016 [online]. Available: http://www.telegraph.co.uk/women/family/how-to-unplug-your-ipad-addicted-child/ [accessed 20.5.16].

Kagan, J. (2010) *The Temperamental Thread*. New York: Dana Foundation.

Kalliala, M. (2011) Look at me! Does the adult truly see and respond to the child in Finnish day-care centres? *European Early Childhood Research Journal*, 19(2): 237–53.

Karmiloff-Smith, A. (2010) Neuroimaging of the developing brain: taking 'developing' seriously. *Human Brain Mapping*, 31(6): 934–41.

Karras, R. (2003) *From Boys to Men: Formation of Masculinity in Late Medieval Europe*. Philadelphia: University of Pennsylvania Press.

Karrby, G. (1989) Children's conceptions of their own play. *International Journal of Early Childhood Education*, 21: 2, 49–54.

Kayhaoglu, H. (2014) Play as seen by teachers and children in Turkey. *Procedia – Social and Behavioural Sciences,* 152, 149–153.

Keck, M.E. and Sikkink, K. (1998) *Activists Beyond Borders: Advocacy Networks in International Politics*. New York: Cornell University Press.

Kehily, M.J. (2009) Children, young people and sexuality. In H. Montgomery and M. Kellett (Eds.) *Children and Young People's Worlds, Developing Frameworks for Integrated Practice*. Bristol: Policy Press.

Kellett, M. (2005) *How to Develop Children as Researchers: A Step by Step Guide to Teaching the Research Process*. London: Paul Chapman.

Kellett, M. (2010) *Rethinking Children and Research: Attitudes in Contemporary Society*. London: Continuum.

Kelly, C. (2007) *Children's World: Growing up in Russia 1890–1991*. New Haven: Yale University Press.

Kenway, J. and Bullen, E. (2001) *Consuming Children: Education – Entertainment – Advertising*. Buckingham: Open University Press.

Kernan, M., Singer, E. and Swinnen, R. (2011) Introduction. In M. Kernan and E. Singer (Eds), *Peer Relationships in Early Childhood Education and Care*. London: Routledge.

Keysers, C. (2011) *The Empathic Brain: How the Discovery of Mirror Neurons Changes our Understanding of Human Nature*. UK: Social Brain Press.

Khoury, A. (2015) VTech 'cannot confirm' if kids' chat logs and photos were compromised by security breach [online]. Available: http://www.digitaltrends.com/web/vtech-security-breach-update/#:xT0f1foTjKOGIA [accessed 20.5.16].

Kiernan, K. and Mensah, F. (2011) *PREview: Maternal Indicators in Pregnancy and Children's Infancy that Signal Future Outcomes for Children's Development, Behaviour and Health: Evidence from the Millennium Cohort Study*. Yorkshire and Humber: CHIMAT.

Kinder, M. (1993) *Playing with Power in Movies, Television and Videogames: From Muppet Babies to Teenage Mutant Ninja Turtles*. Berkeley: University of California Press.

King, P. and Howard, J. (2012) Children's perceptions of choice in relation to their play at home, in the school playground and at the out-of-school club. *Children & Society*, 28(2): 116–27.

King, R. (1979) *All Things Bright and Beautiful? A Sociological Study of Infant Classrooms*. Bath: Wiley.

Kjørholt, A.K. (2007) Childhood as a symbolic space: searching for authentic voices in the era of globalisation. *Children's Geographies*, 5(1–2): 29–42.

Klapisch-Zuber C. (1987) *Women, Family and Ritual in Rennaisance Italy*. Chicago: Chicago University Press.

Kline, N. (1999) *Time to Think, Listening to Ignite the Human Mind*. London: Ward Lock.

Kuhn, T. (1970) *The Structure of Scientific Revolutions* (Second Edition). Chicago, IL: University of Chicago Press.

Laevers, F. (Ed.) (1994) *The Leuven Involvement Scale for Young Children* (manual and video). Experiential Education Series, No.1. Leuven: Centre for Experiential Education.

Laevers, F. (1995) *An Exploration of the Concept of Involvement as an Indicator for Quality in Early Childhood Education*. Dundee: Scottish Consultative Council on the Curriculum.

Laming, W.H. (2003) *The Victoria Climbie Inquiry: Report of an Inquiry by Lord Laming*. Cmnd 5370. London: HMSO.

Landreth, G. (2002) *Play Therapy: The Art of the Relationship*. London: Brunner-Routledge.

Landry, S.H., Smith, K.E., Swank, P.R. and Guttentag, C. (2008) A responsive parenting intervention: the optimal timing across early childhood for impacting maternal behaviors and child outcomes. *Developmental Psychology*, 44(5): 1335–53.

Lane, J. (2008) *Young Children and Racial Justice*. London: National Children's Bureau.

Langacker, R.W. (1987) *Foundations of Cognitive Grammar: Theoretical Prerequisites*. Stanford, CA: Stanford University Press.

Langacker, R.W. (1991) *Concept, Image, and Symbol: The Cognitive Basis of Grammar*. Berlin and New York: Mouton de Gruyter.

Langsted, O. (1994) Looking at quality from the child's perspective. In P. Moss and A. Pence (Eds), *Valuing Quality in Early Childhood Services: New Approaches for Defining Quality* (pp. 28–42). London: Paul Chapman.

Langston, A. (2011) A guide to the revised EYFS: part 2 – observation and planning. *Nursery World*, 4 October.

Lankshear, C. and Knobel, M. (2011) *New Literacies: Everyday Practices and Classroom Learning* (Third Edition). Maidenhead, Berkshire: Open University Press.

Lareau, A. (2000) Social class and the daily lives of children: a study from the United States. *Childhood*, 7(2): 155–71.

Lareau, A. (2003) *Unequal Childhoods: Class, Race and Family Life*. Berkeley, CA: University of California Press.

Lather, P. (1991) *Getting Smart: Feminist Research and Pedagogy with/in the Postmodern*. London: Routledge.

Lee, N. (2001) *Childhood and Society: Growing Up in an Age of Uncertainty*. Buckingham: Open University Press.

Lee, J. and Walsh D.J. (2004) Quality in early childhood programs: reflections from program evaluation practices. *American Journal of Evaluation,* 25(3): 351–73.

Leontiev, A. (1981) *Problems of the Development of Mind.* Moscow: Moscow University Press.

Leontiev, A.N. (1978) *Activity, Consciousness and Personality.* Englewood Cliffs: Prentice Hall.

LeVine, R.A. (2003) *Childhood Socialization: Comparative Studies of Parenting, Learning and Educational Change.* Hong Kong: Comparative Education Research Centre.

LeVine, R.A. and New, R. (Eds) (2008) *Anthropology and Child Development: A Cross-Cultural Reader.* Oxford: Blackwell.

Levitas, R., Pantazis, C., Fahmy, E., Gordon, D., Lloyd, E. and Patsios, D. (2007) *The Multi-Dimensional Analysis of Social Exclusion* [online]. Available: http://www.bristol.ac.uk/poverty/downloads/socialexclusion/multidimensional.pdf [accessed: 20.5.16].

Levy, R. (2011) *Young Children Reading at Home and at School.* London: Sage.

Lewis, I. and Lenehan, C. (chairs) (2012) *Report of the Young People's Health Outcomes Forum.* London: Department of Health.

Lewis, J. (2012) The failure to expand childcare provision and to develop a comprehensive childcare policy in Britain during the 1960s and 1970s. *Twentieth Century British History,* 24(2): 249–74.

Lewis, M.D. (2000) The promise of dynamic systems approaches for an integrated account of human development. *Child Development,* 71: 36–43.

Liebel, M. (2004) *A Will of their Own: Cross Cultural Perspectives on Working Children.* UK: Macmillan.

Lieberman, J.N. (1977) *Playfulness: Its Relationship to Imagination and Creativity.* London: Academic Press.

Lieven, E. (1994) Crosslinguistic and crosscultural aspects of language addressed to children. In C. Gallaway and B.J. Richards (Eds), *Input and Interaction in Language Acquisition.* Cambridge: Cambridge University Press.

Lieven, E., Behrens, H., Spears, J. and Tomasello, M. (2003) Early syntactic creativity: a usage-based approach. *Journal of Child Language,* 30: 333–70.

Lieven, E., Pine, J.M. and Baldwin, G. (1997) Lexically based learning and early grammatical development. *Journal of Child Language,* 24: 187–219.

Lifton, B. (1988) *King of Children: A Biography of Janusz Korczak.* New York: Farrar, Straus and Giroux.

Lillard, A.S., Lerner, M.D., Hopkins, E.J., Dore, R.A., Smith, E.D. and Palmquist, C.M. (2013) The impact of pretend play on children's development: a review of the evidence. *Psychological Bulletin,* 139: 1–34.

Lindon, J. (2001) *Understanding Children's Play.* Cheltenham: Nelson Thomas.

Lipscomb, S.T. and Pears, K.C. (2011) Patterns and predictors of early care and education for children in foster care, *Children and Youth Services Review,* 33: 2303–11.

Liverpool City Council (2016) *The Workplace Wellbeing Charter. National Award for England* [online]. Available: www.wellbeingcharter.org.uk [accessed 7.5.16].

Livingstone, S., Marsh, J., Plowman, L., Ottovordemgentschenfelde, S. and Fletcher-Watson, B. (2014) *Young Children (0–8) and Digital Technology: A Qualitative Exploratory Study.* National Report. London: London School of Economics and Political Science.

Livingstone, S., Mascheroni, G., Dreier, M., Chaudron, S. and Lagae, K. (2015) *How Parents of Young Children Manage Digital Devices at Home: The Role of Income, Education and Parental Style.* London: EU Kids Online, LSE.

Lloyd, E. (2015) Early childhood education and care in England under the coalition government. *London Review of Education*, 13(2): 144–56.

Local Government Association (LGA) (2014) *Public Health in Local Government. One Year On*. London: HMSO.

López Vilaplana, C. (2013) Children were the age group at the highest risk of poverty or social exclusion in 2011. *Eurostat. Stat. Focus* [online]. Available: http://ec.europa.eu/eurostat/en/web/products-statistics-in-focus/-/KS-SF-13-004. [accessed 19.6.16].

Lowe, R. (1980) Eugenics and education: a note on the origins of the intelligence testing movement in England. *Educational Studies, 6*. (1): 1–8.

Luke, A. and Luke, C. (2001) Adolescence lost/childhood regained: on early intervention and the emergence of the techno-subject. *Journal of Early Childhood Literacy*, 1: 91–120.

Lupton, D. (1995) *The Imperative of Health: Public Health and the Regulated Body*. London: Sage.

Lyon, C. (2007) Interrogating the concentration on the UNCRC instead of the ECHR in the development of children's rights in England? *Children and Society*, 21(2): 147–53.

Lyotard, J. (1984) *The Postmodern Condition: A Report on Knowledge*. Minneapolis: University of Minnesota Press.

Mabbott, J. (2010) *The 'Reading War' in Early Childhood Education: A Marxist History*. Unpublished EdD thesis. The University of Sheffield.

MacNaughton, G. (2005) *Doing Foucault in Early Childhood Studies*. London: Routledge.

Maddox, L. (2016) *I Saw Things Children Shouldn't See – Surviving a Troubled Childhood* [online]. Available: www.mosaicscience.com [accessed 27.6.16].

Malaguzzi, L. (1993) History, ideas and basic philosophy. In C. Edwards, L. Gandini and G. Forman (Eds), *The Hundred Languages of Children: The Reggio Emilia Approach to Early Childhood Education*. Norwood, NJ: Ablex Publishing.

Malkovich, A. (2013) *Charles Dickens and the Victorian Child: Romanticizing and Socializing the Imperfect Child*. London: Routledge.

Mandell, N. (1991) The least-adult role in studying children. In F. Waksler (Ed.), *Studying the Social Worlds of Children: Sociological Readings* (pp. 38–59). London: Falmer Press.

Mahon, M. and Crutchley, A. (2006) Performance of typically-developing school-age children with English as an additional language (EAL) on a test of receptive vocabulary. *Child Language Teaching and Therapy*, 22: 333–51.

Manzo, K. (2005) Exploiting West Africa's children: trafficking slavery and uneven development. *Area*, 37(4): 393–401.

Marcus, I.G. (1996) *Rituals of Childhood: Jewish Acculturation in Medieval Europe*. London: Yale University Press.

Marmot, M. (2010) *Fair Society, Healthy Lives. The Marmot Review. Strategic Review of Health Inequalities in England post 2010*. London: Department of Health.

Marsh, J. (2013) Online and offline play. In A. Burn and C. Richards (Eds) *Children's Games in the New Media Age* (pp. 109–32). London: Ashgate.

Marsh, J. (2015) 'Unboxing' videos: co-construction of the child as cyberflâneur. *Discourse: Studies in the Cultural Politics of Education*, 37(3): 369–80.

Marsh, J., Brooks, G., Hughes, J., Ritchie, L. and Roberts, S. (2005) *Digital Beginnings: Young Children's Use of Popular Culture, Media and New Technologies*. Sheffield, UK: University of Sheffield [online]. Available: http://www.digitalbeginnings.shef.ac.uk/final-report.htm [accessed 20.5.16].

Marsh, J., Hannon, P., Lewis, M. and Ritchie, L. (2015a) Young children's initiation into family literacy practices in the digital age. *Journal of Early Childhood Research*, 15(1): 47–60.

Marsh, J., Plowman, L., Yamada-Rice, D., Bishop, J.C., Lahmar, J., Scott, F., Davenport, A., et al. (2015b) *Exploring Play and Creativity in Pre-Schoolers' Use of Apps: Final Project Report* [online]. Available: www.techandplay.org [accessed 20.5.16].

Marsh, J., Plowman, L., Yamada-Rice, D., Bishop, J. and Scott, F. (2016) Digital play: a new classification. *Early Years: An International Journal*, 36(3): 242–53.

Martucci, K. (2016) Shared storybook reading in the preschool setting and considerations for young children's theory of mind development. *Journal of Early Childhood Research*, 14(1): 55–68.

Mathers, S., Ranns, H., Karemaker, A., Moody, A., Sylva, K., Graham, J. and Siraj-Blatchford, I. (2011) *Evaluation of the Graduate Leader Fund: Final Report (RR144)*. London: DfE Publications.

Maude, P., Whitehead, M., Cushing, A. and Crisp, M. (2006) *Observing and Analysing Learners' Movements*. Worcester: Tacklesport Consultancy Ltd.

May, H. and Carr, M. (2016) Te Whariki: a uniquely woven curriculum shaping policy, pedagogy and practice. In T. David, K. Goouch and S. Powell (Eds), *The Routledge International Handbook of Philosophies and Theories of Early Education and Care*. London: Routledge.

Mayall, B. (2000) Conversations with children: working with generational issues. In P. Christensen and A. James (Eds), *Research with Children: Perspectives and Practices* (Second Edition) (pp. 120–35). London: Routledge Falmer.

Mayall, B. (2002) *Towards a Sociology for Childhood: Thinking from Children's Lives*. Buckingham: Open University Press.

Maybin, J. and Woodhead, M. (Eds) (2003) *Childhoods in Context*. Chichester: John Wiley.

Maynard, T., Taylor, C., Waldron, S., Rhys, M., Smith, R., Power, S. and Clement, J. (2013) *Evaluating the Foundation Phase: Policy Logic Model and Programme Theory, Social Research No. 37/2012*. Cardiff: Welsh Government.

McInnes, K., Howard, J., Miles, G.E. and Crowley, K. (2009) Behavioural differences exhibited by children when practising a task under formal and playful conditions. *Educational & Child Psychology*, 26(2): 31–9.

McInnes, K., Howard, J., Miles, G.E. and Crowley, K. (2010) Differences in adult–child interactions during playful and formal practice conditions: an initial investigation. *The Psychology of Education Review*, 34(1): 14–20.

McInnes, K., Howard, J., Miles, G.E. and Crowley, K. (2011) Differences in practitioners' understanding of play and how this influences pedagogy and children's perceptions of play. *Early Years: An International Journal of Research and Development*, 31(2): 121–33.

McNeill, D. (1966) The creation of language by children. In J. Lyons and R.J. Wales (Eds), *Psycholinguistic Papers: The Proceedings of the 1966 Edinburgh Conference*. Edinburgh: Edinburgh University Press.

Meade, A. (2013) *When Adults Join Children in Playful Learning*. Presentation 22 June 2013. Wellington: Victoria University [online]. Available: http://www.victoria.ac.nz/education/pdf/jhc-symposium/winter-2013/A-Meade-TW-SST-in-playful-learning-VUW-Research-Hui-June13.pdf [accessed 20.3.17].

Mead, M. (1954) *Growing up in New Guinea*. London: Pelican.

Mehmet, N. (2011) Ethics and wellbeing. In A. Knight and A. McNaught (Eds), *Understanding Wellbeing: An Introduction for Students and Practitioners of Health and Social Care* (pp. 37–49). Banbury: Lantern.

Messenger, W. (2012) *The Influence of Professional Cultures on Collaborative Working in Children's Centres*. Unpublished PhD thesis: University of Worcester.

Mikulincer, M. and Shaver, P.R. (2007) *Attachment in Adulthood: Structure, Dynamics, and Change*. New York: Guilford Press.

Miller, E. and Kuhaneck, H. (2008) Children's perceptions of play experiences and play preferences: a qualitative study. *American Journal of Occupational Therapy*, 62: 407–15.

Mintz, S. (2004) *Huck's Raft: A History of American Childhood*. Cambridge, MA: Belknap Press.

Mischel, W., Shoda, Y. and Rodriguez, M.I. (1989) Delay of gratification in children. *Science*, 244(4907): 933–8.

Mitchell, C. (2011) *Doing Visual Research*. London: Sage.

Moffitt, T.E., Arseneault, L., Belsky, D.W. and Caspi, A. (2011) A gradient of childhood self-control predicts health, wealth, and public safety. *Proceedings of the National Academy of Sciences USA*, 108(7): 2693–8.

Moll, L.C., Amanti, C., Neff, D. and Gonzalez, N. (1992) Funds of knowledge for teaching: using a qualitative approach to connect homes and classrooms. *Theory Into Practice*, 31(2): 132–41.

Montessori, M. (1967 [1949]) *The Absorbent Mind*. New York: Dell.

Montgomery, H. (2014) Participant observation. In A. Clark, R. Flewitt, M. Hammersley and M. Robb (Eds), *Understanding Research with Children and Young People* (pp. 122–35). London: Sage.

Mortimer, H. (2001) *Special Needs and Early Years Provision*. London: Continuum.

Mosley, M. (2010) *The Story of Science: Power, Proof and Passion*. London: Mitchell Beazley, Octopus Publishing.

Moss, P. (2010) We cannot continue as we are: the educator in an education for survival. *Contemporary Issues in Early Childhood*, 11(1): 8–19.

Moss, P. (2011) *Democracy as First Practice in Early Childhood Education and Care* [online]. Available: http://www.child-encyclopedia.com/documents/MossANGxp1.pdf [accessed 16.3.17].

Moss, P. (2013) The relationship between early childhood and compulsory education: a properly political question. In P. Moss (Ed.), *Early Childhood and Compulsory Education: Reconceptualising the Relationship* (pp. 2–49). Oxon: Routledge.

Moss, P. (2014) *Our Youngest Children Deserve Better than a Fragmented Patchwork of Services*. IOE London Blog, Childhood and Early Education, posted February 5, 2014.

Moylett, H. (2013) *Learning and Teaching in the Early Years: Active Learning*. London: Practical Pre-School books, MA Education.

Moylett, H. and Stewart, N. (2012) *Understanding the Revised Early Years Foundation Stage*. London: Early Education.

Muijs, D., Aubrey, C., Harris, A. and Briggs, M. (2004) How do they manage? A review of the research on leadership. *Journal of Early Childhood Research*, 2(2): 157–69.

Munck, T. (2011) *The Enlightenment*. Oxford: Oxford University Press.

Munro, E. (2010) Learning to reduce risk in child protection. *British Journal of Social Work*, 40 (4): 1135–51.

Munro, E. (2011) *The Munro Review of Child Protection: Final Report – a Child-Centered System*. London: HMSO.

Naidoo, J. and Wills, J. (2016) *Foundations for Health Promotion* (Fourth Edition). London: Elsevier.

Nardi, B.A. and O'Day, V.L. (1999) *Information Ecologies: Using Technology with Heart*. Cambridge, MA: MIT Press.

National Evaluation of Sure Start (2011) *The Impact of Sure Start Local Programmes on Five Year Olds and their Families*. Report of the Longitudinal Study of 5-year-old Children and their Families. London: DfE.

Nederveen Pieterse, J. (2004) *Globalization and Culture: Global Melange*. Oxford: Rowman and Littlefield.

New Zealand Ministry of Education (1996) *Te Whariki: Every Childhood Curriculum*. Wellington, NZ: Learning Media Ltd.

Neuman, M.J. (2005) Governance of early childhood education and care: recent developments in OECD countries. *Early Years*, 25(2): 129–41.

Newman, J. and Yeates, N. (2008) *Social Justice: Welfare, Crime and Society*. Berkshire: Open University Press.

Newton, H. (2014) The sick child in early modern England, 1580–1720. *Endeavour*, 38(2): 122–9.

NHS (2016) *The Family Nurse Partnership* [online]. Available: http://fnp.nhs.uk/about-us. [accessed 20.5.16].

NHS England (2014) *Five Year Forward View*. London: NHS England.

NHS England/Public Health England (PHE)/Health Education England (HEE) (2016) *Making Every Contact Count (MECC): Consensus Statement*. London: Public Health England.

NICHD Early Childcare Research Network (2006) Infant–mother attachment classification: risk and protection in relation to changing maternal care-giving quality. *Developmental Psychology*, 42(1): 38–58.

Nieuwenhuys, O. (1996) The paradox of child labour and anthropology. *Annual Review of Anthropology*, 25: 237–51.

Ninio, A. and Snow, C. (1999) The development of pragmatics: learning to use language appropriately. In T.K. Bhatia and W.C. Ritchie (Eds), *Handbook of Language Acquisition*. New York: Academic Press.

Nivala, V. (2002) Leadership in general, leadership in theory. In V. Nivala and E. Hujala (Eds), *Leadership in Early Childhood Education: Cross-cultural Perspectives*. Oulu: Oulu University Press.

Noble, K.G., Tottenham, N. and Casey, B.J. (2005) Neuroscience perspectives on disparities in school readiness and cognitive achievement. *The Future of Children*, 15: 71–89.

Nussbaum, M. (2010) *Not for Profit: Why Democracy Needs the Humanities*. Princeton, NJ: Princeton University Press.

Nussbaum, M. (2013) *Political Emotions*. Cambridge, MA: Harvard University Press.

Nutbrown, C. (2011) *Key Concepts in Early Childhood Education and Care*. London: Sage.

Nutbrown, C. (2012) *Foundations for Quality: The Independent Review of Early Education and Childcare Qualifications*. London: HMSO.

Nutbrown, C. (2013) *Shaking the Foundations of Quality? Why 'Childcare' Policy Must Not Lead to Poor Quality Early Education and Care*. Sheffield: University of Sheffield.

Nutbrown, C., Clough, P. and Atherton, F. (2013) *Inclusion in the Early Years* (Second Edition). London: Sage.

Nuttall, J. (2013) Challenges, opportunities and capacity building in early childhood teachers' education research in Australia and New Zealand. *New Zealand Journal of Educational Studies*, 47(1): 65–78.

O'Brien, M., Alldred, P. and Jones, D. (1996) Children's constructions of family and kinship. In J. Brannen and M. O'Brien (Eds), *Children in Families: Research and Policy*. London: Falmer.

Ochs, E. (1985) Variation and error: a sociolinguistic approach to language acquisition in Samoa. In D.I. Slobin (Ed.) *The Crosslinguistic Study of Language Acquisition*, Vol. I. Hillsdale, NJ: Erlbaum.

Ochs, E. and Schieffelin, B.B. (1995) The impact of language socialization on grammatical development. In P. Fletcher and B. MacWhinney (eds), *The Handbook of Child Language* (pp. 73–94). Oxford: Blackwell.

O'Neill, O. (1992) Children's rights and children's lives. In P. Alston, S. Parker and J. Seymour (Eds), *Children, Rights and the Law*. Oxford: Oxford University Press.

OECD (2004) *Curricula and Pedagogies in Early Childhood Education and Care*. Paris: OECD Publications [online]. Available: http://www.oecd.org/education/school/31672150.pdf [accessed 16.3.17].

OECD (2006) *Starting Strong II: Early Childhood Education and Care*. Paris: OECD Publications [online]. Available: http://www.oecd.org/edu/school/startingstrongiiearlychildhoodeducationandcare.htm [accessed 16.3.17].

OECD (2012) *Starting Strong III – A Quality Toolbox for Early Childhood Education and Care*. OECD Publications [online]. Available: http://www.oecd.org/edu/school/startingstrongiiiaqualitytoolboxforearlychildhoodeducationandcare.htm [accessed 19.9.17].

OECD (2016) *Education at a Glance 2016*. Paris: OECD Publications [online.] Available: http://www.oecd.org/edu/education-at-a-glance-19991487.htm [accessed 16.3.17].

Oerter, R. (1993) *The Psychology of Play: An Activity Oriented Approach*. Munich: Quintessenz.

Ofcom (2015) *Children and Parents: Media Use and Attitudes Report*. London: Ofcom [online]. Available: http://stakeholders.ofcom.org.uk/market-data-research/other/research-publications/childrens/children-parents-nov-15/ [accessed 20.5.16].

Ofsted (1993) *First Class: The Standards and Quality of Education in Reception Classes*. London: HMSO.

Ofsted (2005) *Firm Foundations*. London: DfE [online]. Available: www.ofsted.gov.uk [accessed 13.3.17].

Ofsted (2012) *Evaluation Schedule for Inspections of Registered Early Years Provision*. Manchester: Ofsted.

Ofsted (2013) *Getting It Right First Time: Achieving and Maintaining High-Quality Early Years Provision*. London: DfE.

Ofsted (2015a) *Early Years Inspection Handbook*. London: DfE [online]. Available: http://www.foundationyears.org.uk/files/2015/06/Early_years_inspection_handbook_from_Sept_2015.pdf [accessed 16.3.17].

Ofsted (2015b) *School Inspection Handbook*. London: DfE [online]. Available: https://www.gov.uk/government/publications/school-inspection-handbook-from-september-2015 [accessed 13.3.17].

Ofsted (2015c) *The Common Inspection Framework: Education, Skills and Early Years* [online]. Available: https://www.gov.uk/government/uploads/system/uploads/attachment_data/file/461767/The_common_inspection_framework_education_skills_and_early_years.pdf [accessed 13.3.17].

Ofsted (2015d) *Early Help: Whose Responsibility?* Ofsted [online]. Available: www.gov.uk/government/organisations/ofsted [accessed 6.7.16].

Ofsted/Children's Services and Skills (2012) *No Place for Bullying*. London: Ofsted.

Olsson, L.M. (2009) *Movement and Experimentation in Young Children's Learning: Deleuze and Guattari in Early Childhood Education*. London: Routledge.

Ord, K., Smorti, S., Carroll-Lind, J., Robinson, L., Armstrong-Read, A., Brown-Cooper, P., Meredith, E., Rickard, D. and Jalal, J. (2013) *Developing Pedagogical Leadership in Early Childhood Education*. Wellington, New Zealand: New Zealand Childcare Association.

Orr, D.W. (2009) *Down to the Wire: Confronting Climate Change*. New York: Oxford University Press.

Osborn, A., Butler, N.R. and Morris, A.C. (1984) *The Social Life of Britain's Five-year-olds*. London: Routledge and Kegan Paul.

Osgood, J. (2015) Reimagining gender and play. In J. Moyles (Ed.), *The Excellence of Play* (pp. 49–60). Maidenhead: Open University Press.

Osgood, J. and Scarlet, R.R. (2016) Putting post-humanist theory to work to reimagine gender in early childhood: when theory becomes method becomes art. *Global Studies of Childhood*, 5(3): 346–60.

Osgood, J., Scarlet, R.R., de Clisson, J., Longstocking, A. and O'Mhaille, G. (2016) Re-imagining anti-bias education as worldly-entanglement. In Scarlet, R.R. (Ed.), *The Anti-bias Approach in Early Childhood* (pp. 183–202). Sydney: Multiverse.

Osgood, J., Albon, D., Allen, K. and Hollingworth, S. (2013) *Engaging 'hard to reach' Parents in Early Years Music-Making*. London: National Foundation for Youth Music.

Oswald, M. (2010) *Teacher Learning During the Implementation of the Index for Inclusion in a Primary School*. Thesis presented for the degree of Doctor in Philosophy (Educational Support), Stellenbosch University. Unpublished.

Oswell, D. (2013) *The Agency of Children: From Family to Global Human Rights*. Cambridge University Press.

Owusu-Bempah, K. (2007) *Children and Separation: Social-Genealogical Connectedness Perspective*. London: Routledge.

Pacini-Ketchabaw, V. (Ed.) (2010) *Flows, Rhythms & Intensities of Early Childhood Curriculum*. New York: Peter Lang.

Page, J. (2016) The legacy of John Bowlby's Attachment Theory. In T. David, K. Goouch and S. Powell (Eds), *The Routledge International Handbook of Philosophies and Theories of Early Childhood Education and Care* (pp. 80–90). London: Routledge.

Paget, A. and Cadywould, C. (2015) *Life to the Full: Care and Support in the UK for Disabled Children and Children with Life-Limiting and Life-Threatening Conditions*. London: Demos/True Colours Trust.

Palmer, S. (2006) *Toxic Childhood*. London: Orion Press.

Palmer, S. (2016) Why the iPad is a far bigger threat to our children than anyone realizes. *The Daily Mail*, 27 January 2016.

Palmieri, M. (2012) *Della Vita Civile*. Charleston, SC: Nabu Press.

Palmieri, M. (1825 [1429]) *Della Vita Civile* [civil life], Vol. 160.

Panksepp, J. (2003) At the interface of the affective, behavioural and cognitive neurosciences: decoding the emotional feelings of the brain. *Brain and Cognition*, 52: 1–14.

Papatheodorou, T. and Moyles, J. (2009) *Learning Together in the Early Years: Exploring Relational Pedagogy*. London: Routledge.

Parliament, House of Commons Health Committee (2015) *Childhood Obesity: Brave and Bold Action. First Report of Session 2015–16* (HC 465). London: The Stationery Office.

Parton, N. (1985) *The Politics of Child Abuse*. Basingstoke: Macmillan.

Pascal, C. and Bertram, A. (1995) *Evaluating and Developing Quality in Early Childhood Settings: A Professional Development Programme*. Worcester: Amber Publishing Co. Ltd.

Pascal, C. and Bertram, A. (1997) A conceptual framework for evaluating effectiveness in early childhood settings. In M.K. Lohmander (Ed.), *Researching Early Childhood, Vol. 3, Settings in Interaction* (pp. 125–50). Gothenburg: Göteborg University, Early Childhood Research and Development Centre.

Pascal, C., Bertram, A., Ramsden, F. and Saunders, M. (2001) *Effective Early Learning Programme (EEL)* (Third Edition). University College Worcester: Centre for Research in Early Childhood Education.

Pearson, B.Z., Fernandez, S. and Oller, D.K. (1993) Lexical development in bilingual infants and toddlers: comparison to monolingual norms. *Language Learning*, 43: 93–120.

Pearson, E. and Degotari, S. (2009) Education for sustainable development in early childhood education: a global solution to local concerns. *International Journal of Early Childhood*, 41(2): 97–111.

Pellegrini, A.D. (1991) *Applied Child Study: A Developmental Approach*. NJ: Erlbaum Assciates.

Pellegrini, A.D. and Bohn-Gettler, C.M. (2013) The benefits of recess in primary school. *Scholarpedia*, 8: 30448.

Penn, H. (2011) Travelling policies and global buzzwords: how international non-governmental organizations and charities spread the word about early childhood in the global South. *Childhood*, 18(1): 94–113.

Penn, H. (2012) The rhetoric and realities of early childhood programmes promoted by the World Bank in Mali. In R. Ames and A. Twum Danso Imoh (Eds), *Childhoods at the Intersection of the Local and the Global* (pp. 75–93). Basingstoke: Palgrave Macmillan.

Peppler, K., Halverson, E. and Kafai, Y. (Eds) (2006) *Makeology: Makerspaces as Learning Environments* (Volume 1 and 2). New York, NY: Routledge.

Percy-Smith, B. (2002) Contested worlds: constraints and opportunities growing up in inner and outer city environments of an English Midlands town. In L. Chawla (Ed.), *Growing Up in an Urbanizing World* (pp. 57–80). London: Earthscan.

Percy-Smith, B. and Thomas, N. (eds) (2010) *A Handbook of Children and Young People's Participation: Perspectives from Theory and Practice*. Abingdon: Routledge.

Perner, J. (1991) *Understanding the Representational Mind*. Cambridge, MA: MIT Press.

Peterson, C. and Siegal, M. (1995) Deafness, conversation, and theory of mind. *Journal of Child Psychology and Psychiatry*, 36: 459–74.

Phillips, D. and Ochs, K. (Eds) (2004) *Educational Policy Borrowing: Historical Perspectives*. Oxford: Symposium Books.

Piaget, J. (1951) *Play, Dreams and Imitation in Childhood*. London: Routledge and Kegan Paul.

Piaget, J. (1952) *The Origins of Intelligence in Children*. New York: Norton.

Pinker, S. (1984) *Language Learnability and Language Development*. Cambridge, MA: Harvard University Press.

Plate, E. (2012) *Staff Support for Inclusion: An International Study*. Unpublished thesis: Canterbury Christ Church University.

Plato (2007) *The Republic*. London: Penguin Classics.

Platt, D. and Turney, D. (2014) Making threshold decisions in child protection: a conceptual analysis, *British Journal of Social Work*, 44: 1454–71.

Plowman, L., Stephen, C. and McPake, J. (2010) *Growing Up With Technology: Young Children Learning in a Digital World*. London: Routledge.

Postman, N. (1985) The disappearance of childhood. *Childhood Education*, 61(4): 286–93.

Pound, L. (2011) *Influencing Early Childhood Education: Key Figures, Philosophies and Ideas*. Maidenhead: Open University Press.

Pramling, I., Sheridan, S. and Williams, P. (2004) Key issues in curriculum development for young children. In OECD, *Starting Strong Curricula and Pedagogies in Early Childhood Education and Care: Five Curriculum Outlines*. Paris: OECD.

Prendiville, E. and Howard, J. (2014) *Play Therapy Today: Contemporary Practice with Individuals, Groups and Carers*. London: Routledge.

Prendiville, S. (2008) *Bringing the Beach Indoors: A Study Investigating Sand and Water Play Opportunities in Infant Classrooms in the Republic of Ireland*. Unpublished Masters thesis: University of Limerick.

Prensky, M. (2001) Digital natives, digital immigrants. *On the Horizon*, 9(5): 1–6.

Pritchard, C. and Williams, R. (2010) Comparing possible 'child-abuse-related-deaths' in England and Wales with the major developed countries 1974–2006: signs of progress? *British Journal of Social Work*, 40: 1700–18.

Project Zero and Reggio Children (2001) *Making Learning Visible: Children as Individual and Group Learners*. Reggio Emilia: Reggio Children.

Prout, A. (2005) *The Future of Childhood*. London: Routledge Falmer.

Prout, A. and James, A. (1990) A new paradigm for the sociology of childhood? Provenance, promise and problems. In A. James and A. Prout (Eds), *Constructing and Reconstructing Childhood: Contemporary Issues in the Sociological Study of Childhood*. London: Falmer Press.

Public Health England (PHE) (2014a) *From Evidence into Action: Opportunities to Protect and Improve the Nation's Health*. London: Public Health England.

Public Health England (PHE) (2014b) *Reducing Unintentional Injuries in and around the Home among Children Under Five Years*. London: Public Health England.

Purdy, L. (1992) *In Their Best Interest? The Case Against Equal Rights for Children*. Ithaca, NY: Cornell.

Qvortrup, J. (2005) Varieties of childhood. In J. Qvortrup (Ed.), *Studies in Modern Childhood: Society, Agency, Culture*. Basingstoke: Palgrave Macmillan.

Qvortrup, J., Bardy, M., Sgritta, G. and Wintersberger, H. (Eds) (1994) *Childhood Matters: Social Theory, Practice and Politics*. Aldershot: Avebury.

Radford, L., Corral, S., Bassett, C., Howat, N. and Collishaw, S. (2011) *Child Abuse and Neglect in the UK Today*. London: NSPCC.

Rai, R. and Pannar, K. (2010) *Introduction to Culture Studies*. Mumbai: Himalaya Publishing House.

Ramani, G.B. (2005) *Co-operative Play and Problem Solving in Pre-school Children*. Doctoral thesis. Unpublished: University of Pittsburgh.

Razavi, S. (2011) Rethinking care in a development context. *Development and Change*, 42(4): 873–904.

Reason, P. and Bradbury, H. (2006) *Handbook of Action Research*. London: Sage.

Reddy, V. (2010) *How Infants Know Minds*. London: Harvard University Press.

Reder, P. and Duncan, S. (2004) Making the most of the Victoria Climbiè Report. *Child Abuse Review* ,13: 95–114.

Rideout, V. (2014) *Learning at Home: Families' Educational Media Use in America*. The Joan Ganz Cooney Center.

Riesman, P. (1992) *First Find Your Child a Good Mother: The Construction of Self in Two African Communities*. NJ: Rutgers University Press.

Ritchie, J. (2013) Sustainability and relationality with early childhood care and education settings in Aotearoa. *New Zealand International Journal of Early Childhood*, 45: 307–26.

Ritzer, G. (2008) *Sociological Theory* (Seventh Edition). Columbus, OH: McGraw-Hill Higher Education.

Roberts-Holmes, G. (2009) Inclusive policy and practice. In T. Maynard and N. Thomas (Ed.), *An Introduction to Early Childhood Studies* (Second Edition) (pp. 190–201). London: Sage.

Roberts, H. (2008) Listening to children: and hearing them. In P. Christensen and A. James (Eds), *Research with Children: Perspectives and Practices* (Second Edition) (pp. 260–75). London: Routledge Falmer.

Robertson, L.H. and Drury, R. (2014) Silencing bilingualism: a day in a life of a bilingual practitioner. *International Journal of Bilingual Education and Bilingualism*, 17(5): 610–23.

Robinson, K.H. (2013) *Innocence, Knowledge and the Construction of Childhood: The Contradictory Nature of Sexuality and Censorship in Children's Contemporary Lives*. London: Routledge.

Robinson, K.H. and Jones-Diaz, C. (2016) *Diversity and Difference in Early Childhood: Issues for Theory and Practice* (Second Edition). Maidenhead: Open University Press.

Robinson, S., Yardy, K. and Carter, V. (2012) The development of obesity in infancy and childhood. *Journal of Child Health Care*, 339–84.

Robinson, V. (2016) Explore the wonderful world of Disney in this crazy new VR app. *TechInsider*, 16 May 2016 [online]. Available: http://www.techinsider.io/disney-movies-vr-launches-on-steam-2016-5 [accessed 20.5.16].

Robinson, V., Hohepa, M. and Lloyd, C. (2009) *School Leadership and Student Outcomes: Identifying What Works and Why*. Best Evidence Synthesis International (BES), Wellington, New Zealand: Ministry of Education.

Robson, S. (2006) *Developing Thinking and Understanding in Young Children*. Oxford: Routledge.

Rogoff, B. (1989) The joint socialization of development by young children and adults. Reprinted in P. Light, S. Sheldon and M. Woodhead (1991) *Learning to Think. Child Development in Social Context 2*. London: Routledge.

Rogoff, B. (1990) *Apprenticeship in Thinking: Cognitive Development in a Social Context*. Oxford. Oxford: University Press.

Rogoff, B. (2003) *The Cultural Nature of Human Development*. Oxford: Oxford University Press.

Rogoff, B., Chavajay, P. and Matusov, E. (1993) Questioning assumptions about culture and individuals. Commentary of Michael Tomasello, Ann Cale Kruger and Hilary Horn Ratner. *Behavioural and Brain Sciences*, 16: 533–4.

Roopnarine, J., Patte, M., Johnson, J. and Kuschner, D. (2014) *International Perspectives on Play*. London: McGraw Hill.

Rose, L. (1991) *The Erosion of Childhood: Childhood in Britain 1860–1918*. London: Routledge.

Rousseau, J.J. (1964[1762]) *Jean Jacques Rousseau: Emile: His Educational Theories Selected from Emile, Julie and Other Writings*. New York: Barron's Educational Series.

Royal College of Paediatrics and Child Health (RCPCH) (2015) *Tackling England's Childhood Obesity Crisis*. London: Royal College Paediatrics and Child Health.

Rubin, K.H., Fein, G.G. and Vandenberg, B. (1983) Play. In P.H. Mussen and E.M. Hetherington (Eds), *Handbook of Child Psychology*, 4. Basel: S. Karger.

Rueda, M.R., Rothbart, M.K., McCandliss, B.D., Saccomanno, L. and Posner, M.I. (2005) Training, maturation, and genetic influences on the development of executive attention. *Proceedings of the National Academy of Sciences*, 102: 14931–6.

Ruffman, T., Slade, L. and Crow, E. (2002) The relation between children's and mothers' mental state language and theory-of-mind understanding. *Child Development*, 73: 734–51.

Rutter, J. (2016) *2016 Childcare Survey*. London: Family and Childcare Trust.

Rutter, J. and Evans, J. (2011) *Informal Childcare: Choice or Chance*. London: Daycare Trust.

Said, E. (1978) *Orientalism*. London: Routledge.

Samman, E., Presler-Marshall, E., Jones, N. with Bhatkal, T. Melamed, C. Stavropoulou M. and Wallace J. (2016) *Women's Work: Mothers, Children and the Global Childcare Crisis*. London: ODI [online]. Available: https://www.odi.org/global-childcare-crisis [accessed 16.3.17].

Sammons, P., Sylva, K., Melhuish, E., Siraj-Blatchford, I., Taggart, B. and Barreau, S. (2015) *Effective Pre-school and Primary Education 3–11 Project (EPPE 3–11): Influences on Children's Attainment and Progress in Key Stage 2: Social/Behavioural Outcomes in Year 5. Full Report.* London: Institute of Education, University of London.

Sammons, P., Sylva, K., Hall, J., Siraj, I., Melhuish, E., Taggart, B. and Mathers, S. (2017) *Establishing the Effects of Quality in Early Childhood: Comparing Evidence from England – Occasional Paper. Early Education* [online]. https://www.early-education.org.uk/establishing-effects-quality-early-childhood-comparing-evidence-england-occasional-paper-march-2017 (accessed 0.03.17).

Saracho, O. (1991) Educational play in early childhood. *Early Child Development and Care,* 66: 45–64.

Saracho, O. and Spodek, B. (1998) *Multiple Perspectives on Play in Early Childhood.* New York: New York Press.

Savage, M. (2012) *Home Literacy and Agency: An Ethnographic Approach to Studying the Home Literacy Practices of Six Multiliterate Children in Qatar.* Unpublished EdD Thesis: University of Sheffield.

Save the Children (2006) *Righting the Wrongs: The Reality of Children's Rights in Wales.* Cardiff: Save the Children.

Save the Children (2012) *Child Poverty in 2012: It Shouldn't Happen Here.* London: Save the Children.

Sawyer, R. (2003) Emergence in creativity and development. In R. Sawyer, V. John-Steiner, S. Moran and D. Feldman (Eds), *Creativity and Development.* Oxford: Oxford University Press.

Schieffelin, B. (1994) Language acquisition and socialization: three developmental stories and their implications. In B. Blount (Ed.), *Language, Culture, and Society.* Illinois: Waveland Press Inc.

Scholl, B. and Leslie, A. (1999) Modularity, development and theory of mind, *Mind and Language,* 14: 131–53.

Schraad-Tischer, M. (2011) *Social Justice in the OECD: How Do the Member States Compare.* Berlin: Bertelsmann Stiftung.

Schraad-Tischer, M. (2015) *Social Justice in the EU – Index Report 2015.* Berlin: Bertelsmann Stiftung.

Schweinhart, L.J. and Weikart, D.P. (1997) The High/Scope preschool curriculum comparison study through age 2–3. *Early Childhood Research Quarterly,* 12: 117–43.

Schweinhart, L.J., Barnes, H.V. and Weikart, D.P. (1993) *Significant Benefits: The High/Scope Perry Preschool Study through Age 27.* (Monographs of the High/Scope Educational Research Foundation, 10). Ypsilanti, MI: High/Scope Press.

Schweinhart, L.J., Montie, J., Xiang, Z., Barnett, W., Belfield, C. and Nores, M. (2005) *Lifetime Effects: The High/Scope Perry Preschool Study through Age 40.* Ypsilanti, MI: High/Scope Press.

Scientific Advisory Committee on Nutrition (SACN) (2011) *The Influence of Maternal, Fetal and Child Nutrition on the Development of Chronic Disease in Later Life.* London: SACN.

Scoones, I. (2007) Sustainability. *Development in Practice,* 17(4–5): 589–96.

Scourfield, J., Gilliat-Ray, S., Khan, A. and Otri, S. (2013) *Muslim Childhood: Religious Nurture in a European Context.* Oxford: Oxford University Press.

Scriven, A. (2010) *Promoting Health: A Practical Guide.* London: Bailliere Tindall.

Scrivens, C. (2002) Constructions of leadership: does gender make a difference? Perspectives from an English-speaking country. In V. Nivala and E. Hujala (Eds), *Leadership in Early Childhood Education: Cross-cultural Perspectives.* Oulu: Oulu University Press.

Searle, G.R. (1976) *Eugenics and Politics in Britain, 1900–1914 (Vol. 3)*. London: Springer.

Sebba, J., Berridge, D., Luke N., Fletcher, J., Bell, K., Strand, S., Thomas, S., Sinclair, I. and O'Higgins, A. (2015) *The Educational Progress of Looked After Children in England: Linking Care and Educational Data*. Research Centre University of Bristol [online]. Available: http://reescentre.education.ox.ac.uk/research/educational-progress-of-looked-after-children/ [accessed 06.07.16].

Seligman, M.E.P. (2011) *Flourish: A Visionary New Understanding of Happiness and Well-being*. London: Nicholas Brealey Publishing.

Selwyn, J., Harris, P., Quinton, D., Nawaz, S., Wijedasa, D. and Wood, M. (2010) *Pathways to Permanence for Black, Asian and Mixed Ethnicity Children*. London: BAAF.

Selwyn, J., Quinton, D., Sturgess, W. and Baxter, C. (2006) *Costs and Outcomes of Non-infant Adoptions*. London: British Association for Adoption and Fostering.

Serpell, R. and Adamson-Holley, D. (2015) African socialization values and nonformal educational practices: child development, parental beliefs, and educational innovation in rural Zambia. In T. Abebe and J. Waters (Eds), *Labouring and Learning. Geographies of Children and Young People*, 10: 978–98.

Seung Lam, M. and Pollard, A. (2006) A conceptual framework for understanding children as agents in the transition from home to kindergarten, *Early Years*, 26(2): 123–41.

Shakeshaft, C. (1989) *Women in Educational Administration*. Beverley Hills, CA: Sage.

Sharp, C., Lord, P., Handscomb, G., Macleod, S., Southcott, C., George, N. and Jeffes, J. (2012) *Highly Effective Leadership in Children's Centres*. Nottingham: National College for School Leadership.

Sheriden, M. with Howard, J. and Alderson, D. (2017) *Play in Early Childhood from Birth to Six Years* (Third Edition). London: Routledge.

Shonkoff, J.P. and Phillips, D.A. (Eds) (2000) *From Neurons to Neighborhoods: The Science of Early Childhood Development*. Washington, DC: National Academy Press.

Shore, A. (2011) *The Science of the Art of Psychotherapy*. New York: Norton.

Shore, A. (2016) *Affect Regulation and the Origin of the Self*. NY: Routledge.

Siegel, D. (1999) *The Developing Mind*. New York: Guilford Press.

Siegler, R.S. (2000) The rebirth of children's learning. *Child Development*, 71: 26–35.

Siencyn, S.W. and Thomas, S. (2007) Wales. In M.M. Clark and T. Waller (Eds), *Early Childhood Education and Care: Policy and Practice* (pp. 135–66). London: Sage.

Sigelman, C.K. and Rider, E.A. (2008) *Life-span Human Development*. London: Thomson. Wadsworth.

Simon, A., Owen, C. and Hollingworth, K. (2015) *Provision and Use of Preschool Childcare in Britain*. London: UCL Institute of Education.

Simons, D. J. (2010) The Monkey Business Illusion. YouTube [online]. Available: https://www.youtube.com/watch?v=IGQmdoK_ZfY [accessed 13.3.17].

Sinclair, I. (2005) *Fostering Now: Messages from Research*. London: Jessica Kingsley.

Siraj-Blatchford, I. (2008) Understanding the relationship between curriculum, pedagogy and progression in learning in early childhood in Hong Kong. *Journal of Early Childhood Education*, 7(2): 6–13.

Siraj-Blatchford, I. (2009) Conceptualising progression in the pedagogy of play and sustained shared thinking in early childhood education: a Vygotskian perspective. *Educational and Child Psychology*, 26(2): 77–89.

Siraj-Blatchford, I. and Manni, L. (2008a) *Effective Leadership in the Early Years Sector*. London: Institute of Education, University of London.

Siraj-Blatchford, I. and Manni, L. (2008b) 'Would you like to tidy up now?' An analysis of adult questioning in the English Foundation Stage. *Early Years*, 28(1): 5–22.

Siraj-Blatchford, I. and Sum, C. (2013) *Understanding and Advancing System Leadership in the Early Years*. Nottingham: National College for Teaching Leadership.

Siraj-Blatchford, I. and Sylva, K. (2004) Researching pedagogy in English pre-schools. *British Educational Research Journal*, 30(5): 713–30.

Siraj-Blatchford, I., Sylva, K., Muttock, S., Gilden, R. and Bell, D. (2002) *Researching Effective Pedagogy in the Early Years, DfES Research Report 356*. London: DfES.

Siraj-Blatchford, I., Sylva, K., Taggart, B., Sammons, P. and Melhuish, E. (2003) *Technical Paper 10: Case Studies of Practice in the Foundation Stage*. London: Institute of Education.

Siraj-Blatchford, J., Smith, K. and Pramling Samuelsson, I. (2010) *Education for Sustainable Development in the Early Years*. OMEP [online]. Available: http://www.worldomep.org/wp-content/uploads/2013/12/combined_ESD_book.pdf [accessed 6.6.16].

Siviy, S.M. (1998) Neurobiological substrates of play behaviour in the structure and function of mammalian playfulness. In M. Berkoff and J.A. Byers (Eds), *Animal Play: Evolutionary, Ecological and Comparative Perspectives*. Cambridge: Cambridge University Press.

Skelton, C. and Francis, B. (2012) The 'Renaissance Child': high achievement and gender in late modernity. *International Journal of Inclusive Education*, 16(4): 441–59.

Skinner, B.F. (1957) *Verbal Behavior*. New York: Appleton-Century-Croft.

Smart, C., Neale, B. and Wade, A. (2001) *The Changing Experience of Childhood: Families and Divorce*. Cambridge: Polity.

Smilansky, S. (1968) *The Effects of Sociodramatic Play on Disadvantaged Pre-school Children*. New York: Wiley.

Smith, B.J., Tang, C.T. and Nutbeam, D. (2006) WHO Health Promotion Glossary: new terms. *Health Promotion International*, 21(4): 340–5.

Smith, J. (2016) *The Jimmy Savile Investigation Report*. BBC [online]. Available: http://downloads.bbci.co.uk/bbctrust/assets/files/pdf/our_work/dame_janet_smith_review/savile/jimmy_savile_investigation.pdf [Last accessed 13.03.17].

Smith, P.K. and Vollstedt, R. (1985) On defining play: an empirical study of the relationship between play and various play criteria. *Child Development*, 56: 1042–50.

Smuts, A. and Smuts, R. (2006) *Science in the Service of Children, 1893–1935*. New York: Yale University Press.

Snow, C.E. (1977) Mothers' speech research: from input to interaction. In C.E. Snow and C.A. Ferguson (Eds), *Talking to Children: Language Input and Acquisition*. Cambridge: Cambridge University Press.

Sokolov, J. and Snow, C. (1994) The changing role of negative evidence in theories of language development. In C. Gallaway and B.J. Richards (Eds), *Input and Interaction in Language Acquisition*. Cambridge: Cambridge University Press.

Soni, A. (2012) Promoting emotional well-being or mental health in England. In T. Papatheodorou (Ed.), *Debates on Early Childhood Policies and Practices* (pp. 172–82). London: Routledge.

Speier, M. (1976) The adult ideological viewpoint in studies of childhood. In A. Skolnick (Ed.), *Rethinking Childhood: Perspectives on Development and Society*. Boston, MA: Little Brown.

Speller, V., Parish, R., Davison, H. and Zilnyk, A. (2012) *The CompHP Professional Standards for Health Promotion Handbook*. Paris: International Union for Health Promotion and Education.

Spivak, G.C. (1988) *In Other Worlds: Essays on Cultural Politics*. New York: Methuen.

Springhall, S. (1999) *Youth, Popular Culture and Moral Panics: Penny Gaffs to Gangsta-Rap, 1830–1996*. New York: St. Martin's.

Stables, A. (2013) The unsustainability imperative? Problems with 'sustainability' and 'sustainable development' as regulative ideals. *Environmental Education Research*, 19(2): 177–86.

Stacey, C. (2011) Psychoneuroimmunology and wellbeing. In A. Knight and A. McNaught (Eds), *Understanding Wellbeing: An Introduction for Students and Practitioners of Health and Social Care* (pp. 67–77). Banbury: Lantern.

Stafford, A., Parton, N., Vincent, S. and Smith, C. (2012) *Child Protection Systems in the United Kingdom: A Comparative Analysis*. London: Jessica Kingsley.

Stalford, H., Thomas, N. and Drywood, E. (2011) Editorial: the European Union and children's rights. *International Journal of Children's Rights*, 19(3): 375–79.

Stanley, N., Miller, P., Richardson Foster, H. and Thomson, G. (2011) A stop–start response: social services' interventions with children and families notified following domestic violence incidents. *British Journal of Social Work*, 41(2): 296–313.

Steedman, C. (1995) *Strange Dislocations: Childhood and the Idea of Human Interiority, 1780–1930*. New York: Harvard University Press.

Steiner-Khamsi, G. (Ed.) (2004) *The Global Politics of Educational Borrowing and Lending*. New York: Teachers College Press.

Steiner-Khamsi, G. and Silova, I. (2008) *How NGOs React: Globalization and Educational Reform in the Caucasus, Central Asia and Mongolia*. Bloomfields USA: Kumarian Press.

Steiner, R. (1919) *An Introduction to Waldorf Education*. GA 24. Anthroposophic Press [online]. Available: http://wn.rsarchive.org/Education/IntWal_index.html [accessed 15.4.16].

Sterling, S. (2001) *Sustainable Education: Revisioning Learning and Change*. Schumacher Briefings 6. Totnes: Green Books Ltd.

Stern, D.N. (1985) *The Interpersonal World of the Infant*. New York: Basic Books.

Stevens, J. (2013) Observing, assessing and planning for how young children are learning. In H. Moylett (Ed.), *Characteristics of Effective Early Learning: Helping Young Children Become Learners for Life*. Maidenhead: Open University Press.

Stewart, J. and Bushell, F. (2011) Built environment and wellbeing. In A. Knight and A. McNaught (Eds), *Understanding Wellbeing: An Introduction for Students and Practitioners of Health and Social Care* (pp. 201–13). Banbury: Lantern.

Stewart, J., Bushell, F. and Habgood, V. (2003) *Environmental Health as Public Health*. London: Chadwick House.

Sturrock, G. (2003) Towards a psycholudic definition of playwork. In F. Brown (Ed.), *Playwork: Theory and Practice*. Buckingham: Open University Press.

Sulzby, E. (1989) Assessment of writing and of children's language while writing. In L. Morrow and J. Smith (Eds), *The Role of Assessment and Measurement in Early Literacy Instruction*. Englewood Cliffs, NJ: Prentice-Hall.

Sulzby, E. and Teale, W. (1991) Emergent literacy. In R. Barr, M. Kamil, P. Mosenthal and P.D. Pearson (Eds), *Handbook of Reading Research* (Vol. 2). New York: Longman.

Sutherland, I. (1987) History and background. In I. Sutherland (Ed.), *Health Education: Perspectives and Choices*. Chicago: NEC Publications.

Sutton-Smith, B. (1979) *Play and Learning*. New York: Gardnet Press.

Sutton-Smith, B. (1997) *The Ambiguity of Play*. Cambridge, MA: Harvard University Press.

Sutton-Smith, B. and Kelly-Byrne, D. (1984) The idealisation of play. In P.K. Smith (Ed.), *Play in Animals and Humans*. Oxford: Basil Blackwell.

Swick, K.J. and Williams, R. (2006) An analysis of Bronfenbrenner's Bio-Ecological perspective for early childhood educators: implications for working with families experiencing stress. *Early Childhood Education Journal*, 33(5): 305–27.

Sylva, K. (Ed.) (2010) *Early Childhood Matters: Evidence from the Effective Pre-school and Primary Education Project (EPPE)*. London: Routledge.

Sylva, K., Melhuish, E., Sammons, P., Siraj-Blatchford, I. and Taggart, B. (2004) *The Effective Provision of Pre-school Education Project: Final Report*. London: DfES/IoE, University of London.

Sylva, K., Bruner, J.S. and Genova, P. (1976) The role of play in the problem solving of young children 3–5 years old. In J.S. Bruner, A. Jolly and K. Sylva (Eds), *Play: Its Role in Development and Evolution*. Penguin: New York.

Sylva, K., Melhuish, E., Sammons, P., Siraj-Blatchford, I. and Taggart, B. (2008) *Effective Pre-School and Primary Education 3–11 Project (EPPE 3–11) Report from the Primary Phase: Pre-school, School and Family Influence on Children's Development during Key Stage 2 (Age 7–11)*. DCSF Research Report 061.

Sylva, K., Siraj-Blatchford, I., and Taggart, B. (2010) *ECERS-E: The Early Childhood Environment Rating Scale Curricular Extension to ECERS-R*. Stoke on Trent: Trentham Books.

Sylva, K., Gott, J., Eisenstadt, N., Smith, T., Hall, J., Evangelou, M., Smith, G. and Sammons, P. (2015) *Organisation, Services and Reach of Children's Centres. Evaluation of Children's Centres in England. (ECCE Strand 3)*. London: Department for Education.

Takhvar, M. (1988) Play and theories of play: a review of the literature. *Early Child Development and Care*, 39: 221–44.

Talan, T., Bloom, P. J. and Kelton, R. (2014) Building the leadership capacity of early childhood directors: an evaluation of a leadership development model. *Early Childhood Research and Practice*, 16(1&2).

Tan, C.Y. and Dimmock, C. (2014) How a 'top-performing' Asian school system formulates and implements policy: the case of Singapore. *Educational Management Administration and Leadership*, 42(5): 743–63.

Tassoni, P. (2013) Learning and development: two year olds: settling in. *Nursery World*, 11 January.

Taylor, A. (2013) *Reconfiguring the Natures of Childhood*. London: Routledge.

Taylor, P.H., Exon, G. and Holley, B. (1972) *A Study of Nursery Education*. London: Schools Council/ Methuen.

Teale, W. and Sulzby, E. (Eds) (1986) *Emergent Literacy: Writing and Reading*. Norwood, NJ: Ablex.

Tech City with NESTA (2016) *Tech Nation 2016: Tranforming UK Industries* [online]. Available: http://www.techcityuk.com/wp-content/uploads/2016/02/Tech-Nation-2016_FINAL-ONLINE-1.pdf [accessed 20.5.16].

TED (2006) *Do Schools Kill Creativity?* [online]. Available: http://www.ted.com/talks/ken_robinson_says_schools_kill_creativity.html [accessed 13.3.17].

The Children's Society (2011) *How Happy are our Children?* London: The Children's Society.

Theakston, A., Lieven, E., Pine, J. and Rowland, C. (2001) The role of performance limitations in the acquisition of verb argument structure. *Journal of Child Language*, 28: 127–52.

The World Bank (2016) *Gross Enrolment Ratio, Pre-primary, Both Sexes (10%)* [online]. Available: http://data.worldbank.org/indicator/SE.PRE.ENRR/countries?display=graph [accessed 1.6.16].

Thomas, L., Howard, J. and Miles, G. (2006) The effectiveness of playful practice for learning in the early years. *The Psychology of Education Review*, 30(1): 52–8.

Thomas, M. (Ed.) (2010) *Deconstructing Digital Natives: Young People, Technology and the New Literacies*. New York: Routledge.

Thomas, N. (2000) *Children, Family and the State: Decision-making and Child Participation*. Basingstoke: Macmillan (paperback edition 2002, Bristol: Policy Press).

Thomas, N. (2007) 'Towards a theory of children's participation', *International Journal of Children's Rights* 15(2): 199–218.

Thomas, N. (2008) Consultation and advocacy. In B. Luckock and M. Lefevre (Eds), *Direct Work: Social Work with Children and Young People in Care*. London: British Association for Adoption and Fostering.

Thomas, N. (2011) *Children's Rights: Policy into Practice* (Centre for Children and Young People Background Briefing No.4). Lismore: Southern Cross University.

Thomson, P. (Ed.) (2008) *Doing Visual Research with Children and Young People*. London: Routledge.

Thorne, B. (1993) *Gender Play: Girls and Boys in School*. New Brunswick, NJ: Rutgers University Press.

Thornton, K., Wansborough, D., Clarkin-Phillips, Aitkin, H. and Tamati, A. (2009) *Conceptualising Leadership in Early Childhood Education in Aotearoa New Zealand*. Occasional Paper, No. 2, Wellington, New Zealand: New Zealand Teachers Council.

Tickell, C. (2011) *The Tickell Review of the Early Years Foundation Stage*. London: DfE.

Tilbury, D. (1994) The critical learning years for environmental education. In R. Wilson (Ed.), *Environmental Education at the Early Childhood Level* (pp. 11–3). Troy, OH: North American Association for Environmental Education.

Timimi, S. (2009) The commercialization of children's mental health in the era of globalization. *International Journal Of Mental Health*, 3: 5–27.

Tomasello, M. (1992) *First Verbs: A Case Study of Early Grammatical Development*. New York: Cambridge University Press.

Tomasello, M. (2000) Do young children have adult syntactic competence? *Cognition*, 74: 209–53.

Tomasello, M. (2003) *Constructing a Language: A Usage-based Theory of Language Acquisition*. Cambridge, MA: Harvard University Press.

Tomasello, M., Carpenter, M., Call, J., Behne, T. and Moll, H. (2005) Understanding and sharing intentions: the origins of cultural cognition. *Behavioral and Brain Sciences*, 28: 675–91.

Trevarthen, C. (2009) *Why Attachment Matters in Sharing Meaning*. Keynote address. SIRCC Seminar, 11 September, Glasgow Marriott Hotel.

Turkle, S. (2011) *Alone Together*. Cambridge, MA: MIT Press.

Twum-Danso, A. (2009) International children's rights. In H. Montgomery and M. Kellett (Eds), *Children and Young People's Worlds: Developing Frameworks for Integrated Practice*. The Open University and Policy Press.

Tyler, S. (2016) Theory of mind. In T. David, K. Goouch and S. Powell (Eds), *The Routledge International Handbook of Philosophies and Theories of Early Childhood Education and Care* (pp. 138–46). London: Routledge.

UNCRC (United Nations Convention on the Rights of the Child) (2006) *General Comment No.7, Implementing Child Rights in Early Childhood, CRC/C/GC/7*. [online]. Available: http://www2.ohchr.org/english/bodies/crc/docs/AdvanceVersions/GeneralComment7Rev1.pdf [accessed 19.06.16].

UNESCO (2000) *The Dakar Framework for Action. Education for All: Meeting our Collective Commitments*. Dakar: UNESCO.

UNESCO (2008) *Early Childhood and its Contribution to a Sustainable Society*. Paris: UNESCO.

UNESCO (2015) *Roadmap for Implementing the Global Action Programme on Education for Sustainable Development*. Paris: UNESCO.

UNICEF (2008) *The Child Care Transition. Innocenti Report Card 8*. Florence: The United Nations Children's Fund.

UNICEF (2011) *Social Protection for All – An Agenda for Pro-Child Growth and Child Rights*. London: UNICEF.

United Nations (UN) (1989) *Convention on the Rights of the Child*. London: UNICEF.

United Nations (UN) (2015) *Sustainable Development Goals*. London: United Nations.

Uprichard, E. (2008) Children as 'Being and Becomings': children, childhood and temporality. *Children and Society*, 22(4): 303–13.

Valkanova, Y. (2009) The passion for educating the "New Man": debates about preschooling in Soviet Russia, 1917–1925. *History of Education Quarterly* 49(2): 211–21.

Valkanova, Y. (2015) Constructions of nature and emerging ideas in children's education and care. In T. David, K. Goouch and S. Powell (Eds.) *The Routledge International Handbook of Philosophies and Theories of Early Childhood Education and Care*. London: Routledge.

Valkanova, Y. and Brehony, K. (2006) The gifts and 'contributions': Friedrich Froebel and Russian education (1850–1929). *History of Education* 35(2): 189–207.

Veresov, N. (2006) Leading activity in developmental psychology: concept and principle. *Journal of Russian and East European Psychology*, 44(5): 7–25.

Vertovec, S. (2012) 'Diversity' and the social imaginary. *European Journal of Sociology*, 53(3): 287–312.

Vincent, C. and Ball, S. (2007) Making up the middle-class child: families, activities and class dispositions. *Sociology*, 41(6): 1061–77.

Vygotsky, L. (1933) Play and its role in the mental development of the child, *Voprosy psikhologii*, 1966, No. 6, trans. Mulholland, C., Psychology and Marxism Internet Archive 2002 [online]. Available: www.marxists.org/archive/vygotsky/works/1933/play.htm [accessed 20.3.17].

Vygotsky, L. (1966) Play and its role in the mental development of the child. *Voprosy psikhologii*, 12: 62–76.

Vygotsky, L. (1978) *Mind in Society: The Development of Higher Mental Processes*. Cambridge, MA: Harvard University Press.

Vygotsky, L. (1986) *Thought and Language*. Cambridge, MA: MIT Press.

Vygotsky, L. (1994a) The problem of the cultural development of the child. In R. van der Veer and J. Valsiner (Eds), *The Vygotsky Reader* (pp. 57–72). Oxford: Blackwell.

Vygotsky, L. (1994b) The problem of the environment. In R. van der Veer and J. Valsiner (Eds), *The Vygotsky Reader* (pp. 338–50). Oxford: Blackwell.

Vygotsky, L. (1997[1926]) *The Problem of Cultural Age. The Collected Works of L.S. Vygotsky: Vol 4*. New York: Plenum.

Vygotsky, L. (1998) *Child Psychology. The Collected Works of L.S. Vygotsky: Vol. 5*. New York: Plenum.

Vygotsky, L. (2004) Imagination and creativity in childhood. *Journal of Russian and East European Psychology*, 42(1): 4–84.

Waksler, F. C. (1991) *Studying The Social Worlds of Children: Sociological Readings*. London: Routledge.

Walker, P. (2012) On public health and wellbeing. In P. Walker and M. John (Eds), *From Public Health to Wellbeing. The New Driver for Policy and Action* (pp. 1–20). Basingstoke: Palgrave.

Walsh, G., Sproule, L., McGuinesss, C. and Trew, K. (2011) Playful structure: a novel image of early years pedagogy for primary school classrooms. *Early Years*, 31(2): 107–19.

Wang, C.C.D.C. and Mallinckrodt, B.S. (2006) Differences between Taiwanese and US cultural beliefs about ideal adult attachment. *Journal of Counselling Psychology*, 53(2): 192–204.

Ward, H., Brown, R. and Westlake, D. (2012) *Safeguarding Babies and Very Young Children from Abuse and Neglect.* London and Philadelphia: Jessica Kingsley.

Warming, H. (2005) Participant observation: a way to learn about children's perspectives. In A. Clark, P. Moss and A.T. Kjørholt (Eds), *Beyond Listening: Children's Perspectives on Early Childhood Services* (pp. 51–70). Bristol: Policy Press.

Weare, K. (1992) The contribution of education to health promotion. In R. Bunton and G. Macdonald (Eds), *Health Promotion: Disciplines and Diversity* (pp. 66–85). London: Routledge.

Weare, K. (2007) Delivering health education: the contribution of social and emotional learning. *Health Education*, 107(2): 109–13.

Weikart, D. (2000) *Early Childhood Education: Needs and Opportunity.* Paris: UNESCO: International Institute for Educational Planning.

Weisberg, D., Zosh, J., Hirsh-Pasek, K. and Golinkoff, R. (2015) 'Talking it up': play language development and the role of adult support. *American Journal of Play*, 6(1): 39–54.

Wellman, H.M. (2002) Understanding the psychological world: developing a theory of mind. In U. Goswami (Ed.), *Handbook of Childhood Cognitive Development* (pp. 167–87). Oxford: Blackwell.

Wellman, H.M. and Gelman, S.A. (1998) Knowledge acquisition in foundational domains. In D. Kuhn and R.S. Siegler (Eds), *Cognition, Language, and Perceptual Development, Vol. 2.* In W. Damon (Gen. Ed.), *Handbook of Child Psychology.* New York: Wiley.

Wells, G. (1986) *The Meaning Makers: Children Learning Language and Using Language to Learn.* London: Hodder and Stoughton.

Wenger, E. (1998) *Communities of Practice.* Cambridge: Cambridge University Press.

Westcott, M. and Howard, J. (2007) Creating a playful environment; evaluating young children's perceptions of their daily classroom activities using the Activity Apperception Story Procedure. *Psychology of Education* Review, 31(1): 27–34.

Westerman, W. (2001) Youth and adulthood in children's and adults' perspectives. In J. Erricker, C., Ota, and C. Erricker (Eds.) *Spiritual Education, Cultural, Religious and Social Differences: New Perspectives for the 21st Century* (pp. 248–59). Brighton and Portland: Sussex Academic Press.

Westermann, G., Mareschal, D., Johnson, M.H., Sirois, S., Spratling, M.W. and Thomas, M.S.C. (2007) Neuroconstructivism. *Developmental Science*, 10(1): 75–83.

Whalley, M. (2000) *Involving Parents in Their Children's Learning.* London: Paul Chapman.

Whitebread, D. and Bingham, S. (2011) *School Readiness: A Critical Review of Perspectives and Evidence.* TACTYC Occasional Paper No. 2 [online]. Available: http://tactyc.org.uk/occasional-paper/occasional-paper2.pdf [accessed 20.3.17].

Whitebread, D. and Jameson, H. (2005) Play, storytelling and creative writing. In J. Moyles (Ed.), *The Excellence of Play.* Buckingham: Open University Press.

Whitebread, D. and O'Sullivan, L. (2012) Pre-school children's pretend play: supporting the development of metacognition, metacommunication and self regulation. *International Journal of Play*, 1: 197–213.

Whitebread, D., Basilio, M., Kuvalja, M. and Verma, M. (2012) *The Value of Children's Play. A report written for the Toy Industries of Europe.* Cambridge: University of Cambridge Publishing.

Whitehurst, G. and Lonigan, C. (1998) Child development and emergent literacy. *Child Development*, 69(3): 848–72.

Wilcox, A. (2006) *An Occupational Perspective of Health.* New Jersey: Slack.

Williams, T., Wetton, N. and Moon, A. (1989) *A Picture of Health. What Makes you Healthy and Keeps you Healthy?* London: HEA.

Wilson, J. (2000) Doing justice to inclusion. *European Journal of Special Needs Education*, 15(3): 297–304.

Wimmer, H. and Perner, J. (1983) Beliefs about beliefs: representations and constraining function of wrong beliefs in young children's understanding of deception. *Cognition*, 13: 103–28.

Winnicott, D.W. (1971) *Playing and Reality.* London: Routledge Classics.

Wohlwend, K. (2009) Early adopters: playing new literacies and pretending new technologies in print-centric classrooms. *Journal of Early Childhood Literacy*, 9: 117–40.

Wolfe, R.M. and Sharp, L.K. (2002) Anti-vaccinationists past and present. *BMJ*, 325(7361): 430–2.

Wood, D., Bruner, J.S. and Ross, G. (1976) The role of tutoring in problem-solving. *Journal of Child Psychology and Psychiatry*, 17: 89–100.

Woodhead, M. and Faulkner, D. (2008) Subjects, objects or participants? Dilemmas of psychological research with children. In P. Christensen and A. James (Eds), *Research with Children: Perspectives and Practices* (Second Edition) (pp. 10–39). London: Routledge Falmer.

Woodhead, M. and Streuli, N. (2013) Early education for all: is there a role for the private sector? In P.R. Britto, P. Engle and C. Super (Eds), *Handbook of Early Childhood Development Research and Its Impact on Global Policy.* Oxford: Oxford University Press.

Woodrow, C. and Busch, G. (2008) Repositioning early childhood leadership as action and activism. *European Early Childhood Research Journal*, 16(1): 83–93.

World Commission on Environment and Development (WCED) (1987) *Our Common Future.* Oxford: Oxford University Press.

World Health Organization (WHO) (1946) *Constitution of the World Health Organization.* Adopted by the International Health Conference, New York 19 June–22 July. Geneva: WHO.

World Health Organization (WHO) (1978) *Declaration of Alma-Ata. International Conference on Primary Health Care*, Alma-Ata, USSR 6–12 September. Geneva: WHO.

World Health Organization (WHO) (1986) *Ottawa Charter for Health Promotion.* Canadian Public Health Association, Ottawa. Geneva: WHO.

World Health Organization (WHO) (2009) *Global Plan of Action for Children's Health and the Environment 2010–2015.* Geneva: WHO.

Worsfold, V.L. (1974) A philosophical justification for children's rights. *Harvard Educational Review*, 44(1): 142–59.

Wyness, M. (2011) *Childhood and Society: An Introduction to the Sociology of Childhood* (Second Edition). Basingstoke: Palgrave Macmillan.

Zeitlin, F. (1995) *Playing the Other: Gender and Society in Classical Greek Literature.* NJ: Princeton.

Zener, R.S. (1999) Revisiting the process of normalization. *NAMTA Journal* 24(1): 87–105.

Zelazo, P.D., Carlson, S.M. and Kesek, A. (2008) The development of executive function in childhood. In C. Nelson and M. Luciana (Eds), *Handbook of Developmental Cognitive Neuroscience* (Second Edition) (pp. 553–74). Cambridge, MA: MIT Press.

Zelazo, P., Qu, L. and Muller, U. (2005) Hot and cool aspects of executive function: relations in early development. In W. Schneider, R. Schumann-Hengsteler and B. Sodian (Eds), *Young Children's Cognitive Development: Interrelationships Among Executive Functioning, Working Memory, Verbal Ability and Theory of Mind* (pp. 71–95). New Jersey: Lawrence Erlbaum Associates.

INDEX